AT HOME IN NATURE

AT HOME IN NATURE

Modern Homesteading and Spiritual Practice
in America

Rebecca Kneale Gould

University of California Press   Berkeley Los Angeles London

Frontispiece: Sign at the entrance to Helen and Scott Nearing's
Forest Farm. Photo by R. K. Gould.

University of California Press
Berkeley and Los Angeles, California

University of California Press, Ltd.
London, England

Library of Congress Cataloging-in-Publication Data

Gould, Rebecca Kneale, 1963–
    At home in nature : modern homesteading and spiritual
practice in America / Rebecca Kneale Gould.
        p.   cm.
    Includes bibliographical references (p.) and index.
    ISBN 0-520-24140-1 (cloth : alk. paper) — ISBN
0-520-24142-8 (pbk. : alk. paper)
        1. United States—Religious life and customs.   2. Country
life—Religious aspects.   3. Nature—Religious aspects.
4. Spirituality—United States.   5. Country life—United States.
6. Nature and civilization—United States.   I. Title.
BL2525.G69   2005
306'.0973—dc22   2004027410
Manufactured in the United States of America
14   13   12   11   10   09   08   07   06   05
10 9 8   7   6   5   4   3   2   1

This book is printed on New Leaf EcoBook 60, containing 60%
post-consumer waste, processed chlorine free; 30% de-inked
recycled fiber, elemental chlorine free; and 10% FSC-certified
virgin fiber, totally chlorine free. EcoBook 60 is acid-free and
meets the minimum requirements of ANSI/ASTM D5634–01
(Permanence of Paper).

In memory of four lovers of gardens and seekers of the Good Life: Helen Knothe Nearing, my maternal grandparents, Ada Kneale Burns and Robert Martin Burns, and Ione P. Smith

And for my sister, Alison Gould, my brother, Kenneth Gould, and my mother, Nadja B. Gould

There is an Adam and Eve in Darwin's plan, too, but they were not set up in business on the home farm, their garden ready planted. They made their own garden and knew how they came by their acres.

John Burroughs, 1883

Amid the decay of creeds, love of nature has high religious value. This has saved many persons in this world—saved them from mammon-worship, and from the frivolity and insincerity of the crowd. It has made their lives placid and sweet. It has given them an inexhaustible field for inquiry, for enjoyment, for the exercise of all their powers, and in the end has not left them soured and dissatisfied. It has made them contented and at home wherever they are in nature.

John Burroughs, 1920

CONTENTS

ILLUSTRATIONS

PREFACE

> We saw our good life . . . as a pilgrimage, for us,
> to the best way we could conceive of living.
>
> Helen Nearing, *Loving and Leaving the Good Life*

Pilgrims

In 1996, I was living in a wood-heated stone house on the coast of Maine. The food I ate came mostly from the garden. The waste I produced went into the soil. I collected seaweed, for the compost, from the Penobscot Bay cove I daily surveyed from my living room window. In ways both large and small, I lived a life dictated by the cycle of the seasons and the pleasures and limits of staying in one place, hour by hour, day by day.

That place was called Forest Farm, a homestead that once belonged to Helen and Scott Nearing. While hardly a household name in mainstream culture, Scott Nearing was well known in academic and socialist circles as early as the first decades of the twentieth century, when he spoke on the lecture circuit with John Reed, debated Clarence Darrow in packed lecture halls, and ran on the Socialist ticket for Congress in 1918 against Fiorello LaGuardia.

Helen Nearing was a less familiar figure, although she was well connected in certain spiritual networks. She was born to parents who were deeply engaged in Theosophy, a nineteenth-century liberal religious movement that grew out of Spiritualism and a burgeoning American interest in Asian religious traditions. Theosophists embraced the concept of reincarnation and encouraged the practice of meditation. They supported the intellectual and spiritual quest for an ancient, perennial wisdom that they believed to be discernible beneath the outer forms of many religious and philosophical traditions. Helen had trained as a professional violinist and, in lieu of college, had traveled to Europe and Asia to pursue further both her musical and her spiritual interests. She became known through her youthful romance with Krishnamurti, a young man from Madras who was handpicked by the Theosophical Society as the next "World Teacher" but who ultimately rejected both the title and the society, although he remained a spiritual leader. Helen also maintained a close friendship with Krishna's brother, Nitya. These intimate connections kept her well placed in Theosophist networks and in the broader, elite circles of Euro-Americans interested in Asian religions and occult spirituality.

Both Nearings were active in vegetarian societies and had traveled widely. But it was only after the publication of *Living the Good Life* in 1954 and the republication of the text in 1970 that the Nearings became widely known in what was only one of their many incarnations: as the "grandparents" of the Back-to-the-Land movement.[1]

In 1932, the Nearings began to turn their backs on their privileged backgrounds to cultivate a largely self-sufficient life in the backwoods of Vermont (from 1932 to 1952) and, starting from scratch a second time, on the rugged shoreline of Maine (from 1952 to 1995).[2] The publication of their books, beginning with *The Maple Sugar Book* in 1950, led to a steady stream of visitors that, in summers, soon became floods. Their correspondence with the public multiplied with every year, as they received letters from scores of strangers seeking psychological, spiritual, and practical advice on how to live a better, saner, more "natural" way of life.

When I came to live at Forest Farm, I inherited many of the Nearings' old roles, including the fascinating task of reading and responding to a new generation of seekers after the Good Life. In the early winter of 1997, I received a particularly compelling letter. The letter writers, a young couple from a suburban New England town, were writing to thank me for sending them a set of books by the Nearings. Dave and Dani Bonta had long been interested in the ways and means by which the Nearings had managed home-based living, fighting the evils of "artificial" city life and the growing culture of consumption.[3] Now the Bontas were actively planning to do the same. Having already purchased a rural homestead site, they were busy making house-building plans (including using the Nearings' slipform method of stonework) and preparing themselves for a move in early 1998. "We hope to live a harmless and purposeful life," they wrote. "What we are living now is more or less [an] existence of day to day 'working for the man,' and working towards our goal of breaking away." The Bontas acknowledged that their quest for the simple life was hardly "simple" when the realities of planning, acquiring skills, and

FIGURE 1.
Helen and Scott Nearing's last stone house and garden in
Maine, 1990s. Photo by R. K. Gould.

making difficult choices were considered. "There are a number of issues to
address in this endeavor and we meet them all head on as best we can," they
reported, "but everything seems to take so much longer than we wish it
would."

The Bontas had faced the very real difficulties of extracting themselves from
the normal routine of "working for the man" and from the dominant consumer
culture that they saw as harmful to themselves, others, and the natural world.
Yet the inspiration of the Nearings' example had kept them going. A brief visit
with Helen Nearing in 1993 was particularly inspirational. As she had done
with thousands of visitors before them, Helen (then a very youthful eighty-
nine) took them into the garden, enclosed by a solid stone wall hand-constructed from rocks picked up on the Maine shoreline and dug out of the earth.
Helen sprang about the property with the energy level of a teenager, pointing
out the neatly arranged compost piles, one of the wooden yurts that graced the
backyard, and the plastic tofu box containing remnants of the hardpan earth first
removed from the land, before the soil had been built up. She then invited the
Bontas into the hand-built stone house and showed off Scott Nearing's books
and papers.

Scott had died in 1983 at the age of one hundred, but Helen remained the enthusiastic publicist of his works. Ever the modest and gracious host, Helen downplayed her own efforts in light of Scott's ideals and practices. At the same time, her seemingly tireless approach to her visitors—the Bontas were only two of a number who appeared that day—betrayed her endless enthusiasm for the way of life she had chosen.

Helen Nearing's evangelical zeal for the principles and practices of homesteading was obviously catching. The Bontas returned home and found themselves telling the story of their pilgrimage to Forest Farm to all who shared their interests. In their letter to me they reflected: "It was only a short visit, but we will replay it in our minds over and over again and as time goes by it will take on the character of a sort of 'witnessing' or 'The Gospel according to' type of event. . . . [And] whatever pursuit we engage ourselves in within the research of our Homestead dreams, we keep coming across 'like-minded' fellows [who] are similarly affected by the Nearing example." The religious language that the Bontas employed to describe their visit to Forest Farm was no mere casual choice of metaphor. Like the visions of many other self-acknowledged "pilgrims" to the Nearing homestead, the Bontas' dream of a new way of living was as spiritual as it was practical. Through the contacts they had made as they began their journey to a new life, the Bontas had discovered a host of others—whom they referred to as "the Faithful"— whose lives had been similarly influenced by reading the Nearings' work or visiting the farm.

Over the years, many pilgrims to Forest Farm have been inspired to make changes in the style and tone of their lives, to slow down, to follow a vegetarian diet, or to experiment with organic gardening in the backyard. Others have experienced more dramatic transformations, laying aside old lives in the cities and suburbs and taking up new ones in rural areas. Today's "modern homesteaders" have built their own homes, planted gardens, preserved their food, worked at ways to make a home-based living, and also have often educated their children on the homestead. The Bontas understand themselves and these others as participating in a growing spiritual shift in late-twentieth-century American culture. In their letter, one of them commented:

> I don't mean to exaggerate [or] offend . . . but sometimes I feel that there is a
> silent movement afoot here with the potential as civilization directing, as impacting as perhaps the influence of Christianity itself. I am not a religious person in the formal sense, but from what I've gleaned of it over the years I see a
> lot of parallels between what the original Christ worked towards, and intended,
> and what the direction of The Good Life principles effect. To consider that two

people, starting with average means, could structure their lives into such a good example of Right Livelihood, as to influence countless numbers of people around the world is truly awe-inspiring.

The Bontas see in the example of the Nearings and in the practice of homesteading, generally, a promising vision for the future. The changes they welcome are not only ones of personal health and well-being but also cultural shifts that are ultimately moral and ethical in nature. The Bontas' vision of the potential impact of homesteading on Western civilization is likely overstated. But their sense that the practice of homesteading has strong spiritual dimensions is not. Countless visitors to Forest Farm, and the majority of homesteaders I have interviewed since 1993, describe themselves as "not religious in the formal sense." Nevertheless, they still speak of their interest in homesteading in profoundly moral, spiritual, and ethical terms.

The anthropologist Clifford Geertz has argued that when humans are pushed to the limits (of their analytical capacities, their endurance, or their moral insight) the "Problem of Meaning" rises to the surface and "religious concepts" are pressed into service so that intellectual, emotional, and moral experience can be given "meaningful form."[4] Homesteaders often embark upon their new lives because they have reached precisely these kinds of limits. For homesteaders, however, it is not only *concepts* (of corrupt culture and redeeming nature) but also, just as important, *practices* (of going "back to the land" and pursuing self-sufficiency) that save them. Whether we prefer the term *spiritual* or *religious*—a matter I shall take up in the pages to follow—we can see in the practice of homesteading a lived response to problems of meaning that are personal and cultural. The purpose of this book is to explore the ways in which these problems of meaning are experienced, challenged, and responded to by those who, like Helen and Scott Nearing, have tried to practice what they preach in the midst of a technological and consumption-oriented American culture they found to be spiritually and ethically wanting. For modern homesteaders living both before and after the Nearings, the complex pursuit of the simple life close to nature became a practice that addressed—although it did not always resolve—a particular cultural version of a perennial moral problem: that the world as it is today is not the world as it ought to be.

By the time I received the Bontas' letter, the profile of themselves that they presented was astonishing to me, not in its uniqueness, but in its utter familiarity. In the course of my own research on homesteading, I had experienced the pleasure of coming to know Helen Nearing personally, the tragedy of her sudden death in the fall of 1995, and the decidedly mixed blessing of being the first person to live at Forest Farm following her death. By the spring of 1996, I found myself unexpectedly living at what the religion scholar Mircea Eliade might have called the "sacred center" of modern homesteading. Suddenly, I was wearing Helen's shoes (quite literally), spending my days tending the garden and filling book orders and my nights (after some initial hesitancy) sleeping in her bed. I answered mail and phone calls, listened to grieving friends and neighbors, and assisted with the difficult birth of a new nonprofit organization that would carry on the Nearing legacy, the Good Life Center.[5] In all of these tasks and the research that preceded them, the stories I so often heard were full of spiritual narratives: of quest and rebirth as old lives and "mainstream" culture are left behind, of pursuing a spiritual life but not in a formal religious setting, of recentering the self amid the wonders (and resources) of the natural world.

Every now and then, I had a chance to write. But the responsibilities of gardening to Good Life standards, administrative work, and receiving a spiritually (and often physically) hungry public were both rich and demanding. Some days I felt more like a therapist or a rabbi than a student of American religion. Other days I felt like a file clerk or a cook. Some late afternoons I was simply a tired farmer, planting the corn for the third time and hoping the birds would not eat the seed *again*. Some days it all drove me to wits' end. Most days I loved it.

Through my daily labors, I began to understand, as never before, the challenges so often felt by the Nearings themselves, wanting to model the Good Life for others and wanting to be left alone to live it. The age-old religious tension between inner-directed contemplation and outer-directed social reform ran persistently as counterflowing streams through the Nearings' lives. Not surprisingly, I sometimes felt caught in the whirlpools their legacies had left behind. Not surprisingly either, these themes (of contemplation and action, of retreat and reform) shaped the interpretation of the stories I tell in this book.

As I settled into my new life on the Nearing homestead, I had the pleasure of experiencing my "interview subjects" (since 1994) becoming my neighbors, warmly welcoming me into their lives, their gardens, and their saunas. No longer was I journeying from Cambridge to Maine to gather stories of "what are you doing and why?" Now I was living my daily life among a fascinating group of creative participants in homestead living. I could also indulge in the Nearings' library, the books and papers not yet archived, and so gain a richer sense of the wider intellectual history of which homesteading is a part.

My duties at the farm allowed me to engage in the practice of homesteading myself. Such engagement admittedly involved a "cushy" existence relative to that of many homesteaders. The hand-built stone house required few amendments, and this last of the Nearings' many buildings was outfitted (unlike the original Vermont home) with electricity, hot water (which I mostly kept turned off), and a phone. The garden needed tending, but in this I was masterfully guided by Helen and Scott Nearing's close friend Nancy Berkowitz. Despite these comforts, my daily labors included a new kind of attention to matters of time, food, work, and leisure. For instance, I spent a great deal of time sawing and chopping wood, knowing that when winter came, if I could not keep warm, I could not write. I often found myself thinking twice about whether it was really worth firing up the cook stove just to make a cup of coffee, yet I never did warm to Helen's suggestion that a morning brew of molasses and water was a truly viable alternative.

In a strange case of life imitating scholarship, I found—while already embarked on the first drafting of this study—that my own patterns of living and my feelings about those patterns closely matched the writing and theorizing I had already done. I was grateful for the opportunity to shift my status from "interviewer" to "participant-observer" and even more grateful that circumstances had unfolded such that I could break the traditional pattern of "going into the field" one year and "writing up" the next. I came to see my scholarship and my thinking as following a spiral pattern that had begun with my reading of the Nearings' works and continued through a series of returns to the Nearing homestead and to the homesteads of those living near them.

But comparatively little of my time was spent on such intellectual musings, for most days I was busy receiving pilgrims. Over a thousand visitors came to Forest Farm in the summer of 1996. They came to touch the stone walls of the house that Helen and Scott had constructed when in their seventies and nineties, respectively, and asked, "Did the Nearings really build this themselves?" (a question that, like many questions about the Nearings, had quite a complicated answer).[6] They wandered into the garden and exclaimed, "This is such a peaceful, spiritual place!" They sat in the wooden yurt behind the house—the creation of a homesteading friend of the Nearings—and meditated on how their lives were touched by the Nearings' example and how they might make Nearing-style changes of their own. The questions the pilgrims brought with them and the vows of transformation they made while visiting resonated with the many letters to Helen Nearing that I had read both before and after my arrival at Forest Farm.[7] A minority of the letter writers and pilgrims were actually homesteaders themselves, but the questions they always raised—about the human relationship with the natural world, about what the "real" priorities in living should be, about how to face the ecological and cultural threats of the late twentieth century—were questions that full-time homesteaders were seeking to answer in the ways that they went about their daily lives.

The questions pilgrims brought began to build, day after day, into a kind of refrain. The questions were not all "new," nor was homesteading a "new" answer to them. As I received visitors by day and conducted research by night, the daily visitations of pilgrims (sociology) and the ongoing story of homesteading as a persistent response to certain problems of modern culture (history) conspired to make the Bontas' letter, and the many others like them, seem age-old. But even though not "new," the stories of homesteaders and of the pilgrims who follow their lead demand our attention. They are an important and revealing expression of a contemporary psychospiritual longing: to find a form of spiritual life outside formal religious institutions and to practice a way of living that is in step with the natural world rather than against it. Yet this contemporary cultural urge is also the latest articulation of an ongoing postindustrial quest to live close to nature and "to suck the marrow out of life" that we first hear in the writing of Henry David Thoreau. The desire to homestead is both revealing of our uncertain spiritual and ecological futures and an important link in the religious and environmental history of what Perry Miller aptly termed "Nature's nation."[8] The story I am telling here, then, is a religious story, an ecological story, and also an American story.

Much personal insight can (and I hope will) be gained by reflecting on the particular choices that homesteaders make. Perhaps some readers will start to grow their own food, make their own compost, and raise vital questions about consumerism and capitalism. If so, all to the good. Scott and Helen would be pleased. But this book is not a study of "practical ethics" as such. It is not a recommendation that we all ought to become homesteaders, nor will it advise readers on how to do it. Nor is it a work of celebration or hagiography. At heart, it is an inquiry into one dynamic version of the complex dance of religion and spirituality in—and with—American culture. For both in the nineteenth century and today, the choice to go "back to nature" is also a choice about the life of the spirit and the relationship between self and culture.

In broad terms, this book considers the decisions some Americans begin to make in the face of rising industrialism and consumerism and in the face of scientific and intellectual challenges to traditional forms of religion that, in the past, provided some sense of moral and spiritual security. I say "some" because the assumption of solid early American religious foundations is often vastly overstated. Problems of meaning in America have always been negotiated in the context of ambivalence and anxiety with respect to institutional religion.[9] But from the late nineteenth century forward, a particularly significant and far-reaching version of such anxiety has come into play as traditional belief in God has been challenged by various forms of religious liberalism (including Transcendentalism), the first influx of religious pluralism, and the influence of Darwinian theory.[10] At the same time, the second wave of industrialism, the rise of the city, the subsequent development of consumer culture, and the perceived decline in "community values" all conspired to pose economic and moral problems that were addressed by a vocal minority of intellectual dissenters.

This book is a study of individual and cultural choices and the meaning that is made from them. Ideally, it is a study for more than one audience. I hope those interested in a history of homesteading, the practice of sustainable living, and the shifting meanings of religion and nature in American culture will find much that is illuminating in the stories and reflections that I bring to these pages. A scholarly audience will find, in addition, an underlying set of arguments that further the discussion of the cultural construction of nature, examine where—and why—such forms of spiritual practice have emerged in modern America, trace the intellectual history of the turn to nature, raise questions about the so-called privatism of contemporary spiritual life, and probe the ambivalences (individual and cultural) present in the choices that homesteaders make. These arguments are laid out more fully in the introduction, are woven into my retelling of homesteaders' stories, and are deepened in the footnotes. My hope is that general readers and a scholarly audience will find a meeting point in this study of life choices and life pilgrimages, for as I have often contended, "real life" and "scholarly life" need not be as separate as they sometimes seem.

Those who have taken up homesteading—whether in the late nineteenth century, in midcentury, or in more recent periods—have all been acting out particular versions of larger experiments in American cultural dissent and spiritual creativity. They have done so through a turn to nature. Choosing to live within the structures, limits, possibilities, and symbolic power of a religious faith is one approach to the problem of meaning. Choosing to live within the structures, limits, possibilities, and symbolic power of a home and life in nature is another. While particular choices about homesteading differ, the practice of homesteading continually articulates an attempt to live a good and moral life, a life that might redeem society or at least the self. Helen and Scott Nearing are perhaps the best-known actors in this narrative, but earlier "modern pioneers" preceded them, and contemporary homesteaders continue their legacy. This book tells some of their stories.

ACKNOWLEDGMENTS

My first debt of thanks goes to the many homesteaders who opened up their homes and gardens to me from 1994, when I began an early version of this study, to the present. Many who hosted me are not profiled closely in this book, and still fewer are mentioned with their real names (see the Appendix), yet the role they have played remains vital. There are others whose printed words gave me sufficient insight into their doings that I chose not to pester them in person and still others whom I met informally through letters, at lectures and workshops, and in wider homesteading circles. There is not room in this book to tell everyone's story, and much more could be written about these many remarkable lives. Their stories and insights, whether shared in the course of pages, mentioned in a single footnote, or hinted at in a broader comment, have made the texture of this book what it is. While the analysis is my own, the lives I have written about are ones that were graciously shared with me. The homesteaders who are the subjects of this book have my deepest gratitude and my enduring respect. To the "A.W.K.W.B.'s" who were my neighbors in 1996, and to those mentioned throughout this text, you know who you are, and you have my special thanks and affection.

A wider circle of individuals who knew the Nearings well as friends, family members, or students of their lives have helped illuminate this study beyond measure. In addition to many of the anonymous homesteaders mentioned above, I have been touched by both the intellectual generosity and the friendship of Nancy and Warren Berkowitz, Ellen LaConte and Dolly Hatfield, John

Saltmarsh and Gisele Grenon, Greg Joly and Mary Diaz, Robert Nearing, and Elka Schumann. Hendrik Gideonse and the Gideonse family provided me a place to hang my hat at various stages of research and are part of this story. Laura Waterman offered reflections on her life, which reverberate through this study and reconnected me to an earlier time when I encountered both her and Guy Waterman through shared work for the Appalachian Mountain Club.

My extended stay at the Nearing's Forest Farm was made possible by the Trust for Public Land and the Good Life Center. A long list of TPL staff and Good Life Center staff, volunteers, and subsequent stewards have added much to this project. Generous support from the Lilly Endowment and the Mellon Foundation on this and related projects throughout my graduate school years have given me the gift of time and have enriched my thinking about religion and American culture. A Charlotte W. Newcombe Dissertation Grant made it possible to write one version of this study and a postdoctoral fellowship from the Center for the Study of American Religion (now the Center for the Study of Religion) at Princeton University gave me the opportunity to envision the project anew as a quite different book. While at Princeton, I received encouragement and advice from Robert Wuthnow and Ann Taves, whose insights have continued to shape my thinking on this project as well as on American religion more broadly. Diane Winston, Susan Myers-Shirk, and Cynthia Eller also generously gave feedback on portions of the text during that year.

The deeper roots of this book go back a very long way. I would not have become a scholar of religion, beginning in my undergraduate years, had it not been for my brilliant introduction to the field by Diana L. Eck, who so wonderfully demonstrates a blend of intellectual rigor and personal compassion. Other model teachers and scholars who influenced my intellectual growth at important junctures include: Dorothy A. Austin, the late William Alfred, John Cort, Jim Engell, Alan Hodder, Missy Holland, Will Marquess, Richard Niebuhr, Bud Ruf, Sharon Welch, and Carol Zaleski. In the still more distant past, Janet Brecher, Dorothy DiDomenico, and Richard Gauthier taught me the arts of infusing work with love.

In terms of this particular project, the intellectual encouragement has been longstanding and exceedingly generous. Nancy Tatom Ammerman first introduced me to the joys of fieldwork and so permanently changed me into a historian with a love of ethnography. Members of the American Religious History Colloquium at the Harvard Divinity School helped to create a rare model of intellectual community. William Hutchison ably co-led the colloquium, opened my eyes to many facets of nineteenth- and twentieth-century American religious history I might have otherwise overlooked, and has been wonderfully supportive over many years. Members of the colloquium and others in the

Graduate School of Arts and Sciences who have played a particularly important role as both friends and scholarly conversation partners include: Chris Coble, Marie Griffith, Jess Gugino, Emily Haddad, Steve Holmes, Lance Laird, Michelle Lelwica, Kimerer LaMothe, John O'Keefe, Sara McClintock, Michael McNally, Tim Morehouse, Brian Palmer, and Kirsten Sword. Lee Warren and the rest of the staff of the Bok Center brightened my days. Elizabeth Lemons and the late Betsy Clark pushed me on the gender questions lurking in this project. I am grateful to them for that and for much else.

Those who have heard portions of this work presented at conferences and have offered enthusiastic support and advice through the years include: Catherine Albanese, Beth Blissman, Courtney Bender, David Hackett, Danièle Hervieu-Léger, Meredith McGuire, Mary Jo Neitz, Robert A. Orsi, Jim Spickard, Bron Taylor, and Rhys Williams.

Many colleagues at Middlebury College have been helpful as I have brought this work to completion. I want to thank, especially, Larry Yarbrough, who has been a model department chair and a gracious colleague, and Charlene Barrett, who makes everything run so smoothly. I am lucky to have generous colleagues throughout the Religion Department and the Environmental Studies program who have expressed interest and support for this project, and I thank them all. John Elder and Robert Prasch read and offered helpful commentary on portions of the manuscript and have cheered this project on. Some past and present Middlebury colleagues who have been especially inspiring and helpful (whether they knew it or not) include: Dan Bedford, Eric and Jennifer Bleich, Alison Byerly, Dan Brayton, Deborah Grant, Heidi Grasswick, Barbara Hofer, Mary Hurlie, Nan Jenks Jay, Antonia Losano, Bill McKibben, Peggy Nelson, Ted Nunez, Burke Rochford, Jaye Roseborough, Ted Sasson, Steve Trombulak, Jacob Tropp, Susan Watson, and Rich Wolfson. Kathryn Morse deserves a special thank you for fielding questions on minutia while keeping me grounded in the big picture.

As this book came into being it was ably shepherded by my editor at the University of California Press, Reed Malcolm, whose enthusiasm and encouragement have been a true gift. The two readers who reviewed this manuscript gave expert advice, for which I am very grateful. Jacqueline Volin and Robin Whitaker served as astute and gracious editors. Jeff Cramer of the Thoreau Institute, Roland Goodbody of the Milne Archives at the University of New Hampshire, Jonathan Greene of Gnomon Press, Tevis Kimball of the Jones Library in Amherst, Massachusetts, Nancy Wood of In Brief Press, and Ann Wilken and Arthur Rodriguez of the School of Living offered timely assistance with photographs and permissions, as well as interesting insights of their own.

Some particularly important people have helped keep me going through the years, some by reading drafts of the manuscript, others by distracting me with good food, sane *bons mots*, and the remarkable gifts of friendship. Special thanks go to Kym Boyman and Beth Robinson, Chris Bensley Drain, Roland Dunbrack Jr., Janet M. Helson, Liz Hutchison, Ruthanna Hooke, Laurel Kearns, Stephanie LeMenager, Pat Rathbone, Kathy Richman, the Smith family, Jody Shapiro, and Sarah McFarland Taylor.

Many gifted people affiliated with the Simplicity Forum and with Elat Chayyim have inspired and in-spirited me as I have finished this work and moved on to new projects that touch our common hopes for the future. A special bow goes to Rabbi Phyllis Berman and Rabbi Arthur Waskow.

David D. Hall and Lawrence Buell, who served as advisers to the project in its dissertation form, deserve special mention. David and Larry have gone beyond the call of duty in every way as teachers, mentors, and models of intellectual engagement. This book would not have happened without them.

Finally, the members of my family demonstrated caring for this project and, more important, for its author. My mother, Nadja B. Gould, while actively engaged in professional life as well as singing and playing the cello, still managed to read numerous versions of the manuscript and to delight me with her witticisms in the margins. My brother, Ken, and my sister, Alison, have expressed boundless support and patience when I managed to bring work with me to every family vacation. While their influence and support go well beyond this project, it is to my mother and my siblings that this book is dedicated.

Many special people have died in the course of my work on this project. Some are mentioned elsewhere in the notes, but I would like to honor them here: Ginny Brereton, Betsy Clark, Gail Disney, Chuck Matthai, Helen Knothe Nearing, Ione P. Smith, Bob Swann, and Guy Waterman.

Beyond a doubt, the person who deserves the most gratitude is the one who lived with this project the longest, my partner, Cynthia S. Smith. In the midst of the process of becoming a physician (a process akin to building a homestead with hand tools), she dedicated herself to being a fabulous partner and a sharp-eyed editor. With Cynthia, I am always at home.

And thanks to Walden Pond, for giving me refreshment when I needed it.

·   ·   ·

Portions of this book have appeared elsewhere, in different forms, in *Worldviews: Environment, Culture, Religion* 3, no. 3 (1999) (Brill Press); *Social Compass* 44, no. 3 (1997) (Sage Publications); David D. Hall, ed., *Lived Religion in America* (Princeton University Press); and Charlotte Zoe Walker, ed., *Sharp Eyes: John Burroughs and American Nature Writing* (Syracuse University Press) and are reproduced with the kind permission of the publishers.

The drawing by Harlan Hubbard, taken from his book *Payne Hollow*, is used by permission of Gnomon Press. Historical photographs of John Burroughs are used by permission of the Jones Library, Inc., Amherst, Massachusetts. Historical photographs of the Nearings are used by permission of the Good Life Center and the Thoreau Institute at Walden Woods; and the photograph from Arden is used with permission of Robert Nearing and the Thoreau Institute at Walden Woods. The image from Myrtle Mae Borsodi's article in *The Silent Hostess* is used by permission of the School of Living (s-o-l.org) and by the Milne Special Collections at the University of New Hampshire.

A HOMESTEADING TIME LINE

1854 Henry David Thoreau's *Walden* is published.

1872 John Burroughs leaves Washington, DC, to take up a life of farming and writing in West Park, New York.

1896 John Burroughs completes the building of his cabin Slabsides and begins living there annually from March to December.

1905 Scott Nearing builds his first cabin and grows his first organic garden at the single-tax community of Arden, Delaware.

1907 Bolton Hall publishes *Three Acres and Liberty*; in 1908 Hall publishes *A Little Land and a Living*, foreword by Ralph Borsodi's father, William Borsodi.

1920 Ralph Borsodi and his family leave New York City and establish their first homestead in Rockland County, New York.

1929 Ralph Borsodi publishes *This Ugly Civilization*.

1932 Helen and Scott Nearing purchase their first Vermont homestead, making it their primary residence in 1935.

1934–35 The School of Living starts up in Suffern, New York, becoming fully established in 1936.

1938 Henry Tetlow publishes *We Farm for a Hobby and Make It Pay*.

1942 Louis Dickinson Rich publishes *We Took to the Woods*.

1944   Carolyn and Ed Robinson publish *The Have More Plan*, based on their homesteading experiment in Norwalk, Connecticut, begun in 1942.

1945   Bradford and Vena Angier read *Walden* and leave Boston for a life in British Columbia, publishing *At Home in the Woods* in 1951.

1948   Louis Bromfield publishes *Malabar Farm*.

1949   Aldo Leopold publishes *A Sand County Almanac*.

1952   Following a shanty boat trip down the Ohio and Mississippi rivers that began in 1943 and lasted eight years, Harlan and Anna Hubbard build a house in Payne Hollow along the Ohio River in Kentucky.

1954   Helen and Scott Nearing's *Living the Good Life* is self-published.

1964   Wendell Berry leaves New York City and reinhabits the Long-Legged House part-time while teaching at the University of Kentucky.

1968   The members of Total Loss Farm settle in Vermont, publishing their collected writings in *Home Comfort* in 1973.

1970   *The Mother Earth News* is launched. *Living the Good Life* is republished.

1973   Gene Logsdon publishes *Homesteading: How to Find Independence on the Land*, to be followed by a series of homesteading books.

1974   *Payne Hollow*, by Harlan Hubbard, is published.

1970s   Helen and Scott Nearing build their last stone house in Maine, when Scott is in his nineties and Helen is in her seventies.

1983   Scott Nearing dies at age one hundred.

1987   Wendell Berry publishes *Home Economics*.

1995   Helen Nearing dies at age ninety-one. The Good Life Center is established to preserve the Nearings' legacy and promote sustainable living.

2003   William Coperthwaite publishes *A Handmade Life*.

Some keep the Sabbath going to church;
I keep it staying at home.

Emily Dickinson

The center of life routine is surrounded by a
circumference of choice.

Helen and Scott Nearing, *Living the Good Life*

Choices

To say this is a book about American religion is—to borrow a phrase from Emily
Dickinson—to tell the truth but "tell it slant." It is a book about choices and negotiating the circumference of choice. It is a book about people who have chosen to be self-conscious about their lives and to shape life with less attention to
economic livelihood and more attention to living itself. The problem of living,
of course, is ultimately wrapped up in the problem of meaning, the question of
how to render one's life experiences meaningful and meaning filled. For some,
this is a philosophical question; for many, it is also a religious and spiritual one.

The problem of meaning and the problem of living are seldom defined or enacted in the same way. In the early 1930s, the socialist Scott Nearing faced the
dilemma of being a public intellectual whose political and antiwar views had
caused him to be blacklisted by universities and publishing houses. In the
1920s, Ralph Borsodi fled his job as an advertising executive for Macy's and
sought to bring the United States out of impending "material barbarism."[1] More
recently, Wendell Berry sampled and then rejected a literary life in New York,
San Francisco, and Paris, choosing, in 1965, to return home to Kentucky and
to daily labor as a farmer and writer.

Lesser-known figures, whom I shall introduce in these pages, have faced similar choices. What do you do, spiritually and practically, after returning from two
tours of duty in Vietnam? If you are a woman who would "really rather live in

the nineteenth century," is it possible to live such a lifestyle when you are firmly planted in the new millennium?[2] How can one be artistic with one's entire life, not just with one's approach to dancing or puppet making? For Helen and Scott Nearing, Ralph Borsodi, Wendell Berry, and a vast array of other adventurers, the practice that answered these theoretical questions was the same: grow your own food, build your own house, live close to nature, and make the home the center of personal, professional, and spiritual existence. Indeed, for these individuals (who call themselves homesteaders), the divide between the personal and professional is actively resisted; so too the division between theory and practice. Homesteading means staying at home but in the richest possible sense.

The practice of homesteading that is the subject of this book is not the same homesteading as that provided for in the Homestead Act of 1862. Indeed, this nineteenth-century legislation, promising 160 acres in exchange for five years of dwelling on the land, was primarily an expression of the dominant American ethos: railroad-produced expansionism, early industrialism, and manifest destiny. Today's homesteaders, although they often are seeking inexpensive land and the same skills and fortitude as earlier pioneers, might see the Homestead Act as an ironic and troubling prelude to their own struggles against industrialism, consumerism, and corporate greed. Homesteading, for today's back-to-the-landers— as well as for the Nearings, the Borsodis, and others who preceded them—means something quite different from participating in a government-sponsored plan of western settlement. It means choosing to center one's life around home, a home consciously built with attention to a particular place in the natural world. The details of that life may vary, but the ethic of living "at home in nature" is an ethic of simple living, of being a producer more than a consumer, and of letting nature set the terms for one's daily choices. As Linda Tatelbaum puts it:

> If it's insane to carry fresh cold water from a stone spring to my house each day, so be it. If it's insane to benefit from the light of day and rest when darkness comes, so be it. If it's insane to share a single reading lamp with my husband as we sit quietly at the end of a day's work, then surely I must be crazy. . . . I like walking down into the cellar for a quart of milk, down into the cool, dark earth. I like the different light that comes in on cloudy days and sunny days and blizzard days.[3]

This homesteader sees the value of creating for herself a circumference of choice. Her written testament of her daily practices and her repetition of "so be it" becomes a refrain of "amen" (literally, "may it be so") to the way of life she has chosen.

But what have such choices to do with religion—either directly or at a slant?

Addressing this question and its endlessly intriguing offspring is the intention of this study. Focusing on homesteading texts as "testaments" to a new way of living—as conversion narratives of a kind—starts us in the right direction. Fittingly, my exploration includes attention to the ongoing legacy of Henry David Thoreau's *Walden*, the original sacred text of homesteading for so many who have followed his lead. Thoreau's experiment at Walden was too fleeting to qualify as a full-fledged homesteading project, but it was a lived expression of Transcendentalist visions of nature and the divine, which set the stage for other similarly post-Christian, but nonetheless religious, experiments in getting close to nature. In terms of tracing the Thoreauvian legacy down to the present, this book is a work of intellectual history.

But this study also includes an examination of the ways in which nature is constructed, that is, how the word *nature* is interpreted and understood by those who consciously seek to live intimately with the natural world. For nature, as we know from the voluminous dictionary definitions given to the term, is no mere unilateral "thing." Although we tend to think we know it when we see it (those green mountains, that pewter-toned river), nature is a moving target. In its broad Western context, for instance, nature is imagined and reimagined through the ancient Roman, Hellenistic, and European lenses of Virgil and Lucretius, Plato and Aristotle, Augustine and Aquinas, Newton and Descartes, Rousseau and Wordsworth, Darwin and Heisenberg. And in American history particularly, we find distinct (but also related) voices that stretch from the Calvinist visions of Cotton Mather and Jonathan Edwards to the Transcendentalism of Ralph Waldo Emerson and on to the environmental ethics of Aldo Leopold and Rachel Carson. All of these writers and thinkers share a Western cultural heritage that shapes some common approaches to the meaning of nature, but each also constructs a vision of nature out of a specific historical context and unique personal experience.

For the homesteaders and back-to-the-landers, who are the focus of this study, nature is most often constructed in a particular way: as sacred, beneficent, and redemptive; or, sometimes in more rational language, as the ultimate source of "order" or "purpose" in life, as the "core" or "true set of laws" around which daily life should be organized. But this book begins with the assumption that neither nature nor religion exists outside of culture. "Nature" and "religion" are *always* shaped by historical and social contexts. These contexts define both the terms themselves and the uses to which they can be put. In that sense, this text is also a work of cultural history.[4]

Finally and of importance, this study is a history of practice. It seeks to examine what people do, why they do it, and how what they do functions as an expression of their most deeply held values and beliefs about what the world ought to be like and how they ought to live in it. For some, homesteading becomes primarily a private, symbolic practice of dissent from the dominant culture. For others, it is a means of radically reforming that culture. For still others, it is a delicate balance of both. In all cases, however, homesteading involves not just practical work but also symbolic, cultural work.

This book investigates certain modern American varieties of the search for meaning, not as they might be theorized by professional philosophers and theologians, but rather as they emerge out of daily lived experience. Given the extent to which homesteaders are motivated by environmental commitments and concerns, some might prefer to call such a study an examination of philosophy or even of politics. Certainly, such terms would not be inaccurate, but the language homesteaders themselves have more often used (both in earlier periods and today) is the language of spiritual searching and spiritual practice.

In terms of ideal types, today's homesteaders fit the category of what sociologists Wade Clark Roof and Robert Wuthnow have called "spiritual seekers."[5] They exercise one version of a growing feature of contemporary American religious life: the tendency to pursue religious or spiritual life outside institutional structures. But as the historical chapters of this book will reveal, such seeking is not necessarily new, nor is the turn to nature only a recent, post-environmental-movement phenomenon. Rather, the search for a spiritual life close to nature is part of a longer American story. This study, then, is not only an examination of contemporary nature-oriented spiritual practice or of modern American forms of rebellion against the culture of consumption. It is also, significantly, an examination of these contemporary practices in light of a long history of the turn to nature as a form of spiritual regeneration and cultural dissent.

The Religious Argument: A Closer Look

Before we imaginatively waltz into the homes and gardens of homesteaders of the past and present, a few caveats are in order. This research began with the relatively straightforward observation that for the homesteaders I had read and interviewed, nature had become the site of meaning and authority once previously occupied (in American history and often in their early lives) by the more traditional religious structures of church, synagogue, or religious education. For these homesteaders, nature had come to serve as the "ultimate reference point" or "ultimate concern" by which good and evil, right and wrong, sacred and profane could be discerned.[6]

Countless homesteading texts are redolent with religious and moral language about nature. Indeed, the excessive use of Romantic tropes sometimes impedes the literary quality of homesteading tales. Sometimes, such language oddly breaks ranks from otherwise dry pages of technical description on how to build cold frames or relocate an outhouse. We think we are getting gardening advice, and suddenly a variation on Gray's "Elegy for a Country Churchyard" or the Book of Genesis bursts onto the page like a volunteer sunflower. Listen, for example, to Sam Ogden's 1957 meditation on contemporary farming norms:

> It seems to me that the whole pattern of our mechanized and materialistic civilization is so tightly integrated that no single aspect of it can be changed or reformed. To change any part the whole must be changed. The overall pattern is unified and tightly knit and is the expression of our cultural values and convictions. . . . The home gardener, on the other hand, is a free agent. . . . He can and should treat his soil with consideration for the laws of Nature, and to do this he must turn his back on most, if not all, of the pronouncements of the latest of scientific agricultural dogma. If this be heresy, make the most of it.[7]

In a similar vein, Paul Corey, in 1944, segues from a scientific discussion of compost to a moralizing rant about how "the masses" may not understand the true nature of nature, including the natural virtues of human waste: "No matter how much you may be shocked by the idea, your own excrement is excellent fertilizer. . . . If you are so fastidious and stupid that you can't bring yourself to utilize your own fertilizer products, then the raising of food is something you should stay far away from—and the eating of food likewise. The food you eat is the result of decay and rebirth and you'd better accept the fact grimly and firmly and exploit it to the utmost."[8] Ogden's and Corey's commentaries are much more than scientific replies to factory-farmers or advice to squeamish suburbanites. They are modern jeremiads urging the reader to get back to the (organic) Garden.

Of course, not all homesteading testimonies are so heavy-handed or draw such sharp lines between the "true believers" in nature and the ignorant apostates of the general culture. Some display a gentler tone, as when Gladys Dimock moves effortlessly from an inventory of her homestead supplies to a deeper meditation on the virtues of gardening: "A garden shows the connection from creation to development to decay to regeneration, in an annual rotation, that is as convincing an argument as any I know for the theory that energy never ends, that it is merely transformed in an unbroken round. . . . [Food] is not the whole of the benefits offered. . . . There is what can only be called the spiritual benefits of gardening. . . . Spend the afternoon in the garden and by suppertime everything will be right, including your own peace of mind."[9] Here Dimock offers a reflection akin to many we will hear in this study: words of reassurance ("all will be well," "the flow of energy never dies") that rest on what I have come to call a "theology of the soil."

In the pages to follow, however, my intention in describing and interpreting the moral and religious language of homesteading is not to support primarily a functional interpretation of religion (homesteading is a way of making meaning; therefore, homesteading is religious). Functional definitions of religion can be applied to a wide range of phenomena. Debating where to draw the line between acknowledged and "implicit" religion is not the most interesting—or revealing—approach to the data before us.

We get a bit closer to the mark, but still risk oversimplification, if we argue that, for homesteaders, among others, nature is conceptualized as sacred; therefore, life lived close to nature is religious.[10] But it is also unwise to begin with the assumption that we can universalize our understanding of what is definitively "sacred" (or "sacred space") and what is not. While earlier sociologists and historians of religion, such as Émile Durkheim and Mircea Eliade, felt confident that the "sacred" could easily be distinguished from the profane, I and others, while indebted to their work, want to argue with their essentializing tendencies.[11] My own approach to the material is not so much to provide static definitions (of "religion" or "the sacred") from without as it is to explore the physical homesteads themselves and the stories that people tell about them, to see what they tell us of the symbolic (and literal) construction of spiritual and ethical living in modern American culture.

My concern in this book, then, is with what some scholars of American religious history have called "lived religion." Of course, all religion is lived to a certain extent. But the term lived religion also refers to an approach to the study of religion. It is an approach in which, as Robert Orsi tells us, "religion is not only not sui generis, distinct from other dimensions of experience called 'profane.' Religion comes into being in an on-going, dynamic relationship with the realities of everyday life." The concept of lived religion does not attend to what is static or "wholly other"; nor does it presume that religion will always serve to resolve personal, social, or cultural tensions. In contradistinction to these earlier ways of describing the nature and function of religion, a lived-religion approach examines the sacred as "the space of activity, engagement, ambivalence and doubleness." Religion, in this view, has to do with what David Chidester calls "that dimension of human experience engaged with sacred norms," yet it recognizes the fluidity and ambiguity of how "the sacred" is constructed and where it may be found. I have argued elsewhere—and will continue to make the case here—that a study of homesteading illuminates our understanding of lived religion in American culture.[12]

For some readers, however, the term religion still bears the burden of signifying stultifying tradition, bureaucratic (and often hypocritical) institutions, expensive buildings, and unchanging dogma, the very aspects of "religion" that most homesteaders rail against! While I am apt to cast a wider and more positive net with respect to what religion might be and might do in the world, in the ethnographic portions of this text, I tend to use the language that most homesteaders and many contemporary readers themselves would use, a language that distinguishes between religion and spirituality.[13]

As a historian of religion, however, I do not make these definitional claims in the same way. My own interest is not to accept these contemporary distinctions at face value but, rather, to probe the connections between them. Thus, because I am putting contemporary homesteading stories in the context of late nineteenth- and twentieth-century precedents, I will also be describing the ways in which placing nature at the center of one's universe of meaning becomes a kind of "religion relocated." That is, I do not submit that spirituality is a static category that is somehow essentially distinct from another static category that we might call religion (sometimes thereby implying "true religion").[14] Rather, I see the very *discourse* of identifying oneself as "spiritual but not religious" as the result of a post-Enlightenment historical process, one more far reaching than is often assumed. This is a historical process in which contemporary homesteaders and a broad range of their peers and predecessors have participated by looking to nature for moral authority and spiritual renewal. The nineteenth-century essayist and farmer John Burroughs, for example, was quite intentionally enacting a post-Enlightenment gesture of "relocating religion" when he entitled a once famous essay "The Gospel of Nature."

It should be clear by now that my interests in this project are not only Durkheimian but also Weberian. That is, I am less interested in the fixed *location* of the sacred or the essential *definition* of religion and more interested in the *ways* in which problems of meaning are worked out by those who construct the sacred and the profane, the religious and the spiritual, in particular ways. I am interested in sacred space but also sacred canopies; the meaning of ritual but also the practice of ritualization; theories of religion but also the daily, lived enactment of a spiritual and ethical life.[15]

Thinking about Homesteading: A Map of the Book

In the chapters that follow, I weave together the intellectual and cultural history of homesteading with an ethnographic study of how daily life is pursued by the individual homesteaders I have come to know in Maine. The ethnographic portions (chapters 1, 2, and 3) precede the historical narrative (chapters 4, 5, and 6), but the two sections of the book are meant to be in dialogue with each other. In the opening chapters, I focus primarily on how choices about homesteading are made and unmade and what these choices mean. I ask a number of questions: In what ways is one "reborn"—indeed, spiritually regenerated—when one chooses to leave a consumer-oriented urban or suburban life behind and take up a rural, partly self-sufficient one? At the same time, in what sense is "getting close to nature" really *about* nature, and in what sense is it about cultivating the self, sometimes—ironically—in spite of nature? How and why is it that when seeking to pursue "the natural," some homesteaders still express a kind of longing for immortality that we might equate with more traditional religious visions? And in broader, more historical terms, in what senses is *nature* being pressed into the service of what is primarily a vision of *cultural* reform? These are the questions that I found percolating up from the pages of a how-to manual or in the pauses of a morning interview.

In the first half of *At Home in Nature*, I am intentionally probing beyond the obvious significance of how-to texts or spoken personal narratives. I want to get past *what* homesteaders do and into the realm of *why* they do it. But I lay no claim to the assumption that I can (or should) cast homesteaders' practices as "texts" that only I can interpret.[16] Rather, I seek to bring to the fore both the lighthearted musings and the earnest rationales that homesteaders *themselves* have offered through the pages of their written testimony or in conversations conducted while picking rocks from a field.

But of equal importance is that these homesteaders have not made their choices in a historical vacuum. My assertion in the second half of the book is that while the search for meaning may be universal, it always takes place in a social and historical milieu. The choice to go "back to the land" is not merely an aspect of the 1960s counterculture, as is often assumed, but a longstanding practice that has a history of its own.[17] Indeed, another important argument of this book is that it is a mistake to see contemporary homesteading as merely a latent "hippie" phenomenon occurring primarily among baby-boomer "seekers." While the homesteaders I came to know most closely in Maine might fit this demographic category, their practices and the way they think about them descend from a long line of visionaries, including not only Henry David Thoreau and Helen and Scott Nearing but also John Burroughs, Bolton Hall, Ralph Borsodi, Mildred Loomis, and other late nineteenth- and early twentieth-century critics of the culture of unbridled progress, capitalism, and consumption. Many contemporary homesteaders trace lines of personal history or intellectual inspiration from back-to-the-landers of previous periods.

Taking a longer view also helps us to begin to see the spiritual dimensions of modern homesteading in historical perspective. As I have stated above, I cannot argue (except by applying crude, functional definitions) that homesteading is "a religion" in the traditional sense. It is not. But we *can* see the ways in which the practice of homesteading often involves religious or spiritualized visions of nature that have a long, dynamic history in American culture. The "conversion to nature" that homesteaders exhibit might be seen as a particularly intense version of what Catherine Albanese has insightfully termed "nature religion."[18] As with the case studies Albanese compellingly brings to light, homesteaders' visions of nature are shaped by a broader story of the American relationship with nature—a story both civic and religious—that has always been marked by love and passion, domination and fear, the longing to "commune" and the desire for control.

Throughout this book, I also put forth the argument that while homesteaders attempt to resist dominant cultural norms, they also often reproduce them. Thus, while conventional religion is resisted by most of these individuals, everyday religiosity is not. Their attempts at solving certain problems of meaning cause them, for instance, to find in nature a source of truth, authority, and immortality that other Americans have sought in a Jewish or Christian concept of God. Relatedly, these middle-class advocates of simple living sometimes hold tightly to their own elite sense of moral authority, even if that authority is enacted in unconventional places. Strains of spiritual perfectionism and exceptionalism are not hard to find in many testaments of homestead living. Here again we find that familiar and persistent themes in American religious life may go underground, but they do not go away.

In analyzing homesteaders' life choices—particularly the choices to farm, write, and urge others back to nature—I am also investigating the evolving cultural conditions that have influenced these choices and to which the new lives of farming and writing are intended to be a response. Thus, while I am still attending to the problem of meaning-making in the latter half of this book, I am adopting a historical approach that argues that the religious work of homesteading can be effectively interpreted only when treated both ethnographically and in the context of the changing social and cultural conditions of late nineteenth- and twentieth-century America.

Homesteading locates itself at the crossroads of at least two stories of American culture: the turn to "nature" and the extraecclesial quest for "the religious." Both of these stories are stories of modern (some would say postmodern) America. The related story, as I am suggesting here, is the story of how certain legacies of religious American culture refuse to disappear in the face of these practices of dissent. As the following chapters unfold, I will occasionally point out how the desire to control the natural world, the quest for immortality, and the tendency toward a sectarian kind of exceptionalism sometimes continue to be subtly expressed by these proponents of a more natural, more embodied, more humble way of living. My point in discussing these underlying themes is not to undermine or unduly criticize what I primarily take to be admirable and instructive ways of living, ways of living from which we all can learn. Rather, I seek to illuminate the complexity and contradictions of religious and cultural action. Homesteaders were and are passionate about what they do, but they are also ambivalent. Ambivalence toward nature is a dominant theme in American environmental history. Not surprisingly, it is also a significant theme of this book.

Throughout this text, the lives of Helen and Scott Nearing serve as a touchstone. It is through the Nearings' books that I first encountered "modern" homesteading, and it is through living at Forest Farm that I experienced the details of homesteading life through my own labors. In this study, the Nearings serve as a kind of linchpin between ethnography and history. I treat Helen Nearing primarily in the ethnographic chapters, not only because I knew her personally, but also because her own interpretations of the meaning of homesteading tend to reflect more recent attitudes. Similarly, while Helen Nearing is certainly a historical figure in her own right, Scott Nearing is the focus of the historical chapters. In part, this is because my knowledge of him is only historical. More important, Nearing's vision of homesteading emerged out of his own early experiments in an alternative community called Arden and his (often unrecognized) passionate interest in the Social Gospel, a movement that held Christianity accountable for the social ills of the early part of the twentieth century. His style of homesteading, while it changed over time, reflects earlier eras and tells us much about them.

It is important to remember, however, that the separate categories of history and ethnography are more hermeneutical than they are real. In larger terms, I am always considering contemporary homesteaders in their historical context and historical figures in terms of contemporary expressions and interpretations of religious practice. In adopting this approach, I am also making an argument about how we might "do" studies of American religious life. In my own experience, the conversations that ensue in ethnographic research are vital in forming the questions one then poses when interpreting primary historical texts. In a complementary fashion, the work done in archives provides the long view of religious meaning-making that sociological and anthropological research alone cannot provide. In the field of American religion today, it is vital that some scholarly investigations bridge the traditional disciplinary boundaries of history and sociology and work back and forth between them. The multidisciplinary approach offered in this study, however, begins with particular people who have devoted themselves to particular places. It is with their individual stories that this book must properly begin.

> I found myself in a new incarnation, enthused
> with the unaccustomed life and enjoying most of
> its features. In a very real sense, I felt as if I had
> been born again.
>
> Scott Nearing, *The Making of a Radical*

Three Re-creations of Home (1995)

I sit at the kitchen table of a home located about fifteen miles from the Nearing homestead.[1] I am surrounded by projects in motion. Children's artwork is scattered at one end of the table. Dried herbs and flowers spill out from the kitchen into the dining room. Books are stacked in piles on and near shelves. One volume of a children's encyclopedia, a staple of home schooling, lies open near the kitchen counter. Few walls separate one room from another in the first floor of the refurbished nineteenth-century house and, seemingly, few divisions among housework, homework, artwork, and play. Robin is in the kitchen cutting tomatoes, and Sally, her seven-year-old daughter, is giving a hand. Dale comes in from the woodlot and heads to the bathroom to wash the grime from his hands. Four-year-old Alden sits down at the table, his wide eyes fixated on the sweet potato pie.

Lunch begins and I embark on my usual round of conversational questions: How long have you been here? What motivated your decision to come here? Has the garden always been this size? What level of self-sufficiency have you reached? What level do you want to reach? Talk focuses on economic limits: Robin is forced to pay capital gains tax on a house she sold to come here. It is an irony that frustrates her, paying taxes to "the system" for having tried to leave the system. Dale and Robin hope to get "off the grid," by which they mean both the local electric supply particularly and life regulated by a consumer economy more generally. They are proud of their productive garden and the dense wood-lot that provides them with heat through the winter. But more often than com-menting on what they have achieved, they upbraid themselves for what they have not. Dale, in particular, chastises himself for not having heeded Scott Near-ing's dictum "Pay as you go." Such an approach would have been ideal, but be-tween taxes, tools needed for the homestead, and health insurance to consider, "Endure necessary debt" has become the temporary real-life motto. Both Dale and Robin recognize that they face some economic burdens that Helen and Scott did not face when they embarked on their homesteading experiment in the 1930s: higher land prices and taxes, rising health costs, less access to inexpen-sive tools and supplies, and, most significant, providing for two young children. Nevertheless, Helen and Scott remain their ideal models, even when remem-bered in the very real context of day-to-day life on Forest Farm.

"What does homesteading mean to you?" I ask, half expecting Dale or Robin to comment on the natural surround: the way the light is falling on the ash trees or the way the birds are flitting through the branches. "It's about home, I guess," Dale replies, "about being at home, about centering your life around home." Dale comments further that homesteading is about recognizing that focus and about reordering one's life around the true center. Robin agrees while offering her own details of what placing home at the center means, commenting par-ticularly on her commitment to food production at all levels, gardening, pre-serving, and cooking. "Knowing where food really comes from" and perfect-ing techniques for raising "healthy food" in a "natural" way are essential to her way of living.[2]

Raising the children at home is also an important priority for both Dale and Robin, although they are also committed to keeping their children involved in local groups so that Sally and Alden will be exposed to other children and to op-portunities to learn off the homestead. While they do not speak harshly of the public school system in academic terms, they are quite concerned about the so-cialization processes that peer pressure can foster: bullying, cliques, and the de-sire for unnecessary things. They offer examples of local kids they know for whom the public school experience has done more harm than good.

While Dale and Robin worry about money and the inevitable ties between needing to make money and participating in a consumer culture they want to reject, they do feel that they have begun to create a haven in their home. They heat their house entirely from wood cut on-site, although Dale admits that cut-ting wood and placing it immediately in the wood stove last winter was a sign of their literal hand-to-mouth existence and of the shortage of time as well as money in these first homesteading years. The vegetable garden is ample, with plenty of surplus for freezing and canning. Fruit trees are growing well and will produce in a number of years. The barn out back has been successfully refurbished into a studio for Dale, whose income comes, in part, from book illustration. While this work is not produced from the homestead in the same way that the Nearings' maple syrup and blueberries were, it is still home based. Dale refers to his artwork, in fact, as his own sort of "cash crop." While not yet self-sufficient, Dale and Robin have managed to create a life that is centered on home. The task that remains is to circumscribe this achievement further, to become less dependent on outside means, both means of support (the electric company and regular pay checks) and means of intrusion (health insurance companies and public schools), often flip sides of the same coin.

The image of a successful homestead that Dale and Robin created in conversation with me is an image of the homestead as island, not a deserted island, but an inhabited and cultivated island, kept up in part by significant ferrying back and forth to the "mainland" of mainstream culture. Fittingly, the homestead calls up images of an island in its physical layout as well. It is bordered on two sides by homes belonging to "summer people," one of whom has become a close friend and loyal supporter of Dale and Robin's homesteading dream, but none of whom attempts to eke out an existence through the harsh Maine winter. The road to town marks the "ferry route," and the woods in the rear extend for some twenty acres and remain inhabited only by deer, squirrels, and the occasional bear. In the center of the yard sits a whimsical play area, a kind of giant sandbox with a mast and sail rigged up in the center. Dale's prehomesteading life was that of a sailor and boat builder. In the midst of the garden, at least one of Dale's boats has found a permanent mooring. A life of the sea has been replaced by a life at home on the land.

But this new life, while more grounded, is still a life lived at some remove from the dominant culture. Although discussions of the importance of home and family pervade that culture, in Dale and Robin's view, they are discussions that are spoken about rather than lived. Their choice to keep their distance is a mixed one. They are dedicated to the homesteading way of life, yet they feel the social and practical pressures of maintaining this "separate" identity. Life would be easier, they sometimes admit, if they just stayed "plugged in" to the school system, to the "grid," to the grocery store, to all conventional ways of living.

Over one hundred miles northeast of Dale and Robin's house another homestead is thriving on the Maine coast.[3] While even more "islandlike" in its remoteness, it resembles a small Mongolian kingdom in appearance. Accessible from the road by a mile-and-a-half-long foot trail, the homestead site consists of a broad clearing cut into the coastal woods, dotted with yurts of various shapes and sizes. A round, four-tiered structure dominates the landscape and serves as the main residence for Bill Coperthwaite, the designer, builder, artist,

FIGURE 2.
Bill Coperthwaite's main yurt beckons from a distance. Photo
by R. K. Gould.

and chief resident of this rustic kingdom. A visitor walking from the main house
to the shoreline will soon stumble upon a guest yurt—capable of housing fifteen to twenty visitors—perched at the end of the slope. At the shoreline itself,
an outdoor shower is rigged up and ready for year-round use by anyone seeking a bracing wash. Around the bend stands an outdoor kitchen with fire pits,
benches, tables, and cookware all ready for the next summer of full-time use.
The boathouse, occupied by several hand-crafted canoes, is situated just below
the kitchen outpost. On the return toward the main house, other, smaller yurts
come into view, though their shape and natural wood coloring keeps them half-
camouflaged in the tall grasses: a study, a "cache yurt" for food storage, and an
outhouse yurt, each with its own whimsical touches.

On my first visit to this homesteading "kingdom"—which exists on paper as the Yurt Foundation—I was reminded of the welcoming haven of a summer camp when visited in the fall: no noisy campers or eager-to-please staff, but shoreline views, a cacophony of birds, and warm, inviting dwellings, each built with both function and natural surround in mind. As with Dale and Robin's homestead, this homestead site is brimming with signs of activity. Birch wood lies piled by the sawhorse, where it will be cut, "Scott Nearing style," by slow, constant draws of the hand saw. The first floor of the main house is busy with projects awaiting attention: canoe paddles to be carved, a homemade wheel-barrow to be perfected, and chairs to be patched. But here the sense of space is different. At Dale and Robin's house, projects overflowed from the home, as if the four walls could not contain them. In contrast, the yurts seem designed for all kinds of building and crafts. One gets an almost palpable feeling of the home-stead calling others to come up and engage in manual, artistic labor.

With room, equipment, and the inspiration of a beautiful setting, the phys-ical site of the Yurt Foundation looks for all the world like an ideal setting for an alternative community. The round houses are built not only for efficiency of labor and maximization of usable space but also to encourage certain kinds of thinking and conversation. To revolutionize society, Coperthwaite argues, is to start by daring to think differently and to encourage consensus and equality in the conversation process. Thinking "round" is more promising than thinking "square." The proliferation of hand tools also encourages both an artistic and a utilitarian mode of living. The many libraries invite others to write, to read the works of Gandhi, Tolstoy, and Richard Gregg, or simply to meditate in the midst of a world of lofty (yet practical) ideas.

Coperthwaite has spent a certain percentage of his time crafting essays as well as building boats and carving spoons. I labor at the sawhorse while he reads to me from one of his published works on redesigning society:

> At the moment, in much of the United States, homemaking is looked down upon as a profession. In reality, it is the most important profession and can be the most exciting of all. . . . The home is our most important social institution and unless we give it the respect that is its due and stop the incessant erosion that is taking place, we will suffer irreparable loss. . . . The home is the focal seat of education and emotional security. More and more the functions of the home have been taken over by the school, but the school is no substitute, no matter how fine the instructors or expensive the equipment. . . . What mental insolvency has overtaken us that we can allow the core of our culture to be den-igrated, weakened and reduced? Far better to burn your house to the ground and live in a cave than to lose the sense of wonder and privilege of making a home.[4]

While personally moved by this modern jeremiad, I find myself thinking that the words Bill Coperthwaite speaks—if lifted from the physical context in which they are being articulated—could easily be coming from mainstream, conservative America. Ironically, Coperthwaite's themes are not far afield from those of today's leaders of the Republican and Christian Right. Homemaking is held up as the most worthy of today's professions, American culture is criticized for overvaluing the purpose and potential of public schools, society is taken to task for a lack of mental fortitude and an inability to keep the "core of our culture" strong and intact. But Coperthwaite's rhetorical devices are made far more effective by the fact that his audience is not the Christian Coalition but readers of a progressive, liberal, "alternative," and decidedly low-tech journal. Coperthwaite takes his readers by surprise, urging that homemaking is not only the most important but, in fact, the most exciting profession of all. With a deft conceptual twist, he argues that going "back" to homemaking is not a regression to a less sophisticated, less enlightened way of life as, we might imagine, some of his readership might assume. In invoking the image of cave dwelling as the alternate "lesser evil" to maintaining the status quo, Coperthwaite suggests that homemaking is a progressive ideal, blending a sense of wonder with a recognition of privilege, bringing the family together with a "common thread or purpose" that goes beyond personal concern for self-advancement.[5]

Coperthwaite locates his discussion of homemaking within a broader discussion of tradition, again blending themes that may strike some as conservative (in both the political and literal sense) with others that are more recognizably countercultural. While acknowledging that some traditions, "like going to war," ought to be dispensed with immediately, Coperthwaite argues that "we change too many things at our peril" without recognizing that traditions, as "something to lean on," are vital to a feeling of emotional security. The tradition to which Coperthwaite feels most sympathetic, is most interested in preserving, is that of the family farm: "The small farm family of a hundred years ago provided most of human needs. People sold little for cash and bought little. Life was hard but in many cases a happy life."[6]

According to his narrative of late nineteenth-century history, "advancement from the family farm" brought Americans to a crossroads of cultural decision making. One choice, the choice that mainstream culture has made, was "to abandon the farm and the husbandman's skill" for the sake of industrial development geared at making life "less physically hard." The other choice, "the path that could have been taken," laments Coperthwaite, would have been to retain the family farm while applying new "scientific and technological skills to make life on the homestead less hard and isolated." Aware of the potential charges of nurturing a romantic, nostalgic, even gauzy vision of the past, Coperthwaite disarms his imagined critics—and perhaps also his lurking internal demons—by emphasizing the essentially progressive, forward-looking nature of his design for living: "Now some in this country are moving in that direction—not back to a former way of life, but forward to a way that blends the best of the past with the best of today. It is with this kind of blending that social design is concerned."[7] Homesteading, Coperthwaite tells us, is about reviving that most important of professions—homemaking—and bringing it to a new "modern" stage of development, such that is at once art, science, and social reform.

Bill Coperthwaite's vision of homesteading and the physical realization of this vision are manifested by a fascinating but also dizzying confluence of opposing forces. We have already noted the ways in which he turns contemporary "conservative" rhetoric on its head, eliciting both shock and a shock of recognition in reform-minded readers. While feminists especially might recoil at the elevation of homemaking to the most noble and "exciting" of professions, they are—by virtue of Coperthwaite's wordplay—forced to reconsider the varied artistic, scientific, and political dimensions involved in a practice of homesteading that has as its ultimate goal, "the blossoming of human culture," the creation of "an Eden on earth."[8] While progressive thinkers may be uneasy with his valuation of the past, they are called to contemplate the ways in which "going back to the farm" is a moving forward, a creative way of responding to the dangers of industrial, technological culture without throwing out science and technology altogether. Skeptics may charge that Coperthwaite's camp of canoes and yurts resembles a childhood retreat from the imperatives of the "real world," but he reminds his readers that for too long Americans have relied on "heroes" and "experts" to make decisions for them, thus keeping themselves "in a state of permanent adolescence," where neither the capacity for creativity nor a psychological maturity can ever be fulfilled.[9] For Bill Coperthwaite, homesteading is a liberating and progressive undertaking. It fosters intimacy with nature, psychological growth, and social responsibility.

But theory and practice are difficult to interweave, even though the unity of theory and practice is a kind of mantra for many homesteaders. In Coperthwaite's homesteading work, several competing claims remain in tension. Despite his valuation of women, Coperthwaite tends to prefer an older notion of "separate spheres" as the most practical means of dividing and distributing labor.[10] Despite his claims to be modern, his primary interest is in folkways—he frequently takes trips abroad to learn how Lappish people build ovens or Norwegians make mittens. Coperthwaite's intent may be to update some designs (such as the original Mongolian yurt), but his larger goal is the preservation of folk arts and techniques that are threatened by global modernization. Finally, despite his philosophical commitment to the idea of community,

Coperthwaite is, in many ways, quite isolated and unable to foster the kind of community he would ideally like to have. Such tensions between theory and practice run through any number of homesteaders' lives.

To consider yet another version of the complex marriage between theory and practice, let us visit one more homestead and the broader vision of community that attends it: the homestead, or more accurately *homesteads*, belonging to Arnold Greenberg in his past and evolving through the years.[11] If Bill Coperthwaite's kingdom of yurts has all the trappings we might expect a homestead to have—unusually shaped and structured buildings made from hand-cut wood, a location reachable only by foot or canoes, home-based systems of water collection and waste management—the homestead belonging to Greenberg is primarily a homestead of the mind.

In 1995, Greenberg was busy running a restaurant–coffee house in a town about an hour's drive from the Nearings' Forest Farm. He struck me first as a "hip" entrepreneur with socialist leanings. He was engaged in everything from baking bread and keeping the counters wiped down to lining up performers at the forefront of the contemporary singer-songwriter scene. His demeanor was both kindly and mischievous. With a wild gray beard and twinkling eyes, he was reminiscent of a Santa Claus staging conscientious objection to shopping-mall duty. His concerns remain chiefly about children, the shape of the future, and the dangers of a consumer society. These concerns have led him through a number of incarnations, beginning with a tour of duty in the navy, then jobs as a teacher and headmaster in an alternative school in Philadelphia, and later a position as founder and head of the Deep Run School of Homesteading in rural Pennsylvania, a school whose intellectual lineage goes back to the particular social visions of Ralph Borsodi and Mildred Loomis, visions I will explore more fully in chapter 6.[12]

While Greenberg has tried on a number of different professional guises in order to realize his visions, he sees homesteading as a matter of approach more than a particular activity. When I first interviewed Arnold on an autumn afternoon, he was—characteristically—in the midst of doing several things at once: pouring coffee for a regular, checking on which high school employees needed to change their work schedules because of after-school activities, arranging meals for the evening's performers, who had just come off an eight-hour road trip. "This," he said gesturing widely to the architecture, the food, and the activity of the café, "this is my homestead."

Greenberg's use of the term *homestead* when others might use *business* rests in part on strictly economic principles. Just as other homesteads described here maintain a fairly high level of self-sufficiency based on home-garden production, so does Arnold's café rely on homegrown fruits and vegetables for the bulk of the food that is sold. The café also is Arnold's home; he sleeps upstairs and arises at four o'clock in the morning to bake bread for the day's crowds. In other ways, of course, business is business: meal and ticket prices diverge little from many Cambridge coffeehouses. In the context of business operations, then, the term *homestead* functions less as a noun representing the actual work or institution than as an adverb describing *how* things get done. For Arnold Greenberg, providing locally harvested food, giving performers an audience, and providing a community (particularly in seasons other than summer) with a place to eat, meet, warm up, and find evening entertainment are all part of a larger social vision. That vision is one that places faith in individual capabilities, local economics, and community cooperation. As Greenberg puts in a recently self-published book: "In suggesting homesteading—either rural, urban or suburban—as a way of life, that is, creating a more home-centered existence, working in your home, educating your children at home . . . by creating a simpler, more self-sufficient life-style, I'm also suggesting creating communities, reinventing neighborhoods, living more cooperatively."[13] While Arnold Greenberg has found the "café-homestead" as one way to work from a home base while nurturing a broader community, he now feels it is time to turn this successful venture over to new hands. He is retiring from his current labors to pursue new versions of the homesteading school he ran in the late 1970s and early 1980s. While the café may have been a kind of a homestead, Arnold feels he must get back to teaching young people the practical and social skills necessary for the new millennium. This means not only setting up an alternative high school but also offering for its thirteenth year a program for students to engage intensely in living, working, and learning "off the land." In both cases, the design for the school has come out of the heads and hearts of local people—many of whom are homesteaders, homeschoolers, or both—who want an alternative to traditional education for their children.

Robin and Dale's homestead, Bill Coperthwaite's yurt kingdom, and Arnold Greenberg's array of literal and symbolic homesteads all occupy significant places on a continuum of relationship between the homestead and the larger community. Robin and Dale find the best way to nurture their values is to seek remove from the dominant society, to focus on the home as the primary locus; Bill Coperthwaite is interested in reforming society through rearticulating the value of homemaking and through creating a model community in his own backyard; Arnold Greenberg takes the vision a further step outward: instead of homeschooling, joining with locals and designing schools themselves to reinvestigate and rearticulate the values of home, community, and living lightly on the land. But all three homesteading stories share common nodes in the narrative net. Each homesteading model represents an "after" that suggests a "before": a time when life seemed purposeless and out of balance, often because a homesteader's inner sense of purpose or balance did not match that of the dominant culture. For Bill, Dale and Robin, and Arnold a desire to live close to nature and to be intimately involved in and respectful toward the natural world was also central to the vision. But none of these homesteaders would describe themselves as environmental activists in the typical political sense or as religious persons in the institutional sense; rather, their environmentalist lives and their spiritual lives emerge from their commitment to the conscious cultivation of "staying at home."

While not as prolific as those advocates of a "sense of place" who have increasingly nourished a hungry audience seeking nature and community, these quiet and largely unpublished homesteaders sound not unlike such nature-writing gurus as Wendell Berry and Gary Snyder. Snyder calls on the wisdom of a Haida elder—"dress up and stay at home"—to remind us that it is in our own backyards that our creativity and spirituality ought most to be cultivated.[14] Similarly, Wendell Berry warns his readers of the practical and spiritual chain of life that is broken when local culture is compromised or destroyed: "The triumph of the industrial economy is the fall of community. But the fall of community reveals how precious and necessary community is. For when community falls, so must fall all the things that only community life can engender and protect: the care of the old, the care and education of children, family life, neighborly work, the handing down of memory, the care of the earth, respect for nature and the lives of wild creatures." The recipe Berry offers for the preservation of meaning in the industrial age is to foster a deep practical and spiritual relationship to a particular place. By living and working "in place," Berry argues, we become aware of the interdependencies that industrial culture seeks to have us forget, deny, or destroy. Being in place is practiced by eating locally, caring for the land, taking responsibility and developing affection for one's home, animals, and natural surround. "Community," writes Berry, "when it is alive and well, is centered on the household—the family place and economy."[15] While unsung in the literary world, the homesteaders of northern Maine articulate similar desires to nurture local culture, a home-based economy, and a sustainable way of living. In many senses, they are the Wendell Berrys and Gary Snyders of their rugged, coastal lands.

Definitions

Beyond recognizing the creative passion of these homesteaders and beyond hearing their voices as part of a broader literary and cultural tradition of dissent, what are we to do analytically with these three visions of homesteading?

How might we define homesteading given the range and variety of expressions, not only today, but in earlier periods of late nineteenth- and twentieth-century American history? In the introduction, I offered some first-order comments about what homesteading is and is not. Now we need to thicken the discussion.

A homestead, wrote Scott Nearing in 1972, "is a habitation in which a family group manages to eke out a living on its own."[16] In defining homesteading in terms of the problem of livelihood and the place where that problem is solved, Nearing offers a classic, and restrained, definition that is clearly the fruit of a former economics professor's reasoning. Even within this rather limited definition, however, a note of idealism persists, for the task of eking out a living on one's own is always performed in the context of wider, unavoidable dependencies. Indeed, no homesteader I have ever met—including, and sometimes especially, the Nearings—has managed the task of complete self-sufficiency, by which I mean complete divorce from the "price-profit" economy against which Nearing and many other homesteaders have defined themselves.

A willingness to acknowledge the impossibility of the self-sufficiency ideal exists on a continuum, like many other aspects of homesteading. Some acknowledge from the outset that they are not purists. "Above all," writes one homesteading couple, "we are pragmatists, rather than romantics. Our living here was not so much an attempt to 'get back to nature' as it was simply to pursue and promote a sane and sustainable way of life."[17] While denying romanticism (which they see as a criticism), this couple also recognizes that the pursuit of sanity and sustainability are intricately bound up with living on nature's terms.

Others have been more openly idealistic, seeking self-sufficiency initially but soon discovering the unanticipated consequences of their cottage industry choices. With the humor that can be afforded only by time and distance, Elizabeth and Charles Long remember how their visions of a backyard milk supply were soon thwarted by nonhuman interests: "There was Isadora the self-milking goat. . . . We tried milking her early, feeding her more, even telling her she'd go blind if she kept it up. But Isadora stubbornly continued to short-circuit the dairy plan . . . in one end and out the other."[18] Still others find that their practices shift with time, changing values, and practical circumstance. Some who started with high degrees of self-sufficiency, selling products produced on the land, later moved to part-time jobs in town, while continuing to grow most of their food at home. While some homesteaders may not be achieving economic self-sufficiency, many strive toward what Janet Chadwick has called "food sufficiency."[19]

But however troublesome the term (and the achievement of) *self-sufficiency* might be, the ideal persists as a model to strive for in many homesteading projects. The ideal is expressed in the desire to grown one's own food, reduce spending, and "make do or do without." "True homesteaders," writes Sophia Hauserman, are those who "spend most of their time directly providing for their own needs." As Jane Dwinell puts it: "The homesteading dream, to me, means simple living, making do with what you have and doing for yourself as much as possible. Providing our own power, heat, food, lumber and skills [is] deeply satisfying to me." While not all the homesteaders introduced in these pages share the Nearings' stated reverence for frugality and asceticism as virtues in themselves, all homesteaders advocate some combination of self-production and self-reliance, whether having to do primarily with food and shelter or work and leisure.[20]

An equally important aspect of homesteading life is a commitment to rural living or, at least, to living "closer to nature" than one has before or than the majority of Americans seem to do. While Catherine Mills forthrightly explains that she is not a purist in the self-sufficiency department, she nonetheless emphasizes the sense of well-being that can come only from a combination of resisting consumerism and living close to the land: "Life in the city can seem easy because, for a price, there are services and products to meet every need. But I can't buy peace to soothe me or an environment to remind me that I, too, am an animal and I need to rest more than I need to buy something. When I am on the land although I have little, I find I want nothing."[21] Similarly, Reed, a homesteader living not far from the Nearings in Maine, spoke to me of his need to leave the world of the academy behind so that "regular contact" with nature would be a significant part of his daily life. To do so, he left a doctoral program and taught himself to craft and sell homemade wines and ciders from the orchards behind his house.[22]

In the realm of "getting close to nature" too, however, ideals and realities blend, for living intimately with nature can mean choosing a distant backwoods retreat as a home site or turning one's suburban backyard into a productive organic garden with room for a brood of chickens and a milk goat. As homesteading advocates throughout the century have suggested, only five acres may be needed for "independence" or three for "liberty."[23] Few homesteaders, in fact, are strict wilderness advocates or John Muir–like retreatants. They may share with Muir the rejection of a religious upbringing in favor of the worship of King Sequoia, but wilderness travel and living are not their primary mode. Although degrees of alteration and manipulation may vary, their very livelihoods depend on having some impact on their natural surround. Having such impact, in fact, is why homesteaders and small farmers have often been overlooked as part of the nature writing or environmentalist tradition, a trend this study hopes to correct.[24]

The point is not "back to the land," Bill Coperthwaite once informed me, "but down to earth."[25] In coining his own definition, Coperthwaite was pointing out the importance of attitude, that *disposition* toward nature matters as much as *where* in nature the homestead is located. As more than one subscriber to an Internet "Homesteading" list has commented: "Homesteading is a state of mind." Another confirmed, "It is more a feeling or experience that is unique to everyone."[26] Editors Jd and Diane Belanger, on the masthead of *Countryside and Small Stock Journal* (one of a number of popular homesteading magazines), directly address the philosophy that binds together the writers and readers of their "how-to" publication. Defining homesteaders as "practitioners of the simple life," the Belangers go on to say that the simple life can have many forms: "It's not a single idea, but many ideas and attitudes, including a reverence for nature and a preference for country life; a desire for maximum personal self-reliance and creative leisure . . . a certain nostalgia for the supposed simplicities of the past and an anxiety about the technological and bureaucratic complexities of the future."[27] That reverence for nature is at the top of the list of defining attributes of homesteaders is not surprising. While homesteaders may disagree on whether to eat meat or live "off-the-grid" (and these points of divergence will surface throughout this study), all express a commitment to *nature*, while constructing the meaning of what is *natural* in a variety of ways.[28]

Contemporary homesteaders vary a great deal in the particular choices they make about their lives. How, then, can we generalize? In my reading of the texts and lives I have come to know in the course of this study, I would argue that homesteaders share a common commitment to on-the-ground environmental ethics, do-it-yourself pragmatics, and an improvisational, nature-based spiritual practice. Practicing the arts of "voluntary simplicity" is often a stated goal of homesteaders, although the voluntary simplicity movement itself (which includes urban and suburban efforts to reduce consumption) casts a considerably wider net.[29] At the same time, the homesteaders I came to know best tended to take themselves with a grain of salt in terms of the voluntary simplicity movement. On several occasions, my neighbors would pile into a sauna after a day of groveling in the garden or hammering on the roof, cursing themselves for having made a commitment to what they liked to call "voluntary stupidity."

While homesteading, then, involves particular practices, the larger ideals to which it points are often what distinguishes homesteading from, say, pursuing farming as a business or choosing gardening as a hobby. Behind the Nearings' definition of homesteading stood the unwavering vision of the Good Life, a life that homesteading makes possible. One of Scott Nearing's characterizations of the Good Life was that it constitutes a spirit and practice of "affirmation," affirmation of the values of human life and of the significance of the earth and all of its creatures. Living the Good Life, in the broadest terms, means living "in and of the universe, as a glad, responsible, participant in a magnificent enterprise."[30] Each homesteader I have interviewed or whose story I have read has expressed some vision of what the Good Life means. That vision runs through their homesteading experiment like a cool spring through a homestead's back forty, or back five.

Conversion Narratives

"I used to be a dancer in New York City and now I raise leeks." This one-sentence conversion narrative was uttered to me one December morning as a neighbor came to drop by a holiday offering of a tree ornament, a handmade felted carrot.[31] Both the comment and the carrot resonated symbolically. The ornament's referent was the way of life its creator had chosen, a life of gardening and home-based artistry, far removed from the urban center of artistic life where she once had lived. Amid the pragmatic, there is always an ethic. Particular visions of the Good Life, or of a good life, may vary, but—revealingly—they are often written against the backdrop of the "bad life" that homesteading might overturn or resist. It is in this sense that the decision to homestead is often described in the language of conversion, a word that literally means turning from one situation to another.

Written testaments of homesteading often begin with the Thoreauvian trope of answering questions posed by those still occupying the cultural world of the "old life." Thoreau tells us, perhaps disingenuously, that he would not have written *Walden* without such questions: "I should not obtrude my affairs . . . if very particular inquiries had not been made . . . concerning my mode of life. . . . Some have asked what I got to eat; if I did not feel lonesome; if I was not afraid and the like."[32] Whether these questions were actually posed or not, Thoreau uses this opening interrogative model to establish for his readers that the questions "society" asks are not ones that he is terribly worried about. Thoreau is ultimately more interested in cultivating beans as a means of coming to know himself and of experiencing intimacy with the natural world than he is in growing beans for mere food or economic gain. But he needs to "set up" his text by referring first to the world he has left behind and inferring that society's typical concerns are rather silly ones.

Countless stories of homesteading begin on this same boundary between the life left behind and the new life being chosen. "Before I came here," the narrator begins and goes on to describe a previous life of personal confusion, unhealthy surroundings, a work life that was fast-paced and unrewarding, a way of living that seemed disconnected from what was really important. In offering a definition of homesteading as "living closer to the earth with the people you love without outside interference," one homesteader clarified not only what she held dear in her current life but also what she sorely lacked in her former one.[33]

Other homesteader-authors follow suit. Harlan Hubbard claims he was often asked, "Why did you choose to live in this forsaken hollow on the fringe of society?" The soft-spoken testaments of his book constitute his reply: the social "fringe" of life lived on the edge of the Ohio River is the spiritual "center." Louise Dickinson Rich reports being queried, "Isn't the way you live escapism?" She responds, "It is not escapism," but rather "the exchange of one set of problems for another." For example, she offers, she has exchanged "the problem of keeping out from under car wheels for the problem of not getting lost in the woods . . . or the problem of being bored to death by one's neighbor for the problem of being bored to death by oneself."[34]

It has often struck me that homesteaders tend to produce as many texts as they do vegetables. Like Thoreau, many homesteaders express innocence in their motivations for writing, though they also admit that writing itself—however "unplanned"—helps support the homesteading venture, often more than selling homegrown carrots or potatoes does. Rich, for instance, relates how a trial submission to the Saturday Evening Post is almost accidentally accepted. Brad and Vena Angier marvel at how a piece of fiction is fortuitously jettisoned in favor of an article on wild foods that, ironically, provides eighty dollars of badly needed grocery money.[35] Similarly, in a desperate move to continue homesteading while earning a graduate degree, the young Gene Logsdon bangs out a story about "amusing things that happened on the farm at home" and finds to his shock and amusement: "Magic. A check for $200 came back."[36] The sense of wonder at receiving cash for homesteading tales allows the authors to express a certain remove from the culture of consumption they are explicitly resisting. But the tone of marvel at their good fortune also serves as a kind of testimony to their sense of "rightness" about the lifework they have undertaken. Circumstance and fate conspire to give them the support when they most need it and to provide the reassurance that others want to hear about the lives they have chosen.

Regardless of their mixed motivations, homesteader-authors provide valuable insight into the world of meaning-making through homesteading. Homesteaders gravitate toward authorship not simply because writing is a potentially lucrative "cash crop." The proliferation of texts demonstrates a need to tell the story, to give one's own accounting of what kind of life had to be rejected and what kind of rebirth was initiated, regardless of the physical, emotional, and financial hardship that such conversions involve. Like more traditional conversion narratives, these stories are told because they have to be told, because they bear witness to right ways of living and encourage others to follow suit.

It is important to recognize that these conversion narratives are not the testaments of just post-1960s spiritual seekers. Reflecting on his own turning-point year of 1920, former advertising and marketing consultant Ralph Borsodi recalled:

> We lived in New York City—the metropolis of the country. We had the opportunity . . . to use the speedy subways, the smart restaurants, the great office buildings, the libraries, theaters, public schools—all the thousand and one conveniences which make New York one of the most fantastic creations in the history of man. . . . [But] how could we enjoy them . . . when we lacked the zest of living which comes from real health and suffered all the minor and sometimes major ailments which come from too much excitement, too much artificial food, too much sedentary work, and too much [of] the smoke and noise and dust of the city . . . when our lives were barren of real beauty, the beauty which comes only from contact with nature and from the growth of the soil[?][37]

Bolton Hall, a friend of Borsodi's father and an advocate of urban homesteading in Philadelphia, put his vision of personal and social reform through homesteading in more explicitly religious terms. Preceding the publication of Borsodi's *Flight from the City* by almost thirty years, Hall wrote in *Three Acres and Liberty*: "Life belongs in the garden. Do you remember—the first chapters of Genesis show us our babyhood in a garden—the garden that all babyhood remembers, and the last chapters [of the Apocalypse] leave us with a vision of the garden in the holy city, on either side of the river, where the trees yield their fruits every month and bear leaves of universal healing. Just so will it be in our holy cities of the future—the garden will be right there 'in the midst.' "[38]

In the 1930s we hear not only the witty testament to country living of Louise Dickinson Rich but also the more earnest exhortations of William Duryee. Duryee served as both a family homesteader and an assistant to the president of Sheffield Farms Company in New York. His narrative clearly follows a "sin and redemption" model: "The family attracted to the city by the lure of high industrial wages and by crowded avenues finds . . . that it has lost its moorings. In seeking means of reestablishment free of the terrifying complications of industrial life, the mind turns to the country, to the soil. . . . The open country seems ready to welcome back her errant children graciously and to enfold them within her protecting bosom."[39] Today, some ecofeminists might recoil at Duryee's portrait of "Mother Earth [as] a generous but exacting parent" eager to forgive the sins of wayward (male) industrial capitalists and to welcome back the prodigal children. Religious pluralists may find Bolton Hall's references to Genesis a bit quaint and outmoded. The point here, however, is not to offer a critique of homesteading authors' tone or use of metaphor, though many passionate advocates indeed succumb to a certain degree of purple prose. The point, rather, is to see that these narratives are *conversion narratives* of a kind and thus, not surprisingly, occasionally overeager and overblown.

The persistent trope of homesteading narrative as conversion narrative continues from its first expression in Thoreau's desire to "drive life into a corner" while at Walden to the more explicitly environmentalist expressions of the 1960s and beyond. Here too, however, the spiritual motif persists, with fewer biblical references, perhaps, but with no less evangelical fervor. Consider a piece of Wendell Berry's early writing in which he reflects on his days spent at "the Camp," a rustic family outpost not far from his boyhood home in Port Royal, Kentucky. In 1961, on the eve of his departure for a literary fellowship in Paris, Berry reflects on his time at the Camp:

> In those days I began the long difficult realization of the complexity of life in this place. Until then . . . I had thoughtlessly accepted the common assumption . . . that the world is merely an inert surface that man lives on and uses. . . . And that summer, I remember, I began to think of myself as living within rather than upon the life of the place. . . . That summer I began to see, however dimly, that one of my ambitions, perhaps my governing ambition, was to belong fully to this place, to belong as the thrushes and the herons and the muskrats belonged, to be altogether at home here. . . . It is a spiritual ambition, like goodness. The wild creatures belong to the place by nature, but as a man I can belong to it only by understanding and virtue. It is an understanding I cannot hope to succeed in wholly, but I have come to believe that it is the most worthy of all.[40]

Berry's choice to return to the region of his childhood and to farm was not preformulated as a sustainable plan for his life. It is not as if Berry had said to himself, "I think I will farm part-time and then become a prolific writer and sought-after cultural critic." The pattern of Berry's life has unfolded as a conversion process wherein one makes the primary commitment of the heart and then shapes one's life according to that commitment. A serious Christian might call this process "growing in God," while Berry might term it "growing in place." But for Berry—a cranky, subversive, and thoroughly committed Christian—the two go hand in hand.

Cultural Sin

Of course, not all homesteading narratives are as infused with explicitly spiritual language as those of Wendell Berry or Bolton Hall, but every narrative I have read or heard has a similar dynamic. It tells a story of meaning-making, infused with a plot of being "lost" in a world of consumerism, industrialism, rampant individualism, and, more recently, environmental degradation, until "found" again in a life lived close to nature. A desire for intimacy with nature, new forms of self-cultivation and self-knowledge, and the fostering of community and local culture are all at work here. Not surprisingly, we find similar desires at work in more traditional, institutional quests for a religious life. The pursuit of the Good Life is a practice that attempts to heal the wrongs of the world—sometimes through broad visions of reform, as in the work of Ralph Borsodi and the Nearings; sometimes through more privatized, small-scale efforts at "doing no harm" and living lightly on the land. To borrow language from Protestant theology, conversion to homesteading—making the decision to resist industrialization, consumerism, and artificial living—functions as a kind of "justification," a realization that one has been living wrongly. The daily practice of homesteading, in turn, becomes a way of living a kind of sanctified life. The ultimate reference point, however, is not usually God (though it is for writers such as Berry) but nature itself as the source of goodness and authority.

While most homesteading texts tend to be bright-eyed and optimistic—sometimes to a fault—a sense of sin lurks within these stories and plays a role in making them not mere autobiography or how-to but stories of conversion. The Nearings, for instance, were both famous and infamous—depending on the audience—for their professed asceticism. On Thanksgiving, for example, Helen was fond of abstaining from food while others feasted, feeling that a personal practice of refusing food would be an important commentary on (and way of healing) American habits of overindulgence. The Nearings staunch work ethic, unyielding vegetarianism, and strict fasting regimes (more consistent in textual representation than in practice) will be discussed in more detail in chapter 3. But they are worth noting here as a way of elucidating how homesteading practices and texts are, whatever else they may be, *symbolic* commentaries on what is "wrong" with the dominant culture and what is "right" with the newfound way of life.

Of course, such practices can be taken to an extreme, and the danger of such extremes was noted by one of the Nearing neighbors, Ernest, whose vision of homesteading is more defined by the model of French country hedonism than by the Nearing post-Protestant style of abstention and rigor. "Healthy-minded homesteaders are not apt to pursue extreme self-sufficiency," he remarked. "The homesteader who tries to live an almost cavemanlike existence is always caught up in trying *not* to do things, not to use any power tools, not to eat meat, not to buy things. But they're usually running away from something and are being extreme. Healthy-minded homesteaders are moving toward something. They are more apt to be productive."[41] Quite unintentionally, Ernest adopts the language of William James to characterize a variety of homesteading practices. While it is not my purpose to apply Jamesian theory to homesteading practice for the purposes of any lengthy analysis, I do think that it is worth meditating a moment on Ernest's accidental reference to the author of *The Varieties of Religious Experience.*

In James's study of individual religious experience, he employed the language of "healthy-mindedness"—and its opposite—to make a kind of catalog of religious types. James's typology helps us to conceptualize certain homesteaders' experiences as spiritual journeys of the "sick-soul" toward what James called the hard-won "healthy-mindedness of the twice-born." For some, homesteading becomes the conversion process through which the sick soul remakes itself while the body is building a garden and house. The choices homesteaders make, however, differ from those of practicing Christians—James's primary examples—in some important ways.

The sick soul, as James describes it, is characterized by one of several dispositions: an awareness of the vanity of mortal things, a sense of sin, and a fear of the universe (a literal terror of the evil at work in the natural world and of the insecurity of life).[42] With regard to this last category, of course, most homesteaders appear not to suffer from a particular fear of natural evil, for they actively welcome nature into their daily lives. An awareness of the vanity of mortal things and a sense of sin, however, are more recognizable features in the character of some homesteaders or, more particularly, in their self-descriptions of who they were before they began to homestead. The feeling that mortal things are vain tends to express itself particularly in a rejection of the materialism of American culture. While homesteaders, unlike traditional religious converts, do not then reach out toward a life of prayer, membership in a religious community, or contemplation of an otherworldly, spiritual realm, they do tend to cultivate a kind of "spiritual materialism" in which natural things have spiritual value, while artificial products or conveniences are treated as polluting in both a literal and a moral sense. Raymond Mungo remarks that life at Total Loss Farm was a quest for "the truly material . . . not the fake comforts of Buick or Sylvania, but the richness of soil and the texture of oatmeal bread."[43] The sense of sin comes not from remorse about breaking religious behavioral codes but from a drive to repent a previous life of poor health, consumerism, political apathy, and nonecological thinking or behavior. The "cure" is not relocation to heaven but relocation to a new piece of earth. The work performed on and in that earth constitutes an inscription of a new, "healthy-minded" self. Homesteading texts are often unintentionally rich with a Christian language of sin and redemption or inflected with Jewish themes of choosing to return (*teshuvah*) to the source of life. Or the reader may hear a more general, spiritualized evocation of loss and recovery: the loss of self, nature, and community; the recovery of these through a re-creation of home.

Remaking the Sacred and the Profane

Homesteading is about much more than simply a return to nature. But nature occupies the symbolic center of homesteading, even if the turn to nature is an ambivalent one. Before probing this ambivalence, however, it is worth lingering on the more common constructions of nature that come to the fore through interviews and texts; this is the construction of nature as "sacred." The range of vocabularies here is wide. Wendell Berry, for instance, draws on traditional Christian language while pushing the implications of that language toward the boundaries of cultural and political radicalism. Berry writes of the farm as a literal and symbolic manifestation of the "Kingdom of God" on (and in) earth. His examples of living in right relationship with the topsoil are most often grounded in the books of the Bible, the religious texts with which he and his readership are most familiar.[44] At the same time, Berry notes that his chosen phrase is merely a "local term," one that may easily be exchanged with the Great Economy (the earth's *oikus* or household), the Buddhist economy, or the Tao. Berry makes the religious case for his farming life clear when he asserts: "The [so-called] drudgery of growing one's own food . . . is not drudgery at all. . . . It is—in addition to being the appropriate fulfillment of a practical need—a sacrament, as eating is also, by which we enact our oneness with the Creation, the conviviality of one body with all bodies."[45] Berry is no fan of institutional Christianity, which he sees as more concerned with building funds and self-perpetuation than with nourishing the spiritual needs of the community.[46] Instead, Berry proposes a mode of sacramental life through participation in nature—not simply recreational visits to "the outdoors."

Just as Berry recounts for readers the myriad ways in which farming is a sacrament, so does his friend and colleague Gene Logsdon rely on traditional Christian imagery, even while giving such imagery a rebellious tweak. Logsdon describes homesteaders as "pioneers, seeking a new kind of religious and economic freedom" whose God "does not reside in the inner sanctums of cathedrals, but walks with us, hoeing in the fields."[47] For Logsdon, like Berry, the use of Christian language is far from circumstantial. Logsdon's first career choice was to be a priest. (Relatedly, one of Scott Nearing's early interests was to be a minister.) Like Nearing, Logsdon ultimately concluded that institutional religion was corrupt and confining, not a fair judgment in all cases, perhaps, but one that emerged authentically from his life experiences, including time spent in seminary. For Berry, Logsdon, and many others, the sacralization of nature comes, in part, from a preexisting religious stance toward the world that remains even after the commitment to institutional religion has been rejected. The ideals inherent in the religious worldview persist, even while nature moves to the center of a new, extraecclesial religious life. Thus, the "mainstream" world is still seen as "fallen" in the sense that the priorities of American culture seem to be extreme individualism, financial gain, and the perpetuation of self-interest. But now simple living close to nature is seen as the way out of this fallen world, a means of nourishing community, spiritual life, and a way of living in which human interests are not always at the center.

Other homesteaders are less apt to use explicitly Christian language but speak of being "connected" to plants, rocks, and animals; of feeling included in and comforted by the ongoing seasonal cycles of birth and death made visible in the garden; of experiencing the pleasurable dissolution of the self in the face of the larger forces of the natural world, such as a bold prairie wind or a star-soaked alpine sky. While many of these homesteaders are contemporaries of Logsdon and Berry, they are not as comfortable with the traditional language of church and synagogue, even if that language is being used in the service of cultural critique. At the same time, their ways of talking about what they do frequently invoke the word *spiritual* or choose images for the human-nature relationship that resemble familiar images of the relationship between humanity and God. They may depict nature as all-powerful and all-knowing, nature as beneficent parent, nature as the source of the mysteries of life and death, or nature as the ideal model of harmony, balance, and goodness. Whether recognizably Jewish or Christian or more broadly and eclectically spiritual, the language that homesteaders use to talk about nature is a language that tends to portray nature as sacred.

If—as I am proposing throughout this study—homesteaders are engaged in a complex negotiation of religious and cultural work, a major part of this work is the *sacralization of nature,* a term several scholars have coined to describe a phenomenon that mediates between secularization and more traditional religious thought.[48] In using this term, I may seem to be arguing that sacralizing nature is something that homesteaders consciously *do:* they identify nature as sacred and then adjust and refine their actions in nature accordingly. Yet in homesteaders' lives, the relationship with nature is rarely enacted in such a plodding, self-conscious, or one-directional manner. They do not see themselves as making nature sacred; rather, nature is profoundly—and sometimes unexpectedly—*experienced* as sacred, in ways not unlike the experience of divine revelation, whether slowly over time or suddenly in the biblical "twinkling of an eye." Such experiences may inspire an individual to a life of homesteading, or they may occur and accumulate in the context of homesteading practice.

In talking about the sacralization of nature, then, I am consciously walking a middle path between the competing hazards of implying either that nature is not sacred but that homesteaders make it so or, on the other hand, that nature is sacred and that an investigation of homesteaders' experiences and actions must begin with this fundamental acknowledgment.[49] As with any study of religious or spiritual experience, we must keep our ears attuned to the ways in which the people we study think and talk about their experiences, as well as become aware of where our own presuppositions may lie. In this book, that means paying attention to how homesteaders enact and talk about their spiritual experiences in and with nature, in other words, the way they construct nature and themselves. At the same time, my interest as a student of religion, history, and culture is to explore and interpret the means by which the possibility of experiencing the natural world as sacred becomes available in our "cultural repertoire."[50] Just as we might ask how American Protestant commitment to the idea of predestination moved away from the center of theological life in the eighteenth and nineteenth centuries, we must also ask how and by what means do the experiences of nature we are discussing here enter onto the cultural stage?

The most obvious factor in late twentieth-century America is the decline of traditional religious objects and practices: church and churchgoing, God and prayer to God, heaven and living in ways that secure one's getting there. While both popular literature and formal sociological studies assure their readers that religious activities such as prayer and church attendance are as vibrant as ever, certainly in some sectors of contemporary American society (generally the socially and politically liberal ones) this is not the case.[51] While America may not be as secular as once was feared by some, certain segments of the population express persistent suspicions about what was once undeniably "sacred" in traditional Jewish and Christian contexts. Among the liberal, educated, and scientifically inclined, there is a kind of poverty of language about the sacred.

What we see at work in the lives of homesteaders is the expression of religious or spiritual experience with and in nature that for some individuals (or their ancestors) used to occur in traditional Jewish or Christian contexts and that for many continues to occur today. These experiences in nature (about which we will hear more in ensuing chapters) may involve a private sense of the dissolution of the self, say, by performing the daily ritual of carrying water from a well, or they may be a shared experience of feeling connected to the "All" of the natural world through regularly performing a group ritual such as cooking together, observing a seasonal festival, or gathering for a sauna. For the more traditionally devout—or in earlier times—these same experiences of the expansion or dissolution of the self may have occurred privately "before God" or "in the hand of God," as in daily morning prayer or in the social context of enacting one's connection to a power larger than the self, such as participating in a church liturgy. As with religious experiences of loss or dissolution of the self before God, these experiences in nature can occur as profound life-changing moments or as less intense daily reminders of the proper relationship between nature and the self. Significantly, these experiences are not just momentary happenings, such as the psychospiritual "peak experience" that one might have climbing a mountain and that, depending on one's religious orientation, might be interpreted alternately as "communing with nature" or finding oneself in the "true hand of God."[52] The experiences of homesteaders, while similar, are ones that occur in the context of lives that have been dramatically transformed in part *because* of such experiences. In this sense, they are akin to more traditional religious experiences (of divine transcendence and immanence and of self-expansion or self-dissolution) that either incite conversion or occur in the daily lives of those who count themselves among the converted.

If we understand the transformation of the self in nature (as opposed to the self before God) as one aspect of a ritual life of homesteading, we begin to see more clearly the mutually reinforcing aspects of these processes. The nature of the experience may differ for individual homesteaders, just as conversion may be instantaneous or evolutionary. In most cases, however, encountering nature's sacredness involves either losing the self in nature or finding oneself to be intimately connected to all of nature, an experience that, in turn, reinforces the understanding of nature as sacred. At the same time, we must remember that these experiences of "loss of self" or "expansion of self" are also about the construction of the self in and through the experience of what is sacred. Like more traditional religious experience, this is a multivalent process, one that cannot be "explained away" as being psychological but not spiritual, or vice-versa.

A life of homesteading ritualizes a complex relationship with nature, one in which nature is placed at the center of life, as the source of meaning and authority. These ritualizations (both the original choice to homestead and the daily practices of homesteading), then, often bring about more experiences of nature in which the self is lost before or taken up by a power that is "greater." Or nature may be redefined to emphasize the spiritual in a way that scientific naturalism would not, as when nature is seen as a source of immortality.

In choosing to engage in daily practices that are as symbolic as they are pragmatic and to cast these practices in explicitly religious or vaguely spiritual terms, most homesteaders are simultaneously engaged in acts of rebellion and revitalization. While some are rejecting the religious traditions to which they are born or those that they find oppressively dominant in American culture, many are also redefining these same traditions, or choosing new ones, in that recognizably American way of "shopping" for spirituality.[53]

An important aspect of this dynamic of rebellion and revitalization—of linking daily farm labor with old and new religious practices—is a longing for ritual itself. Indeed, the quest for ritual among the religiously disaffected in modern American culture is often synonymous with the quest for religious experience.[54] Homesteaders who speak of gardening as "meditation," of building from locally harvested materials as a "discipline," of working outdoors in the nude as "attuning" oneself to the sun and soil, frequently interpret their actions as responses to what they see as missing in the lives they led before they took up homesteading.

While the longer history of getting close to nature as a spiritual practice will be told in later chapters, we should take an initial glance at more recent decades. Among the most explicitly "spiritual" readings of nature by American back-to-the-landers are those given by the countercultural youth of the 1960s and 1970s who headed for hills, forests, and deserts in droves, particularly in the period between 1968 and the late 1970s. While relatively few of the 1960s back-to-the-land efforts—particularly communal ones—remained successful in later decades or were even able to establish a stable economic and social world during the time they were in operation, Total Loss Farm, despite its name, was a notable exception.[55] Its membership shifted with the seasons, but among its more permanent and better-known figures were Raymond Mungo, Alicia Bay Laurel, Pete Gould, Marty Jezer, and Verandah Porche.[56] Like many of the homesteaders we have met and will meet, the members of Total Loss Farm were highly educated individuals, dissatisfied with the educational, religious, and professional status quo and looking for meaningful lives and livelihoods. While discontent with the religious upbringings of their youth was just one of their common cultural complaints, frustration with the restrictions and inadequacies of organized religion is a recurrent theme in many of the essays written for a collective reflection on life at the farm, entitled Home Comfort.[57] Some of the denizens of Total Loss Farm had come to see their confirmations, first communions, and bar mitzvahs as initiations into a bourgeois world of social distinction and moral hypocrisy, in which they wanted no part. Others were intellectually and spiritually persuaded by the religious traditions of the East, took up graduate study as an alternative path to religious enlightenment, but ultimately "dropped out" in search of more experiential means of learning sacred mysteries. Still others articulated a sense of having been generally "lost" until finally "found" through the daily work of sowing, weeding, reaping, milking, and wood chopping.

In an essay appropriately titled "Who's in Charge," Richard Wizansky begins by describing work patterns on the farm and concludes with a meditation on farm life that accentuates its essentially religious aspects:

[This is] what I think happened here. That the wind and the snow, the explosions of green and summertime blew us all down, taught us lessons about time and sequence of events and especially where direction comes from.

Now the rhythm of our work is that rhythm. And the farm as a whole, its plantings, plowings, harvests, business transactions, decision makings etc. can be seen as a mirror image in the larger picture of what each one of us learned in his relationship with . . . whatever it is that's out there. . . . In the image, the farm becomes a power or an idea or a movement greater than each individual or even the group as a whole, which like a simile for what's out there, has a rhythm, a process which gives cues, and which one, not necessarily submitting to, becomes a part of [first ellipses in the original].[58]

Wizansky's language is certainly less precise than that of a Wendell Berry. While evocative, it is also stumbling and inarticulate, hesitating to name the force or power beyond the self that he acknowledges exists for each of his fellow farmers. His diction is indicative of the vague searching and finding that is emblematic of the religious lives of American youth in the 1960s.

Despite their inability to capture their experiences with precision and their unwillingness to rely on explicitly Christian interpretations, the authors of Home Comfort share Wendell Berry's notion of farming as a sacred act and his notion of the familiar round of farming chores as a liturgy full of daily sacraments. Verandah Porche, in an essay on milking and cheese making (wittily entitled "The Making of a Culture Counter") praises the blessings of having to do daily devotions to Bessie, the cow: "Bessie has taught me many lessons: care of the cow brings good fortune. . . . She taught me that dawn and dusk are the most ineffably beautiful parts of the day, and that repetition is often prayer instead of drudgery."[59] In Porche's words we hear the echo of Berry's remarks quoted above: what is drudgery for some is sacrament for others. Not surprisingly, however, the sacramental nature of farming is more often celebrated by those who have freely chosen to leave their old lives behind and to convert (or return) to farming when life in the city or suburbs has ceased to have meaning.

Wizansky and his fellow farmers are all involved in the creation of an emergent (and therefore fuzzy) theology of the farm. Accompanying this theology is an attendant liturgy of farm-based labor. Here we see that pragmatic theologies of nature may inspire new religious language—or the reconstitution of ancient (or imagined) pagan imagery—but they also frequently involve a relocation of the very religious images (or doctrinal themes) that these newfound farmers are trying to escape.

An example of such relocation of traditional religion into the world of the homestead can be found in the testament of one of Total Loss Farm's most magnetic personalities, Raymond Mungo. In his portrayal of homesteading life in *Total Loss Farm: A Year in the Life*, Mungo depicts his journey from religious disaffection to spiritual renewal, wherein life on the Vermont farm plays a pivotal, if not final, role.[60] Like so many of the 1960s youth who headed to the backwoods with vans full of tents and Rodale gardening books or who trekked up to the Nearing households for homesteading lessons and personal advice, Mungo had little but hostility for the church of his youth. "They say there is no more virulent anti-Catholic than a former one," he writes. "I'm living proof of the bigotry that comes of rebellion to indoctrination."[61] But once established on Total Loss Farm, Mungo writes of the practice of gardening in a particularly revealing manner. This self-described virulent anti-Catholic chooses his words with uncanny resonance. Mungo writes: "I travel now in a society of friends who heat their houses with hand-cut wood . . . [who] weed potatoes with their university-trained hands, pushing long hair out of their way and thus marking their foreheads with beautiful penitent dust. We till the soil to atone for our fathers' destruction of it."[62] We might say of Mungo that while you can take the city boy out of the Catholic Church, you cannot take the Catholic Church out of his new life on the farm. His practice of homesteading and his understanding of nature is not simply religion newly discovered or created; it is religion relocated from the childhood church to the fields of young adulthood.

Yet another version of constructing nature as sacred is expressed when a religious reading of nature is borrowed from a religious tradition perceived to be more positively "nature-oriented" than the tradition (or absence thereof) with which they grew up. Kate spoke to me of her interest in homesteading as coming not only from remembrances of happy childhood experiences playing in the woods but also, later in life, from reading and talking with others about Native American practices.[63] Similarly, Fran began homesteading out of her own beliefs and impulses about what was "the right way to live" in relationship with nature but later felt challenged by the absence of reinforcement for the lifeways she had chosen. A Boston-area woman in her forties who started homesteading shortly after graduating from a prominent New England college, Fran found that while many shared her convictions in the 1970s, few in her immediate area seemed like-minded or even supportive. Settled in a semirural area in Massachusetts, she experienced the encroachments of both "suburban buildings and suburban thinking" on her chosen way of life. But when she started attending the meetings of a regional "medicine society" led by a Native American elder (but attended by many nonnative participants), she found both psychological and spiritual support for her own practices.[64] While in no way claiming (or wanting) to be living a tribal way of life, Fran, through her emerging knowledge of Native American cultures, has found a way to link her own practices with a particular spiritual tradition. In so doing, her vision of nature no longer exists in isolation or as a cultural aberration. While still proudly swimming against the cultural mainstream, Fran has found an alternative culture that provides her with a context (social, intellectual, and spiritual) in which to further contemplate and celebrate the intimate and reverent relationship with nature, one that she upholds each morning as she milks her goats and feeds her home-schooled children a breakfast of homemade bread and goat cheese.[65]

In homesteading narratives, the symbolic legacies of Judaism and Christianity are still clearly evident in the readings of nature that we see, though often these legacies are revitalized and reinterpreted as nature takes its place at the center of meaning. At other times, these legacies are downplayed in favor of a cultural "turn East" or a revitalization (sometimes ethically problematic) of native religious traditions.[66] While recently the importance of nature (and, in particular, a healthy environment) has begun to gain some attention within institutional religious traditions themselves, an emphasis on nature was not the norm of early religious experience in the homesteading lives I studied. Rather, what we see in homesteading texts and testaments is the way in which a spiritual critique of "worldliness," a view of dissent from a dominant culture, moves out of traditional religious contexts and into the realm of nature.

This move has many precedents and many complex historical threads going back, at least, to the unfolding of the Enlightenment, which the historian Peter Gay aptly deemed "the rise of modern paganism."[67] But this transformation also has one particular precedent in American history, a cultural hero of the turn to nature as a spiritual center and of the use of a living close to nature as a means of dissent. That is Henry David Thoreau. But just as contemporary homesteading is not merely about a turn to nature, so also was Thoreau's experiment at Walden not simply an experiment in seeking intimacy with the natural world. Thoreau's experiment was, in the tradition of Unitarian thinking, an experiment in self-cultivation. That experiment sometimes involved ambivalent responses to the natural world. It is to a beginning exploration of ambivalence that we now turn, probing the legacies that Thoreau has left us.

2

GETTING (NOT TOO) CLOSE TO NATURE

We talk of communing with nature, but 'tis with
ourselves we commune.

John Burroughs, *The Heart of Burroughs's Journals,*
November 27, 1877

The Legacy of Thoreau

When I first asked Helen Nearing what thinker had most influenced her life, she
instantly replied, "Thoreau." Subsequent conversations turned up a rotating
repertory of writers and activists who were touchstones for her: Scott Nearing,
of course, whose notebooks Helen frequently reread; Krishnamurti, her first
great romantic and spiritual companion; Olive Schreiner, an early feminist
writer whose books were often at Helen's bedside; and, Pearl Buck, a fellow Vermont intellectual and writer who had encouraged the Nearings in their first
publishing venture. But Thoreau's work was the most consistent foundation.[1]

As I have already shown, homesteading conversion narratives often model
themselves on Thoreau's example and on *Walden* as a ideal text. Certainly, his
writing serves as a template—offering a "why I did it" opening that many
homesteaders imitate. Homesteaders' testaments of their own efforts to "know
by experience" often borrow Thoreau's narrative structure (four seasons), his
objects of inquiry (visitors, animals, sounds, beans), and his rhetorical strategy
of moving from descriptions of "natural facts" to meditations on the "spiritual
facts" to which the natural observations point.[2] But the Thoreauvian influence
extends well beyond that of a literary model. *Walden* represented the essence of
"right-livelihood" for those ready and willing to follow his example.

Throughout the Nearings' texts, we find evidence of their admiration for
Thoreau's tightwad economics, his blend of personal optimism and social cyn-

icism, and his self-styled crankiness. Indeed, the Nearings welcomed those who characterized *Living the Good Life* as the "twentieth-century *Walden*." At the same time, however, some aspects of the Transcendentalist mind Helen and Scott chose to neglect or ignore. As with many readers, Helen never hesitated to point out that Thoreau was not truly *self-sufficient* at Walden, having ready access to the town and to the maternal cookie jar. Moreover, Thoreau liked to insist that a day of idleness was as worthy a pursuit as any. His portrait of a good day at Walden—"It was morning and lo, now it is evening, and nothing memorable is accomplished"—is an intentional send-up of the intense productivity depicted in the creation story of the book of Genesis.[3] Such pronouncements hardly resemble the Nearings' insistence on a "four-four-four" formula for patterning their days (four hours of farm-based "bread-labor," four hours of leisure time, and four hours of "association," i.e., building community and contributing to social reform). While the Nearings publicly recommended leisure—and certainly resisted dominant cultural models of "going to work"—their homesteading vision was inscribed with a strict Protestant work ethic that outclassed any ideal types Max Weber might have imagined.[4]

In fact, the four-hour block originally designated for leisure is elsewhere described as a time for "professional interests," such as violin playing and teaching (for Helen) and, together, writing, giving lectures, answering correspondence, and developing the Social Science Institute to further their reform work. Moreover, real life at the Nearing homestead, especially with the constant influx of visitors, was often a life in which private time had to be rigorously protected and sometimes did not exist. The Nearings' daily patterns often involved much more attention to "productive" and "serious" work than their early descriptions of sun bathing and music making suggested to hopeful readers.

Excerpts from *Walden* pepper the epigraphs that open the chapters of *Living the Good Life* and *Continuing the Good Life*, but these selections reveal a particular version of Thoreau, one who seems to be nodding with approval at certain aspects of the Nearing project: performing hard physical labor, simplifying daily wants, and keeping strictly vegetarian. But this is not the Thoreau who wants to ingest a woodchuck raw, infusing its wildness directly into his very being, nor is it the Thoreau who (surprising the unsuspecting reader) trembles with the fear of wilderness on the upper reaches of Kataadin. It is also not the Thoreau who praises idleness for its own sake or is content to leave the shores of Walden once his "experiment" is concluded. The Thoreau that appears in the Nearings' texts is Thoreau as ideal homesteader.

All readers of *Walden* have their own Thoreau. The text and the writer exhibit an enduring and fascinating complexity that allows him to be possessed by everyone and no one—so I found as I expanded the circle of my interviews and discovered that almost every homesteader had something to say about the curmudgeon of Concord. For Simon, Thoreau became a kind of mentor, speaking from a nineteenth-century text into his mid-twentieth-century situation. In the 1960s, living in New Hampshire in a wood-heated cabin, Simon was practicing a certain level of "simple living" while wondering if he was pursuing an important "life path" or simply living out of step with a society that he really ought to "get it together" to join. Taking a course on Transcendentalism at the local college was a turning point for him. "Suddenly I felt I had a philosophy to back up what I was already doing by instinct," Simon told me one day as our paths crossed on the road from his house. "When I read [*Walden*] I felt like Thoreau was telling me that what I was doing was OK, was the right thing to do, was a good thing to do, that, in fact, I should be living my life *more* as he did." In later years, when Simon built his own homestead in Maine and began to practice yoga and meditation on a regular basis, he found that Thoreau continued to serve as a guide. His wife, Grace, remembers how at a group meditation session they were supposed to focus their minds' eye on a spiritual guide, the guru of their particular practice, perhaps, or an image of the Buddha. Simon closed his eyes, but all he could see was Thoreau. Luckily, their teacher had no problem with this particular avatar, and Simon's experience reinforced in him the deep extent to which Thoreau served as a touchstone and model. Thoreau became as much of a guru as the Indian spiritual teacher was.[5]

Joshua also remarked to me that it was Thoreau who gave him permission to drop out of the mainstream but, ultimately, to drop *into* a commitment and dedication to a single place in nature. In the late 1960s and early 1970s, Josh had wondered if an agriculturally based life might be a solution to the social and ecological problems he saw dominating the American landscape. Out of interest in his religious heritage and curiosity about the mysteries of "real" agricultural work, Josh traveled to Israel and spent time on a kibbutz. As with some other kibbutzim, he soon realized that little about communal living and the daily grind was romantic. Not unlike Nathaniel Hawthorne's Miles Coverdale, who feared his thoughts at Blythdale (the fictional stand-in for the Transcendentalist Brook Farm) would become "cloddish" because of too much time spent digging in the soil, Josh worried that his old intellectual life might fall prey to the new agricultural one. What would happen to his mind if he spent his days reading only about "how to cultivate artichokes"? Would his thinking soon become only "artichoke" thinking? While traveling across the country and living out of a van following his return to the United States, Josh read and reread *Walden* with intensity. As with Simon, it was Thoreau who saved him. Walden provided a model for living close to nature in which "living meanly" was not simply an agricultural pursuit but also a spiritual and intellectual pursuit.[6]

In contemplating the impact and legacy of Thoreau on the lives of contemporary homesteaders we see an appreciation, then, primarily for the spiritual and intellectual Thoreau, one who provides philosophical foundations and, hence, legitimizing authority to those seeking to negotiate between a life of urban or suburban complacency and a rural life that could be dominated by physical labor without occasion for reflection. While a farmer of sorts, Thoreau consciously distinguishes himself from the conventional (eponymous) "John Field," who is bound by his work and who has no freedom to crack a book or write a poem. Field is Thoreau's antitype, a "man of the soil" only in the shallow sense. For while Field works in the soil, he does so to support habits that Thoreau is eager to persuade him to give up. Thus, in *Walden*, Thoreau reminds us that "as he [Field] began with tea, and coffee, and butter, and milk, and beef, he had to work hard to pay for them, and when he had worked hard he had to eat hard again to repair the waste of his system."[7] While Thoreau's reflections on Field are certainly patronizing—and elsewhere blatantly anti-Irish—his meditations in the "Baker Farm" chapter of *Walden* are intended to emphasize the distinction between farming as employment and the kind of "moral farming" in which he is engaged.

When taken to extremes, however, such a vision of agriculture as spiritual practice can even lead one to leave agricultural practices behind. Such ironies pervade Thoreau's work, most notably when he claims that growing fewer beans and more self-knowledge is his new plan for agricultural reform. His labor is not so much economic as it is an exercise in gnosis: "What shall I learn of beans or beans of me?" he wonders at the outset of his project. He openly relishes the fact that his bean field will not show up in the state commissioner of agriculture's survey, that it is a "half-civilized field," with birdsong rather than soil amendments serving as top dressing. And he vows that, in the next summer, he will "not plant beans and corn with so much industry . . . but such seeds, if the seed is not lost, as sincerity, truth, simplicity, faith, innocence and the like."[8] Thoreau's remarks confirm for us why criticisms about his proximity to town may be misplaced. His was not an experiment in self-sufficiency or wilderness living so much as it was an experiment in self-cultivation, a long-standing Unitarian virtue—extolled by Ralph Waldo Emerson, William Ellery Channing, and others—and put into practice at Walden.[9] The homesteaders in this study all surpass Thoreau in the longevity of their projects, but the fact that some homesteaders (including the Nearings) are not absolute in their self-sufficiency puts them in continuity with Thoreau more than in contrast with him. The symbolic dimensions of their work take precedence over the purity of economic independence.

It is important to read *Walden* as a text primarily about the experience of gaining spiritual knowledge and knowledge of the self (processes that, for the Unitarians and Transcendentalists, were conceptually intertwined). By understanding the significance of Thoreau for homesteaders and by recognizing the Walden experiment as a spiritual exercise of self-knowing, as much as an experience of nature, we are then better equipped to understand other homesteading efforts as being only partly about nature as such. As in the case of Thoreau, contemporary homesteaders go back to nature for a complex constellation of reasons. Living close to nature figures prominently in the life of homesteading, but nature is variously defined and not always as central as it may first appear.

A Tale of Two Gardens (1994)

What are the legacies that Thoreau has left us? What is sought in going "back to nature" and what is found? What aspects of homesteading pertain to nature—and the many ways it can be constructed—and what have to do with the self? To get a closer look, it is fitting to wander into the garden.

For most homesteaders, the garden is the center of a self-sufficient livelihood. While the cash crop may come in the form of blueberries, puppets, dried wreathes, or handcrafted cabinets, food for the family comes from the garden. But the garden is not simply "a store in the backyard," as homesteaders make clear through both actions and words. It is also the center for aesthetic expression and ethical decision making. Do you add animal products to your compost? Do you grow flowers as well as vegetables? Do you plant only the seeds you have saved yourself? The garden is also the place where nature is simultaneously welcomed and resisted, nourished and controlled. These choices are revealing, not only of the many ways in which nature is constructed in contemporary American culture, but also of the ways in which the self is made in and through these constructions of nature. Let us enter some gardens then, for a closer view.[10]

The first garden still thrives at the Good Life Center in Harborside, Maine.[11] The model for homesteaders past and present, it is distinguished by a hand-constructed stone wall that surrounds the fifty square feet of rich topsoil that once was barren clay. The Nearings collected stones for this wall on the shores of Penobscot Bay. They constructed the edifice using the same movable slip-form techniques that they had developed to build their home and outbuildings in Vermont. On the north side of the garden stand several compost bins, each six feet square, each spaced evenly from the other and arranged in diminishing heights, resembling a series of steps. Within the garden is a series of raised beds, a plot for asparagus and strawberries and rows for lettuce, carrots, broccoli, and kale. Each section is marked off by paths of sawdust, and a traditional hand cultivator is still in use.

The garden at the Good Life Center is a miniature version of its predecessor up the hill. On the first Maine homestead, the Nearings kept a garden four times the size of the one that now remains. It was circumscribed by a hand-built wall made of 420 feet of stone. The Nearings' decision to build a walled-in garden in Maine began, we are told, with the discovery of local deer breakfasting on their grapevines and raccoons snacking on their corn. But the Nearings' remarks in their homesteading books reveal that their love of stones and stonework played as much of a role in the decision to wall in their garden as did the deer and the raccoons. Building structures of stone had been, in many ways, the Nearings' signature activity in their Vermont years. Over a dozen stone buildings remain as testimony to their homesteading ventures.[12] Yet the stonework also betrays Helen and Scott's particular style and approach to their projects. For the Nearings, building in stone enabled them to put into practice the principles that they accepted as crucial to their homesteading plan: to build from local materials, to use hand tools only, and to create structures that are indistinguishable from their surroundings in order to create the illusion that the building was a part of the environment from its beginnings and has been "growing up with the environment ever since." Finally, the Nearings insisted that the style of the building should express the character of the inhabitants and "be an extension" of themselves.[13]

It is this last principle that is of particular interest, for it shows the Nearings' sense of themselves as being reflected in their buildings. Their comment invites us to consider what the architecture says of the architects. Environmentalist readers to whom I have introduced the Nearings' work often remark on the significant contrast between the Nearings' elaborate building projects and their own "leave no trace" environmental ethics. Yet the Nearings themselves seem aware of these disjunctions, at least indirectly. While proudly boasting of the multiple outbuildings they fashioned in Vermont, they hint that some tension might exist between their commitments to nature and their commitments to art, between the pull of human creativity and the desire to humble oneself before the natural world. The tension reveals itself, for instance, in the amateur masons' multiple warnings that the placing and pointing of the stones should be done in a way that resists "stylized and formal lines" and lets "each stone tell its own story in its own form and color."[14] Thus, while willing to impose on nature with multiple, long-lasting, and not easily compostable structures, they still insist on conducting their work "naturally."

This same tension is revealed in the explanation of the initial decision to build the garden wall. As the Nearings admit, while hungry animals were a reason for building at least a wire fence, the decision to replace the fence emerged from

FIGURE 3.
A stone wall in Helen's garden. Photo
by R. K. Gould.

the longing to build again in stone. They express the desire to have an occasional
project that carried with it the "absence of any compulsion" and would serve,
in their words, as "our tennis and our golf" for the fourteen years it took to construct.[15] Clearly, the wall was built for Scott and Helen's sake as much as for the
sake of the garden. While a fence would have been sufficient to protect their
food, the act of building the wall fed other human hungers.

The second garden, when I first walked through it, belonged to a neighbor
whom Helen thought I should visit. In 1994, Sal was actively experimenting
with a style of gardening and homesteading that flouted much of what the
Nearings stood for, but Helen found his rigorous approach to homesteading ad-

mirable in certain respects. In the late 1980s, Sal, together with his wife, Kate, and their children, had moved down to the Nearings' neighborhood on Helen's invitation. Helen had heard of Sal and Kate's homesteading efforts in a different state and was aware of the economic limitations under which they were living. Having seen a newspaper article in which Sal was pictured bathing in a tiny washbasin, Helen apparently wrote him with an invitation for a proper bath. The invitation itself tells us something: that Sal's asceticism was admirable to Helen but that Helen also wished to convince him that homesteading was possible without unnecessary privation. The competing themes of asceticism and pleasure that run through so many homesteading experiments were themes that emerged in the first contacts between Helen and Sal. Stated and unstated differences on these same matters also ultimately separated them.

At first, Sal worked for Helen, helping her with the garden. When he began to assert his own views (adding animal manure to the compost, broadcasting seed rather than planting ordered rows), they parted ways. Eventually, another of Helen's neighbors leased Sal and Kate some land. With hand tools, a portable mill, and a seemingly limitless supply of sweat equity, they built their own home and garden, both of which were flourishing when I first met them in 1994.

Sal's home was a kind of yurt, a circular dwelling made with wood cut on-site. Inside was a large central kitchen and living space. The bedrooms, loft, and a composting toilet were all apportioned in spaces created by partial divisions coming out from the center of the house like spokes on a wheel. Outside, the garden—once it became distinguishable—recapitulated the home's circular design. It seemed to emanate from the house in widening circular patterns, as if the home were dropped into a green pond of grasses, grains, and midsummer vegetables.

My difficulty in distinguishing the garden, when I first visited at the height of its July flowering, was an intentional effect on Sal's part. The garden was planted so that low, fast-growing plants, such as lettuces, would grow as protective soil-nourishing weeds for taller, sun-seeking beans and peas. Squash, carrots, and radishes seemed to be sprouting randomly. Sal spoke to me of his intention to eventually develop a "walking garden," one that he would plant largely by walking up and down a path and casting the seed abroad. Already, he had planted some of the garden in this manner, and he reveled in the way certain plants appeared in spaces unexpectedly, each one finding its place of "opportunity."

Sal's primary principle was to maintain a "no-till" garden in which the soil is prepared by mulching and composting only.[16] Seeds, if planted at all, are merely pushed into place in the small compost and mulch hills, and the soil is broken only by the water-seeking roots of the plants themselves. But Sal's rea-

FIGURE 4.
Sal's homestead and sauna express a contrasting approach to
the Nearings' strong sense of order. Photos by R. K. Gould.

sons for no-till planting go far beyond the intention of maintaining a fruitful garden, just as Helen and Scott's reasons for building stone walls were not simply utilitarian.

In our conversation, Sal linked the idea of the walking garden with both Zen practices and early Native American methods of sowing. In so doing, he evoked themes I would later hear in many conversations with other homesteaders: a desire to look back to an earlier, presumably simpler period in American history was complemented by an interest in "turning East," taking cues from Asian methods, in which agriculture practice and spiritual practice appear to be more closely intertwined. Of course, such nostalgia for a more pure and less industrialized America, coupled with a Romantic interest in the religious traditions of the East, had already been introduced by Thoreau and Emerson. But for Sal and the other homesteaders I spoke with, such themes were often articulated as fresh insights.

Sal's approach to gardening is clearly a particular agricultural method, but it reaches beyond practical theory to include a philosophy and a kind of theology. On the first day that I visited his garden, Sal spoke to me about the practical details and how-tos of its maintenance. Amid this pragmatic litany, however, he hinted about the presence of a "spirituality" both in the walking garden he was trying to develop and in the gardens he had already made. That spirituality is one of digging into the earth, aerating it, and letting things come up into the sun. On the second day I visited, I asked Sal to clarify his remarks on the spirituality of till and no-till gardening. His response charted a kind of cultural history:

> [Tilling] has been part of our past evolution . . . [of] bringing things to light. . . . Tilling the earth was part of that process. [But now] you can recognize forces where they are. . . . In other words, things appeared to be so dark before that it was necessary to throw light and air on things in order to see truth and have order. I think in the future we'll be capable of realizing that there's no need for imposed order; that order is there—it's a chaotic sense of order. It's such a large and interwoven sense that it appears chaotic, but it's a much more divine sense of order.[17]

Sal's comments on his gardening technique suddenly take us to a much wider agricultural world where culture itself is being consciously remade. In making these wider connections, Sal is not unlike Wendell Berry, who sees culture and agriculture as being inextricably linked. For Berry, "the definitive relationships in the universe are . . . not competitive, but interdependent. . . . We can build one system only within another. We can have agriculture only within nature, and culture only within agriculture." Thus, Berry argues, the rise of the factory farm is a crisis not only of agriculture but also of culture.[18] For Sal, tilling also locates itself in a wider complex of cultural moments, moments in history that we would be fortunate to get beyond: the relentless desire for "truth and order" and the exercise of "too much human control" over the natural world.

In Sal's view, the health of the garden, the productivity of the garden, and the health of the humans relying on the garden are all intertwined: "Tilling the soil is a remedial process. . . . [You] bring your garden to a kind of fulfillment by the end of the year. But then you break it again, so that the garden never heals beyond a certain point. You have a limited potential for building the garden, and that's because you have a limited potential for it to be healed." Thus, no-till gardening is not only representative of a cultural process in which the need to impose order is relaxed; it is also a choice to respond to nature on nature's terms, so that both natural health and human health are kept in balance.

Sal's gardening practices give a portrait of the gardener, just as the Nearings' stone walls evoke the builders. Sal's voiced perception that the search for "truth" and "light" often accompany the need for order is not a casual remark. It is a commentary on the culture from which he is dissenting, a world of utilitarian dominance over nature in the name of human progress. But it is also a response to the Nearing approach to homesteading.

The Nearings were no postmodernists. The search for universal principles by which to live was a stance Scott took seriously, in academic life, in political activity, and in personal pursuits. In the Nearing world, planning lay at the heart of their homesteading vision. Before they moved to Vermont, they drew up a carefully reasoned ten-point plan to guide them in their work.[19] *Order* was Scott's watchword. Even his personal letters to Helen often began with a statement of principles, followed by a logically reasoned, carefully enumerated set of elaborations. Helen, meanwhile, also sought truth, though in mystical as well as rational form. She measured her own spiritual growth by a plaque on the living room wall proclaiming the Theosophical dictum: "There is no religion higher than Truth." A quest for "light" as well as Truth is also apparent in the Nearings' everyday practices, as my discussion of food and eating in the subsequent chapter will underscore. While the Nearings and Sal both enacted expressions of cultural rejection of the commodified American mainstream, Sal also eventually overturned the Nearing ideal model of dissent. Whether intentionally or otherwise, Sal's garden is an interpretive response to the Nearings' work. The stone house and square garden are replaced by a round wood home barely distinguishable from the trees and a circular garden just visible through the weeds.

What kind of nature is Sal "getting back to"? Running through Sal's rationales for no-till gardening is the assumption that he is responding to the way nature *really is*: a divine sense of order that appears chaotic, a complexly structured environment to which humans should accommodate. For Sal, this understanding of nature—which historians might call a "construction" of nature—emerges from his early experience with formal education. "Ever since I was young," he remarked to me, "there seemed to be a part of the world that was available to me, but the conventional schooling that I was going through didn't seem to offer it." Sal originally pursued a college major in wildlife biology, a field that appealed to him because it involved being out in nature. His decision to switch majors and eventually to leave college in order to pursue wood carving and carpentry full-time came, in part, from disappointment with his original discipline: "You weren't really out [in nature]. You weren't out in the sense of being available to what was there. You were going out with a predetermination of what you were looking for and a schedule. You know, a schedule of things that had to be accomplished and it was all . . . determined already. Nothing entered in except *by accident* . . . [and then] often you aren't prepared for it and you don't have the proper energy to access it." (The italics reflect Sal's vocal emphasis.) In this description of his frustrating educational experiences, Sal exhibits an approach to nature in sharp contrast with that of Scott and Helen Nearing. To have a schedule, to make a plan, to see nature as a "laboratory" for human "experiments," as Helen and Scott often put it, is, according to Sal, a way of closing oneself down to the real lessons that nature has to teach.[20]

Sal and the Nearings are not polar opposites. They share a desire to learn by doing and to learn from direct experience with the natural world. Certainly, they share a critique of the dominant consumer culture and the capitalism and industrialism that support it. Yet they clearly differ in their styles of homesteading practice. These variant styles symbolize differences in ethics, aesthetics, and assumptions about nature and the self that underlie the daily work of homesteading. Of course, I do not mean to suggest that Sal's and Helen's different approaches to gardening and house building are *exclusively* symbolic, but I do want to emphasize that these actions always resonate symbolically.[21] Building a stone wall around a garden, for instance, emphasizes the role of human control in the natural arena and also guarantees that a certain legacy remains. As one visitor to Forest Farm remarked, "All of these stone walls and buildings tell me something—that Helen and Scott wanted to be remembered for what they did." Helen Nearing's own musings on their legacy underline the extent to which she and Scott wished their homestead to be preserved:

> Who will reap what we have built here
> In this house and on this land?
> You and I will be forgotten
> But our work and house will stand.
> Other folk will come and go here;
> Others take their places, too.
> We will leave our blessings for them:
> Happiness in what they do.[22]

While the Nearings were deeply concerned about human impact on the environment—and became increasingly so during the years of building their last home and garden (the late 1970s)—they also sought to inscribe themselves in the land and to have that inscription stand the test of time. Such acts of inscription have multiple meanings. They reflect the environmental values of the builders (keep the masonry simple, local, "natural," and unadorned) while also underlining the sense of significance that the builders had with respect to their work.

In contrast, Sal's approach to gardening seems to articulate a humbler ethic and aesthetic. Sal appears to be letting nature take the lead while claiming only the supporting role for himself. But the conscious construction of a round, rough-hewn house and a chaotic-looking garden is also a manipulation of symbols, a testament to both himself and others of a particular view of nature (as redeeming and beneficent in its original state), and a particular articulation of the "proper" human response (to leave nature alone). For Sal, self-cultivation requires a rejection of the themes of discipline, control, order, and legacy building that we find in the Nearings' experiments.

Both Sal's and Helen's gardens—and their spoken and written words about them—express a profound reverence for nature. In both cases, their approaches to gardening express a sense of nature as sacred, worthy of reverence and respect. The act of homesteading itself involves the sacralization of nature, in which nature becomes both the physical and the symbolic center of one's existence. At the same time, these self-conscious and attentive gardening practices express some underlying ambivalences with respect to the human relationship with the natural world, ambivalences that will continue to surface throughout this study. Much of this ambivalence stems from the extent to which the act of getting close to nature can be about the process of self-construction as much as (or more than) it is about actual intimacy with the natural world. For Helen and Sal, this process of self-construction in nature is more implicitly acknowledged. For another neighbor, Henry, it is a clear raison d'être.

"Doing Things Yourself Is a Spiritual Process": Henry (1995)

"I had the idea that this is what I wanted do before I ever met Helen and Scott," Henry remarked to me early on in our first conversation.[23] Henry and his first wife, Pat, were on the verge of buying a sizable plot of land in the interior of Maine for seven thousand dollars, a "steal" even in the early 1970s but a stretch for a young, unemployed couple. Having come upon Helen and Scott's *Living the Good Life* by accident in the library, Henry remembers thinking, "Yes, these folks are doing the same kind of thing I'm trying to do. I don't agree with everything, but they have the right idea." Henry and Pat decided that since they were already venturing out from their home state to peruse their potential homestead site, they might as well pay a call on the Nearings. With a certain hint of pride in his voice, Henry recounted how upon arriving at the Nearing place he immediately took his ax and maul from the car and helped Scott split wood. "I was more of a bull then," remarked the now slightly graying but still barrel-chested man. "We got a fair amount of wood split that day." Apparently, Henry's approach to visiting the Nearings—a departure from that of numerous visitors whom the Nearings have chastised for being eager to "talk philosophy" but averse to hard work—helped establish his credentials.[24] Two days after Henry and Pat had returned home from their visit, they received a certified letter from the Nearings telling them not to buy land until they paid another call on Forest Farm. They returned promptly, and Henry walked part of the Nearing land with Helen. She did not simply want to offer it to him, she wanted to know what he thought of its uses: Could it make a good homestead? Would it support a family? Was it possible to build a house from the material on the property and to raise enough vegetables to maintain self-sufficiency? Henry thought so, and the land was theirs at a rock-bottom price.

But Henry did not begin his story with the day he read the Nearings' work or the moment he was invited to buy some of the Nearings' land. He began with Vietnam. Having fought for his country "as only a naive, patriotic nineteen-year-old knows how to do," Henry returned from the Southeast Asian jungle to find that he was the enemy on his own college campus. Finding no support in the dorms for his personal choices and no meaningful context for learning in large lecture halls, Henry resisted several visits from his dean and his own pride in having completed honors work and decided to leave in his junior year. The sense of regret that accompanied this choice still crept into our conversation as Henry simultaneously defended his choice and wondered aloud what might have happened differently if he had not made it. After twenty-five years, Henry still commented on the high grade point average he attained before leaving school. He remembers it to the second decimal.

The theme of Henry's tour of his homestead was that of personal accomplishment in the face of uncertain beginnings. The refrain did not amount to mere boasting—his pride in a job well done was more than justifiable; rather, it was one of making distinctions. When I commented on the familiar set of compost bins near the garden, Henry remarked, "Scott's system worked well, but I've made some improvements on it as you can see. I pride myself on having bins that don't decay." Indeed, the squares were more square, the poles thicker and sturdier than the ones at Helen's house. Inside Henry's home, the massive stone fireplace dominated the room. Henry guided me through the natural history of its construction. The bottom of the fireplace had a rough, slightly uneven look. Several feet up, however, the stone was more tightly packed, the shapes more balanced. Close scrutiny of the final stage of the chimney from the vantage point of the second floor revealed a more graceful line at the corners, more balanced hues in the stones selected and significantly less use of mortar. "We could have followed others' advice on this," Henry commented, "but we found we learned so much more by doing it ourselves. We can remember what we learned—and you can see it too—each time we look at the chimney."

Henry's apologies for various household imperfections faded to the background as he took me down a wooden ladder into the room that was among his favorites, the root cellar. Jar upon jar of canned summer fruits and vegetables lined the wooden shelves of the earthen room. Henry launched into exquisitely detailed descriptions of favorite winter recipes whose secrets depended on the contents of the root cellar. Upon returning from the cellar, Henry remarked that all this was possible for me, or anyone, to do. "But make sure you get advice from technically able professionals," he warned. "I might have ruined my foundation if I had kept mixing cement the way Scott told me to," he added. "And remember to write in your book "that the currency of homesteading is hard work. Hard, backbreaking work."

As a young man, the college environment from which Henry had extracted himself had chastised him for playing by one set of rules (serving your country through military service) and simultaneously asked to abide by another (listening to lectures, earning good grades). Satisfaction came only when he was able to relocate himself physically and psychologically onto his own land, a land to which he owed nothing but his hard labor and from which he expected only self-generated rewards. Yet he acquired his land because of two visionaries who recognized in him a familiar disaffection for the dominant culture and a capacity for hard work.

Truly to ground himself on his new land, however, Henry had to separate himself even from his like-minded elders. Although he never articulated that separation from the Nearings was a necessary part of the homesteading process, even—or especially—when homesteading on old Nearing land, his conversational refrains included making distinctions between his process and theirs, pointing out self-made achievements, and gently mentioning the ways in which the Nearings did not always live up to their public image. Along with similar remarks from other "Nearing neighbors," Henry's comments revealed a certain Oedipal tension with respect to the Nearings' role as "parents" of the neighborhood. Making distinctions between his own work and theirs helped Henry mark out the territory that was his.

"Doing things yourself is a spiritual process," Henry remarked while telling me how he cleared his tangled, stony acres without chain saws, back hoes, or tractors. We were talking in his wood shop surrounded by electric band saws, drills, and lathes. "I don't go to church or anything. My spirituality comes in building things myself. In knowing I've done all this from the ground up." But what of the band saws and his current "cash crop" of cabinetmaking? Henry told me that he had not anticipated that this is what he would be doing today. Previously, he had pursued other means of gaining supplementary income for the homestead. He had sold vegetables and hens' eggs as cash crops and had been a sought-after livestock slaughterer in the community, until he quite literally threw in the towel one day when "all that killing" finally got to him. He had worked on construction projects and still accepts contracts from time to time. But he turned to cabinetmaking because he experienced it as artistry, less taxing on the body than house construction, and uniquely satisfying in terms of the product made. "Now I *could* use a hand planer and only hand tools to make my cabinets," he admitted. "But think of the price tag I would have to put on those cabinets. And how long it would take. If the product is well-designed and well-crafted, it ceases to matter whether it's planed by hand or planed with an electric tool. You're never truly self-sufficient, see? You always need some tools. And once I begin to look at it that way, I realize that there is no real difference between this [he holds up a tape measure] and that [he gestures to a table saw]. One is just an extension of the other." In talking about his craft, Henry placed hand tools and power tools quite close together on his technological continuum. In his current frame of mind, a high-tech piece of equipment seems little different from a hand-held, human-powered tool.

While Henry is quick to point out the inconsistencies between Helen and Scott's life as portrayed in books and Helen and Scott's life as actually practiced (for instance, the Nearings' reliance on scores of visitors for help in constructing their "one man and one woman" houses), he made no self-conscious mention of his own inconsistencies or reversals; rather, his conversation charted a kind of natural progression of his homesteading project, from the rejection of all but the barest tools to the acceptance of complex technology as not only a help but also an artistic enhancement.

The key to understanding Henry's journey from the hard pursuit of self-sufficiency to the gentle appreciation of a balanced, healthy lifestyle lies in his comment that "doing things yourself is a spiritual process." The notion that making things yourself is a spiritual activity is a notion that Henry was at once most passionate about and most inarticulate in developing conceptually in conversation. This is not surprising, for it is common that the word *spiritual*, after being distinguished from institutional religion, is left to explain itself. What we hear in Henry's story, however, is that the journey from self-sufficiency to a positive, healthy style of life is a journey in which doing things yourself and remaking the self are simultaneous and intertwined. On the continua of technology and rigor, Henry has moved toward more conventional poles, rejecting an ascetic lifestyle and a purist approach to avoiding technology. But in order to create himself, and to create himself as a "self-made" man, Henry had to begin near the opposite poles. His spiritual progression began with the acceptance of an appealing countertradition to the ones he had known. In the Nearings, he found a model of living that was in dissent both from the military-industrial complex and from those in the counterculture who resisted work, discipline, and authority. But in order to make himself anew, Henry eventually needed to dissociate himself from the Nearings as well. He chose to remain in a loose-knit community that was Nearing-defined but to be the keeper of the "true stories" about the Nearings as models. By clearing his land by hand, making compost piles that were bigger and better than those of the Nearings', and building a house from the ground up without depending on a steady stream of visitors to assist the construction, Henry simultaneously nurtured and constructed a self. By limiting technology and pursuing a livelihood of constant physical and mental rigor, one dependent on nature and on his ability to live effectively in it, Henry eventually brought himself to a point where more complex technologies could be welcomed, additional human impact on the natural world could be accepted, and a movement toward pleasure and away from rigor could be interpreted as "healthy," balanced, and more realistic.

Homesteading as Self-Construction

Henry's current "softer" approach to homesteading is more the norm than the exception in the community of homesteaders inspired by the Nearings. "Compared to the Nearings," began one homesteader with a twinkle in his eye, "we're all terrible hedonists!" In fact, the theme of moving away from strict concepts of purity—and wondering, even obsessing, about whether such as move is "OK"—reverberates through many homesteaders' narratives. "I don't *want* to make my own Grape-Nuts or grow my own mustard seed!" Linda Tatelbaum declares to herself in 1987. "I've stopped reading *Mother Earth News* and other back-to-the-land magazines that extol the 'simple life.' Call it enough to eat from your garden year 'round. Call it enough to be minimally responsible for the world's pollution. . . . I've come to believe in compromise. I believe that conforming to anything warps a life, that keeping up with the Nearings is just another form of rat-race."[25]

But to get to this point of self-aware humor about purity and to be able to defend one's new standards, most homesteaders have to go through a process like Henry's, a process whereby the practice of purity—of getting as low-tech, do-it-yourself, close to nature as you possibly can—enables them to experience nature and themselves anew. Again, not unlike converts to a religious way of life, a strict approach to behavior and ritual may often be the first step, and a relaxation of norms may come later. Craig described this process to me when explaining his decision to stop felling large trees on his property with a two-person crosscut saw and, eventually, to acquire a chain saw. "You just have to go through 'doing it the hard way' first," he explained. "It's like crawling on your knees, through broken glass, up a mountain so you can see the virgin." Craig pointed out that he did not generally see his life as "spiritual," which he interpreted as ascribing hidden meaning to natural events ("For me, if an owl comes to your window, it doesn't mean anything. It's *just an owl*"). But his interpretation of his early attempts at avoiding any kind of harm to the natural world were rich with the language of ritual process. He spoke of his experiments with purity as "a kind of pilgrimage," which, once attained, need not be repeated. While Craig is yet another homesteader who read the Nearings' *Living the Good Life* in one sitting and decided the next day to change his life, he also resists following precisely in their footsteps. He has done enough research to confirm that the Nearings' were not as "pure" as they said they were, and while admiring their work immensely, he has learned his own lessons about purity. Eventually, the pilgrim returns home, dramatically changed perhaps, but no longer in the heat of journey. The pilgrimage of homesteading, while never truly finished, often gives way to pragmatism, to leading a life that is not only ecologically but also personally sustainable. There are limits to what the body can tolerate, and Craig can do other things with his time when not using hand tools for all of his work: there is more time for gardening, family, pursuing the intellectual life, and building community in his town.[26]

Making Bread and Making Meaning (1995)

Meaning-making processes compete for space. They coalesce, conflict, interrupt one another, and work at cross-purposes. As we have seen, the sacralization of nature is a central, persistent theme in the cultural work of homesteading. But "making the self-made self" is a corresponding, and sometimes competing, theme. Henry, in fact, speaks little about getting close to nature as a conscious intent, though, in his case, actions such as building a summer tree house to sleep in or keeping his refrigerator in an outbuilding speak louder than words. Sal, on the other hand, speaks voluminously about what nature means to him. Yet when I saw Sal a year after my initial interviews, his homestead was largely deserted and his life and work were relocated to a commercial business in town. Sal had taken out loans, bought electronic scales and temperature gauges, and become a baker.

Sal's reincarnation from homesteader to baker was not the only radical transformation he experienced in the year between my visits. Sal also endured the breakup of his marriage, the tragic deaths of two close friends, and bouts of emotional and physical exhaustion that accompanied these. These changes influenced Sal's move from his homestead to his bakery, but the decision to pursue bread baking preceded them and, not surprisingly, became the quest that made these tragedies more bearable. But my interest here (in part out of consideration for the individuals involved and in part because these personal matters are not central to this study) is not to hypothesize about the ways in which Sal's transformation into a baker may have served either a compensatory or an aggravating function with respect to the personal challenges he had to face. My purpose, rather, is to investigate Sal's own understanding of how this transformation affects and sheds light upon his earlier experience as a homesteader. In so doing, I want to illustrate how a meaning-making process at work in homesteading—the process of cultivating the self—can actually lead a person out of homesteading and into another practice.

The change that struck me the most upon visiting Sal in October 1995 was a change not in Sal himself but in the environment surrounding him. Sal had moved from a cabin that had served as a semipermeable membrane between him and the natural world to a thick-walled bakery-café behind a general store in a small Maine town. His days were no longer spent hauling water, chopping wood, lighting his home with candles, or harvesting vegetables. Now they were filled by hours of labor spent indoors, mixing dough, kneading bread, selling loaves to customers, and delivering (by car) bulk orders to local restaurants. Sal was already experimenting with bread baking in the summer when I first met him. He had crafted a brick oven from Maine clay, harvested by the shovelful on the home site. In one sense then, his life as a baker was nothing new; it was an extension of his previous experimentation with the art. At the same time, however, I was struck by how radically his life seemed to have changed. No longer was he working in order to create and live in a place where he could "truly dwell"; now he was, not unlike a Wall Street broker, eating and sleeping in the place where he worked. Yet this contrast in ways of living was more apparent to outside observers than it was to Sal himself. In Sal's mind, the move indoors was a literal, psychological, and spiritual shift, but one that grew—we might say "organically"—out of his earlier practices.

On one visit, Sal mentioned to me that he had spent a recent day off with his children, picnicking at a friend's pond near his homestead. I asked him if he missed such days, days that were the norm only a year before. "Sometimes I miss the sun on my back and being able to work in the fresh air," he replied. "But I don't find myself missing it too much, because my relationship to nature has changed." Sal's initial comment evolved into a thoughtful discourse on the evolution of the self. "I used to go to nature with a feeling of yearning or emptiness," he began.

> Or rather, I experienced a kind of yearning and emptiness and I went to nature to be fulfilled. I used to look at a sunset and think, "How grand!" but I would push away something like this (he indicated his digital flour scale) as not being grand, as interfering with the experience of nature. But once you live close to things and especially if you've done it, like I have, for a very long time, you start approaching things differently. You begin to see the divinity in things, in the elements, and that can lead you to see it in manmade things as well.[27]

Like Henry, Sal intertwines a discourse about the self with a discourse about tools. Also like Henry, Sal has come to embrace technology that he would have shunned earlier in life. But Sal's explication of this change is slightly different. While Henry charts a shift in his way of *being*, from mastering self-sufficiency to cultivating a lifestyle, Sal speaks more particularly about a change in his way of *seeing*, from going to nature for something (fulfillment) to going to nature with something (awareness of the inherent divinity in material things). In religious terms, we might speak of this transformation as a shift from experiencing spiritual transformation (or revelation) to perceiving incarnation. These terms fit in particularly well with Sal's liberal use of such phrases as "experiencing grace" and "seeing divinity" to describe the differences between earlier and current phases of his life. This latter phase, Sal remarked, was "a more *mature* approach," one of approaching people, things, and experiences with "a sense of belonging to them."

Of course, we might ask whether Sal's new life and new job are not being somehow psychologically justified and rationalized by this philosophical discourse on divinity, perception, and spiritual maturity, but we might ask the same questions of a churchgoer who, having undergone painful personal transformations, has found a new life, a more mature life, in Christ. While spiritual transformations may serve psychological functions, my purpose with respect to both Sal and his imagined Christian counterpart is not to explain away these experiences in terms of what they do psychologically but rather to unfold the dynamics of such experiences in terms of the broad category of meaning-making to which both psychological and religious experiences belong. More particularly, in the context of homesteading, I want to explore how one category of meaning-making (making the self) can interfere with or render irrelevant another category (sacralizing nature). In Sal's case, the process of being available to what nature has to teach, a process that led him into a self-consciously low-impact, unordered style of homesteading, became sufficiently fulfilling to take him out of nature and into a different setting for practical and spiritual education. The external practice of living close to nature became subordinate to the internal practices of honing perception and nurturing a sense of connection to other people and things, practices that Sal interprets in the language of spiritual growth and psychological maturity.

When we consider the possibility that making the self became the primary process of meaning-making in Sal's homesteading efforts, at least in the final years, a shift occurs in the way we interpret his new life. With a new lens to look through, the incongruities and inconsistencies that glared back at our first glance at Sal's latest profession may fade, somewhat, from view. The continuities appear first in the external similarities. Sal has not become an industry baker; rather, he is the inventor, designer, and builder of a wood-fired bakery. He mixes his recipes by hand, not only in the sense of avoiding electric mixers, but also in the sense of preferring his hands to spoons. As with his work as a gardener and woodcarver, Sal minimizes the amount that he reads about his craft. He prefers to learn from the ingredients themselves, even if the "price" of the trial is error. As the proprietor of his shop, he also educates his customers about the physical and spiritual benefits of consuming bread that is whole-grain, homemade, and wood-fired.

A painted mural above the oven (the work of yet another homesteader) is a testament to the bread of life. Mother Earth is depicted in her wheat-sprouting bounty. Reapers, millers, and bakers from a variety of traditional cultures are depicted transforming the wheat into bread. Each stage of the process involves intergenerational, communal, and hand labor. The golden land dominates the mural, but a dark city (looking suspiciously like Boston) lurks in a far corner. Though I was told the effect was accidental, the Grim Reaper, scythe in hand, appears to be heading straight toward it. The mural tells a story of bread, of the bounty of nature, of the value of community, and of the dangers of an urban culture that sees itself as separate from essential natural processes. In a corner underneath the mural stands a stone fountain, not yet in operation, which will bring the soothing sounds of a flowing stream into the world of the bakery, offering a kind of musical accompaniment to the artwork above.

The bakery, as Sal has fashioned it, expresses both an aesthetic and an ethos. We could argue that if Sal were to use mixers, dough hooks, and the like, he would save time and get out into nature more. But Sal brings nature indoors through the design of the bakery, the ingredients he uses, and his approach to the bread-making process. Sal speaks of having attained a more mature place in his relationship with the world, of being no longer dependent on nature for fulfillment or revelation, but he still comes to his new work with the same kind of cultivated ignorance (an attitude Thoreau also praised) with which he approached woodcarving and gardening. He sees baking bread as a new learning process, one in which *matter itself* is the teacher, a process through which both technical and spiritual knowledge is attained. While there may have been some defensiveness in Sal's comments to me about his not having "changed as much as people think," there was also discernment in regard to what change and continuity really are. To some extent, Sal's practice is still one of making the everyday world and everyday practices sacred.

If we think of the decision to homestead as a kind of conversion, we have in Henry and Sal two different models of what that conversion can look like. For Henry, the initial process of homesteading was pursued with a kind of intensity and quest for purity (in terms of making things by hand) that softened into a more relaxed practice over time. If we call on our Jamesian categories once more, we might say that Henry stands somewhere between James's portrait of the healthy-minded *Homo religiosus* and that of the impassioned convert. Henry's homesteading life has permitted a return to an original healthy-mindedness that the Vietnam experience and the dislocations of the 1960s disrupted. Sal's experiences, on the other hand, point *beyond* James's sketch of the twice-born self, a sketch that captures the intensity that Sal projects but maps only a one-time conversion experience. Sal consistently puts himself through painful, urgent rebirths. Each new incarnation (from woodcarver, to homesteader, to baker) carries forward some continuities with the old, but the most striking continuity of all is the commitment to making the self over as many times as is necessary to perceive truth and contribute that truth back to his world.

Once Henry constructed a self-made self, the need to maintain an ethic and aesthetic of rigor retreated accordingly. But the practice of homesteading continued to be vital to the process of what Peter Berger has called "world-construction" and "world-maintenance."[28] Having created the self anew through the process of creating a miniculture on a plot of land in Maine, Henry found himself rooted to the spot. For Henry, nature, culture, and the self are bound up in one another; they are literally and metaphorically intertwined in a particular piece of earth. For Sal, being close to nature continues to be significant. His sense of the sacredness of the natural world, or, better, his construction of nature as sacred, is much more frequently and explicitly expressed than Henry's is. But when the commitment to living in nature came up against the calling to remake the self, living in nature was simultaneously sacrificed (as a phase outgrown) and redefined (as a process never truly given up).

·   ·   ·

Going "back to nature" is pursued by many in order to find in nature an experience of the sacred that is perceived to be unavailable either in the disenchanted culture of capitalism or in the doctrinally bound culture of organized religion. But going back to nature also involves discovery of what the self can do in and in spite of, with and against, the natural world. These two "reasons" for going back to nature—whether articulated or implicit—have fused, interlaced, and competed with each other on the American scene at least since Thoreau wrote of his classic homesteading experiment at Walden Pond or, as Raymond Williams suggests in the European context, ever since "the country" emerged as a cultural category distinct from "the city."[29] Because of the twin impulses of sacralizing nature and remaking the self, nature itself becomes something of a shape-shifting entity. At times, nature is highly personalized (most often feminized) as a being with whom one seeks intimacy, from whom one hopes for revelation, in whose maternal arms redemption and comfort are sought. At other times, nature is a site, or even a laboratory, for human invention and experimentation. Depending on the experiment conducted, nature's significance can fade.

Walking in Walden Woods one day, Thoreau came upon a woodchuck. Not for the first time upon meeting up with a wild animal, Thoreau tells us, he was "strongly tempted to seize and devour him raw." Thoreau goes on to elaborate the particular nature of this desire: "Not that I was hungry then, except for the wildness that he represented. Once or twice, however, while I lived at the pond, I found myself ranging the woods like a half-starved hound, with a strange abandonment, seeking some kind of venison which I might devour, and no morsel could have been too savage for me. The wildest scenes had become unaccountably familiar."[30] Thoreau's hunger for nature is not physical hunger but concerns *incarnational experience*. Living in nature is sometimes not enough for him, taking nature into the body is a communion for which he longs at various intervals.[31] But Thoreau also holds this very longing at bay, interpreting it as savage and ultimately threatening to the spiritual purity he is seeking to attain. "I found in myself, and still find," Thoreau writes, "an instinct toward a higher, or, as it is named, spiritual life, as do most men, and another toward a primitive rank and savage one, and I reverence them both."[32] It can be argued, as the use of the word *reverence* in this passage suggests, that Thoreau's hunger for nature and his pursuit of Higher Laws are both spiritual quests. Certainly, Thoreau's construction of *Walden* as a text would bear out this interpretation.[33] But in Thoreau's mind a division still exists between the experience of sacralized nature and the cultivation of a spiritual self. The subsequent meditations on vegetarianism, chastity, and the dangers of coffee and tea that follow the more celebrated woodchuck passage underscore (among other things) Thoreau's concern with the development of the self, a concern that portrays nature—and, relatedly, the body, sexuality, and loss of control—as simultaneously desirable and dangerous.

Almost 150 years after Thoreau's encounter with the woodchuck, another nature-seeking writer describes a similar encounter near her home not far from Hollins Pond. Annie Dillard depicts herself relaxing on a tree trunk, enjoying a sunset, when suddenly she locks eyes with a wild weasel: "Our look was as if two lovers, or deadly enemies, met unexpectedly on an overgrown path when each had been thinking of something else: a clear blow to the gut. It was also a bright blow to the brain, or a sudden beating of brains, with all the charge and intimate grate of rubbed balloons." The moment of "enchantment" is fleeting, the weasel disappears, and Dillard finds her "spirit pleading" for the wild animal to return. She sees herself as having "missed her chance" with the weasel, a chance for intimacy and for the incorporation of its wildness into herself. "I should have gone for the throat," Dillard writes. "I should have lunged for that streak of white under the weasel's chin and held on . . . for a dearer life. . . . I could very calmly go wild."[34]

Calmly going wild is not only a clever play on words; it is also a recognition that going wild is not a strange behavior. For Dillard, like Thoreau, the wild can sometimes seem "unaccountably familiar." The desire for an experience of nature that is separate from daily human existence is also a desire that is human and thoroughly "natural." The sacred is apprehended in and through nature, and this is why Dillard comes to Hollins Pond, "to learn, or remember how to live . . . [to] learn something of mindlessness, something of the purity of living in the physical sense and the dignity of living without bias or motive." Yet a reader of Dillard will recognize that this going to nature *does* have a motive: it is a self-imposed choice, a discipline that has as its goal the remaking of the self. Just as Thoreau retreats to Walden in order to "drive life into a corner," so Dillard hunts nature bare-handed, seeking "to locate the most tender and live spot and plug into that pulse." In truth, of course, Dillard is hunting nature not with her hands but with her mind. In so doing, she equates this practice with other spiritual disciplines: "People take vows of poverty, chastity and obedience—even of silence—by choice. The thing is to stalk your calling. . . . Then even death cannot you part."[35] Dillard portrays herself seeking intimacy with nature, but she does so while testifying that developing such intimacy is a form of spiritual practice that (like monastic vows) can help her to overcome the limits of her life, including that most natural limit of death.

How much Dillard's weasel encounter is consciously modeled on Thoreau's near consumption of the woodchuck, how much is re-created from actual experience, we may never know.[36] But the anxiety of influence is not our only subject here. What we see in the writings of Thoreau and Dillard is an anxiety about nature, an anxiety that reproduces itself in the lives of both those homesteaders who write about their practice and those homesteaders whose practice is their act of inscription. For these individuals who have built a home in nature, the desire for intimacy with nature and for sacred experience is incorporated into and sometimes also simultaneously pitched against the construction of the self.

To the extent that humans see themselves as removed from nature and removed from their "true selves," the pursuit of intimacy with nature is necessarily an ambivalent pursuit. Nature is sought but sometimes resisted, inhabited but sometimes "grown out of." When we consider these inherent ambivalences, as well as the personal risk and "backbreaking" labor of homesteading, one wonders what keeps some homesteads successful and some homesteaders persistent through the years. Our cue may be taken from Dillard—that, for homesteaders (perhaps more than for many nature writers), it is not "ideas" of nature that sustain them, even when nature is seen as sacred in itself or vital to spiritual growth; it is the *experience* of making the self at home in nature that is paramount. Like the taking of vows (which concern not only belief but even more how to live), homesteading involves a lived commitment to a particular place with natural challenges and limits. The everyday work and play of homesteading become symbolic enactments of this commitment: a "naturalized" form of spiritual practice, an ecologically oriented ritual life.

3

> Ritual is, above all, an assertion of difference . . .
> a means of performing the way things ought to
> be in conscious tension to the way things are.
>
> Jonathan Z. Smith, *To Take Place*

When Thoreau set up one-room housekeeping on July 4, 1845, he was engaged in two kinds of activity: the practical work of establishing a rustic home in the woods and the symbolic work of expressing his personal declaration of independence from the "mass of men" whose culture he wished to reject. His goals and the means by which he achieved them were both symbolic and utilitarian.

Thoreau's sojourn at Walden has been a touchstone throughout this exploration of homesteading, yet so far Thoreau has not been brought into the center of the discussion as an "official" homesteader himself. Why? Even given my open and flexible definitions of homesteading, Thoreau stands somewhat outside the parameters, in that I am primarily investigating those who have made more dramatic and permanent commitments to a new way of life. Most homesteaders have left one world for another and have not planned to return to the former. Thoreau's actions were comparatively more tentative in both place and time. He lived at Walden for two years, within walking distance of his family home and Concord center. Historically, too, Thoreau's experiment in living is best seen as a *preface* (though, indeed, a prescient one) to the critique of urban life and the growing influence of science and technology that were to come in the late nineteenth and early twentieth centuries. These later developments brought force to the "cult of nature" that burgeoned at the turn of the century and made John Burroughs—the first modern, post-Darwinian homesteader— so popular among the urbanized middle class.

I shall take up Burroughs's story in chapter 4. About Thoreau, however, we might say that neither is he fully a homesteader, nor is his historical context the same kind of "modernity" against which later homesteaders have strived. And yet, as we have seen, homesteaders are almost unanimous in claiming Thoreau as a kind of cultural hero. While most relish the opportunity to point out his relatively comfortable arrangements at Walden, they also judge what they do by Thoreau's example. Moreover, homesteader-authors tend to see their texts as mini-*Waldens*. While Thoreau may not fully belong to the same circles of those who have practiced the arts of self-sufficiency for thirty or more years, he nonetheless gives them guidance and inspiration. Those who are apt to dismiss Thoreau may be quick to observe that his momentary journey back to the land was "merely symbolic," not "real." But it is precisely on symbolic grounds that Thoreau ought to be invited into the circle. For whatever else it may be, homesteading is a kind of symbolic action, in fact, a kind of ritual action.[1]

"Playing at Farming": Symbolic Action

If we think back over the homesteaders we have met in the preceding pages, we find that what they offer in texts and interviews is more than just "readings" or ideas of the natural world. While spoken and written testaments are a main source of access to the lives of homesteaders, what homesteaders are speaking and writing about is *practice*. In describing their practices, homesteaders are often self-conscious about the symbolic work in which they are engaged. When the self-described "mad professor" Linda Tatelbaum recounts what is involved in getting ready for work in the morning, for instance, she knows that her commitment to the many complexities of "the simple life" is a commitment to the symbolic maintenance and ritualizing of a certain relationship with nature as much as it is a commitment to literal self-maintenance.

In an essay entitled "Résumé: A Homesteader's History," Tatelbaum provides the following self-reflective entry for 1981:

> I go back to work as a professor, part-time. I get up in the dark and eat breakfast by kerosene light. Dressed up in my new clothes, I haul water trying not to perspire or spill water on my stockings. Our dirt road is the last in town to get plowed, so I leave extra early in snow, and then mud, to make the hour commute for an 8 o'clock class. I read student papers by Aladdin lamplight at night. At college I feel like a creature from another planet, until I find out my colleague in the next office, who had me fooled with his three-piece suit, lives in a log cabin and has to ski out to his car in the dark each morning. I begin to see how funny it all is.[2]

We might say that Tatelbaum's sense of humor about her situation emerges from what Catherine Bell has called a "sense of ritual."[3] It is not physically necessary that she haul water from a well or grade papers by the flickering light of a kerosene lamp, but it is symbolically and ritually necessary for her to do so. At home, the ritual life of homesteading is predominant. At work, the everyday life of the dominant culture looms large. Finding herself in the liminal space between homesteading and conventional academia, she feels like an alien, yet laughs knowing that she (and others) have chosen this alien identity as the only sane way to live, a way that seems considerably less sane when out in the "real world."

Just as Tatelbaum recognizes that she is a "mad" rather than an ordinary professor, so did the members of Total Loss Farm recognize that they properly belonged neither to the conventional world of white-collar professionalism nor to the rural world of the Vermont farmer. Nowhere did this realization come home more clearly than when they found themselves neck high in mud attempting to dig a well by hand. "I can assure you that subsequent wells, if needed, will be done with backhoes," writes one recounter of the well-building story, "[but] this first one had to be done by ourselves." He continues: "We are just playing at farming, you see. That's why we dig wells by hand, hew beams from great hickory trees with an adz, make our own furniture, build stone chimneys and make clothing. . . . How little we are understood by our fathers and teachers. We are not serious. I, one of many, intend to still be playing farmer when death comes."[4] Like much play, the play at Total Loss Farm was both fun and serious, a rigorous way of living and a cultural performance. It involved creativity, imitation, and voluntary work. The labor was intense, but the intensity was self-chosen, freely accepted as a kind of strenuous living that the "play farmers" had both the time and resources to enjoy. At the same time, these farmers paid the price of voluntary poverty in order to give themselves the leisure to ritualize their lives in this way. If they had not been satisfied by earning a crude living from their gardening and writing, or if the garden had failed and their health had declined from the lack of pure water, the well most certainly would have been dug with a backhoe in a day.

When we remember that homesteading life is a life to which one has "converted" from a former life of urban and suburban living, we gain a more complex sense of the dynamics of work and play in which homesteaders engage. In the case of Total Loss Farm, for instance, the project was dedicated to letting "the natural flow of events determine the structure" of daily life. In accounting for how "things get done" on a farm where "process" (what the Nearings called "planning") is never explicitly discussed, one member used the image of a jazz band. "Freedom," he asserted, "gives us form."[5] But such freedom, as we shall soon see, is as much a source of anxiety as it is a source of relief. Because self-chosen farmwork is not simply a job but also a ritualization of a new way of life, it takes on a web of meanings that include both how to distinguish oneself from "the world" (the same "come-outer" motif that runs through many more traditional religious movements) and how to respond to role models such as the Nearings.

Among the many essays in *Home Comfort*, nowhere does the assertion of freedom and the right to do nothing at all get a more celebrated hearing than in Marty Jezer's essay "Maple Sugaring: Our Finest Hour," a mischievous (though also admiring) spoof on the Nearings' *Maple Sugar Book*.[6] In the original Nearing text, an overriding sense of accomplishment is apparent throughout. Although the Nearings' pride in their labors may well be justified, it is also a persistent refrain. The Nearings adopt a (by now familiar) characteristic stance when they inform their readership of their capacity to "outsugar" their neighbors. The blend of humility and exceptionalism here, as elsewhere, produces a curious effect. While claiming that "anyone with perspicacity" can learn to sugar, the Nearings also make an effort to emphasize the ways in which their own approach to the maple sugar business was unique and more effective. While their neighbors were producing maple cream for the market, the Nearings refused "to join the procession on the sheep run" and chose instead to make "old-fashioned grained sugars such as the Indians made."[7] While native Vermonters used galvanized metal for the stacks of their sugarhouses, the Nearings thought a permanent concrete stack would be more effective and, after "finding no record of a sugarhouse with a concrete stack," went ahead and built one anyway. Later, they constructed a second sugarhouse, also with a concrete stack. "[The stacks] are among the most satisfactory features of our setup," the Nearings concluded.[8]

The Total Loss farmers found the Nearings' book on maple sugaring provocative and were "properly inspired" by the contents. They immediately began to plan a syrup business of their own and even went so far as to have a rubber stamp made, which proudly announced the formation of "The Total Loss Maple Producers Cooperative." But the stamp was as far as the project evolved. Other projects continually interceded, and the weight of guilt for not building the sugarhouse continually bore down on the shoulders of the aspiring syrup makers. Plans were made and aborted, first month after month, then year after year. Finally, one day, writes Marty Jezer, "I decided to say 'fuck the sugarhouse.' It was my finest hour." No sooner had Jezer reached this conclusion than his feelings about the sugarhouse became the farmers' motto. Expletives toward the sugarhouse were relayed over hill and dale from one gleeful member of the farm to another until the four erstwhile most-invested proponents of the syrup business "went tripping across the meadow to enjoy the fading autumn light."[9]

"Maple Sugaring: Our Finest Hour" is a playful rejoinder to the Nearings' text. It is also a morality tale about work, one that, at first glance, seems to uphold our notions of what 1960s homesteading must have looked like. But this tale of triumph over the work ethic is really a tale of anxiety about work, one that Jezer himself confesses when he informs his friends, " 'Better to take an objective view of the situation and act from a position of strength than to throw ourselves into a project we obviously can't finish and admit defeat.' "[10] While Jezer and his farm family were waxing victorious over their ability to put off sugarhouse building into perpetuity, they admitted that they were also otherwise engaged: an old barn needed to come down, cordwood needed hauling, apples were being turned into cider, and a pipe needed to be run from the well to the working barn. Much of this work was being done late in the season because of the time it took to build the well by hand.

Again we are reminded that *ritualization*, this "playing at farming," is serious business. In choosing to live "free" of the conventional separation between work and leisure—or, as they often saw it in the lives of their parents, between work and life—these farmers have imposed upon themselves a heavy agenda of physical and emotional labor. The joy in abandoning the sugarhouse project was not just one more expression of the pleasure principle; it was also the joy taken in the temporary breaking of unwritten rules. It was the joy of recognizing that the "serious play" of homesteading is sometimes just too much work to take on.[11] But the serious work interlaced with the play is not only that of physical effort and self-imposed labor; it is also the work of ritualization itself, work that is often "misunderstood" whether by the Total Loss farmers' parents or by Tatelbaum's office mates. Choosing to carry water from a well or to dig that well by hand—from an outsider's perspective—seems to make no sense, but if understood as ritualized behavior that both bears witness to and helps to maintain the sacredness of nature, such actions make much sense indeed.

What do I mean when I say that the work of homesteading involves a sense of ritual, that homesteaders actions ought to be understood as ritualized ones, that homesteaders are engaged in ritualizations of everyday life? Scholars of religion or anthropology may be quick to take sides on whether Tatelbaum's choice to carry water rather than install an electric pump is ritual in the same way as taking communion is ritual or celebrating a bat mitzvah is ritual. Still other scholars might argue that even conventional notions of ritual (communion, bat mitzvahs) are worthy of inquiry. These scholars claim that there is no fundamental, "essential" form of behavior that we can point to and call ritual.

To use the label "ritual," they argue, is to overlook the ways in which the term itself comes from contingent scholarly categories.[12] Such categories shift and change with time, cultural knowledge, and academic fashion. Thus, in academic circles, there is ongoing disagreement about whether ritual is only religious or can also be secular, whether ritual is a subset of ceremony or encompasses all forms of symbolic behavior (theatrical performances, sports, festivals). Some wish to dispense with the term *ritual* altogether, but the debate about ritual rages on.[13]

Catherine Bell has laid out masterfully the history of these debates and the assumptions about the dichotomy between theory and practice that has led scholars to paint themselves into interesting corners by analyzing the meanings of ritual based on the very categories they have invented and imposed.[14] But however fascinating these arguments are, I do not wish to engage them fully here. Rather, I want to take up the most interesting and more constructive part of Bell's discussion, which suggests that the term *ritualization* is preferable to *ritual* because it seeks not to define a particular event, action, or ceremony as ritual but rather to characterize a way of behaving that is on a continuum of human activity (particularly communicative, performative activity) but is not synonymous with "everything" that humans do. For Bell, ritualization is a strategy people choose: "[It] is a way of acting that is designed and orchestrated to privilege what is being done in comparison to other, more quotidian activities. . . . [It is] a matter of variously culturally specific strategies for setting some activities off from others, for creating and privileging a qualitative distinction between the 'sacred' and the 'profane.' "[15] For most of us, daily activities cannot get more quotidian than digging a well by hand or carrying water to one's house! But Bell's definition does not have to do with the *what* so much as the *why* and the *how*. Within the "culturally specific" context of twentieth-century, highly educated, middle-class American culture, making such choices is anything but quotidian; rather, it "privileges" activities that are environmentally ethical and "close to nature." If ritual is, as Jonathan Z. Smith has argued, the assertion of what "ought to be" in the face of what "is," then these activities—if we temper Smith with a dose of Bell—can be seen as ritualizations. They are ritualizations of how to live in the face of a dominant culture that celebrates the artificial, exploits the environment for the sake of "economics," and confines spiritual life to that which takes place in buildings, often in reference to transcendent, denatured gods. In contrast, homesteaders' actions tend to identify nature as sacred and American emphasis on competitiveness, consumption, and greed as profane.

To put this process in laypersons' terms, Bell wants to make clear to her readers that while ritual actors may well be aware of how, why, and to what effect they are engaging in certain kinds of ritual activity, they also do not see themselves as merely "making things up." We might think of members of an Episcopalian liturgical planning committee. They may want to bake their own communion bread and have folk guitar accompaniment, but they do not see the ritual of the Eucharist itself, and the meaning of Christian life to which it points, as fabricated. While members may disagree about the nature of Christ's presence in the communion ritual and may question their own commitments to a Christian life, they take a leadership role in creating this ritual out of some sense of the authenticity of the ritual itself.[16]

Just as ritual experts, while manipulating symbols and rites, do not necessarily doubt the efficacy of their ritual actions, so also do even the most self-conscious homesteaders—those most willing to describe and analyze their actions as purposefully symbolic—continue to engage in symbolic work for the sake of the profound and very "real" experiences gained. The experience of nature that occurs in and through symbolic and ritualized activity remains authentic and, for many, transformational. It is this experience of transformation and renewal, in fact, that keeps many homesteaders rooted to their homesteads despite the hard physical labor and isolation they sometimes face.

What kinds of transformations are we talking about? And how do they relate to an understanding of nature as the source of personal meaning-making? What I have found in most homesteading texts and oral testimonies are descriptions of the expansion or dissolution of the self in the context of contact with the natural world. In some cases, the experience is one of enlargement, a feeling that one is "connected to all living beings" or "part of the cycles of life and death occurring in the garden." As the Nearings often put it, work in the woodlot or the garden reinforced their sense of being part of the "All-That-Is." For others, the process goes beyond a mere loosening of the boundaries between the self and the outside world to an almost mystical dissolution of the body and soul in the larger body and soul of the natural surround. Harlan Hubbard speaks of woodcutting as a kind of time out of time. When collecting river driftwood, he writes: "I was lifted out of present circumstances. I became a voyager passing strange shores. . . . Whenever I lift axe and saw from their pegs . . . my spirits rise. . . . The practical business of getting fuel is transcended. To me the winter would be well spent if I did nothing but gather wood to burn in an open fire, where I could watch its sublimation into smoke and ashes."[17] The Nearings might object to Hubbard's impractical leanings—the admitted longing to collect and burn wood for its own sake—but they would share in his larger sentiments, the sense that living and working in the woods, while also a means of livelihood, is a path to the "exquisite living that you can experience from the beauty of nature" and a means of experiencing "the one life in all things."[18] Indeed, Hubbard, at times, explicitly describes his homesteading life as an act of

faith, one that departs from traditional Christianity while bearing family resemblances to it. In his journals, Hubbard comments: "Much as I admire the
Christian principles and teaching . . . for myself I require a more direct revelation, not one that must come through so many minds before it reaches mine. I
must have a faith that I can see and hear."[19] For Hubbard, the sawing, cutting,
and burning of wood all play a role in keeping these experiences of "direct revelation" present in his daily life.

Whether the self expands or is dissolved or undergoes some combination of
both, homesteaders often report experiencing a blurring of distinctions between the self and the natural world. It is as if the self, in particular moments,
is made up of permeable membranes that open up to let the whole of nature in
or break down to become one with the larger environment. No longer is nature
the Other; now nature is experienced as part of the self while also being larger
and often more significant than the self.

Lest this description of what happens to the self in the context of intimacy
with the natural world seem hopelessly abstract, let us return to some of the
homesteaders we have already met in these pages to hear their renderings of
such experiences. Consider, for instance, the way Sal approached the construction of his house, from local wood and with no more tools than a chain saw and
a small, attachable mill. For Sal, choosing to dwell in one place carries responsibilities of relationship to that place. Thus, he writes of the process of building his home: "As I cut a hundred living trees from which to shape our home,
I did not triumph, I grieved. This is a relationship with profound exchange—
in pouring out my life energy to mingle with the dying exhalation of a tree, the
depth of the transaction fed my soul."[20] For Sal, constructing a building to protect and preserve his own life was, at the same time, an act that involved the sacrifice and death of other lives. For someone who does not see nature as sacred,
trees would serve as mere resources, the means to the end of a house; but for
Sal, trees played a significant role in the larger commitment to live a life close
to nature. In order to establish a new self, a homesteading self, Sal also had to
give himself over to the larger processes of profound exchange, in which
human life must recognize its interdependence with other life forms; with that
recognition comes the felt experience of nature's pain.

A similar language of intimacy emerges in Laura Waterman's reflections on
the difference between the experience of nature common to her and her late
husband, Guy, and those of their visitors. Laura and Guy maintained both summer and winter walking trails in and out of their homestead near a mountain-
ous section of rural New England. Having maintained a high level of self-
sufficiency, they rarely used a car except when restocking dry goods or coming
and going from frequent hiking trips. When returning from such ventures, they

Alone in the woods
closed in by dark
trees and snow
With axe and saw
chopping sawing
splitting his thoughts
which he will bring home
in billets on his wheelbarrow

FIGURE 5.
Harlan Hubbard's drawing suggests that home construction and self-construction go hand in hand. By Harlan Hubbard, taken from his book *Payne Hollow* and used by permission of Gnomon Press.

kept the car several miles away and packed in their supplies. Visitors, on the other hand, drove toward the homestead as far as their cars would take them. Reflecting on this distinction, Laura Waterman writes:

> [In response to] the idea of nature being in control [and] not us humans . . . [Guy] and I felt this particularly when we'd see that people had tried to drive up our steep

hill and in the process had churned up the road, flattened the water bars, but by God they got up! It just seemed to us that we looked at things so differently. It hurt, I mean we felt it physically, to look at the sad mess of our road—the wound. But it is the American way to get over the obstacles that nature imposes, isn't it?[21]

While Laura realizes that her homesteading practices necessarily involve a home-based version of getting over nature's obstacles (by harvesting wood for fuel in the winter, cutting back undergrowth, clearing and planting a garden), she contrasts these practices with a dominant American ethic that rarely allows nature to set the terms for livelihood. Like Sal, Laura feels the sacrifices nature makes to the human will on both a moral and a physical level. In situations in which others exert themselves over nature unnecessarily, she experiences the natural world as being in pain and feels that pain as her own.

Gene Logsdon also expresses an intense, empathetic relationship with the natural world, again, especially in those instances when he exerts his human needs and interests over against his understanding of nature's own course. Drawing on the images of his early education in seminary, Logsdon speaks to the notion of ritual directly, demanding that the sacrifice of nature be given rich, symbolic attention:

> Cutting down a large tree should be an act charged with ritual: candles burning, incense smoking, plump bishops in high hats holding forth in senatorial prayers. A tree that has experienced two centuries or more of life on earth deserves that kind of respect. . . . I justify my felling of it only because it is dying and by thinking how its wood will now become furniture at my son's hands, burnished and beloved by generations of humans. In ending the tree's green life, I release its woody soul to a sort of life everlasting.[22]

Sal's, Laura's, and Gene Logsdon's understanding of the self as not separate from nature bears much in common with Arne Naess's philosophical notion of "Self-realization!" as the goal of human experience, a goal reached by pursuing practices that recognize that the individual self is not separate from the Self of the larger natural and cultural worlds.[23] But these homesteaders are not consciously attempting to "apply" Deep Ecology theory; rather, they report experiences of intimacy (including that of self-expansion or self-dissolution) that emerge from their felt sense of the sacredness of nature.

For Linda Tatelbaum, the practice of carrying water from her well every day carries with it a similar relationship of profound exchange, although this time the exchange is one of pleasure rather than pain. Certainly, sacrifice is also involved: Tatelbaum's sacrifice of time and physical effort in the drawing of the water and the sacrifice involved in using a natural resource that is not boundless. But it is working within both of these constraints, writes Tatelbaum, that makes this daily labor both meaningful and meaning filled. As Tatelbaum puts it:

> The lowering and raising of the bucket centers me. All thoughts become purified in the clear stream of water as it swirls through the funnel into the jug. This is my existence. Here is where I am.
>
> Not just the act of carrying water engages me, but the way of life that goes with that act. I am aware of water, of drops, of dowsings. To live with a quantity of daily water that I am willing to carry, I must live simply. . . . The water that moistens bean sprouts can wash my face. The water that scrubs potatoes can feed the house plants. . . . I love water. . . . I would no sooner throw out a half cup of clean water than I would discard the last of a fine old wine. The water is sacred to me. I am a vessel, preserving.[24]

In this poetic passage, the very rhythms of which evoke the pulling and hauling of buckets, Tatelbaum offers several variations on both the sacredness of nature and the expansion and dissolution of the self. In the first sentence, the self becomes contracted, centered, focused only on existence in the present, on being as it is currently unfolding. The self also moves in limited circumstances—the necessity of reusing water; yet, in this reuse, awareness expands, the relationship with all kinds of water (with drops of dew or downpourings of rain) becomes possible and significant. Finally, the self is extolled not in its own right but is celebrated as a vessel for water, a container for that which is sacred.

A page later in her essay, Tatelbaum elaborates on this notion of the self as vessel or vehicle for water: "I cease to be involved in it all," she writes, "I am the motor behind the work, the woman carrying water. . . . I dip into earth's bounty, and I am washed clean."[25] Here she emphasizes the process of self-emptying, a familiar theme in many religious traditions, in which the self is cleansed to make way for the divine presence. In the homesteading version of this idea, the self becomes important by virtue of the essence of nature that it holds.

While both Sal and Linda Tatelbaum cast their daily labors as ritualizations that involve the dissolution of the boundary between the self and the natural world, no one makes this process of giving up the self more explicit than Raymond Mungo does. As he draws his readers into the world of Total Loss Farm, Mungo's earlier remarks about the sacred act of gardening turn into an unabashed testament of faith and submission: "The garden . . . is where long afternoon is most striking, it is church, it is synagogue, it is peace on earth and plenty. We are never higher or nobler than when we are weeding eggplants. . . . [Our friend] who speaks the least, who finds it hardest to put his concerns into words, spends most of his time here. He talks like an ear of corn: ripe and fleshy with positive energy."[26] Mungo suggests that the nobility of the farmer goes hand in hand with his or her ability to give the self over to the natural world. The highest compliments are reserved for that member of the farm who has become most like the fruits of the earth, who is nature incarnate. Here the anthropocentric strain of a rejected Catholic faith is replaced by a generalized spirituality wherein humanity takes its best cues from nature. Mungo states this ethic much more succinctly when he explicates the meaning of the successful farm he and his friends have dubbed a "total loss": "It's called Total Loss Farm because it produces nothing visible to the mature eye—all the livestock, machinery, seeds, and such tools and not even one peach or can of maple syrup makes it to the market. And nobody who goes in there to stay has ever been seen alive again. Total Loss Farm: *lose yourself.*"[27] But if homesteaders are lost in nature, they are also found. Although the members of Total Loss Farm believed they were, in some sense, dying to the selves they once were and would "never be seen again," they also believed they were being reborn and renewed.

Such a dynamic of self-loss and self-recovery is to be expected. It is an essential feature of religious experience. But when it occurs in the context of a reverence for nature—in the context of a this-worldly rather than an other-worldly concept of the sacred—the consequences are particularly interesting and complex. The work of spiritual self-discovery and self-fashioning when performed in the context of nature can mean that nature itself is sometimes resisted or seen primarily for its beneficial or salvific aspects. While nature's intrinsic value may be explicitly praised, its uses for humans persist. I have engaged this dynamic already in the previous discussion of "self-culture." Now I want to investigate it further, with a focus of one of the most symbolically rich aspects of homesteading practice: food and eating.

Eating Right: Rituals of Food

Food and eating are symbolically significant for all of us. Eating is a central activity in the construction of self. In a certain sense, we "are what we eat" physically, socially, and culturally. A person who articulates a preference for frozen dinners and fast-food chains conjures up a certain image: of one who is constantly pressed for time and money, perhaps, or one who places a strong value on consistency and reliability. What social and cultural communities we see ourselves as belonging to is also suggested by how, what, and where we eat. Does a festive occasion of eating and drinking mean pizza and beer, a clambake on the beach, or a dinner in a French-Cambodian restaurant? Do we cook only for our family and close friends, or do we invite large group of acquaintances into our homes for a meal? Is it important to invite the minister to lunch? How significant is it to keep kosher even if we never go to synagogue services and our theology is only loosely Reform? Decisions about what should or should not be taken into the body are sometimes the last realm of individual choice in a constrained or homogenizing culture.[28] At the same time, community is often preserved or destroyed on the basis of socially constructed rules (both written and unwritten) about food. Eating in a certain way can be a means of political protest, a strategy for maintaining social and cultural distinctions, or an embodied practice leading toward spiritual experiences of transcendence or communion.[29] Like homesteading itself, then, eating is a symbolic gesture that can perform both cultural and religious "work."

For homesteaders, the decision to homestead is, in a fundamental sense, a decision about food. To engage in homesteading is to place food at the center of one's life and livelihood or, as many would prefer to put it, to recognize "where food really comes from" and to adjust one's life appropriately around this recognition. The choices made about food and eating are many and varied. One may reject consumer culture by minimizing the hype around food and trying to live simply. One might acknowledge the essential spirituality of eating mindfully and choose, say, to develop rituals of gratitude around eating, to eat meat from well-loved animals, or to make sure that one eats locally only. Eating is always a physical activity, but it is also always a symbolic activity and may, in addition, be a ritual one. As we have seen in the foregoing discussion, the ritual element in the daily lives of homesteaders is often accented, performing the symbolic work that all of our daily actions perform but with particular emphasis in the context of the "new lives" to which they have converted.

"Our first realization that ritual was a part of farm life centered around food," a Total Loss farmer remembers:

> Even in the first lean winter of living here the hours of dusk set in motion some crazy energy in the kitchen which caught up the whole house in the animated preparation of food. . . . We found out that we were all, every last one of us, crazy for food. I guess it was then, too, that we realized how important it was that this place become a farm so that we could be close to what we ate, and have what we wanted always at hand. If we were unduly poor and loved eggplant it was obvious that we would grow eggplant and freeze eggplant and eat eggplant out of season.[30]

In these reflections we hear several interconnected themes coming into play. The first is the acknowledgment of the practice of eating as a ritual one. In this case, eating is recognized as the primary instance and locale of ritualized activity from which other ritualized elements of farm life later develop.[31] The second theme is the recognition that rituals, particularly food rituals, are what bind the community and give it purpose. Finally, we hear a link being made between eating and gardening, a link that emphasizes both the "connection" that the farmers want to feel with their food (and the "nature" it represents) and the desire for certain tastes and longings to be fulfilled.

The ritualization of eating may happen in a daily way, such as the Nearings' tendency to use only wooden bowls and chopsticks when eating, a decision that Scott made early in life and Helen later adopted. Other homesteaders ritualize eating on a daily basis (enacting a commitment to eating what one has produced for oneself) and on special occasions (setting aside particular days to celebrate the harvest or the appearance of the first peas of the season). While not acknowledging any divine presence out loud, Bill Coperthwaite will pause for silence before each meal, drawing the attention of even the most reluctant to the gifts of bounty on the table. At the same time, he refuses hot drinks, tending to see these as unnecessary luxuries, usually involving labor that is unnecessary (firing up the stove) or undesirable (using "the grid") for such a passing fancy. The families of homesteaders who were inspired by the Nearings and who bought neighboring land celebrate and formalize their commitment to the homesteading way of life through a weekly sauna and potluck dinner, a community tradition we will explore more fully later.[32] Embodied in all of these physical practices are larger notions of "right eating" that go beyond strictly nutritional conceptions of "eating right."

Choices about food in the homesteading world reflect the broader cultural dynamics of eating and drinking in which we all engage. At the same time, these decisions are heightened in the context of lives and livelihoods created by the raising of food. Moreover, because homesteaders—more than the average city dweller—experience and foster an awareness of where food comes from, they are more apt to articulate (in word and deed) the particular connections between food and nature. While scholars such as Pierre Bourdieu tend to downplay the animal need for food in favor of the ways in which eating practices function as markers of cultural and social distinction, homesteaders, by contrast, are more apt to emphasize eating as a "natural" process in which the animal and vegetable kingdoms all mutually participate. In this cyclical schema, humans are understood as a part of nature feeding on other parts of nature while engaging in daily work that helps to nourish the natural world (animal or vegetable) on which they feed. Such an approach mirrors Gary Snyder's assertion that we "are all each other's prey sitting at one big table."[33]

Emphasizing such connectedness, of course, is another means of creating social and cultural distinctions ("aware" homesteader vs. "ignorant" suburbanite; "healthy" farmer vs. "unhealthy" city dweller, "spiritually minded" producer vs. "materially minded" consumer), but it is also an engaged attempt at closing the symbolic distance between nature and food. In exploring the ritualization of food and eating, then, I want to bring both of these aspects of eating to the fore: eating can be cultural behavior only dimly connected to the natural requirements of self-nourishment; and, at the same time, for homesteaders especially, eating is a symbolic behavior that invokes and emphasizes "the natural." "Eating naturally" is thus a cultural act.

The rite of the Eucharist (depending on how it is interpreted) is a means by which a Christian may take into herself either the actual body and blood or the memory of Christ. Physical ingestion becomes a means of incorporating one's deepest values and commitments into one's spiritual self. While this ritual emerged from traditional gatherings for meals (in which the bread and wine were blessed as gifts of God's creativity in and through nature), the bread and wine soon came to symbolize something distinct from ordinary food; indeed, it no longer was considered to be food in the everyday sense at all. In homesteaders' lives, the lines between everyday practice and ritual practice are—as we have already seen—considerably less distinct than we would find in institutional religious settings. But here, too, eating has symbolic dimensions and must be seen in the broader context of the life to which one has converted. For homesteaders, eating naturally is not only a utilitarian matter; it is also a means to "reconnect" with nature through the act of (alternative) consumption. How then, and with what range of practices and interpretations, does such ritualized eating happen?

"What We Eat and Why": The Nearing Disciplines of Eating

In the Nearing household, the eating of particular foods—and periodic abstinence from all food—was understood to be not an end in itself but a recipe for health. A recurrent testimony in the "Good Life" books is that in the fifty-plus years of their homesteading life together neither Helen nor Scott once visited a doctor.[34] Despite these occasional boasts, however, the understanding of health put forth by the Nearings does not restrict itself to the absence of disease but rather encompasses their entire way of acting and being in the world. The Nearings understood health as something that needs to be "practiced," and they interpreted that practice in a number of ways. They saw practicing health as a skill that needs to be worked at and perfected; it is a way of life that ought to be pursued daily, and it is a spiritual discipline that leads to the "human virtue" of healthfulness.[35]

The locus of health is food, which, taken together with air, light, sunshine, and "more or less obscure sources of electro-magnetic, cosmic energy," provides for "wholth or wholeness," the "primary, positive principle" that the Nearings referred to when trying to define health.[36] That the Nearings also considered air, sunlight, and unnamable energy as vital elements to be taken into the body along with food (or as another kind of food) suggests the more mystical elements in their thinking. But the practical work of the growing, harvesting, and eating of vegetable food occupied the center of the Nearings' homesteading experience. Their relationship with nature and their critique of culture began at the broad wooden plank that served as their table.

Both Helen and Scott had developed "unconventional" attitudes toward food and eating early in life. Helen's Theosophist parents, Maria and Frank Knothe, practiced Spiritualism, meditation, and vegetarianism. Unlike her brother and sister, Helen remained much in tune with the spiritual attitudes and daily practices of her parents and, if anything, was more committed to her parents' principles than they were.[37] Vegetarianism was not an area of compromise for Helen. She liked to tell of refusing elegant dinners thrown by well-meaning admirers. One of her favorite stories was of refusing to eat a meat-laden Austrian feast presented in her honor by fellow Vermont transplant Maria von Trapp. Remembering her early courtship with Scott, she reflected: "We talked of vegetarianism and I was glad to hear he also was a non-carcass-eater. He said he was a pacifist and did not like killing—of man, bird, or beast. It was this side of him that appealed to me most. I think if he had not been a vegetarian, I would not have tied up with him."[38] As Helen's actions and language suggest, the boundary between meat eating and "non-carcass" eating was a boundary that would not be crossed. For her, being a vegetarian was essentially a ritualization of her Theosophist, pacifist, and, later, environmental ethics.

Scott Nearing did not become a strict vegetarian until 1917, at age thirty-five, "a turning point in his life." His decision to give up meat eating and discard fashionable clothing symbolized a conversion to a new way of being in the world. This "new life" was a response to his dismissal from academia and his hard-won acquittal from a federal trial, in which he was charged with treason for his public denouncement of the United States' participation in World War I.[39] Yet Scott's interests in health and diet preceded these midlife transformations. His new resolutions represented an affirmation of prior commitments as much as a dramatic reversal of thought and conduct.

Beginning in his youth, Nearing was a regular reader of fitness guru Bernarr Macfadden's *Physical Culture* magazine and a "devotee of his good health formula," which included a large dose of outdoor activity and regular fasting.[40] Along with such well-known promoters as William James and Theodore Roosevelt, Nearing participated in the crusade for renewed physical vitality that was advanced in highly moral, masculinized, distinctly Protestant terms. Between the years of 1906 and 1915, when he was in his twenties and early thirties, Nearing also summered at Arden, Delaware, a single-tax intentional community where he first experimented with organic farming and vegetarianism. These early endeavors came to shape not only Nearing's choice to maintain this style of living in later years but also his tendency to continue to interpret his choices in the familiar language and tone of the Progressive Era's rigorous idealism with respect to self-culture.[41] Both Helen and Scott Nearing, then, brought already-existing foundational attitudes toward food, health, and vegetarianism to their experiment at Forest Farm.

In *Living the Good Life*, the Nearings write that their guiding principles of "wholeness, rawness, garden freshness and one or a few things at a meal" resulted in a simple, largely unwavering regime: "fruit for breakfast; soup and cereal for lunch; salad and vegetables for supper."[42] Twenty-five years later, they provide in *Continuing the Good Life* a remarkably similar account: "our own herb teas and fruit for breakfast; soup and grains for lunch; salad, one cooked vegetable and some applesauce for supper."[43] In both books, the Nearings refer to their leanings toward mono-diets, decreasing variety in favor of simplicity, and, Helen characteristically adds, making "little work for the housewife."[44] In *Continuing the Good Life*, the Nearings report their experiments with mono-diets and fasting with greater precision:

> We have gone on mono-diets—for example, eating only apples for days on end, or subsisting on juices, or fasting on water only—for ten days at a time. . . . One day a week we aim at twenty-four hours on just liquids, either juices or water. We enjoy these days of fasting and look forward to them as one of the high points of the week. . . . Just as shaving the head completely of hair can give one a godlike feeling of lack of clutter, so going without food can give one a feeling of freedom and release that is real emancipation.[45]

The detailed descriptions given here suggest that the rigorous dietary regimes mentioned in their earlier book were more frequently put into practice as their homesteading years accumulated. The Nearings elsewhere report that their earlier use of dairy products gave way to a largely (though not exclusively) vegan diet, with allowances made for ice cream on festive occasions.[46]

Whether or not all readers breathe a collective sigh of relief upon learning that the Nearings, like the best of us, indulged in ice cream, we can detect in even these slight descriptions of their "food practice" a number of resounding themes: the importance of holistic and organic gardening; the deep significance of the circular pattern of harvesting, eating, and composting one's own produce; and the valuation of all life forms. But in addition to hearing those themes that sound familiar to twenty-first-century, environmentally attuned ears, we can also detect in the Nearings' reports a persistent (and perhaps less familiar) theme of rigor and self-discipline.

If we return to a number of passages in which the Nearings discuss their nutrition decisions, we can see how seamlessly their words flow from the language of harmony and balance to that of discipline and self-rule. In speaking of the importance of eating in time with the seasons, the Nearings begin with a simple testament to the sensibility and enjoyment that comes from this practice. They write: "By following the seasons, we got a succession of foods—each at its peak. We enjoyed each in turn. We tired of none, but always looked forward to it coming in the growing season."[47] With a gesture to Thoreau (they cite his remark, "I love best to have each thing in its season only, and enjoy doing without it all other times"), the Nearings put forth their ideas in the language of commonsense thinking, while also explicitly linking their practices with the Transcendentalist tradition of self-culture.[48]

The sense given here is that nature should set the menu for the human guests and not the other way around, as is so frequently the case in supermarkets.[49] But at another moment within this same general discussion, we detect a similar statement on eating "in season" that bears a slightly different message and tone. Beginning with the warning that "there is something extravagant and irresponsible about eating strawberries in a cold climate," the Nearings go on to assert: "Such practices ignore the meaningful cycle of the seasons. Those who dodge it or slight it are like children who skip a grade in school, pass over its drill and discipline, and ever after have the feeling that they've missed something."[50] Here the Nearings move beyond a focus on nature and the importance of eating and living according to the cycle of the seasons to a judgment of those people who do not live in this way. The shift is slight, but it is a significant one in that it gives us access to the large role that discipline plays in the Nearing project.[51]

If this exhortation to live according to the seasons takes on the tone of a parent rebuking a child, an even more unrelenting approach comes to the fore when the topic of vegetarianism is considered. Within their chapter "Eating for Health," in *Living the Good Life*, the Nearings again present their views with something of a double approach. In one paragraph, they present their philosophical principles in a simple, flowing style that seems to match the ease and common sense with which they arrived at their convictions: "We were looking for a kindly, decent, clean and simple way of life. Long ago we decided to live in the vegetarian way, without killing or eating animals; and lately we have largely ceased to use dairy products. . . . This is all in line with our philosophy of the least harm to the least number and the greatest good to the greatest number of life forms."[52] But the Nearings' gentle philosophical extension of Jeremy Bentham's thesis is not the only means by which their views are expressed. In the same pages, the Nearings move from a peaceful espousal of "the vegetarian way" to a more militant condemnation of the opposite alternative when they write: "Carnivorism involves (1) holding animals in bondage (2) turning them into machines for breeding and milking (3) slaughtering them for food (4) preserving and processing their dead bodies for human consumption."[53]

Their most stringent remarks go one step further when the subject of milk drinking is broached. They write: "Milk is a highly concentrated infant food, especially designed to stimulate rapid growth in the early stages of development. Human milk should normally be for baby humans, cow's milk for calves. . . . Adults of any breed should have been weaned and past the milk stage of feeding."[54] Calling to mind the earlier remark that eating food out of season is like skipping a crucial year in grade school, the Nearings bestow on any dissenters the status of a child. The reader, and certainly American culture generally, is accused of having not yet grown up. Here the Nearings' words suggest again that how they eat reflects not only their concern for nature but also their individual and cultural development. Proper "food-practice" is thus tied to concepts of maturity and purity that are in fact as human-focused as they are nature-focused.[55] The dynamic relationship between sensitivity to the interconnectedness of the ecological world, on the one hand, and the drive to control the self's relationship to that world, on the other, demonstrates both the unique combination of forces that maintained the Nearing experiment and the tensions that ran through it.

The Pleasures of Eating

In contrast to the Nearings' approach-avoidance dance with nature, food, and the self, others engage in practices and interpretations of what they do that emphasize different values, such as celebration, intimacy, pleasure, and affection. Like the Nearings, for instance, Wendell Berry wants to put food back in its proper place. He resists the notion of food as a commodity, a "product" to be produced without concern for social and physical health, and he objects to the idea that growing and harvesting food should be conducted under rigid market principles. In The Unsettling of America, Berry writes against James Bostic Jr., former deputy assistant secretary for the Department of Agriculture, who once hailed a future where "ninety-five percent of the people can be freed from the drudgery of preparing their own food."[56] Berry's attention to food here reflects his general conviction that our current agricultural crisis is symptomatic of a larger crisis of human character and culture that ought to be healed. In response to Bostic, Berry writes: "Only by restoring the broken connections can we be healed. Connection *is* health. . . . What our society does its best to disguise from us is how ordinary, how commonly attainable, health is. We lose our health—and create profitable diseases and dependencies—by failing to see the direct connections between living and eating, eating and working, working and loving."[57]

In Berry's view, our culture has cast as drudgery that which is our only means of connection to the life processes that fuel our being. To be released from it would be the equivalent of being "released" into a cultural prison where we are cut off from all knowledge of and contact with our actual support systems. To step into the circle of relationships among ourselves, our food, and the natural world—a circle that, Berry argues, we are already in though not necessarily *aware* of—is to participate in an act of necessary worship and communion. He writes, "Eating with the fullest pleasure—pleasure that does not depend on ignorance—is perhaps the profoundest enactment of our connection with the world."[58] Like the Nearings, Berry interprets personal and cultural health as "wholeness," a concept against which American culture pushes its capitalist and materialist agenda.

The Nearings might well agree with Berry's initial assertions. But if we look more closely at Berry's writing, we hear a language and tone that departs from the themes of discipline and rigor that run through the Nearings' works. Most obviously, the word *pleasure* occurs, a word that seldom appears in the Nearings' writings, although the reader cannot miss the sense of enjoyment and satisfaction they undeniably gained from their homesteading practice.[59] In contrast, pleasure is an explicitly emphasized value in Berry's thought and writing. The word is so dominant that it constitutes its own particular ethic and aesthetic. Of his diet Berry writes:

> If I am going to eat meat, I want it to be from an animal that has lived a pleasant uncrowded life outdoors, on bountiful pasture, with good water nearby and trees for shade. And I am getting almost as fussy about food plants. I like to eat vegetables that have lived happily and healthily in good soil. . . . People who know the garden in which their vegetables have grown . . . will remember the beauty of the growing plants, perhaps in the dewy first light of morning when the gardens are at their best. Such a memory involves itself with food and is one of the pleasures of eating. . . . The same goes for eating meat. The thought of the calf contentedly grazing flavors the steak.[60]

Here Berry's less rigid approach to what food he may eat is accompanied by a greater openness and effusiveness in the way he writes about his food. For Berry, pleasure emerges from those situations in which intimacy, positive memory, and gratitude are all present in the context of dynamic relationships both among people and between humans and other living beings. Thus, Berry will include among the pleasures of eating not only the pleasure of knowing the animals he may eat but also the pleasure of working with animals—and overcoming "estrangement" from them—as part of the small-scale agricultural process.[61] In contrast, the Nearings' policy on animals was a curious mix of reverence for their lives and resolve to keep them at bay.[62]

A kind of "middle path" between the ethics and aesthetics of rigor (as epitomized by the Nearings) and the ethics and aesthetics of pleasure (as exemplified by Berry) can be found in the various approaches to food that Helen's former neighbor, Sal, has adopted. Sal's decision to eat meat, like his practice of no-till gardening, emerges from and is supported by his broader views of history and of the self. Choosing to eat meat, after previously being a vegetarian and having experimented with fasting, is a decision that locates itself within the larger complex of building and gardening practices and ideas about nature and culture that we have heard Sal express. Sal interprets his previous experiments with intense fasting and vegetarianism as phases, tests in freeing the body from its dependence on food. Moreover, Sal understands vegetarianism as another aspect of that moment in history when people sought truth and light through strategies of force. While homesteading, Sal and his family ate meat on occasion, interpreting that choice as located somewhere between the factory farming of consumer culture and the pursuit of "otherworldly" perfectionism that some vegetarians seemed to seek. Yet Sal's interest in getting to a "more mature place" personally and culturally—in part by eating meat—resonates (again ironically) with the Nearings' comments on the vegetarian way of life as an appropriately "grown up" and enlightened practice.

As we can see, Sal, Wendell Berry, and Helen and Scott Nearing are all engaged in ways of eating that articulate ways of living. In each approach to eating, nature figures strongly as something to be valued and protected, but in each case also the self is being created and nurtured. Like all cultural acts involving taste, these different practices of food and eating also function as means of enacting personal and cultural distinction. Ritualizations in response to nature are also, always, ritualizations in response to the dominant culture. The effects of such ritualization are often mixed. The Nearings' vegetarianism, for instance, was one of the most troublesome elements in their attempts at creating community in Vermont, but it was a position on which they refused to compromise. Remarking that their dietary practices were the source of "the most consistent and emphatic disapproval" from their neighbors, the Nearings ultimately blamed the problem on inbred rural attitudes rather than the stringency of their own practices. While admitting that their eating habits were deviant in the eyes of their neighbors—"We ate food raw . . . that should have been cooked, and we cooked weeds and outlandish things that never should be eaten at all"—their final assessment of the problem reads as follows:

> In a community which serves pie, cake and doughnuts for two if not three meals a day, conduct such as ours was not only unbelievable but reprehensible. . . . To the credit of Vermont conservatism it must be said that during the two decades of our stay, after innumerable discussions and long-drawn-out arguments on the subject of white flour, white bread, white sugar, pies and pastries, the necessity for eating raw vegetables, and the revolting practice of consuming decaying animal carcasses, no native Vermont family of our acquaintance made any noticeable change in its food habits.[63]

Here the Nearings seem surprised that the local community—whose families had been farming and maple sugaring for centuries before they had—could not understand the error of their ways. As with the locals' "dependence" on farm animals and their tendency to let tools rust in the yard, their food practices, in the Nearings' eyes, were symptoms of a larger problem: a lack of discipline, an absence of concern for health, a refusal to approach "the problem of living" through respect for nature and control of the self. Yet, as with many "flatlanders," the Nearings were dependent on the locals for learning the art of sugaring, for borrowing equipment, and for help with numerous gardening and building projects. The Nearings rarely acknowledged their neophyte status or dependence on others to the extent that neighbors and locals would have liked, in part because of their need to define themselves as "different" with just the kind of exceptionalist language we hear in the doughnut and carcass diatribe above.[64]

Wendell Berry's food practices, by contrast, help link him to the local community. He eats as they do, raises animals as they do, and, to the chagrin of some of his readership, supports tobacco growing as they do.[65] But Berry explicates meat eating in a way in which the farmer up the road might not, using the traditional Christian language of communion to support the practice while also borrowing rationales from the more "alternative" campaigns for organic gardening and free-range animal husbandry. His way of eating—and of interpreting what he eats—keeps him connected to the local community while also pushing its boundaries. Furthermore, he redefines community itself to include the community of plants and animals on his farm.

Berry's choices, however, keep him apart from those proponents of simple living who feel that raising and eating animals does harm to the earth and to the self. Helen Nearing's attitude toward Berry, in fact, was one of considerable caution. Whatever private admiration she may have had for one whose simple homesteading life and sense of the sacredness of nature so closely resembled her own, her public statements were begrudging: "He's a good farmer, I suppose," she once remarked to me, "but he's not a vegetarian."[66] While choosing livelihoods that in so many ways mirror one another, Wendell Berry and the Nearings are kept separate from each other not only by the particular food practices they prefer but also, and perhaps more important, by the aesthetic styles and ethical principles that underlie them.

Mary Douglas's discussion of purity and danger is a useful interpretive guide to the range of practices we are exploring here, one that helps us to understand that these choices about food and livelihood are more than whims or mere pigheadedness. In describing dirt as "matter out of place," Douglas emphasizes that notions of dirt and pollution (whether ancient or contemporary) are based not only on hygienic and aesthetic considerations but also on religious values and notions of the sacred. "Our pollution behavior," Douglas writes, "is the reaction which condemns any object or idea likely to confuse or contradict cherished classifications."[67] Purity, by contrast, is defined according to order, to the place an object or idea holds within, and often at the center of, these cherished classifications. With Douglas's distinctions in mind, we might argue that, in the Nearings' view, meat is understood as life that has been cruelly treated and unjustly terminated, brought in from the "outside" and consumed by the unenlightened. In Berry's view, there is appropriate and inappropriate meat; some meat is sacred, other meat is profane. Sacred meat comes from the "inside," within the family farm at best or at least from a local farm whose ethical animal-raising practices are well-known. If the animals were raised and killed within the proper order of things (organic farming practices, healthy soil, fresh pasture, loving caretakers), then the food is pure, indeed, holy.[68]

Douglas gives us some broad categories for understanding how eating is a symbolic and ritual practice, but her understanding of purity and pollution can be limited by a static Durkheimian view of the sacred and the profane. James Wharton, however, offers a more historical and particularized perspective by interpreting dietary practices within the context of American health reforms in the Jacksonian period, the Progressive Era, and, more briefly, in the late twentieth century. Wharton demonstrates that dietary practices have *always* played a significant role in what he calls "American hygienic religions." Like Catherine Albanese, whose more comprehensive treatment of noninstitutional forms of "nature religion" includes attention to health reform, Wharton argues that health practices (water cures, vegetarianism, mono-diets, fasting), while located in the body, invoke notions of nature's ultimate goodness. Natural goodness, in turn, is equated with spiritual goodness, and human health is understood as a moral imperative. Eating right (along with exercises, baths, and other embodied practices) is performed for the glory of God, the fulfillment of the self, or the making of the social good, and often all three.[69]

With respect to Scott Nearing in particular, biographer John Saltmarsh also makes the case that this "non-believer's" practices emerge clearly out of a history of Christian perfectionism. In commenting on the particularly meaning-laden aspects of vegetarianism in the Progressive Era, Saltmarsh places Scott Nearing's choices in broader, historical terms. He notes that vegetarianism "expressed both a religious orientation and an optimistic confidence in scientific progress," the very blend of impulses that shaped Scott's life and work. In terms of religious contexts of meaning, Saltmarsh reminds us: "Christian physiology explained the human body as God's temple, making physical purity not only a moral duty, but a prerequisite for social purity. Consistent with millennial notions, physical health blended with ethics into a form of strenuous Christianity suitable for resurrecting full vitality in the individual so that he or she would be fit for service."[70] Saltmarsh's gloss on the religious and intellectual significance of vegetarianism is helpful to our readings of the Nearing's project as a whole. While vegetarianism expresses a certain kind of nature-based altruism, as James Wharton suggests, it also expresses a rigorous commitment to the cultivation of the self.[71] This turn toward self-cultivation, while publicly justified as concern for nature, also involves concern for how the self can be mastered and purified. While respect for nature informs the practice, like many forms of respect, it is based on keeping one's distance.

Taken together, Douglas, Wharton, and Saltmarsh help us to see that the choice to eat certain foods in certain ways may go beyond the realm of both practical circumstances (the garden is overflowing with zucchini) and even psychological disposition (a tendency to favor order and control). These choices pertain also to a profound sense of who one is (or can become), how one distinguishes oneself from the world, and what one sees as moral and spiritual imperatives in daily living. The most intriguing (and revealing) consequences of these practices, however, are the ways in which they may keep individuals at a certain distance from nature itself. As I have argued, the choice to homestead carries the weight of deep conviction and the spiritual and psychological impact of conversion, but the daily practices within homesteading can be more paradoxical and uncertain. A persistent and underlying ambivalence, I am arguing, is an ambivalence about how close to nature we should (or can) actually get.

Theologies and Rituals of the Soil

If homesteading is an act of conversion, then it is no accident that it might invoke notions of immortality and in some cases involve an explicit quest to achieve it. But notions of immortality also strike us as oddly discordant when the lives of homesteaders are considered. The homesteaders we are discussing here are ones who have rejected traditional religion and its institutions, in part because of the perceived emphasis on the spirit over nature, heaven over earth, and the next life over daily existence in this world. Homesteaders, by contrast, are particularly apt to embrace—indeed, to celebrate—embodiedness, this-worldliness, and the materiality of the natural world. Yet operating alongside these explicit gestures embracing the body and the earth are other gestures of resistance, gestures that suggest a certain longing for immortality, even while mortality is being affirmed as that most natural of processes.

When Helen and Scott Nearing speak of fasting as giving one a "God-like feeling of lack of clutter," they compare the act to that of shaving the head. The comparison is not just an apt choice of metaphor; it is based on their own experience. In the early years of their homesteading life, Helen and Scott shaved their heads and later proudly published pictures of themselves as self-made acolytes on their Vermont farm.[72] Both fasting and head shaving, along with the more "everyday" activities of highly disciplined gardening, planning, and bookkeeping, expressed the Nearings' concern with purity, order, strong principles, and consistent practices. Yet these matters of aesthetics and psychological orientation were also matters of spiritual and ethical concern, as our discussion of vegetarianism makes clear. Along with the commitment to do no harm to living creatures and to celebrate the "at-oneness" of all creation, the quest for immortality is an important feature of the spiritual life of homesteading, even if it is less obviously articulated.

We have already noted the strains of perfectionism and exceptionalism that can be heard in the Nearings' exhortations to eat according to the seasons and in the disdain they directed toward their unenlightened neighbors in Vermont. This sense of exceptionalism underlies our hunch that the Nearings saw themselves as somehow "saved" from the beliefs and practices of the dominant culture from which they had fled, a culture that respected neither personal health, nor social justice, nor the value of the natural world. But their attitudes toward death both embraced and resisted an understanding of it as a natural process. Certainly, both the Nearings would be among the first to claim that death is a natural event. Both shunned the idea of dying in a hospital. Both made prior arrangements to be cremated and to have their ashes scattered on the lands and waters that were special to them. Both wanted their "crossing over" to be celebrated rather than mourned. For many, the Nearings have come to be models of "conscious living and conscious dying" that represent a challenge to common Western cultural readings (whether secular or religious) of death as an unnatural, evil, and frightening event.[73]

At the same time, both Nearings held to firm notions (based on a blend of Eastern principles of karma and reincarnation and on Theosophist and Spiritualist notions of eternal life) that the physical body was merely an external vessel of the self and that continuance of the self or rebirth in another form was inevitable.[74] While neither endorsed a Christian notion of eternal life, both of them shared a confidence in the spiritual continuity of the self after the death of the physical body. This view of the self existing "above and beyond" nature is, in my reading, a view held not only with respect to the moment of death but also with respect to the daily context of living. Fasting is a particularly recognizable and familiar form of expressing this view, as is the generally ascetic style with which both Nearings engaged in their work.

Homesteaders' reverence for nature often includes a fascinating resistance to nature. For instance, Helen Nearing understood her choice to be vegetarian as a response to her care and concern for all living things. Thus, wrote Nearing: "I acknowledge that leaving-off meat-eating means taking the lives of plants when we cut off their lives, swallow and digest them. And I apologize to the radish, the carrot, the head of lettuce, the apple, the orange, when eating them. . . . Who am I to take their lives in their prime?"[75] Such expressions of humility and gratitude suggest a deep sense of connection with the natural world, a sense that taking the life of a plant is on the same continuum as the taking of any form of life (though certainly not at the same point on the line as the taking of animal life). At the same time, however, this statement expresses a certain discomfort with some essential aspects of human existence: eating and enjoying eating, harvesting and taking pleasure in the act of harvesting. Those who knew Helen Nearing knew that pleasure was a part of her daily life and played a role in making that life satisfactory. But asceticism was the public face, and with that asceticism came a certain tone of exceptionalism and a hint of immortality. "I'd like to be able to live on light alone," Helen Nearing was fond of saying.[76] As she put it to others, by way of spreading the word: "Some day, I hope, we shall be able to live on sunlight absorbed through the skin and deep breaths of clean air."[77] Such visions of human existence do not sever the connections with nature. In fact, Helen Nearing's words amount to a poetic description of photosynthesis and a desire to live as if she were a plant. At the same time, however, these remarks give the sense of one who desires to live differently from most humans, of one who is living in the world but is not of the world, of one who is close to nature but not too close.

While the case of the Nearings may be particularly revealing, still other versions of "getting close to nature" are less ascetic, seeming to permit a much greater proximity and intimacy and yet also articulating a certain longing for transcendence and immortality. Berry's emphasis on connection and communion, for instance, is still interwoven with a kind of anthropocentrism that sees the farmer's relationship to a particular plot of land as mirroring that of God's relationship to all of creation.[78] If God created the universe "for his pleasure," Berry suggests, then the farmer is husband to the land also for the sake of pleasure as well as for the sake of responsibility as God's steward.[79] But the rationale for farming still circles back to what the practice of farming can do for the life of the self and the life of the spirit. Even more than providing pleasure and enacting responsibility, the art of farming turns theology into praxis. Ideas of immortality are translated into experiences of an eternal life, one that is at once more this-worldly than traditional Christian notions of heavenly existence and more recognizably Christian than pagan or scientific.

In a book of poetry entitled *Farming: A Handbook*, Berry invites his audience into what appears to be a practical guidebook for farm living, only to reveal that the foundational principles of farming are essentially spiritual ones. In his opening poem, "The Man Born to Farming," he writes:

> The grower of trees, the gardener, the man born to farming,
> whose hands reach into the ground and sprout,
> to him the soil is a divine drug. He enters into death
> yearly, and comes back rejoicing. He has seen the light lie
>   down
> in the dung heap, and rise again in the corn . . . [80]

A more accurate (and autobiographically appropriate) title might read "The Man Re-born through Farming"; for here farming is portrayed as a kind of godly addiction that, without its inherent promise of rebirth, might not be undertaken at all.

While Louis Bromfield's demonstration farming experiments in the 1930s may be too vast in scale to qualify as homesteading, his conversion from Hollywood writing to organic farming is an intriguing historical preface to Berry's choices. Like Berry, Bromfield rejected a literary life and returned to his native soil, but with radical ideals for soil conservation and natural living that distinguished him from his farming neighbors. Like John Burroughs before him and the Nearings after, Bromfield's model of dissent touched a cultural nerve that made his farm another popular (rural) pilgrimage site, well before organic farming had entered the broader culture. Bromfield's choice to farm should also be understood as a ritualization, a desire to remake culture and the self. In company with Berry, he understood his farming practices in theological terms:

> For me religion and faith have never come through churches and rarely through
> men. These things have welled up in me many times in contact with animals

and trees and landscape, at moments when I was certain not only of the existence of God, but of my own immortality as part of some gigantic scheme of creation, of an immortality that had nothing to do with plaster saints and tawdry heavens but with something greater and more profound and richer in dignity, the beautiful dignity of the small animals of the field, of a fern growing from a damp crevice in the rock, or a tulip tree rising straight and clean 100 feet toward the sky.[81]

Both Berry and Bromfield offer deftly conceived visions of nature that can appeal both to religious readers and to atheistic champions of composting.

A similar assertion is made, although in less explicitly Christian language, by the inhabitants of Total Loss Farm. Like Berry (and echoing Jefferson), Mungo views farmers as a kind of "chosen people."[82] In Mungo's view such chosen people have access to a kind of perpetual life that "outsiders"—those bound by the conventions of materialism, religious doctrine, and social expectation—cannot hope to gain.[83] "We are going to die on Total Loss Farm," writes Mungo near the conclusion of his book. "We will die very soon . . . and yet live here forever. That is how we survive, in our souls, and in the beauty in earthly nature which seizes our bodies for organic waste."[84] In predicting that the Total Loss farmers will die very soon, Mungo is speaking of the kind of spiritual death and rebirth that is so often a part of the initial turn to homesteading. But he is also anticipating how the life of homesteading can accommodate the problem of *physical* death. Mungo understands farming as a kind of practical theology that resolves the problem of mortality in a way that is at once spiritual and natural.

For Berry, Bromfield, the Total Loss farmers, and others, the promise of a kind of immortality may be the ultimate lure of homesteading. The practice of better living and healthy eating are genuinely appealing, but, in ontological terms, they are merely surface attractions. Both Berry and Mungo express faith in a kind of "spiritual materialism," which on the Berry side leans in Christian directions and on the Mungo side leans toward a broad (and somewhat vague) blend of earth-based spirituality, mysticism, and Eastern religious ideas. In each case, however, an ambivalence toward nature and a purely naturalistic or utilitarian assessment of it is expressed. Nature is embraced and pursued on its own terms, but getting close to nature is enacted in part out of what nature can provide for the *self*: a means of somehow getting beyond the very natural limits of human mortality.

Yet another version of this kind of spiritual materialism can be found in the approach that Sal takes toward matter. As we have seen earlier, Sal's various decisions about the growing and eating of food represent a struggle in which ideals of progress are both embraced and resisted. In the same vein, Sal also seems to seek a kind of immortality, even while objecting to the way Western culture has so actively pursued this goal. Sal's preference for "being available" to the practical and spiritual lessons already present in nature, for cultivating a chaotic sense of order in his garden, for resisting how-to books in favor of becoming "a living book," all reveal a Thoreauvian desire to "know by experience." Eating meat in moderation and with awareness of the animal's life and death fits into this schema. It represents a way of accepting the embodiedness of other beings and the interdependence of these bodies in a way that vegetarianism does not. On the other hand, the desire to progress "past technology," to cultivate a walking garden in which nature *seems* to take the lead, also represents a desire to solve human problems—both those that emerge within individual life histories and those that belong to the human condition.

As Sal relates his first steps away from conventional education and toward the natural world, we hear these existential strains:

> I never really needed a specific teacher or ever sought one out because I was too busy; there was just too much going on. . . . Everything immediately would lead to the next thing. . . . [With] no one there to lead you . . . you're going purely by either sense or instinct. . . . However, once those things are crossed, the information is [he pauses], is you. You see what I mean? It is you fully and *nothing* can take it away. There's no set of circumstances—accidents or physical death even or whatever—that can part you from that information. It becomes your very flesh itself, your bones, your structure of your body.[85]

In Sal's view, knowledge that is attained through self-sufficiency and through living intimately with the natural world is taken into the body. Yet somehow this knowledge outlasts the body and the natural processes of death.[86] This valuation of the body and embodiment is the larger context in which Sal's approach to gardening and eating needs to be understood. In one sense, this valuation is a response to his earlier experiences of formal education. It is a rejection of rational "head" learning for fully embodied experiential learning. Yet as Sal's words reveal, embodied learning and embodied living involve much more than a rejection. When he learns from nature directly, nothing can separate him from what he has learned. While Sal rejects the kind of perfectionism that the Nearings strive for and with which he himself once experimented, he remains invested in both the idea of progress and the quest for immortality. His approach, however, is a more incarnational one, a yearning for the *real presence* of things through direct, spontaneous experience. But his, too, is a practice of living that responds to the fact of dying, a creation of culture that simultaneously embraces and resists the processes of nature.

Sauna: A Habit of the Body and Spirit

Sal's comments on gardening and food reveal a highly theorized and recognizably "post-Catholic" interest in incarnational experience.[87] But from the 1980s to the mid-1990s, Sal also participated in a broader neighborhood culture that gives us yet another revealing portrait of the ritual life of homesteading. The other homesteaders in the Nearing neighborhood who are known by most as "the Sauna crowd" (but who refer to themselves by their own special collective name) exhibit exuberant attitudes toward food. Their approach serves as a kind of jovial defiance of the Nearings' aesthetics of rigor. At a typical gathering, Henry and Jo, Simon and Grace, Karl and Kim, and others hover over tables and counters—waiting for a signal to dig in—with a kind of intensity of focus more properly reserved for the truly food deprived. Ernest celebrates the delights of Reed's homemade apple wine and, after several glasses, discourses—with a gleam in his eye and the Nearings in mind—on the unsung virtues of using copious amounts of butter. Like the Total Loss Farmers, Sauna members indeed seem "crazy for food," delighting in their homegrown dishes and homemade wine while also never being averse to a store-bought bag of chips or a large tub of ice cream.[88]

Here again we see the articulation of an aesthetics of pleasure, one that, in many ways, is purposely distinct from the aesthetics of rigor that pervaded the Nearing household. The immoderate eating of all manner of decadent foods (and wine) operates in many ways as a symbolic rebellion against the homesteading ways of the Nearings, who once functioned, for some, as "spiritual parents." At the same time, these practices also embody some of the same principles on which the Nearings' homesteading work was based: emphasizing the connections between gardening well and eating well, choosing to eat primarily homegrown (and home-preserved) food, and generously sharing food with those who are part of the community or who are visitors interested in the homesteading way of life.

In thinking about food and the way that homesteaders talk and write about it, we need to maintain the interpretive perspective that the growing and eating of food are a mode of livelihood but also a ritualization of dissent from the larger American—and, increasingly, global—culture. This dominant culture sees food only as a product of market forces, manipulates food genetically, and rarely considers the connections among food, place, environment, and health in the way that Berry, the Nearings, or their less prominent neighbors conceptualize it. While the actual practices may differ, growing, eating, and celebrating food in the context of the homestead constitute a particularly symbolically rich way of ritualizing a life of cultural and spiritual resistance to the mainstream. But the

Sauna crowd stands out in their ritualization of homesteading life, reminding us that homesteading is not merely a matter of rugged individualism and quirky expressions of taste. Let us linger, a moment, on their sense of ritual.

On the most fundamental level, this community of homesteaders is held together by a weekly ritual: Sauna. Sauna takes place every Wednesday evening. It has been an active tradition since the late 1970s, although the cast of characters attending has changed. Newcomers are welcomed while some old-timers have moved away either physically or emotionally from the Sauna crowd at various points in time. Although the weekly gathering was originally held on the same site each week—a former fruit and vegetable stand refurbished as a sauna—on land once belonging to the Nearings, it has, in recent years, become more like a progressive supper moving up and down the neighborhood.

The significance of Sauna is underlined, in part, by the very development of this progressive supper model. While some neighbors have told me that the early purpose of Sauna was primarily to get clean at a time when most people did not have electricity or running water, this initial rationale later became less relevant. Many of these homesteaders have had electricity, running water, or various solar and wood-fired water-heating systems put in as the time, resources, or change in attitude toward technology has made it possible for them to do so. Nevertheless, they also have built saunas. On the road to the Nearings, almost every homestead has a sauna, and other more far-flung homesteaders also have one, even if it requires the Sauna crowd a half-hour drive to get there. For those whose saunas still *are* their only means of getting clean, the building of them has not led to the homesteader's attitude of "I've got my sauna now, so I don't need yours." Instead, building a sauna has become a way to step into the Sauna tradition more fully.

By hosting Sauna, one facilitates not only the Sauna meal but also the cleansing that precedes it. Henry, one of the longest-standing homesteaders in the neighborhood, has seen his children off to college and recently brought his elderly mother closer to the area. Finally, he has found the time and energy to build his sauna, a work of love and of art; constructed out of timbers harvested on site, it is massive in proportions. The oval entrance is decorated with curved tree trunks, suggesting, to Henry's mind, the meeting of two dragons at the entrance. Others tease that the symbolism is more likely sexual than mythological. In any case, Henry's attentiveness to its construction reflects not only his attentiveness to all the work that he undertakes but also the importance of the Sauna as both a place and a ritual that belongs to the community. At the height of its construction, many neighbors came by, eager to check on the progress of this structure. Now that it is complete, the Sauna rotation itself is complete, with each hosting homestead offering its own sauna, as well as a room for supper.

However the oral history of Sauna is told, it becomes clear as a participant that Sauna is not now, and probably never was, primarily about getting clean. Wednesday evenings are protected and held dear. If someone is missing for more than one Sauna in a row, they are asked about with concern. A group meal without a preceding sauna-bath is never an option, regardless of the winter weather, which may require the Sauna host to drop what she is doing and attend to the fire several hours before the evening begins. Gathering to sweat, scrub clean, and "be comfortably naked together" is crucial. Indeed, one member of the Sauna crowd volunteered that being comfortable with group nudity is the physical and metaphorical foundation of Sauna: "Being naked together brings us all down to one common denominator, and there's no hiding behind anything with people you go to Sauna with. That's probably why Helen and Scott never participated; they didn't want to be a part of that leveling experience."[89] Others might argue that Helen and Scott's reluctance to participate in Sauna had more to do with their discomfort with the spirit of hedonism that pervades this group. Few participants would deny, however, that their attraction to Sauna comes, in part, from the trust that is necessary for men and women in the neighborhood to be comfortable with their own and one another's nakedness.[90] Being comfortable with nakedness, in fact, is one of the ten "Sauna Beatitudes" that one homesteader has inscribed on a plaque outside his sauna. Not all the beatitudes are so philosophical: "bring your own towel" and "wash the sand off your feet" are two of the others. His posting of "beatitudes" rather than rules, however, is a philosophical and spiritual statement: Sauna is a space, time, and event set apart from the rest of the week. To enter into Sauna properly one must prepare the body, the mind, and the heart. "Rules," however, are against the rules, as other Sauna members are quick to observe.

The trust that has been established by the Sauna tradition is celebrated as a kind of safety net that extends beyond Sauna itself and into the conversations that emerge and sometimes erupt over dinner. No one would argue that the group is constituted of anything but a collection of strong-minded individuals who do not always agree, whose opinions span a range of political and social convictions, and whose personal styles run the gamut from quiet retiring types to nonstop talkers and jokesters. "That's what makes our group work," Martha commented to me at one Sauna coming on the heels of a contentious local meeting. Contrasting the ethic of the Sauna crowd with the ethic of the meeting, Martha remarked, "There's room for everybody here. No one agenda can dominate. No one person can set the agenda. If they try, they'll get a lot of shit for it." The prevailing attitude toward Sauna reflects Martha's comments. If there is physical and psychological room in the sauna for persons of every age, shape, size, marital status, and sexual orientation, then there is also room for all kinds of opinions and ways of expressing them.

"Sauna is sacred," Henry commented to me on a ride home one Wednesday night "It's family. It's the place where I can be myself. I may have to take a lot of crap about something, but everybody takes it and everybody gives it out equally. Nobody is special or above the rest. Everybody can get taken down. But that's like family. We all love each other and respect each other."[91]

Two themes emerge in Martha's and Henry's remarks: the feeling that there is "room for everybody" at Sauna and that agendas and ideologies are not allowed. These themes, which function as both the stated and, more often, unstated ethic of Sauna, obviously go together, yet they can work at cross-purposes. When summer visitors get invited and nonhomesteaders begin to appear on a regular basis tensions can brew. As Maggie mentioned to me one afternoon, "If anyone can come, then it's not Sauna anymore. It's not a community." Maggie would prefer that the boundaries of Sauna not become too loose, that not anybody who lives in the area can become a regular part of the Sauna crowd.

In Maggie's comments we hear a dissenting voice. While she appreciates the concern about rules, ideologies, and agendas, she needs to know that some people are "in" and others "out." "It's not about being unwelcoming," Maggie reflects: "It's about knowing who my community is. I have more in common with these people than anyone [else] in Maine. I have more in common with them than with the [nonhomesteading] neighbors I've known for some twenty years. But if people like my neighbors or like the rich tourists start coming to Sauna, then it won't be my community anymore."[92] Here Maggie expresses a common anxiety: how to belong to an open community and yet still feel a sense of belonging. As is often the case, the dynamics of belonging to a community and maintaining distinction from the larger culture are shot through with difficulty. The ritual of Sauna, like more traditional religious rituals, is a ritual that performs "difference," underlining the extent to which homesteading life is not the same as everyday life, even though it involves deep commitment to the everyday.

But the negotiations of this ritual, like the negotiations of all ritual, involve competing claims and needs. In expressing their commitment to a set of virtues that are both environmentally responsible and deeply fulfilling in a personal and spiritual sense, some cannot help but be evangelistic (as the Nearings certainly were) about the ways of life they have chosen. On the one hand, Sauna members are eager to share, even to show off their homesteading ways of life to visitors and neighbors, but on the other hand, they seek to keep the boundaries of the Sauna crowd distinct.

Their collective distaste for the rigidity and ideological tendencies of the Nearings also makes most members reluctant to preach about why and how to live life in a certain way. Thus, talk in the sauna tends to be more about practical matters ("What do *you* leave in your garden after the first frost?") or personal news ("How's your daughter doing in her first week at college?") and less about potentially contentious issues of homesteading philosophy. No one will try to convince others, say, that everyone should raise and eat their own turkeys or refuse to build with chemically treated wood. Thus while some Sauna members are certain that "if everyone saw simple living as fun and not sacrificial, then everyone would do it" (Ernest), only a small amount of public discussion is spent talking explicitly about the value of living simply or the ways in which different choices about homesteading should be made. This group is nonevangelical in its conversation but, at the same time, subtly evangelical in its behavior. By welcoming many nonhomesteaders into its midst, the group seems to be saying, "We've got something special here. Try it, you'll like it."

The idea of any group having a single voice is, of course, misleading. The group consists of individuals, and for some individuals such permeable membranes of membership are both problematic and self-deceiving. Maggie sees the group, however iconoclastic and resistant to ideology it may be, as bound together by shared values: simplicity and restraint in "getting and spending," belief in producing more than consuming, and love and respect for the natural world. While Maggie is personally humbler than most about the way she has articulated these values in her own life, she believes that a certain kind of group "exceptionalism" based on these values is crucial: "We are different from my neighbors and most people in Maine. But if we don't maintain that difference there's no reason to get together. Then Sauna is just like a party, and that's not what it is for me."

Indeed, few people have claimed that Sauna is just like a party, although its occasional partylike atmosphere has sometimes grated on the nerves of the Sauna's quieter members. "It's church," said a former neighbor simply, when I asked her about what it meant to the others. "It's my religion," commented Kim, when I asked her why she attended. Whether stated directly or enacted by means of keeping a commitment for over twenty-five years, Sauna is a ritualization of homestead living par excellence. The practice both responds to the Nearing precedent and sets its own; it makes room for a range of homesteading visions but serves as the overarching ritual that quietly articulates and affirms the meaning of homesteading itself. It may serve the bodily needs of bathing and eating, but its function goes far beyond that, becoming, in its own way, a form of baptism into and communion with a way of life that has home and nature at its center.

Homestead Ritual: A Habit of the Heart

More than one point is to be made through these religious comparisons. On the one hand, we see in the Sauna ritual an embodied affirmation of each member's "conversion" to homesteading life as well as the making of distinctions between homesteading culture and "outside" culture. That is, we see an expression of an alternative form of spiritual life. But we also see a form of spiritual *practice* that extends beyond most scholars' readings of spiritual commitments to nature in contrast to traditional Jewish and Christian concepts of God.

Contemporary sociologists of American religious life, such as Robert Bellah, tend to see a concern for nature and the environment as a form of "expressive individualism" rather than a form of engaged commitment shaped by community life and shared tradition. Thus, when one of Bellah's interviewees, Cassie Cromwell, speaks of her conviction that "we are a product of this life system and are inextricably linked to it," her ecological commitments to protecting the "holiness" of the earth are interpreted by him as a form of individualistic "mysticism." More broadly Bellah sees those who value "harmony with the earth" as people who "lack a notion of nature from which social norms could be derived."[93] While he is correct in pointing out that commitment to nature involves the construction of the self (one of our ongoing inquiries here), Bellah chooses not to name self-construction as *also* being a part of religious experience in institutional settings. Rather, Bellah holds up traditional religious institutions as fostering community in a way that "alternative" forms of spiritual practice cannot possibly do. Similarly, Wade Clark Roof and Robert Wuthnow, while less openly critical than Bellah, also cast interest in nature under the category of "seeking," implying a privatized, individualistic model.[94]

For Bellah, most Americans operating outside the "strong community" model (best exemplified by a neighborhood church) are members not of communities but of "lifestyle enclaves," wherein they express their identity through "patterns of appearance, consumption and leisure activities."[95] But homesteaders such as the members of the Sauna crowd are not merely expressing themselves or gathering in lifestyle enclaves, as Bellah might have it. Rather than being loosely bound together by patterns of consumption (which they resist) or leisure (which they either do not have or have radically redefined), homesteaders form community in the "strong" sense. While not gathered in "intentional communities" (each homestead architecturally and economically stands independently), the network of neighbors living in the vicinity of the Nearing homestead have formed a kind of "unintentional community," which fosters interdependence and interchange. Members share food, tools, advice, emotional support, and encouragement in the lifeways they have chosen.

In the Nearing neighborhood, some share a personal history with one another that goes back twenty or thirty years. But even far-flung homesteaders participate in community in Bellah's definition of the term. They do so within wider webs of interdependence (books, magazines, Internet "advice swapping" lists) as well as through forming local networks of homesteaders. They also participate in an intellectual and moral tradition, another factor that is important to Bellah. Yet this tradition is not biblical but, rather, has Thoreau as a spiritual ancestor and the Nearings as more recent inspiration. Most important, however, they participate in *practices* that are, as Bellah defines it, "ethically good in themselves."[96] These practices are obviously "environmental," but they are also spiritual expressions of commitment to nature and to life lived on nature's terms (to the extent that "nature's terms" may be discernable). Furthermore, these practices perform a criticism of the more prevalent American worldview, which celebrates materialism, consumption, and the utilitarian use of nature. While homesteaders are certainly rugged individualists in some senses, they actively resist the worst legacies of American individualism, choosing instead to nurture home, community, and a relationship with nature through practices that both enact and symbolize ongoing commitment.

A revealing comparison can be made between homesteaders and Bellah's ideal models when we consider a memorable respondent in Bellah's *Habits of the Heart*: Ruth Levy, a therapist and a self-identified liberal Jew who had recently become more involved in her local synagogue. In explaining her renewed participation in the life of the *shul*, Levy says: "You need to put into the pot. You need to be there if something needs to be done. To make courtesy calls and sympathy calls and to deliver food. . . . On the joyous occasions, a bris or a wedding . . . [the] event itself is wonderful. It's magnified when you have other people as happy as you and you can share other people's happy occasions." In addition to becoming more active in her religious community—even while feeling quite uncertain about the content of her faith—Levy also chose to keep a kosher home. She explains her decision this way: "I keep kosher because of structure, because at some point I remember thinking, twelve years ago or so, you know the universe is chaotic, there is so much going on, so much turbulence, and the only thing that provides meaning isn't some external source—God, or the Communist Party or whomever—that's not where it comes from."[97]

Bellah offers an interpretation of Levy's commitments that sheds as much light on his own position as it does on Levy's. On the one hand, Bellah worries that Levy's lack of theological certainty and distrust of external authority ("God, the Communist Party or whomever") suggest that her participation in the Jewish community is merely for the sake of practical and psychic gain. Bellah asserts, "If there is no grounding in reality" (by which he seems to mean faith in God), "communal ties and religious commitments can be recommended only for the benefits they yield to the individual." On the other hand, Bellah's praise for Levy's renewed practice of *kashrut* underlines the central preoccupation (and title) of his book: "We cannot know who we are," Bellah writes, "without some practical ritual and moral 'structure' that orders our freedom and binds our choices into something like habits of the heart."[98] While Bellah and his coauthors seem to wish that Levy were more theologically secure, they do praise her participation in a community that is more than a "lifestyle enclave," and they value her commitment to practices that hold the freedom of rampant individualism in some kind of check.[99]

Homesteaders who have chosen to reorient their lives according to nature's limits share significant common ground with the Ruth Levys of the world. While homesteaders' traditional theological commitments are considerably more attenuated than the commitments of those whom Bellah celebrates, homesteaders' choice to orient their lives around "nature's rules" involves self-chosen practices of discipline (cutting one's lumber with a hand saw, eating mostly "root-cellared" food in the winter) and community participation (sharing the harvest, pitching in at apple cider making time). These and other practices mirror the activities of those whom Bellah presents as positive exemplars of turning away from individualism and toward "tradition," "community," and other commitments beyond the self.

If we listen to a member of Total Loss Farm speaking about the farm labor as not merely a chore but a *practice*, these grounds of comparison become more apparent. In an essay entitled "Who's in Charge," Richard Wizansky muses on the significance of rejecting indiscriminate freedom in favor of the discipline of farm life:

> [It was] simply a matter of learning who the real manager is and learning the
> rules which are set down all over the face of the earth, in the ground which has
> to be tilled for food . . . in the teats of Bessie the cow which have to be, just
> plain have to be, milked at morning and when the sun goes down. Some of us
> hear the call of some of these things more clearly than others. . . . But Bessie,
> like the farm growing and calling all over, won't take no for an answer. And
> she'd stamp her foot, and you'd know it as simple as that.[100]

While such self-acknowledged "hippies" as Wizansky are often represented as "seekers" of freedom from rules and authority, what we see in their praise of life on the farm is the recognition of and desire for a new kind of discipline and structure, one in which nature is understood to be both authoritative and redemptive.

Such remarks on the necessity (and benefits) of living according to the discipline of nature reverberate throughout the written and spoken homesteading testimonies we have heard. From Helen and Scott Nearing's remarks that it is "extravagant and irresponsible" to eat fruits and vegetables out of season, to

Linda Tatelbaum's praise of carrying water daily from pond to home as a healing and renewing practice, to Henry insisting that creating a home and garden with hand tools was a vital "spiritual process," the refrain we hear is one of choosing to live by nature's limits and seeing these limits as ethical "goods" for both nature and human society.[101]

The "homemade ritual" of homesteading life centers on the daily practice of living close to nature. The actions involved can be understood as ritualizations of a way of life, not unlike the ritualization of one's Jewishness by keeping kosher. Such actions do not always make practical sense, but they make do ritual sense. They are means of enacting one's ultimate commitments, commitments that transcend individualistic notions of the self. Practices such as eating only the food one has raised, digging wells and ponds by hand, and refusing to buy what one can barter or make for oneself may have economic benefits, but they are also symbolic actions by which the actor identifies her strongest allegiances and inscribes herself into a particular community and culture. In this sense, homesteaders engage in those "habits of the heart" that transcend the realm of mere expressive individualism, against which Bellah has railed.[102]

We also might say that homesteading is a form of spiritual practice in the way that Robert Wuthnow has interpreted (and celebrated) "practice." Wuthnow has argued that in the broad shifts of twentieth-century American religious life, we have moved away from a period in which American spirituality took the form of "dwelling." In this period (holding roughly through the 1950s), individuals were "cradle-to-grave" members of particular Jewish or Christian institutions and expressed their spirituality primarily through participation in church and synagogue life. From the 1960s forward, however, a "subtle reordering" has taken place in how Americans understand "the sacred," a reordering characterized by "seeking," often outside the institutions and among competing ideas of what the sacred might be and where it might be found. In Wuthnow's analysis, the down side of such seeking, however, is that it led first to personalized and socially unstable quests for freedom and then was followed by the reaction of a "desire for discipline" that ultimately served surface-level therapeutic functions rather than significant personal or social transformation.[103]

A middle way between a largely outmoded spirituality of dwelling and a privatized, individualistic spirituality of *seeking* is a spirituality of *practice*. Speaking in more traditional religious terms, Wuthnow argues for a practice-oriented spirituality that is characterized by time and effort spent in intentional discernment of the nature of spiritual life (through prayer or meditation, for example). Practice-oriented spirituality is also social, embedded in institutions, whether a congregation, a retreat center, or a network of friends reading the same books and reflecting on similar spiritual questions. Moreover, the deliberate practice of spirituality involves conscious reflection on the moral dimensions and responsibilities of human life as well as commitments to action and service that emerge from such moral reflection. Building on Bellah's contributions, Wuthnow makes the case that practice mitigates the tendency toward religious (and cultural) individualism in America and offers possibility for serious, meaningful engagement with concepts of the sacred as well as sustained pursuits of the kind of commitment and community that Bellah and others hope will return to American life.

While located outside the set of more traditional exempla that Wuthnow cites in developing the idea of practice, the daily work of homesteading attends to the central characteristics of practice. While not primarily engaged in developing concepts of God, the ritual life of homesteading becomes a form of practice-oriented spirituality, with nature and home as central orienting concepts. While it is clear that self-construction is part of this practice—and sometimes even takes over—the practices of homesteading are not shallow and therapeutic at heart. They enact and symbolize commitments to the self-imposed limits of living more directly with nature. Indeed, they dramatize the ecological dependence and limits that all of us *experience*, although only a few of us see directly. Homesteading practices also exist in a social world and, again, articulate human interdependence (with nature and with one another) by putting to the fore the matters of ethically procured food, shelter, and livelihood.

Homesteaders engage in serious reflection about what the Good Life actually means, a process of discernment that incites first a conversion to a new way of living and then, in a daily way, informs and is informed by practices that embody moral responsibility, to the self, to a wider community, and to the natural world. Of course, as Wuthnow also point outs, practice can be "messy," and homesteaders' ambivalence suggests that their practices are no different from other forms of spiritual practice. But these messy ritualizations of daily life are practices that inscribe homesteaders more deeply in the human and natural communities they have chosen to live in. They enact a new kind of dwelling, infused with a spirit of seeking.

INTERLUDE: INTERPRETING AMBIVALENCE

Homesteading as Spiritual and Cultural Work

I am two with nature.

Woody Allen

When Woody Allen commented on the "twoness" of his relationship with nature, his quip was intended to sum up the attitude one would expect from an angst-ridden, lifelong New Yorker. But a move to the country does not guarantee that this twoness will go away. Such twoness belongs to the human condition. We long to break down the boundaries of artifice and culture that separate us from nature, and, alternately, we celebrate the consciousness and creativity that enable us to erect these boundaries in the first place.

In the exploration of modern homesteading conducted so far, we have visited gardens, homes, and saunas. We have encountered testimonies of personal transformation both from those whose lives have changed in response to a deeply felt connection with nature and from those (sometimes the same individuals) who sometimes pursue a kind of transcendence of nature's limits. We also have contemplated the extent to which homesteaders are what they eat (and what they grow) and have considered how they may be bound together, or divided, by these acts of production, consumption, and communion. In all of these practices, oneness with nature is sought, but twoness also persists.

The work of homesteading, what homesteading *does*, is a response to culture and also a remaking of it. Certainly, the work of homesteading is utilitarian, but it is also a highly symbolic practice. Whether examining gardening or eating, work or play, it becomes clear that the daily practices of homesteading involve certain kinds of spiritual and cultural work. The processes of sacralizing nature, constructing the self anew, and embodying a sustainable future (sustainable spiritually, economically, and ecologically) have emerged as particularly significant themes.

The realm of everyday action, then, is also the "extraordinary" realm of ritual, a realm in which embodied action on and in nature enacts a vision of what the world should look like and how it ought to function.[1] Culture provides the means and vocabularies, the stage on which the symbolic work of homesteading can take place. The symbolic work of homesteading expresses itself in terms of inherited understandings of what nature, the self, spirituality, and the Good Life *have* meant and in terms of what these concepts might mean in the future. In some cases, this symbolic work is expressed (or interpreted) in the language of the therapeutic. More often, or simultaneously, this work engages "the religious." Homesteaders may describe themselves as experiencing a connection with nature that they (or we) might call mystical. Or they discover, through daily contact with nature, a sense of grace or holiness. Some use less explicitly spiritual language but perceive in the pattern of nature a cosmology that fits into the accepted world of science yet fills that seemingly disenchanted world with new meaning. Because homesteading is both practical work and symbolic work, both cultural and religious, it is also, at times, deeply ambivalent.

The ambivalences of homesteading, once seen, have a kind of chaotic quality. They seem to be endlessly replicating, overlapping, mutually defining one another, and deferring to one another. Ambivalence about how to spend time, for instance, involves ambivalence about work and play, about freedom and control, about order and chaos, about rigor and pleasure. Although these various ambivalences may be scattered about like so many musical notes on a composer's page, notions of maturity and spiritual development run through these notes of ambivalence like the lines of a staff. But these seemingly solid lines are also occasions of ambivalence. Is progress being desired or resisted here? Is homesteading a "mature" response to certain cultural norms or a regressive, self-protective means of escape? Is homesteading a rejection of "outmoded" religious behavior or traditional institutions or a relocation of persistent religious activity (the quest for connection, transcendence, and immortality) to an extraecclesial world? Or both?

While recognizing the dangers of oversimplification, I think it is helpful to group these ambivalences into more manageable categories. The categories I am proposing, however, are not those of *what* these ambivalences are but, rather, *why* these ambivalences persist. Proposing some tentative explanations here is not only a way of interpreting the recent and contemporary practices of homesteading presented in the preceding chapters but also a way of anticipating how to put the work of homesteading into historical perspective—the task of the remaining chapters.

Why do certain ambivalences in the practice of homesteading persist? One possible explanation is that the work of homesteading raises certain unanswerable questions about the "nature of nature," that is, the nature of physical existence (both human and otherwise). Is the physical environment simply "natural" (physical, mechanical, explainable by science), or is it also an embodiment or an expression of something mysterious, something "else": the God behind nature, the divine in nature, or, as it is for most homesteaders, the inherent spirituality of natural processes themselves. From Wendell Berry, to the Nearings, to Raymond Mungo and Sal, each of these models of nature and spirit have been invoked and are often intertwined. Age-old theological concepts including "the argument from design" (the existence of God "proved" by the order of nature), panentheism (God is in all things and all things are in God), and pantheism (the divine and nature are one in the same), are all suggested here, raising questions that replay themselves when the essence of human life and mortality are considered.

In the realm of human existence, the prevailing questions seem to be: Is the physical body all there is? Are we just another part of nature or somehow separate from it? Is it important for human life to persist somehow after death? These are heady questions, questions with which the study of both religion and science have been engaged and questions with which most individuals struggle, at least in moments of crisis. Homesteaders do not necessarily seek to answer these questions, but in putting themselves in a particularly intense relationship with nature they do intend to live them with attentiveness. In living the questions that others may rarely entertain and still others may claim to have decisively resolved, homesteaders put themselves in ambivalent worlds, in part to gain access to experiences that will fuel their intellectual and spiritual development. Of course, some homesteaders themselves feel they have a corner on the existential "answer" market. Public resistance to overly gauzy "spiritual" readings of nature (and the Nearings) is a theme among the Sauna crowd, while the use of recognizably Christian language to describe the workings of nature is a constant trope in Berry's writings, a trope that others resist. But as we have seen, actions may speak louder than words for the unintentional community of homesteaders in Maine, and Buddhist, pagan, and secular-scientific readings of nature are often hiding behind the "local" biblical terminology that Berry prefers.

While homesteading locates itself in the realm of unanswerable questions about the nature of nature (both human and environmental), it also raises questions about whether back-to-nature" efforts are really about nature at all. Although homesteading involves much more than the pursuit of the therapeutic, an ongoing argument of these last two chapters has been that the acts of getting close to nature are often also about the construction of the self (self-development, self-discovery, self-loss, self-transcendence, and self in community with like-minded others). If it is important to ritualize a way of living in nature with others who are doing similarly (e.g., Sauna), are these ritualizations about nature, about the self, about the self in nature, or about the self in community? Each Sauna member would answer this question differently. Some would dismiss it altogether, saying that Sauna is simply fun, a way of getting clean, or a way of taking a breather in the middle of the week. But the ritualizations of homesteading (both individual house building and communal sauna taking) consistently pose the question of why pursuing such ways of life (simplified, "natural," do-it-yourself) are meaningful at all. The task of making meaning circulates through these questions about nature, human society, and the relation of the self to both.

Finally, the work of homesteading is ambivalent because, while it is an act of resistance to culture (in the sense of culture as "the public, standardized values of the dominant community"), it is also, necessarily, culturally determined action.[2] In saying this, I do not intend to be circular in my argument; rather, I mean to illuminate by bringing the obvious to the fore. At first, homesteading is intriguing because it seems different in so many respects from the standard cultural worlds of working at an office, buying one's food at the grocery store, and either worshipping in a church or synagogue or adopting a scientific "secular" view of the world. But it becomes even more interesting because of the ways in which it is *not* different, the ways in which it cannot help being part of the cultural trends it attempts to resist. And in tracing the ways in which the religious continues to percolate up through the apparently secular practice of homesteading, I also have been asking how different homesteading really is from other forms of religious expression, particularly in their more liberal Protestant, Catholic, and Jewish varieties.[3]

By reminding ourselves that homesteading performs cultural work that is culturally determined, we can sort through the many ambivalences of homesteading with a clearer mind and perhaps a clearer conscience. The latter is important to consider; for in pointing out ambivalences, ambiguities, and ironies, I am not casting blame on those who fail to be consistent or unambivalent in the lifeways they have chosen. I am suggesting, rather, that like many kinds of conversion, the choice to homestead may be expressed as an absolute necessity, a profound experience of rebirth, or a pursuit of a long-anticipated personal path. Such proclamations of conviction, however, are never without practices that complicate the convictions themselves. The complications, ironies, and ambivalences that arise come out of the very nature of human cultural action.

But we need to go beyond theoretical propositions about why these ambivalences might be present in the lives of contemporary (or recent) homesteaders.

We also need to explore the historical sources of these ambivalences. As our occasional historical forays with respect to the Nearings already suggest, the ethics and aesthetics of purity, discipline, and control, combined with a certain tendency toward mysticism, come out of the particular social and intellectual history in which the Nearings participated. As I will argue in chapter 5, this is a history of Progressive reform, Social Gospel idealism, rising consumerism, and radical reassessments of religion and science, the body and health, nature and God. Similarly, the dynamics of both self-realization and self-loss in the context of nature—which I have explored here in more recent contexts—has its roots in late nineteenth-century notions of "self-culture" as well as in early twentieth-century valuations of nature as source for spiritual renewal.

In chapter 4, I shall consider the case of John Burroughs, who as homesteader and nature writer attracted an enormous public following in the first decades of the twentieth century. His ethic of self-culture, his nostalgia for a distant past, and his pursuit of the divine in nature are in some ways oddly predictive of recent homesteading efforts, revealing similar ambivalences toward religion and science, work and play, nature and society. Like many homesteaders of today, Burroughs's pursuit of nature was often intertwined with the pursuit of the self, and his experience of the religious in nature often placed him in an ambiguous position with respect to social change. John Burroughs and Scott Nearing each chose a life of homesteading (and of writing about it) as a personal and cultural solution to the problems of their age. Yet the style of homesteading they each pursued sometimes coalesced and sometimes stood in opposition with the choices of the other. These continuities and discontinuities were shaped by the historical distance between them, the particularities of their religious and psychological dispositions, and the mode of cultural dissent in which they were engaged. Each saw himself as objecting to certain aspects of the American pursuit of "progress," yet each defined what he was doing as a progressive and enlightened response to the general drift of culture in the era through which he lived.

In his masterful history of the experience and interpretation of "country" and "city" in English literary culture, Raymond Williams warns his readers that the retrospective glance toward "Old (Rural) England" means different things at different times and that, at various moments, the longing for Old England has performed different kinds of criticism (religious, political, humanist, and so on). My point here is much the same. The decision to go back to nature for spiritual renewal, to challenge culture by remaking it in one's own backyard, to create a life that is financially lean but spiritually and symbolically rich is nothing new. The choice to homestead performs different kinds of cultural work in different cultural moments, and our attention to ironies and ambivalences calls us to think more historically about the different kinds of cultural work home-steading *has* performed, in order to understand more fully the many kinds of cultural work—often simultaneous and contradictory—homesteading is per-forming today.

By placing homesteading in historical perspective, primarily through an ex-amination of the lives of John Burroughs, Scott Nearing, and some of their lesser-known contemporaries (Bolton Hall, Ralph Borsodi, Mildred Loomis, and others), I am emphasizing the persistent cultural power of certain Ameri-can norms: the importance of self-fashioning, the value of nature as a source of renewal, and the preference for scientific forms of knowledge, which is nego-tiated alongside the ideal of personal, spiritual development. These cultural norms come to the surface with varying degrees of intensity and submerge again at various periods of twentieth-century American history. Homesteading is one of several cultural acts that are a reaction against such norms as well as an articulation of them.

But in saying this I do not mean to suggest that a particular mode of home-steading is merely determined by the historical period in which it is undertaken. The questions I am pursuing here are not only illuminated by attention to what Williams calls "structures of feeling" variously expressed over time. Home-steading is shaped by and expresses any number of structures of feeling: the longing for nature, the idealization of the past, the desire to remake the self, the pursuit of "authentic" community.[4] But these structures of feeling are articu-lated in and through a logic of practice, a logic that is often illogical and con-tradictory.[5] In exploring the ways in which homesteading is a cultural gesture of dissent that nonetheless reverberates with the times, I also want to affirm the importance of exploring cultural action in fully embodied terms. We can in-terpret homesteading through its history and its literatures, but we must always keep in mind the ambivalent ways in which it is lived.

4 | THE REENCHANTMENT OF THE FARM

John Burroughs Goes Back to the Land

How can a man take root and thrive without land?
He writes his history upon his field.

John Burroughs, "Phases of Farm Life," 1886

Leaving Washington

By the close of the year 1872, John Burroughs had begun to establish himself as both literary critic and nature writer. Although Burroughs had self-published his first book, *Notes on Walt Whitman as Poet and Person* (1867), he was warmly invited by publisher Oscar Houghton to send material for a new volume. Burroughs's occasional essays, appearing in such magazines as *Putnam's*, the *New York Leader*, and the *Atlantic Monthly*, were becoming increasingly popular, and Houghton, a personal fan of Burroughs's work, anticipated a growing readership for such pieces. *Wake-Robin* emerged in 1871 as a gathering of nature essays old and new. It was well received by the critics and widely read by the public. Among the educated middle-class, Burroughs was beginning to become a familiar name.[1]

After years of eking out an existence with short-term teaching jobs and the occasional foray into unlikely business ventures, Burroughs had also managed, finally, to establish some financial security for himself and his wife, Ursula.[2] He had obtained a position as a clerk with the newly formed Currency Bureau of the U.S. Treasury Department in January 1864 and had risen steadily through the ranks, serving ultimately as the chief of the Organization Division of the Bureau of National Banks. Significantly (for Ursula especially), Burroughs had also managed to clear up his debts sufficiently to be able to buy land and have a house built. By 1867, after ten years of marriage, John and Ursula had settled into a comfortable domestic life at 1332 V Street, just north of Washington's city center.[3] From their new vantage point, Burroughs could reap the advantages of both country (room for a cow and a garden) and city (frequent social visits from his friend Whitman and a host of other literary and bohemian Washingtonians). Following a tumultuous start in acquiring gainful employment, literary recognition, and domestic stability, John Burroughs, by 1872, seemed to have created for himself a successful Washington existence. But in that same year, Burroughs suddenly resigned his position with the Treasury Department, agreed to take a temporary position as receiver of a failed bank in Middleton, New York, and returned to his homeland to begin a life of farming and writing, particularly writing about life in and around his farm.

By the turn of the century, Burroughs's farm at West Park on the Hudson and later his nearby cabin, known as Slabsides, became a pilgrimage site for thousands.[4] Having refreshed themselves with Burroughs's nature essays, these seekers pursued both Burroughs himself and their own firsthand experiences of his natural surround. Burroughs soon became an Emersonian "representative man" for a middle-class culture caught up in the first flush of a back-to-nature craze.[5] In hindsight and in terms of future fame, fortune, and literary success, Burroughs's move back to the land was a success. But Burroughs neither predicted nor particularly desired such success. Moreover, his life in Washington seemed well situated to produce the modest success he did desire: a means of making a living, access to the natural world, and opportunity to write. His job at the Treasury provided not only money but sometimes also the time and space (both physical and psychological) to do the literary work that Ursula deemed "scribbling" at home.[6] More important, Washington proved to be an ideal city for a nature lover such as Burroughs.

From the perspective of the twenty-first century, we may find it difficult to imagine how Washington would have provided sufficient grist for Burroughs's literary-naturalist mill. But Washington in the post–Civil War period was still a young city from which access to outdoor rambles could be acquired simply by foot. The essays in *Winter Sunshine* (1875)—many of which are based on his weekend rambles in Washington, Virginia, and Maryland—reveal a seemingly limitless selection of trails, mountains, farmlands, and birds' nests for the young author-ornithologist to explore. Burroughs's comments on the Washington sunshine reveal that the atmosphere of the capital city was rarefied in more than the political sense. "It seemed as if I had never seen but a second-rate article of sunlight or moonlight until I had taken up my abode in the National Capital," Burroughs writes in his title essay. "The days are softer and more brooding, and the nights more enchanting. . . . It is impossible not to dilate and expand under such skies."[7] And yet there did come a time in his Washington life when Burroughs felt himself no longer able to dilate and expand.

Why would Burroughs have risked personal, professional, and financial up-heaval to make what, at least on the surface, appeared to be an unnecessary move? The case has been made that Burroughs took up farming to establish a secure economic base for his family.[8] Certainly, we have evidence that Burroughs was a shrewd businessman who knew when to expand his holdings, how to adjust his crops to the needs of the market, and how both to manage his hired help and to work beside them. In terms of farming and managerial skills, in fact, Burroughs ultimately surpassed his brother Hiram, who had never left the family farm of their youth. But no one would argue that the life of the farmer was inherently stable or risk free. A week of rainstorms or a late frost could (and sometimes did) wipe out a year's labor and investments in a single stroke.[9] Burroughs's concern for the business end of farming did not come out of a need for job security. His success in farming came out of a desire to make life on the farm sufficiently feasible so that no other employment was necessary. It came from a feeling that any life but the rural life was unacceptable. For Burroughs, rural life created a unique way of being in nature and simultaneously afforded an opportunity to reflect on that relationship. Writing and farming were activities that could mutually inform one another. They brought physical work and intellectual work into an even relationship. The self could expand under such conditions. This is what Burroughs wanted.

Like so many back-to-the-landers of succeeding generations, John Burroughs was embarking on a process of spiritual and psychological reformation. Such a process was a conversion of sorts, not unlike the other conversions to home-steading described in these pages. While Burroughs's literary and intellectual development required an early departure from the farm of his youth, his spiritual growth and sense of well-being ultimately demanded a return to the daily rituals of rural living. Excursions into nature and the "exhilarations of the road" were no longer enough.[10] The dilation and expansion of the self demanded the making of a new life through a return to the country. Significantly, this return was not just a return to a place (his native land); it was also return to a set of activities. At this juncture in his life, Burroughs craved the everyday practices of farming, home construction, and writing. The return to the soil was necessarily labor in the soil. By cultivating nature (as opposed to just visiting it), Burroughs hoped also to cultivate the self.[11]

Farming as Vocation

"It is a common complaint," Burroughs wrote in the mid-1880s, "that the farm and farm life are not appreciated by our people. We long for the more elegant pursuits, or the ways and fashions of the town. But the farmer has the most sane and natural occupation, and ought to find life sweeter, if less highly seasoned, than any other."[12] Essays such as "Phases of Farm Life" reveal a strikingly modern sensibility. While Burroughs's diction is nineteenth-century, the content of his essays, his call to go back to the land, has a curiously familiar sound. Indeed, Burroughs's example alone demonstrates how longstanding the postindustrial "back-to-the-land" impulse has been. Even while many had not yet left the family farms of their youth, city dwellers were being called by Burroughs to return to the land and, thereby, to a simpler, healthier, more spiritually satisfying existence.

Burroughs's popularity as essayist and public figure marks the beginning of a cultural shift in the late nineteenth century, particularly among middle-class, educated, liberals. The ways of living that Burroughs sought—the ability to structure his own space, time, and notions of work and the opportunity to live in intimate connection with the natural world—were the very ways of living being threatened by the new structures of work and domesticity emerging in the industrial age.[13] Not surprisingly, those who expressed concern about the rise of the city, growing monopolies, and the change in the rhythm of labor and daily life saw nature as an optimal resource of health, morality, and a "pure" spirituality. For Burroughs's more liberal readers, looking for "sermons in stone walls" and acknowledging the "rural divinity" of the cow made a certain kind of psychological and spiritual sense.[14] For those questioning the claims of traditional religion but increasingly uncomfortable with the prospect and consequences of a scientific world without meaning, a spiritual reading of nature resolved a growing cultural tension. For some, the idea of nature, or its accessibility through texts and occasional visits, was enough. For others, the commitment to getting close to nature needed to be personally enacted.

The case of John Burroughs gives us access to both of these aspects of the growing interest in nature at the turn of the century. Burroughs's popularity as a writer who practiced what he preached is indicative of the wide cultural concern for nature as a source of relief from the city and as a means of building character in those subjected to the perceived immoral and emasculating influences of urbanization.[15] But before Burroughs gained national attention, his highly personal—and, at first, seemingly eccentric—decision to forgo urban literary life for the life of a writer-farmer is predictive of the path that later homesteaders would choose. It involved a choice to go against the mainstream of contemporary culture and to pursue a "calling" that was at once religious, therapeutic, aesthetic, and economic. The daily practices of work, play, and improvised worship in intimate relationship with the natural world that Burroughs chose are echoed throughout the twentieth century by those such as the Near-ings, Ralph Borsodi, Raymond Mungo, Sal, Bill Coperthwaite, and Wendell Berry. Indeed, all of the homesteaders in this study would find something of themselves in the work and writing of Burroughs.

While I will return in chapter 5 to consider further the significance of the broader cultural appraisal of nature at the turn of the century, here I want to keep a focus on Burroughs himself. In paying attention to the choices he made and the ambivalences about nature, the self, and society that remained in the midst of these choices, I hope to place in historical context some of the themes of homesteading that are now familiar to us. Like many of the homesteaders we have come to know in this study, Burroughs spoke of his return to the farm with the utter assurance of a convert. But in a larger sense, his life choices demon-strate the flexibility of a skilled cultural improviser. The understandings of na-ture and the self that Burroughs developed suggest a fascinating fusion of some of the primary influences on his personal and literary life, those influences, for instance, of Emerson, Thoreau, Whitman, and Darwin. Yet his essays reflect much more than a mere intellectual stew. They emerged also, significantly, from a *practice of everyday life* that Burroughs perfected into a balanced discipline of work and leisure, homemaking and excursion, farming and writing. As a whole, Bur-roughs's art of living enabled him to negotiate between the dawning of the twentieth century (that he both welcomed and feared) and the closing of the nineteenth century (to which he so often wished to return). This negotiation involved several competing claims: the desire to get out from under Transcen-dentalist influence and the continuing appeal of Emersonian and Thoreauvian views of nature and self-culture; the longing for his father's evangelical faith amid his own rejection of Christianity as irrational "superstition"; and the (re-lated) commitment to representing nature scientifically amid his highly spiri-tual experiences of it. Later in Burroughs's life, we also find him wrestling with a vision of the return to nature as a form of cultural reform and the simultane-ous tendency to withdraw from the active work of social transformation, a par-adox that many homesteaders have confronted.

While there is not room in this chapter to deliver a short biography of Bur-roughs (and these already exist), I shall address each of these significant nego-tiations in turn, and, in so doing, I hope to underline the depth and complexity involved in Burroughs's return to nature. In an exploration of Burroughs's pur-suits, the contemporary stories of homesteading we have just heard should con-tinue to resonate in the context of this relatively more distant tale. What we hear is that the quest for self-realization, for a reenchanted world of nature, and for the creation of a society attuned to nature's limits and nature's "simple gifts" is hardly a recent (i.e., post-1960s) preoccupation. While the language articulating that quest has changed and social circumstances (such as the Depression or the rise of an affluent "youth culture") have altered the key in which the back-to-the-land tune is played, the larger themes (the sacralization of nature, the making of the self, the expression of resistance to the dominant culture) became well-established in Burroughs's time and were made familiar by his writings.

Of course, Burroughs himself also changed within his own life span. The Burroughs who wrote the essentially theological (although naturalistic) treatise *The Light of Day* (1900) at the turn of the century was undoubtedly a different man from the young Burroughs in Washington, who was only beginning to make the case for experience in nature as an alternative to traditional religion. And the Burroughs who went to Washington hungry for social and intellectual stimulation was not yet the Burroughs who would celebrate farming as the best possible method for "drawing out the poison" bred in cities.[16] Of course, part of the transition we see was one of growth and maturity. Burroughs went to Washington when he was twenty-six. He published *Signs and Seasons* (1886), containing his first full-fledged treatises on his life as a farmer, when he was forty-nine. But the change in Burroughs's sense of self and of nature that we can detect in his writings was not simply the change from youth to middle age. Burroughs's sense of *vocation* grew and changed as well, and this sense of vocation was inherently intertwined with the aesthetic and spiritual dimensions of his life on the land. Burroughs answered a call to baptize himself in the natural world and then to become the prophet of the blessings such a baptism can bring. As his experience in the practical and spiritual work of farming deepened, so did his writing acquire both depth and breadth. His essays became, first, testaments of the spiritual and psychological riches to be found in one's own backyard and, later, sermons preaching the virtues of farming life to a public increasingly hungry for at least a vicarious experience of "direct and loving contact with the soil."[17]

But let us begin at the beginning. Before attending to the personal and cultural improvisations—and tensions—in which Burroughs engaged, I want to highlight the early development of his views of nature and the self during the time of his transition from Washington literary figure to New York farmer. Here I will attend particularly to some essays appearing in three books that Burroughs produced in this period: *Winter Sunshine* (1875), *Locusts and Wild Honey* (1879), and *Signs and Seasons*.[18] These essays all played a significant role in establishing Burroughs as literary figure and "true man of the soil" by the turn of the century, but they are first and foremost testaments of his conversion to homesteading and interpretations that reveal the meanings he made of it.[19]

The Exhilarations of the Road and a Longing for Home

The tone and content of *Winter Sunshine* is one of exhilaration and the excitement of exploration. The young Burroughs delights in detecting the first breath of spring along the Potomac and in detailing the particular pleasures of walking a southern road in Virginia. Yet scattered throughout these essays, like the green shoots of spring he finds buried under autumn leaves, are hints of the life that Burroughs remembered and longed for: the life of the farm. In "A March Chronicle," for instance, Burroughs interrupts his journalistic observations with a six-page reverie on the finest symbol and activity of early spring: maple sugaring. His memory takes him to a childhood grove: "I have in mind now a "sugar-bush" nestled in the lap of a spur of the Catskills, every tree of which is known to me and assumes a distinct individuality in my thought. . . . Ah! I am there now! I see the woods flooded with sunlight; I smell the dry leaves, and the mould under them just quickened by the warmth. . . . I see the brimming pans and buckets, always on the sunny side of the trees, and hear the musical dropping of the sap." His attachment to the trees runs deep. Like those homesteaders we have heard expressing a sense of pain when nature is harmed or altered, Burroughs remarks: "[When] I find [a tree] has perished or fallen before the axe, I feel a personal loss." While John Burroughs writes in and of Washington, in over half the essay he is somewhere else: back home, on the farm, engaged in the "most delightful farm work" of all.[20]

It is true that Burroughs's attraction to farming was fueled, in part, by the kind of nostalgia that he exhibits in the excursus above. He himself admitted to suffering from a "homesickness which home cannot cure." His most recent biographer, Edward Renehan Jr., rightly understands Burroughs's nostalgia as not only personal but also cultural. "His nostalgia was a consuming one," Renehan comments, "and it included in no small way a deep yearning for a certain preindustrial pastoral innocence that perhaps had never actually existed in a pure form."[21] Yet Burroughs himself displayed considerable insight into these complex workings of heart and soul. He knew that even a return to his boyhood farm (where he vacationed annually and lived intermittently throughout his life) would never satisfy his longings. "The soul's thirst can never be slaked," he admitted. "My hunger is the hunger of the imagination."[22] Burroughs's nostalgia, then, while romantic, was not naive. More important, it was the desire for spiritual renewal, not merely nostalgia, that motivated his return to farming life.

Another essay in *Winter Sunshine* permits us an early view of Burroughs's understanding of seeking intimacy with nature as a spiritual practice. In "The Exhilarations of the Road," Burroughs engages in an extended meditation on the virtues of walking, one that is uncannily reminiscent of Thoreau's own explanations of why he is a *saunterer*.[23] Like Thoreau, Burroughs claims that walking is a moral activity. He establishes this comparison (both serious and playful) between walking and religious devotion in his opening paragraph. Nothing pleases him more, Burroughs writes, than a glimpse of the naked, human foot. "It is the symbol of my order," he proclaims, "the Order of Walkers." In the ensuing pages, Burroughs goes on to enumerate the manifold benefits of taking to the open road on foot: it unites the mind and body, it is inexpensive and democratic, it encourages the cultivation of the senses, and it brings one into contact with the unique character of a nation or region. But the most persistent trope in this essay is the religious one.

Time and again Burroughs exhorts his readers to walk the back roads and byways because it will bring them into right relationship with themselves, with nature, and with God. Embracing simplicity is one aspect of moral reformation, Burroughs tells us. Americans, he observes, particularly crave "the astonishing" and "the exciting." This craving leads to blindness, Burroughs warns: "[We] do not know the highways of the gods when we see them,—always a sign of the decay of the faith and the simplicity of man." Elsewhere, in a more aphoristic mood, he announces: "We have fallen from that state of grace that the capacity to enjoy a walk implies."[24] Further along in the essay, Burroughs becomes more mischievous as he draws institutional religion into the realm of his concerns. Playing the hypocrisy of the church off his own "true religion" of outdoor rambles, Burroughs enters into a deft criticism of his father's evangelical faith while simultaneously putting forth a more spiritually pure alternative.

Burroughs praises the charm of the country church, but only by way of offering a passing concession to the opposition. "I think I should be tempted to go to church myself," Burroughs muses, "if I saw all my neighbors starting off across the fields . . . and I were sure I should not be jostled or run over by the rival chariots of the worshippers at the temple door." The problem with religion, claims Burroughs, is the problem of vanity and insincerity whereby congregants place priority on fine dress, proper carriages, and the prospect of "being seen." But Burroughs proposes a solution: "I think it would be tantamount to an astonishing revival of religion if the people would all walk to church on Sunday and walk home again." If congregants were to follow this discipline, Burroughs promises, they would find themselves spiritually renewed: "[How] their benumbed minds would warm up beneath the friction of the gravel; how their vain and foolish thoughts . . . would drop behind them, unable to keep up or to endure the fresh air! They would walk away from their *ennui*, their worldly cares, their uncharitableness, their pride of dress; for these devils always want to ride, while the simple virtues are never so happy as when on foot." In Burroughs's view, walking in the natural world can absolve most of these sins of pride, but for those who refuse to walk, he advises, "get an ass."[25]

Calling on the image of Christ's entry into Jerusalem, Burroughs is quick to charge the "churched" as being quite *unchurched* when it comes to true Christian values. Such clever games of spiritual one-upmanship (showing how nature outchurches the church) would become characteristic of Burroughs's later writings. Although Burroughs seldom shed his beneficent persona, his essays increasingly served as jeremiads aimed at the spiritual hypocrisy and material excesses of the Gilded Age.

"Next to the laborer in the fields," Burroughs writes at the conclusion of this piece, "the walker holds the closest relation to the soil."[26] It is revealing that in an essay devoted to the primacy of walking, Burroughs refuses to give walking the ultimate pride of place. This quiet aside alerts us to the life change Burroughs is about to make. If he is to follow his own dictum, it is not surprising that walking becomes, at a certain juncture in his life, insufficient to feed the soul. It is spiritually akin, perhaps, to church attendance once a week. For Burroughs, the spiritual life cannot be found only in lay activity, nor can an occupation (work for the Treasury) lead to fulfillment. At the age of thirty-five, Burroughs chose a *vocation* over a job. That vocation combined farming and writing and did so in the context of staying at home. It is important that these choices enabled Burroughs to engage in a process of *ritualization*. Like the Total Loss farmers almost a century later, he responded to nature's sacredness by "playing at farming" (in a serious way) and writing about it. Decades before Wendell Berry lived, yet sounding startlingly like him, Burroughs experienced the blessings—and then sang the praises—of returning to local agriculture and local culture.

Phases of Farm Life

In the months preceding his departure from Washington, Burroughs wrote to his friend Myron Benton of his eagerness to leave the city for the farm. According to his biographer Clara Barrus, he "felt like a fowl with no gravel in its gizzard. . . . He was hungry for the earth, could eat it like a horse if only he could get at it."[27] In the years between 1872 and 1879, Burroughs vigorously responded to this hunger for soil. He built a stone house on the banks of the Hudson, established reliable orchards and vineyards, and while still doing occasional work as a bank examiner became known to his neighbors as a successful farmer. Of course, although he did not advertise his literary ambitions to his neighbors, he remained also a writer. And the new writing that emerged from the farmer began to show a difference.

We can detect this difference in an early book of essays that was written (not merely edited) at Riverby. *Locusts and Wild Honey* (1879) is a testament of Burroughs's baptism in the woods and fields of his local surround. Indeed, the title refers quite directly to the life of John the Baptist, who was said to have lived on such a diet during the early days of his preaching. In choosing the title, Burroughs seems to imply that *he* might be a John the Baptist of a slightly different kind. Indeed, he shares with the biblical John the conviction that a taste of wild honey can bring enlightenment, although, "about the other part, the locusts . . . as much cannot be said."[28] But whatever the preferred morsels, Burroughs unreservedly recommends "divinity-school days in the mountains" as proper theological and vocational training. Such training, Burroughs suggests, not only helps us to develop "sharp eyes" to see nature's dramas but also gives us a sharp mind to interpret what we see, for the "writing is in cipher and [the observer] must furnish the key."[29] In *Locusts and Wild Honey*, then, Burroughs not only engages in his own acts of interpreting the Good Book of Nature, he also calls his readers to do the same, to plunge into the purifying waters of the natural world and be born again.[30]

In some senses, of course, *Locusts and Wild Honey* does not strike the reader as radically new. But essays such as "The Pastoral Bees," "Strawberries," and "Is It Going to Rain?" are no longer essays of an afternoon or weekend rambler, nor are they simply boyhood reminiscences; rather, they depict the life of a man who has stayed *in place* and whose birds, bees, crops, and rain clouds are well-known neighbors. Burroughs himself noted the difference upon receiving the first copy of the *Locusts* text. "I like it better than I thought I should," he noted in his journal. "The later pieces are richer in tone and color than the other books."[31]

Seven years later, in *Signs and Seasons*, Burroughs's writing reaches a certain maturity, as did the man. Writing in the fourth decade of his life, at a time when he was becoming increasingly engaged in the life of the farm and ultimately disengaged from work for the banks, Burroughs no longer *implies* the significance of his choice to take up farming; he preaches it outright. The opening essay in *Signs and Seasons*, "A Sharp Lookout," exhibits remarkable similarities to "Sharp Eyes" in *Locusts*. Both exhort observers of nature to develop keen senses, to be willing to "take a hint" and follow it through, to be patient, curious, yet confident in their ability to interpret what they see. But in "A Sharp Lookout," Burroughs moves beyond a focus on what kind of person will be an effective reader of nature's book to what kind of place this person ought to inhabit in order to be a good reader. (The difference in essay titles reflects this: from "sharp *eyes*" to a "sharp *lookout*.") "Nature comes home to one most when he is at home,"

Burroughs asserts, adding that for those who wander and constantly seek "the new," nature remains a stranger.[32] While Burroughs the farmer would not deny that the exhilarations of the road are still attractive to him, here he lays out a recipe for living that, in his view, offers more than a walk down an unexplored path ever could: "One's own landscape comes in time to be a sort of outlying part of himself; he has sowed himself broadcast upon it, and it reflects his own mood and feelings; he is sensitive to the verge of the horizon: cut those trees and he bleeds; mar those hills, and he suffers. How has the farmer planted himself in his fields; builded himself into his stonewalls, and evoked the sympathy of the hills by his struggle! This home feeling, this domestication of nature, is important."[33] As if purposefully refining the earlier case made for walking over hurrying along in a carriage, Burroughs makes clear that his preference is for keeping one's rambles close to home: "[The] place to observe nature is where you are; the walk to take to-day is the walk you took yesterday."[34]

Burroughs's call to stay in place, to inscribe the self in the soil, is part rhapsody, part elegy, and part exhortation. Literary critics today might scoff at his weakness for the "pathetic fallacy"; deep ecologists might express concern for his anthropocentric views; and wilderness lovers may take exception to Burroughs's preference for tended gardens.[35] But in light of Burroughs's spiritual, psychological, and literary development, this celebration of farm life is neither romantic nor threatening to the natural world. Indeed, it is predictive of the (sometimes overwrought) attention to "sense of place" themes in contemporary nature writing. At Riverby, and later at Slabsides, Burroughs found a way to live in nature that was attentive both to nature's sensitivities and to his own. For Burroughs, farming fosters greater intimacy with nature; with intimacy comes deep knowledge and a sense of responsibility and care. Taken together, intimacy, knowledge, responsibility, and care contribute to the expansion of the self, the "dilation" Burroughs had ceased to experience in the Washington air.

The Gospel of Nature and the Work of Self-Culture

It is almost a truism that Emerson's essay Nature is, at closer inspection, an essay on the self. More particularly, it is an essay on self-culture. In Nature and in much of his later work, Emerson meditates on the ways in which contact with and contemplation of nature will enable the "poet-seer" to develop divine capacities to see the spiritual lessons inscribed in the world and to transform them through the work of the imagination, making them available to the reader. The poet, in Emerson's view, is no mere creator of rhymed verse. The poet (more generally, the artist) "breathes in" the spiritual "signs" of the world through a carefully cultivated perception, then breathes these messages out again, via the imagination.

Burroughs's view of nature and of the self borrowed much from Emerson's thinking, but it was a kind of borrowing that moved from the direct imitation of an admiring youth to a more mature transplanting of Emersonian ideals into a real set of life choices and a particular native surround.[36] Burroughs likened his early experience of Emerson's writing to that of difficult digestion. Emerson, he observed, first "tasted like wild green apples." But not long afterward, Emerson's influence moved into the circulation system and to positive effect. "I read him in a sort of ecstasy," Burroughs later wrote to Clara Barrus. "I got him into my blood and he colored my whole intellectual outlook. He appealed to my spiritual side."[37] For two or three years, Burroughs read little other than Emerson. "I kept Emerson close at hand and read him everywhere," he remembered. "I would go up under the trees of the sap-bush there at home and read and be moved to tears by the extreme beauty and eloquence of his words. For years all I wrote was Emersonian. It was as if I was dipped in Emerson."[38]

The heavy weight of Emerson's influence, and of *Nature* particularly, is evident in one of Burroughs's schoolboy entries in his early journals. At the age of seventeen, while at Cooperstown Seminary, Burroughs wrote, "Poetry is spiritual facts represented by natural symbols. . . . Nature when rightly seen is but a representative of spirit."[39] The ambitious entry amounted to an awkward rewording (without credit given) of Emerson's cryptic Transcendentalist recipe: "Words are signs of natural facts. Particular natural facts are symbols of particular spiritual facts. Nature is the symbol of spirit."[40] Given the extent to which Burroughs found himself under Emerson's sway, it is not surprising that in his maturing years he should inherit a devotee's familiar dilemma: how to pursue the Emersonian recommendation of self-culture and self-reliance and yet do so without following in Emerson's footsteps? The passage was an uneasy one, for Burroughs's first entrée into the literary world (at age twenty-three) was the publication of his essay "Expression," in the *Atlantic Monthly*. Lowell was so convinced that Burroughs had plagiarized Emerson that he searched high and low for evidence of an original before finally conceding that "Expression" was, indeed, Burroughs's work.[41] While flattered by the case of mistaken identity, Burroughs also recognized the necessity of developing a voice of his own. "It was mainly to break the spell of Emerson's influence and get upon ground of my own that I took to writing outdoor themes," Burroughs later recalled. "The woods, the soil, the waters, helped to draw out the pungent Emersonian flavor and restore me to my proper atmosphere."[42]

Burroughs first recognition as an "original" writer came from this turn away from nature in the abstract and toward actual, rural subjects, the literary market for which was growing as early as the 1860s. But Burroughs's choice to return to farming was not driven by this literary market; it was very much in tune with Emerson's emphasis on self-reliance and self-culture.[43] In writing of the delights of maple sugaring, plowing, and butter churning, Burroughs recognized that his own practice of self-culture involved a return to agriculture, a return to the very roots from which the term *self-culture* was derived.[44]

"Nature makes the poet," the twenty-three-year-old Burroughs wrote in "Expression," "not by adding to, but by taking from, she takes all the blur and opacity from him, condenses, intensifies; lifts his nerves nearer the surface, sharpens his senses, and brings his whole organization to an edge."[45] In this youthful essay, we can hear hints of Emerson's "transparent eyeball" passage ("all mean egotism fades"), as Burroughs suggests that going to nature will purify the self, elevating it to an ideal condition. But in Burroughs's later descriptions of farm life—those based not on memory but on actual experience—we find a more substantive, less abstract religion of nature, one in which embodied, earthy communion is celebrated as the greatest spiritual good. Echoing the comments made to Myron Benton when on the verge of leaving Washington, Burroughs writes in *Riverby* of the hunger for the soil that spring awakens in him. In "Spring Jottings," a diary of seasonal changes on the farm in 1891, Burroughs writes: "We plow the ground under the hill for the new vineyard. In opening the furrow for the young vines I guide the team by walking in their front. . . . At night I glowed all over; my whole being had had an earth-bath; such a feeling of freshly plowed land in every cell of my brain."[46] The same passage exists in the original journal, followed by such other comments as "one could almost eat the turf" and "[listening to bird song] we went up on Reservoir Hill . . . and tried to drink deeper draughts of this April nectar."[47] Here the specter of Emerson's transparent eyeball is replaced by the incarnational image of Burroughs consuming the earth and being consumed by it. A few paragraphs later in "Spring Jottings," Burroughs returns to this theme of consumption and communion, remarking that "the freshly turned soil looks good enough to eat" and that he longs to eat of the earth "like a horse."[48] He echoes this sentiment in a subsequent essay, "Lovers of Nature," in which he writes: "Your real lover of nature does not merely love the beautiful things which he culls here and there; he loves the earth itself. . . . [how] good the earth, the soil, seems! One wants to feel it with his hands and smell it—almost taste it. Indeed, I never see a horse eat soil and sods without a feeling that I would like to taste it too. The rind of the earth . . . which has hung so long upon the great Newtonian tree, ripening in the sun, must be sweet."[49] What we see in Burroughs's version of self-culture is a gradual shift from recognizably "Emersonian" philosophical idealism to a testament of nature spirituality that is based in daily *practices* such as plowing, planting, and listening to the local birds. The imagery is no longer that of idealized nature but that of nature as *spirit incarnate*. The intrinsic relationship between cultivating the soil and cultivating the self is emphasized here. Self-culture is no longer primarily an activity of the mind and soul; it is also, perhaps more important, an activity of the *body* engaged in working on the natural world, while the natural world, in turn, "works on" the transformation of the self.

Eight years passed between the publication of Burroughs's *Signs and Seasons* and the next book of local essays, *Riverby* (1894). Only one publication appeared in the middle of this period, *Indoor Studies* (1889), which, as the title suggests, was largely literary criticism, much of it already scripted.[50] Burroughs's biographer, Edward Renehan Jr., characterizes this period as one of "barrenness," referring not only to Burroughs's lack of literary production during this time but also to the persistent feelings of loneliness and melancholy Burroughs endured in response to the successive losses of his parents (his mother in 1880, his father in 1884), of Emerson (1882), and, finally, of Whitman (1892).[51] But while Burroughs often felt himself to be orphaned and drew further into the realm of childhood memory and nostalgia in these years, he also threw himself into the work of his farm, even noting contritely in his journal that the "saddest thing of all" was that while he dreamed of his mother constantly, he continued cheerfully to attend to the affairs of the farm ("and sleep and read and laugh") with her newly in the grave.[52]

In fact, as journal entries and the later essays based upon them reveal, the last two decades of the nineteenth century were a time when Burroughs's farming life held the highest appeal. Even Renehan provides evidence to this effect, citing a letter from Burroughs to Benton in which the grape cultivator noted, "The hoe-handle is better for me now then the pen and I mean to stick to it." In a letter to the aging Whitman, Burroughs similarly commented, "The world has not been so beautiful to me for a long time as this spring; probably because I have been at work like an honest man," and he once again deployed the phrase "The earth seems good enough to eat."[53] Burroughs found the spring months to be particularly evocative, full of "a sort of spirituality [that] can be had at no other time," and felt the pull of manual labor to bring intimacy with nature well beyond that of writing. In May he remarked: "Still at work in the fields and quite well and happy. One cannot keep his love for the land, the soil, without work. Work brings him close to it; he embraces it and loves it, and strikes his roots into it. . . . Every drop of sweat I let fall into these furrows came back to me in many ways. My sleep is restored and my interest in things much keener."[54] This was a time not of barrenness but of fullness, of fullness so complete that Burroughs found writing (particularly in the active farming seasons) to be an unnecessary and even unsatisfying distraction. As Whitman acutely observed, "He

FIGURE 6.
John Burroughs walks by the celery field in front of Slabsides.
Used by permission of the Jones Library, Inc., Amherst, Massachusetts.

is the farmer first—the man before the writer."[55] This matter of identity was essential not only to Burroughs's literary success (as Whitman noted) but also to his sense that he was successfully pursuing his own version of the Good Life.

Negotiating Religion, Nature, and the Self

Burroughs' transition from a world of books and ideas to a world of living close to the soil, yet still very much in connection with books and ideas, is based first and foremost on his sense that the farming life was necessary for the preservation and fulfillment of the self. That Burroughs also understood the turn to farming as a religious activity is in little doubt. Burroughs often drew direct parallels between the fervor of his father's primitive Baptist faith and his own passion for nature. "I reckon it is the same leaven working in us both," he tended to remark. "Father experienced religion, I experienced Nature."[56] Burroughs's pithy summary of the situation, however, does not quite do justice to the subtleties involved. Burroughs was fond of saying that the "time spirit" was responsible for the theological differences between himself and his father, Chauncey. In The Light of Day (1900) he wrote: "[It is] impossible for me to read the Bible as father . . . did, or to feel any interest in the questions which were so vital; not because I have hardened my heart against these things, but mainly because I was born forty years later than they were, with different tastes and habits of mind. The time spirit has wrought many changes in men's views, and I have seen the world with other eyes and through other mediums."[57] While Burroughs's theological departures from his father are in some sense neatly representative of the cultural shifts of his generation, they were reached with greater complexity than we might initially assume.[58] They were not the result of a mere shift in Zeitgeist but were the product of Burroughs's very active engagement with the more liberal dimensions of this shift.

Burroughs arrived at skepticism about his father's religious faith only after first experiencing fear, awe, and his own attempts at conversion. Among his earliest memories are those of his father hotly debating doctrinal issues with a Methodist neighbor. "I can see him now as he sat with the Book open on his knees," Burroughs remembered decades later, "a tallow dip in his hand, his face flushed, his voice loud, hurling Paul's predestinarianism at his neighbor's free salvation Methodism." Having once come upon his father deep in private prayer, Burroughs fled in fear. His own religious feeling, he identified early on, was not in the Bible or in prayer but in the ecstasy of literature and walks in the open air. Barrus cites two instances in Burroughs's childhood when he felt "lifted out of himself" in the same way that the elder Burroughs reported he was "neither in the body nor out of the body" when listening to the local pastor. These two early occasions of ecstasy were incited by reading aloud from The Life of Washington and walking on top of a stone wall on the crest of a hillside one early summer morning.[59]

As a young teacher, Burroughs succumbed to the social pressures of respectability (but not his father's theological views) and attended the local Methodist church, primarily he admitted later, for making the acquaintance of the young ladies in town. But recognizing in himself a certain "religious feeling," he also attended camp meetings and on one occasion found himself called to the anxious bench. "So much had been said about what was to be gained by doing this that I expected it would result in some miraculous change in me," he recollected. But when the leaders of the revival questioned him, he remarked— as an honest observer of nature, including his own—that he felt more or less the same as he had before. The following night the preacher prayed for his soul and for the flock of students Burroughs was likely "taking down to hell with him." From that moment on, Burroughs "decided to work out my salvation in another way." This included deciding to "give [his] heart to Nature instead of God" but also emphasizing that "God is nature . . . [and that] there is some sort of omnipotent intelligence underlying the manifestations of power and the orderliness that we see in the universe."[60] In committing himself to a life in nature rather than to a life in the church, Burroughs found a way to maintain a religious life while rejecting the "superstitions" he associated with formal religion.

Burroughs's insistence that there is nothing of theological value beyond nature, but that nature is divine and not merely mechanistic, reflects his ongoing process of relocating the religious in nature. Like Thoreau and Emerson before him and countless homesteaders and nature writers after him, Burroughs found himself in confronting modernity with a blend of acceptance and resistance. Religious life did not disappear altogether from his cultural landscape, but neither would nature be transformed into a mere machine. His scientific approach to the natural world had long prevented him from abiding by what he believed to be superstition, even when others brought the language of science to their defense.[61] At the same time, however, Burroughs wrestled constantly with the troublesome notions advanced by scientifically minded secularists that nature was nothing more than its component parts following immutable (and humanly knowable) laws. While Burroughs adamantly resisted the idea that "personality" is present in nature—a popular stance that Burroughs challenged in the celebrated "nature faker" controversy—he also could not accept that nature is not infused by a "vital force" or an intelligence.

In subsequent years, Burroughs recognized his dilemma for what it was—a competition between warring sides of his own heart and mind—and addressed the matter directly to his reading audience. In one of his later books, The Breath of Life (1915), Burroughs spoke plainly of the competing forces within him:

> I am aware that two ideas, or principles, struggle in my mind for mastery. One is the idea of the super-mechanical and the super-chemical character of living things; the other is the idea of the supremacy and universality of what we call natural law. The first probably springs from my inborn idealism and literary habit of mind; the second from my love of nature and my scientific bent. . . . An explanation of life phenomena that savors of the laboratory and chemism repels me, and an explanation that savors of the theological view is equally distasteful to me.[62]

Burroughs's dilemma represents, among other things, the competing influences of Emerson and Darwin on his own view of nature. Barrus writes that Burroughs's interest in nature was more for "what lies back of Her" than for nature itself and, in saying this, refers directly to the influence of Emerson, whom Burroughs considered his "spiritual father."[63] But Barrus, ever eager to put Burroughs in the best literary light, here plays up the Emersonian connection more than she should. Important differences between Burroughs and Emerson are found not only in Burroughs's comparatively greater involvement in tilling the soil and rustic living but also in his development as a scientifically informed observer of nature. While Emerson was Burroughs's spiritual father, Darwin was Burroughs's scientific confrere.

Burroughs came late to Darwin, first reading *The Origin of Species* and *The Descent of Man* in 1883. His praise of Darwin was unflagging. Burroughs's experience of reading him was akin to "breath[ing] the air of the largest and most serene mind." Burroughs instantly interpreted Darwin's texts as highlighting the best of humanity, not the "lowest," as Darwin's Christian critics often maintained. Turning the traditional Christian criticism on its head—a typically "Burroughs" device—the farmer-naturalist affirmed that Darwin's book "convinces like Nature herself" and "adds immensely to the glory of the race." Burroughs elaborated by asserting: "Who has not felt what a mechanical, inartistic view of creation that which the churches have so long held is? But that all these vast, complex results and forms of life were enfolded in the first germ—*that* view makes the universe alive, the veritable body of God, the organism of a vast, mysterious, all-embracing, eternal power, impersonal, unhuman in its general workings, but manifesting conscience and beneficence mainly through the human race."[64] Taking the most liberal aspects of liberal theologians' accommodation of Darwin, Burroughs argued to himself and, later, to his readers that the Darwinian theory of natural selection confirmed a scientifically responsible view of the world without detracting from any ultimate sense of wonder or "Godliness."[65]

In Burroughs's reading, Darwin grounded nature in scientific observation rather than philosophical speculation. But Darwin also maintained a genuine "religious feeling," and it was this aspect of Darwin's writing that equally appealed to Burroughs.[66] Burroughs's careful blending of Emerson's and Darwin's influence with his own experiential conclusions is evident in his attempt to resolve the dilemmas confessed in his introduction to *The Breath of Life*: "I crave and seek a natural explanation of all phenomena upon this earth, but the word 'natural' to me implies more than mere chemistry and physics. The birth of a baby and the blooming of a flower, are natural events, but the laboratory methods forever fail to give us the key to the secret of either. . . . To the rigid man of science this [poetic, religious sense of nature] is frank mysticism; but without a sense of the unknown and unknowable, life is flat and barren."[67] For Burroughs, life is flat without a religious sense of nature, and a daily life that does not marvel at the birth of babies and flowers is a daily life hardly worth living.[68]

In the end, Burroughs's decision to hold fast to the Wordsworthian principle that there is always "something far more deeply interfused" in the natural world than a scientific catalog is both a pragmatic and a religious kind of choice. It is a choice about making meaning through the cultural world and the personal history that are available to him. In setting out before his public what he perceived to be a highly personal dilemma, Burroughs also gave voice to the cultural anxieties of his age, anxieties about having to choose between outmoded Christian doctrine and a secularized world without meaning. As we have seen, such anxieties persist into the present and are given particular expression by those homesteaders of today who reject "religion" as such but who discover, in their daily practices, a deeply satisfying spiritual way of life.

Like more recent homesteaders, Burroughs's creative fusion of the religious and the secular (in his case, "science")—and his accompanying ambivalence about that fusion—makes itself most plain when the subject of immortality is addressed. Burroughs treats this subject quite directly in his journal and later more formally in the texts *The Light of Day* and *Accepting the Universe* (1920). A relatively early comment, made when he was forty, reveals his impatience with questions that cannot be resolved scientifically: "Immortality is something to be reasoned about and proven is it? a question to be established by a subtle metaphysical argument? Then away with it, and away with all such questions! If they do not prove themselves like the day or night, or health and disease, if they are not self-evident then I will have nothing to do with them."[69] Here Burroughs exhibits his long-standing distrust of religious beliefs that lack scientific grounding or commonsense evidence. But while Burroughs claims he will have nothing to do with the questions of immortality, his interest in the subject is as persistent as his need to dismiss it. His very first publication, at the age of nineteen, was an attack on Spiritualism, which was published in a local paper (the *Bloomville Mirror*, May 13, 1856). In his editorial remarks, Burroughs accused the Spiritualists of being irrational and egotistical in their assumptions that "celestial beings . . . [would] descend to this obscure corner of creation for the mere purpose of satisfying the idle curiosity of particular individuals! . . . And why must they make their appearances under the cover of darkness?" he queried. "Why not make their visits in the light of day?"[70] Burroughs reclaimed this very phrase in 1900, using it as the title for his book and subtitling it "Religious Discussions and Criticisms from a Naturalist's Point of View." It is in this text that his arguments against religion but for a religious view of nature are most clearly laid out.

In *The Light of Day*, Burroughs makes it plain that he is discontented with the other-worldly emphasis of all but the most liberal Christian churches. He is even less patient with Christians' tendencies to create God in their image. Preceding Wendell Berry's comments on the Great Economy by over eighty years, Burroughs's analysis nonetheless sounds strikingly like Berry's.[71] Burroughs warns his audience: "The universe viewed in the light of anything like the human economy . . . is not the right view. We must get rid of the great moral governor, or head director. He is a fiction of our brains. We must recognize only Nature, the All, call it God if we will, but divest it of all anthropological conceptions. Nature we know; we are of it; we are in it. But this paternal Providence above Nature—events are constantly knocking it down." In his praise of nature and his begrudging acceptance of the possibility that some might *have* to call it God, Burroughs performs a deft act of theological conservation. He believes in clearing his natural temple of false gods, yet he is no fan of the strict scientific materialism or burgeoning capitalism of his day. Nature is still the "All" that demands respect, humility, and the giving over of the self to nature's power. And nature is significant as the foundation not just of physical life but of moral life as well. "The whole order of the universe favors virtue and is against vice," Burroughs writes. "Things have come to what they are, man has arrived at what he is, the grass and the flowers clothe the fields, the trees thrive and bear wholesome fruit . . . through the action of the same principles by which we see that virtue is good and vice bad." Having thus established the moral order of the natural world, Burroughs advises humans to keep their place. "Nature is first and man last," he proclaims, and to live rightly we must adjust ourselves to live "in harmony with immutable laws through which the organic world has been evolved."[72]

In Burroughs's words we find an intriguing blend of the critique of established religion and a reverence for one of its most persistent themes: that there is a power beyond the human self to which the self must be relinquished. For while Burroughs wants humanity to keep its place, with nature first and humanity last, he also urges his readers to take comfort in what a life lived close to nature has to teach: "This vital Nature out of which we came . . . and to which again we all in due time return, why should we fear or distrust it? . . . It looked after us before we were born; it will look after us when we are dead. Every particle of us will be taken care of; the force of every heart-beat is conserved somewhere, somehow. The psychic force or principle of which I am a manifestation will still go on. There is no stoppage and no waste, forever and ever."[73] Humanity may be last in Burroughs's view, but if humans adjust themselves appropriately to the mysteries and rhythms of nature, somehow the last shall be first.

Once again, the theme of exceptionalism—however humbly introduced—persistently accompanies ideas of "naturalized" immortality. The step away from traditional Christian notions of "chosenness" is followed by a slight shuffle back toward a certain *kind* of chosenness: that which is provided by nature itself. The slippery character of this post-Christian pose is made most clear in a journal entry in 1866 in which Burroughs expresses both sides of the paradox in a matter of pages. He opens with the claim that "nature exists for man no more than she does for monkeys, and is as regardless of his life or pleasure or success as she is of fleas." Several paragraphs later he drives his point home with the assertion that while "man is at the top in his own estimation . . . Nature values him only as manure—squanders him as recklessly as autumn leaves." Such decidedly naturalistic and almost fatalistic interpretations of nature, however, are accompanied by a more redemptive reading on the following page: "Nature will not be conquered but gives herself freely to her true lover—to him who revels with her, bathes in her seas, sails her rivers, camps in her woods and, with no mercenary ends, accepts all."[74] In a passage where Burroughs is surely describing himself to himself, the young man who has not yet returned to the soil of his youth is already predicting the grace he will experience there. While quick to judge the exceptionalism of the Christian variety, Burroughs is *less* insightful when it comes to recognizing his own versions of the same tendency. Although his vision of nature eventually goes beyond Thoreau's and Emerson's Transcendentalist views, Burroughs recapitulates here and elsewhere the Transcendental emphasis on the special qualities available only to the practiced poet-seer.

Domesticity

In his intellectual life, Burroughs never fully resolves the many tensions we have reviewed here: the tension between secular-scientific and traditional religious views of life, between mortality and immortality, between an indifferent or a humanized nature. He does, however, engage in a series of improvisations that help him to navigate the shifting cultural landscape of the late nineteenth and early twentieth centuries. These improvisations include a general relocation of the religious into the natural world and the development of a notion of immortality that is linked to the cycle of the seasons and the natural processes of growth and decay. Included in both of these reconceptualizations of traditional Christianity is a conscious attempt at doing away with the notion of humanity as enjoying a special status "above" other aspects of nature, an attempt that is mediated—and sometimes undermined—by an understanding that those who love nature and live closely to her are themselves exceptional individuals who enjoy a special relationship with the natural world. All of these themes we have seen before in the lives of contemporary and recent homesteaders. Burroughs's particular articulation of these themes reminds us that the broad religious aspects of the choice to go "back to nature," as well as the myriad tensions that accompany this choice, were already well in play in the late nineteenth century.

Burroughs was sometimes well aware of the intellectual double binds in which he found himself, as his introduction to *The Breath of Life* illustrates. But he never seems terribly worried about what he willingly admits are tensions and "contradictory points of view" in his writing.[75] While attempting to articulate an understanding of nature that was both empirically valid and spiritually inspirational, Burroughs gave the best of his literary and practical attention to the duties and pleasures of daily life on the homestead. Daily labor in the soil and walks in the woods enabled him to reinscribe his competing views into the *experiential realm* of his encounter with nature. The original move to Riverby was the first step in this process, but the practice of farming would prompt him to cultivate an even greater domestic simplicity, one that would foster a closer relationship with the natural world as well as a growing criticism of "civilization."

Through his practice of everyday life, Burroughs was able to defer those tensions that he could not—and did not necessarily *want* to—resolve intellectually. In light of the homesteaders we have already studied, the choices Burroughs made are familiar ones: the decision to leave urban life was followed by the development of daily practices that symbolize intimacy with nature, self-determination in the structuring of work and leisure, and an ethics and aesthetics of simplicity.

Burroughs's emphasis on domestic simplicity grew hand in hand with his increasing dissatisfaction with life at Riverby and culminated with annual removal (from March to December) to Slabsides in the summer of 1896. Both his contemporaries and his biographers have suggested that Burroughs's increasingly strained relationship with Ursula played a large role in his "retreat" to Slabsides. An article in a New York magazine suggests that Ursula—by all accounts a near clinically obsessive housecleaner—had both literally and metaphorically swept her husband out of the house.[76] Burroughs's relationship with Ursula was indeed troubled, and Burroughs did little to cooperate with Ursula's wishes that he maintain at least a veneer of professional and domestic respectability. His approach to her was a mixture of goading and ignoring. In this sense, the decision to spend the majority of his time at Slabsides was clearly both a symbolic protest and a literal avoidance of Ursula.[77] But it would be myopic to conclude that Burroughs's removal to Slabsides was simply a gesture of escape from his wife.

While seeking distance from Ursula herself, Burroughs was also seeking distance from the world of social convention she had come to represent and the world of business she had always hoped he would enter. The desire to live in a house "with the bark still on it" was a desire to move further away from the aesthetics of opulence and commerce that Burroughs felt was encroaching upon him. Withdrawing from the banks of the Hudson was one aspect of this transition, for Burroughs felt increasingly that the Hudson played host to "yachts of millionaires flaunting up and down it. . . . The Hudson . . . hasn't the domestic and winning qualities that a smaller stream has," he commented. "Its commercial aspect is always intruding, and the dweller on its banks find its disturbing sights and sounds continually jarring on his sensibilities."[78] Removal into the woods meant further removal from the world of getting and spending, even if Burroughs's farming activities continued to link him partially with the very world he increasingly criticized.

The desire to build a home that resisted all elements of affectation was another aspect of Burroughs's Slabsides project, one that he clearly articulated when criticizing his home at Riverby as being insufficiently plain and "absurd" in its elaborate, three-story layout.[79] The admiration of simplicity in domestic structures, however, had been an ongoing motif in Burroughs's writing, beginning with *Signs and Seasons*.[80] Whatever his later regrets, Burroughs stressed the significance of building his Riverby home with an emphasis on the natural and the functional, dedicating an entire essay—"Roof-Tree"—to the aesthetic and moral dimensions of house building. In passages that resonate with Helen and Scott Nearing's words of praise for stone work, Burroughs writes with conviction and enthusiasm of his first building experiences: "I say, therefore, build of stones by all means, if you have a natural taste to gratify, and the rockier your structure looks, the better. All things make friends with a stone house,—the mosses and lichens, and vines and birds. It is kindred to the earth and the elements and makes itself at home in any situation." Just as the Nearings would urge later, Burroughs argues against any obviously "artistic" placing and pointing of stones, urging his readers that "mortar plays a subordinate part in the structure" and should be covered with sand to maintain the stone wall's "rocky, natural appearance."[81] The important relationship between the process of gathering stones and building with them is also stressed, as the Nearings would similarly emphasize almost seventy years later.[82] "It seems to me that I built into my house every one of those superb autumn days which I spent in the woods getting out stone," Burroughs wrote in 1886. "I quarried the delicious weather into memories to adorn my walls. Every load that was sent home carried my heart and happiness with it."[83] While Slabsides was made with "rough and ready" timber rather than rugged stone, it represented a further step—both symbolic and literal—in the direction of simple living.

An important element of Burroughs's Slabsides life was that it enabled him to control for himself the domestic practices that had so long been Ursula's domain. The rituals of domesticity, then, were also *ritualizations*, repeated symbolic gestures toward both the childhood that Burroughs longed for and the virtues of simple living that he felt were vital for the success of future generations. At Slabsides, Burroughs practiced housekeeping in ways that likely would have horrified Ursula but that were "very much simpler" and more satisfying. Having once failed to recapitulate Ursula's baked cherry pudding, for instance, Burroughs found that placing cherries on top of crackers was pudding enough. He used wooden slabs for plates that, after serving duty for several meals, he threw into the fire. His only gesture toward appearances was the eventual replacement of his newspaper-made tablecloth with a white, oilcloth covering.[84] When unexpected guests arrived, Burroughs would slip a few more potatoes into the ashes of his fire, not unlike the way Helen Nearing would add another cup of buckwheat to the pot on the wood stove. Both aimed to be gracious hosts but to do so by showing their guests how appealing simplicity could be.[85]

Unlike the Nearings, however, Burroughs also liked to demonstrate the relaxation and ease (relative to the domesticity of Riverby) inherent in the simple life. His days at Slabsides included leisurely walks in the woods, for their own sake, and plenty of dozing on the rocks and in the fields. While ascetic in some respects—he is said to have fed the rabbit under his study conservatively for fear of "corrupting him with too lavish a meal"—he also craved leisure and retirement.[86] At times, Burroughs attributed this tendency to his "lax moral fibre." "Austerity would ill become me," he remarked and doubtless surprised his audience. "My edge is much easier turned than was that, say, of Thoreau. . . . Yes, there is much soft rock in my make-up. Is that why I shrink from the wear and tear of the world?"[87] At other times, Burroughs drew on the example of Whitman, underlining the importance of "loafing and inviting my soul."[88] Burroughs's life at Slabsides involved daily practices that the visiting public would construct as ascetic (making his own meals, chopping wood daily, procuring food from his fields and root cellar). But Burroughs himself understood these practices to be liberating.

Perhaps the most significant aspect of Burroughs's relocation to Slabsides, however, was the extent to which the decision *was* based on a certain kind of labor, labor in the soil. The story of Slabsides, as Burroughs tells it, began not with the construction of a building but with the transformation of an overgrown swamp into an immensely productive celery and potato field. The work of cabin construction, of building furniture from local "sticks of Nature's own fashioning," and of transforming cooking and cleaning into a simple round of daily chores all played a role in making life at Slabsides more desirable and meaningful than life at Riverby. But it was always the earth itself that had the most magnetic effect on the ever soil-hungry Burroughs: "It has been the land that has given me most pleasure in my wilderness house. It looks different from other land. It is land I have made and it is more precious than any I could buy. . . . If someone had given me a nice piece of tillable land, I wouldn't have thought anything of it as compared with my swamp."[89] For Burroughs, home-

FIGURE 7.
John Burroughs at his desk at Slabsides. The
desk and mantle show his love for wood
"with the bark still on it" and were made by
Burroughs from trees on his property. Used
by permission of the Jones Library, Inc.,
Amherst, Massachusetts.

steading begins with the domestication of the soil and the cultivation of the self.
The art of domesticity emerges from these foundations and seeks to reempha-
size their significance. What fosters intimacy between nature and the self is welcomed; what imposes distance is resisted, if not always intellectually, at least in
the realm of daily practice.

Burroughs and the Public Eye:
"Back to Nature" as Cultural Reform

No sooner had Burroughs retired to Slabsides than the public came trailing after him. In 1905, Burroughs published *The Ways of Nature*, his public response to the "Nature Faker" controversy, which began in 1903.[90] The book and the controversy that preceded it confirmed Burroughs's rising status as a household name, a process furthered by the author's friendships with such national figures as Theodore Roosevelt and Henry Ford.[91] Throughout the first two decades of the twentieth century, Burroughs found himself entertaining thousands of pilgrims at his "private" retreat. His photograph appeared in numerous popular magazines and John Burroughs societies began springing up in high schools and youth groups across the country.[92] The flocks of visitors came to see a man who practiced what he preached. They came to see Burroughs's hut in the woods, to photograph him getting supplies from his root cellar or sitting at his homemade desks. They came to ask Burroughs for advice on nature observation and the arts of simple living. In the first years of the twentieth century, Burroughs's symbolic status catapulted from literary figure to national representative of "natural living" American style.

Burroughs was ambivalent about his growing popularity. Like Helen Nearing (who was always more of a hostess than Scott was a host), Burroughs enjoyed the attention, particularly from those who had a certain degree of cultural influence. Having felt uncertain, for so many decades, of his proper calling in life (and moreover, of its respectability in the eyes of Ursula and others), Burroughs found support and reassurance for his approach to living in his budding friendships with Roosevelt, Ford, and Thomas Edison. But also like the Nearings, he grew weary of the constant visitations from outside, which came to threaten the peaceful existence he sought in the mountains.[93] Burroughs's desire to please was great. He could not say no to correspondents, visitors, and photographers, who, by publicizing Burroughs's whereabouts and his genial nature, brought still more visitors to Riverby and Slabsides. Just as Forest Farm's status as a pilgrimage site sometimes endangered its very nature as a self-sufficient homestead, so did Burroughs's Slabsides become endangered by a cultural hunger for back-to-nature symbols, a hunger that threatened to commodify Burroughs's gestures against an increasingly commodified culture.

Burroughs's conflicted feelings about his popularity was wrapped up in a similarly ambivalent sense of his role as cultural critic, an ambivalence the Nearings largely did not share. The Nearings used their two forest farms (in Vermont and then in Maine) as outposts from which to continually project their manifestos of cultural criticism into the public sphere and, as we have seen, were sometimes so strident in their principles as to alienate those with whom they might have otherwise associated. Depending on the interpretive angle one adopts, Burroughs can be seen as more accommodating—or less principled—in his interaction with those representing the cultural forces he opposed. For instance, he was temporarily enchanted with Henry Demarest Lloyd's *Wealth against Commonwealth* when he eagerly devoured it in 1896. He instantly urged his friends to read the book and unsuccessfully lobbied his editors to give voice in their magazines to Lloyd's condemnation of monopolies and railroads.[94] But Burroughs's enchantment with Lloyd was something of a summer love affair, one that did not lead him to criticize openly the monopolizing and industrializing tendencies of such publicly "showy" associates as Jay Gould and Henry Ford.[95] In addition, with respect to his particular friendship with Ford, Burroughs was also something of a fair-weather friend. Having written essays in which he criticized the car for polluting areas of natural beauty, he became one of Ford's greatest champions after receiving a gift of a Model T and learning of Ford's own nostalgic yearnings for the simplicity of rural life.[96]

Burroughs, as Renehan importantly recognizes, "was generally mute with regard to the industrial excesses of his era" (if by mute Renehan means unwilling to engage in direct social and political criticism).[97] Burroughs was aware that his response to the larger social world was more one of retreat than of engagement. "I know I have gone a-fishing while others have labored in the slums and given their lives for the betterment of their fellows," he confessed to Barrus.[98] But while Burroughs's reforming tendencies were indeed restrained, they were never entirely absent. It is in the careful articulation of the details and the value of his daily practices, in fact, that Burroughs was most effective in publicly voicing his cultural critique. This call for reform sneaks up on us, as it likely did on Burroughs himself, who required several years of labor before recognizing that his personal solution to the problem of vocation was also a cultural response to the evils of industrialization. Nevertheless, the reforming urge periodically breaks through the placid waters of Burroughs's nature essays, not unlike a shimmering trout. One of these early fortuitous appearances is the essay "Phases of Farm Life."

"Phases of Farm Life" demonstrates Burroughs in his prime, moving from the descriptive details of his own practices to a call for reform that urges his audience "back to the land." This is the first essay in which Burroughs considers the farming life as a cultural "sign," a designation of maturity that ought to be the goal of individuals and cultures. In the opening paragraphs, Burroughs puts forth his argument that "a good test of civilization . . . is country life." The city is "older" than the country, Burroughs proposes, even though we are likely to think the opposite. While Burroughs would admit, if pressed, that the first humans did not live in urban centers, he plays on the notion of city and country to point out that the city is the testing ground for "rude and barbarous" people to learn their proper relationship with themselves, with others, and with the natural world. Once "man . . . became sufficiently civilized, not afraid of solitude, and knew on what terms to live with nature," Burroughs proclaims, "God promoted him to life in the country."[99]

Burroughs invokes his trademark nostalgia when he bemoans the lost arts of cornhusking bees, of spinning with flax, or of using old tools such as "crackles" and "swingling knives," but he maintains a tone of perpetual optimism throughout.[100] While remarking that in the age of the railroad "all has changed," Burroughs goes on to defend the charm of the farm which "remains and always will remain": the cow is still the center of the daily routine, good mowing with a scythe is a skill still mastered by few, and "the distilled essence of the tree" is still to be found in maple syrup.[101] Burroughs concludes his meditations on farm life with a direct address to the reader infused with an evangelical tone: "Cling to the farm, make much of it, put yourself into it, bestow your heart and your brain upon it, so that it shall savor of you and radiate your virtue after your day's work is done!" As if his own poetic force may not be enough, Burroughs turns to the Bible to cap his sermon: "Be thou diligent to know the state of thy flocks and look well to thy herds," Burroughs exhorts, ". . . and thou shall have goat's milk enough for thy food."[102]

As the years unfolded, Burroughs increasingly sensed that he was promoting an appealing and potentially transformational life, for the self and society. It was Burroughs's *embodied practice* of an alternative to the dominant cultural flow that was significant for those who read him and those who visited. Nowhere was the importance of the practice of simplicity more succinctly and effectively captured than in Burroughs's article in *Cosmopolitan* in 1906, "What Life Means to Me." He expanded the article to an essay, "An Outlook upon Life," and in each case the public reception was enormous. Of his daily life at Slabsides he wrote:

> When I depart [from the simple life] evil results follow. I love a small house, plain clothes, simple living. . . . How free one feels, how good the elements taste, how close one gets to them, how they fit one's body and one's soul! To see the fire that warms you, or better yet, to cut the wood that feeds the fire that warms you; to see the spring where the water bubbles up that slakes your thirst, and to dip your pail in to it; to see the beams that are the stay of your four walls, and the timbers that uphold the roof that shelters you; to be in direct and personal contact with the sources of your material life; . . . these are some of the rewards of the simple life.[103]

Burroughs's practical and sometimes seemingly self-serving choices were also *ritualizations*. They continued to remind both him and his many admirers of the difference between what life is and what it ought to be. Whether it is in warning that departure from the simple life leads to "evil results" or in concluding his essay on farm life with an extended quotation from Proverbs 27:23, Burroughs consistently reaffirms his status as a preacher for the religious life of homesteading.

.   .   .

My purpose in the preceding pages has been to trace the pattern of Burroughs's practice of homesteading as well as the literary life that developed alongside and in relationship to these practices. What we have seen is Burroughs's conversion and developing commitment to a way of life that put him in direct daily contact with a particular natural surround and allowed him to construct a vocation at some remove from the demands of an increasingly industrialized society. This way of life was, for Burroughs, a religious life, one in which nature was quite consciously substituted for God and became an enduring source of authority, solace, and meaning.

An undercurrent in this discussion has been the relationship between Burroughs and his reading public. In attempting to resolve certain vocational and theological problems for himself, Burroughs symbolized the dilemmas of a liberal, urban, middle-class culture longing for just the kind of beneficent, sympathetic "Nature" that he created in his essays. While Burroughs borrowed heavily from Emerson and Thoreau in these essays, he also took the edge off the most intellectually and morally challenging aspects of their work. In him, the reading public found a symbol of what going back to the land might mean in America at the turn of the century. But Burroughs—relative to Thoreau before him and the Nearings after—represented appeal rather than challenge.

Burroughs's enormous popularity is revealing of the desire of his readership for a certain kind of symbol. The publishing world fanned the flames of this desire through photographs and profiles in magazines. Through Burroughs, readers could vicariously experience an intimacy with the natural world that they knew he was experiencing on a daily basis. He represented the possibility that one could engage in religious life away from the church, pursue both intellectual and physical labor, and bring work and leisure together.[104]

But however much Burroughs's life at West Park included the real work of farming, it did not involve a rigorous commitment to self-sufficiency, nor was it intended as a strong public act of dissent from the dominant cultural norms. Burroughs's later removal to Slabsides (and, to a lesser extent, his temporary fascination with Lloyd) was, in part, an expression of his uneasiness with his status as a gentleman farmer. More so than many homesteads, Slabsides was essentially symbolic. Life at Slabsides depended on the resources of the main house and on the resourcefulness of Ursula as a homemaker. Yet the *symbolic* nature of Burroughs's life at Slabsides reminds us of the extent to which modern homesteading is always a *ritualized* expression of dissent from conventional religion as well as from the conventional world of work and consumption. Although the extent of rigor, self-sacrifice, and public protest involved may vary, homesteading is a decision that its practitioners have had the leisure to make. The way of life chosen is not so much an expression of actual circumstance as it is a symbolic expression of the world as it "ought to be," spiritually, economically, and culturally.

When we take the long view of Burroughs's life and evaluate him in the context of other homesteading visions, it is difficult to assess him in the end. On the one hand, we may take a critical stance toward his life and work. No doubt aware of the back-to-the-land movement in Britain, Burroughs chose not to advocate the return to nature as a mode of radical social reform, as C. R. Ashbee and Edward Carpenter did on the other side of the Atlantic; nor did Burroughs seem to take interest in more local reforms such as Bolton Hall's attempts to make homesteading a means of independence and self-respect for the poor and an opportunity for healthy, "honest" labor for the middle class.[105] Even Burroughs's popular representations of nature invite our criticism. Although he championed Darwin and inveighed against the "Nature Fakers," his own readings of nature were consistently sentimental and anthropocentric. While Burroughs, like other homesteaders, longed to dissolve the boundaries between the self and the natural world, he also understood himself as a special reader of nature's code and often projected not simply "humanity" but particularly "Burroughs" onto his immediate landscape.

A less critical stance to take, however, is to see Burroughs as the "rule" more than the exception of homesteading life. While his understanding of nature and self-culture is clearly turn-of-the-century, it seems remarkably predictive of the concerns and limits of many contemporary homesteaders and their 1960s predecessors. The drive for self-sufficiency may be stronger in more recent periods, but the tendency for some to turn to nature primarily to resolve private dilemmas of spiritual, psychological, and vocational identity is remarkably resonant with Burroughs's life. While the Greenbergs and Coperthwaites may doggedly pursue means of establishing community and reforming society, other homesteaders are content with pursuing (and writing about) what living close to nature means on a highly personal level. Even faithful readers of the Nearings' writings are more apt to praise the "environmental" aspects of their work, without necessarily recognizing the links the Nearings made between homesteading and social reform.

As our analysis moves from Burroughs to Scott Nearing, then, we need to keep Burroughs in mind, in one sense, as a paradigmatic homesteader (leaving behind city life, sacralizing nature, ritualizing simple living, rearranging patterns of work and leisure) and, in another, as representative of what the more accommodationist aspects of homesteading can be. In contrast, Scott Nearing's life strikes us as radically "other": socially oriented, relentlessly confrontational, and rigorous in the commitment to the rituals of simplicity. Like Burroughs, however—although through a quite different series of life events—Nearing also created a life in nature that was an alternative to the mainstream, a life that emphasized "practice" and was ultimately religious.

Scott Nearing . . . was in harmony with the high
ideals he professed. He was in tune with his
universe. He was a man who tried to live what he
believed, who practiced what he preached. He was
essentially religious, but member of no church,
adherent to no religious group; a man of letters,
but a grubby gardener; a public figure and a happy
hermit.

Helen Knothe Nearing, *Loving and Leaving the
Good Life*

Arden, Delaware (1905)

At the age of twenty-two, Scott Nearing built his first house and planted his first
organic garden. In the growing single-tax community known as Arden, Nearing bought one of the last remaining plots abutting the common green, hand
built a wood and stone home that he called Forest Lodge, and reclaimed a poor
section of land with compost and manure.[1] Soon he would become well known
in Arden and beyond for his ability to create fine stone structures and to grow
some of the best pole lima beans in the vicinity. Looking back on the ten years
he spent residing at Arden—off and on as his scholarly schedule in Philadelphia
permitted—Nearing recalled this as one of the most meaningful experiences of
his early adulthood. "There was a reality and completeness about it that was satisfying and uplifting," Nearing wrote almost fifty years later. "[In] a very real
sense, it was the good life in miniature."[2]

The year that Nearing began his first homesteading experiments at Arden was
the same year that John Burroughs published *The Ways of Nature*. While there is
no direct evidence that the young Nearing was a reader of John Burroughs,
Nearing's first experiment in going back to the land occurred at the same time
as Burroughs had become a familiar name in the culture of the literary, educated
middle class.[3] While Nearing was becoming increasingly well-known in liberal
and radical circles in this same period, it would take until the 1960s for him to
become a rediscovered public figure and an additional decade before he would

be lionized as the patron saint of the countercultural back-to-the-land movement.[4] By the early years of the 1970s, Scott and Helen Nearing would be receiving visitors at Forest Farm in numbers far surpassing those who journeyed to Slabsides. But given his past association with the Communist and Socialist parties, the elder Nearing would never attain the mainstream national status that Burroughs temporarily acquired.[5]

If Nearing's first experiments at Arden had led him early on to be primarily an advocate of going back to nature as the solution for the social and spiritual evils of the day, the story might have unfolded differently. Yet the personal, social, and spiritual concerns that first led Nearing, at twenty-two, to become an active participant in the Arden community also—somewhat ironically—kept him from an early life of full-time homesteading and from keeping nature at the forefront of his cultural critique. Nearing took up homesteading as a way of living, however, only *after* his professional and political career was put to rest by the very cultural developments he tried to resist.

Nearing's return to nature as something of a last resort says as much about the strengths and limitations of American culture as about Nearing's own strengths and limitations. Just as Burroughs could not have known that his decision to leave Washington and take up a life of farming and writing would bring him public recognition and success, so Nearing could not have known that taking up a dual career as a university professor and social activist would ultimately force him into a life of farming and writing, shutting him out of public life until his later "discovery" by 1960s and 1970s youth.

"Nature" at the Turn of the Century

As our story of homesteading shifts from Burroughs to Nearing, our lens for viewing this era of American history also changes. Looking at Burroughs, the "representative man," provides us with a view into the late nineteenth and early twentieth centuries and a demonstration of the growing interest in nature as a physical and spiritual salve for the wounds of industrialization. In examining the first four decades of Nearing's life, on the other hand, we see American culture through a lens of *opposition*. The cultural forces that ultimately propelled Nearing into a productive life of homesteading were forces that first constructed him as a renegade, a failed radical, a threat to public safety in wartime, and a menace to American progress. While the American public was willing to go to nature for relief from the ills of industrialization, it was not willing in these early decades to question the structures of capitalism that enabled urban decay (and class inequity) to flourish. For Nearing, however, homesteading was first an act of resistance to unrestrained capitalism and only later—as American culture underwent another shift—an example of home-based environmentalism.

Before I begin to investigate Nearing's early career—as Ardenite, as professor, and as cultural critic—let me linger for a moment on the cultural conditions and shifts suggested here. Why was Burroughs's return to the farm seen as exemplary activity while Nearing's actions (as professor, writer, and homesteader) were first viewed as embittered dissent and later often dismissed and ignored? What dominant strains of the Progressive Era brought Burroughs into the public eye while simultaneously banishing Nearing? At the same time, which of these strains became incorporated into Nearing's own life and work, even as he publicly lashed out against the capitalism of his time? I shall address these first two questions below and return to the third later on when we examine Nearing's choices more closely.

As has been suggested throughout this work, an important clue to the preoccupations of this—and any—period is the construction of nature that occurs in and through the culture of the day. As we began to see in chapter 4, the last decades of the nineteenth century and the first decades of the twentieth—the so-called Gilded Age and Progressive Era—were increasingly characterized by a tremendous revival of interest in nature. To put it more accurately, nature became, for the first time in American history, more than a physical context for home and farm or a symbolic backdrop for humanity's spiritual errand.[6] While still and always both physical and symbolic, nature now became a place to be visited or an experience to have. It was something to be interpreted, protected, and possessed. By the turn of the century, in fact, America found itself in the midst of its first full-fledged "nature craze." The enthusiasm for natural and simple living was proclaimed on every front, in the pages of Lyman Abbott's *Outlook* and Edward Bok's *Ladies' Home Journal*, in the school reform movements in which the virtues of nature-study classes and open-air exercise were extolled, and by Ernest Thompson Seton's newly formed bands of "Woodcraft Indian" boys.[7]

The expressions of this cultural interest in and affection for the natural world were manifold, and the impulses behind them were varied and often intertwined. But it helps us to artificially separate them first, in order to see this phenomenon more clearly. In so doing we may speak of three aspects of the growing nature craze: the general popularity of nature as something to be enjoyed, especially during leisure time; the turn to nature as one aspect of the liberalization of religion; and the (significantly less popular) belief that living close to nature is an appropriate alternative to emergent social problems and future social crises.

At the most popular level, the new reverence for nature was a sweeping response to a dramatic change in social and environmental conditions. For the first time in America's young life, the population of the countryside diminished dramatically while the population in the cities increased with equal force.[8] Correspondingly, Americans' understanding of themselves began to change. In the midst of growing industrialization, many found themselves to be profoundly "out of nature" and wanting to get back into it. Not surprisingly, the enthusiasm for nature found its force in the city and its most sustained expression in books and magazine articles written by elites and consumed by a rising middle class. Given its social location, the nature craze was, for the most part, a *response* to industrialization and industrialism (the ethos of promoting industrialization as the "answer" to America's cultural problems), rather than an *alternative* to it. Nature was constructed as a place to go rather than a place to live in. It treated the symptoms but not the source of the cultural disease, a problem that, William Cronon has noted, persists in contemporary environmentalists' preference for wilderness over inhabited landscapes.[9] The general assumption was that periodic dips into nature on weekends and in summers could restore the body and soul sufficiently to make life in the city tolerable. And if physical journeys to the country were impossible, vicarious travels through the texts of popular nature writers, such as Burroughs, were the second best option.

The growing popularity of Burroughs and other nature writers, however, is explained by something in addition to the corresponding popularity of nature in a general sense. It is also explained by the emergent interest in nature as a place and means of *spiritual* renewal. In this period, nature becomes, to borrow a phrase from Thoreau, "startlingly moral." For the educators and essayists praising the benefits of life lived closer to nature and the urban dwellers heeding their calls, nature was as much a moral and spiritual category as it was a physical place where one might retreat from the vexations of urban living. Ministers and parishioners alike found in nature a purifying force. For some, nature became a point of access to divine lessons that were more available to the average congregant than the theology of the city. Nature provided a way to meet God, without the necessity of complex intellectualizing and theological hairsplitting on the one hand and demanding social challenges on the other. Sojourns into nature served as a kind of experiential frosting on the established creedal cake. In 1903, for instance, the religious educator Earl Amos Brooks instructed ministers to plan outdoor activities into the church program and to develop skills by which to transform each challenge of a camping trip into a spiritual lesson about God's handiwork or the making of Christian character. It is not surprising, then, that by 1912 over a fourth of all Boy Scout masters were ministers, and two-thirds of the existing scout troops were sponsored by Methodist, Presbyterian, Congregationalist, and Baptist churches.[10] While nature may have once played a significant role in the conversions of the camp meeting, now camping itself was coming to be defined as a religious (Christian) experience, to which large numbers were being converted.

The particular theology of nature that we find in Burroughs's writing may have occupied a liberal position on the continuum of emerging Christian paeans to the great outdoors, but it was by no means outside the realm of the evolving liberal debates about the nature and existence of God and the potentially competing claims of science. It is the very liberalizing of Christianity, in the context of the scientific and social scientific critique of religion, in fact, that partly accounts for Burroughs's wide acceptance.[11] While unorthodox in the eyes of his evangelical neighbors, Burroughs never went so far as to exclude God entirely from his vocabulary or from the realm of his concerns. Turning toward nature *was* turning to God, a god appropriate to the modern era but still familiar to the eye and ear and still able to offer the comforts of the Christian God of old. John Muir, his less popular counterpart, was more heterodox in his modes of expression and more activist in his concern for the preservation of nature, especially in its wilderness state. Muir preferred a kind of immediate pantheism that was radical and ecstatic. Only a minority would join John Muir in praising King Sequoia over King Jesus.[12] By retaining a familiar religious diction and keeping himself within certain theological bounds, Burroughs avoided alienating his readers and most likely seduced them into thinking that his natural theology was more Christian than it actually was.

But while Burroughs spoke of going back to the farm as a truly "civilized" mode of cultural reform, what of going back to nature as a solution to social crises? The public "yes" to Burroughs must be understood simultaneously as a general "no" to nature as a source of radical social change. The back-to-nature craze of the early twentieth century was, as both Peter Schmitt and David Shi have convincingly argued, a largely urban movement and a largely conventional one. Of course, such a broad movement posed challenges to industrial magnates and their Christian supporters alike. But these challenges were not so much resisted as absorbed.[13] The call to go back to nature was a call for reform, and the reformation advocated was of a gentle kind. On the one hand, returning to nature was seen not only as good for the individual soul but also as good for society. On the other hand, the benefits advertised were personal and interior, involving a kind of healing of symptoms. Going back to nature was rarely advocated as a revolt against existing institutions or social structures or as a means of getting at the root of social problems. Going apple picking was good for the individual and the social body—and good for the soul of each—but upsetting the apple cart was not.

Competing Claims: Arden and the University

When Scott Nearing took his first steps onto Arden soil, it was in the context of a public construction of nature as a tonic for the ills of the city. Yet Arden teetered on the edge between the mainstream, urban construction of nature on the one side and more radical alternatives on the other. Certainly, Arden offered a means of escape from the city, providing fresh air, sunshine, and homegrown vegetables to residents and flocks of weekend visitors. The single-taxers, however, were clearly "a small but vocal minority" whose efforts were diminished by the dominant culture's large-scale dismissal from without and internal dissent by the socialists from within.[14] But in its philosophical foundations and practical economic principles, Arden was more than an idealist vision or a place of escape. Its permanent residents were attempting to live out Henry George's philosophies of single tax in practice and, by so doing, to model the viability of such a social system for the rest of the country.[15]

Perhaps it was Arden's cultural location on the border of radicalism and convention that made it at once a such captivating place for young Nearing and at the same time a place in which he did not want to remain captive full-time. Interestingly, Nearing's retrospective comments on Arden run in more than one direction. In *The Making of a Radical*, Nearing speaks of Arden as a "vacation area" that, had he remained in academic life, would have been a place of leisure and recreation. In *Man's Search for the Good Life*, however, Nearing's interpretation of Arden is more profound.[16] In the opening chapter he acknowledges Arden as the stepping-stone between his early education and his ultimate realization of the Good Life at his homesteads in Vermont and Maine. If life at Arden was, indeed, "the good life in miniature," then it had to have been more than a place of leisure, even for a man who understood leisure as "strenuous."

Nearing's biographer John Saltmarsh offers a reading of Arden that is helpful here. Saltmarsh also understands Arden to be more than a place of temporary escape supported by the kind of "naive reformers" who, some historians suggest, ultimately defer to the social order rather than transform it. Progressive America established sufficient "cultural openness," Saltmarsh argues, for the creation of sustained alternative values, even if the model might be—as it initially was for Nearing—to develop these values slowly over time while continuing to work within the established social order.[17] Experiments such as the one at Arden occupied a genuine place on the continuum of back-to-nature efforts, a place less compromised than that of the *Ladies' Home Journal* or the Boy Scouts.

While other expressions of back-to-nature enthusiasm voiced dismay at the prevailing culture, Arden actually *enacted* an alternative vision. For Scott Nearing, it was this enactment, this yoking together of theory and practice, that was particularly significant and attractive.

Why was it, then, that the young Scott Nearing did not become a full-time Ardenite and later chose to leave Arden altogether? A clue can be found in the opening sentence of *Man's Search*: "My quest for the good life began in a back office in Philadelphia and led on to a Delaware community called Arden, and eventually to two forest farms in New England."[18] Arden's role in Nearing's life—whatever it may have been in the lives of others—was primarily *educational*. Together with luncheon meetings in the office of the director of the Philadelphia Ethical Society (where Nearing first learned about Arden), life at Arden served, for him, as a dramatic counterpart to conventional schooling, where "pabulum" was absorbed and "regurgitated." Writing in 1974, Nearing reflects: "Arden provided me with a liberal education. High school and university had pumped subject matter into me. . . . School seemed to start and end with book-learning. Arden was different. It minimized theory and emphasized practice, both individual and social. . . . From this beginning I was to work out further aspects of the good life in both Vermont and Maine."[19] Like most serious students, Scott Nearing sought learning experiences that had the ring of truth, vitality, and relevance. He found them at Arden. But also like such students, Nearing was eager to re-create such experiences for students of his own. The profession of teaching would become, for Nearing, a kind of ministry in which he would work "for the liberation of the individual soul."[20]

Perhaps the best clues for Nearing's relationship with Arden can be found in his unpublished work of fiction, "Arden Town," written in 1913 under the pseudonym "Max Worth." In this Progressive Era novella, the hero, Fred Allen, is a typically ambitious Philadelphia businessman, earnest and harmless on the surface but, in his dedication to the bottom line, willing to look the other way when a broken fire escape is made to look functional for the inspector. While Allen squirms temporarily at the notion of child labor, he encourages his manager to hire one or two children, arguing that "in some ways we must cut the costs in this department."[21] A dramatic change of consciousness soon sweeps over Allen, however (conveniently in the form of a strong, healthy, "natural" beauty, Ruth Wade), when he spends the week at the shore with an old college roommate and his suffragette cousin. Ruth is a member of "Arden Town," an idyllic single-tax community where social distinctions are leveled, work and rent is cooperative, living close to nature has made doctors irrelevant, and art is created from within through regular dances, singing parties, and Shakespearean productions involving all members of the community.

In time, Wade enchants Allen sufficiently for him to give up his pursuit of a society girl and to spend the late summer at Arden. Arden's "spirit," as others refer to it, soon works its magic upon Allen, and he decides he must give up his old life, sell his business, and live as a full member of the community. "I think I was made for this life," Allen effuses. "The other is so sordid, so narrowing, so barbarous that I have learned to despise it—since I came to Arden."[22]

But one of Allen's newfound Arden friends (Will Evans) reveals to him that the pursuit of righteous living is more complex than meets the eye. Evans confesses to Fred that his failure as a businessman transpired as a result of a business partner squeezing him out when he (Evans) was busy patching his life together after the death of his wife. The partner, it turns out, was Fred Allen's father, who amassed a fortune by ruining Evans. While Allen reels with the news of this history and attempts to reconcile it with Evans's having treated him like a dear brother, Evans makes his point: "I want you to continue in your business—in our business. I want you to pay fair wages. I want you to breathe into it the spirit of art. Do not come to Arden; take the Arden spirit with you to the city. We would love to have you; they need you."[23]

Certainly, Nearing's own biography differs somewhat from Allen's. Nearing had steered clear of an entrepreneurial life, was already an active reformer by the time he was Allen's age and, in 1913, was speaking out vociferously against child labor while also being reprimanded for his politics by the Wharton School administration. But Nearing's resemblance to Allen (even in physical description) is clear, as is the resemblance between the fictional Ruth Wade and Nellie Seeds, Scott's first wife and a formidable educator and human rights activist in her own right.[24] Allen's decision to remain "in society" and to work with Ruth (who follows him) to invest the workplace with "the spirit of Arden" mirrors Scott's own life in this period. Having already been chastened by Wharton for his views (being denied promotions that he had clearly earned), Nearing worked side by side with Nellie Seeds Nearing (also a PhD), using the academy as a basis for social transformation. The year before drafting "Arden Town," Scott cowrote with Nellie the controversial *Women and Social Progress* (1912).[25] Scott and Nellie enacted in their own lives much of what Fred Allen and Ruth Wade promised to do in their fictional ones.

Nearing's reasons for maintaining a professional life outside Arden, then, were both personal and political, emerging from what he liked to call "the web of circumstance." Effecting social change in the face of unbridled capitalism was not only responsible social behavior; it was also imperative moral behavior. In Nearing's view, such social change was not merely to be modeled through alternative social experiments; it was to be lobbied for by confronting capitalist interests directly, through writing, lecturing, and teaching. Living the Good Life

FIGURE 8.
Scott (far right) in the company of coauthor and economist
Frank Watson and coauthor and first wife, Nellie Seeds, on the
porch of Forest Lodge, Arden, September 1909. Courtesy of
Robert Nearing and the Thoreau Institute at Walden Woods.

at Arden was, for Nearing, not a sufficient response to the social crises he saw
looming beyond the fields. This does not mean that Arden itself was not a compelling "alternative America."[26] But for Nearing, *even* Arden represented a kind
of escapism that, however persuasive, threatened to keep Nearing from his calling to a public life of teaching.

Social Gospels and Socialisms: Nearing's
Early Callings

If there was a religion of nature in the first two decades of the twentieth century, there was also a religion of the city, which seemed better suited to speak
to emerging social crises.[27] In its liberal Protestant form, the movement to hold
Christianity accountable to social problems became known as the Social
Gospel.[28] While many Christians of all persuasions involved themselves in social reform, Social Gospelers distinguished themselves as leaders and thinkers
who placed a premium on social salvation while correspondingly deemphasiz-
ing (though certainly not eliminating) the importance of personal salvation.[29]

While membership in the Social Gospel movement continues to be a matter of historical and theological debate, it included professional ministers and theologians as well as lay social scientists who saw their work as "applied" research in the service of Christian social reform.[30] The work of economist Simon Patten, Nearing's influential teacher at the University of Pennyslvania, falls into this latter category. Patten's writing bears remarkable similarities to Social Gospel texts and sermons of the early twentieth century. Patten and Nearing after him would take aspects of the Social Gospel message into their own work as economists and teachers. Like many Social Gospelers, Patten believed that the "liberating of individual souls" should be accompanied by a social vision grounded in Christianity and at the same time critical of the individualism and social indifference that the institution of Christianity has supported and produced. A closer look at Patten's writing and its influences on Nearing will help us to see the dynamics of this Progressive Era blending of social science and social religion.

In *The Social Basis of Religion* (1911), Patten's intention—much in the spirit of the times—is to give religion "a scientific foundation" and to move religious doctrine out of the realm of religious institutions alone and also into that of social science.[31] Patten's agenda, however, clearly goes beyond that of relocating religion under the social science umbrella. In the eighth chapter of his text, entitled "Social Religion," Patten takes the institutional church to task for its failure to create an authentic social religion, a religion of service that has as its best expression "the teachings of Christ." While allowing for contextual factors in the early centuries of Christianity, which originally produced a "state religion" based on war, want, and fear, Patten insists that such religious institutions will ultimately fail to satisfy humanity's "religious instinct," which seeks both "joy and liberty" and "peace and plenty." A religion of service, argues Patten, is a different creature from a religion of sacrifice, which the state religion of Christianity has been historically. He encourages his readers to let go of old notions of Christianity that mistakenly focus on Christ's death and resurrection, a focus that Christ himself would never have wanted. What we need now, Patten urges, is to "find the conditions and institutions" to make a religion of service, Christ's true religion, effective in the world.[32]

While Patten begins his text as a seemingly distanced economist interested in including religion in the emerging discourse of social science, he pushes toward his conclusion with a reformer's voice and a prophetic tone. The traditional religion of personal salvation, founded in the midst of "a world of deficit," is no longer appropriate to the times, writes Patten. In the current age, he argues, economic abundance is rising, and "the basis of enduring progress has been secured," although such progress has not yet touched everyone. In the context of the early twentieth century, before the Second Coming (of which Patten feels assured), Western culture must recognize that another, "purer" religion lies in the background of evangelical faith and institutional religion. The "stable society" of today is helping people "to put into practice doctrines distinctly Christ's. The Holy Spirit he promised us is with us as social spirit. In it we have a natural guide to conduct and an effective stimulus to coöperative action."[33] Here Patten's vision is clearly less concerned with social science in theory than with the making of the "good society," to which the church may or may not chose to contribute. His notion of the millennium is the Social Gospel notion of a "new heaven and a new earth" brought on by compassionate social action in this life.

In sounding the twin notes of progress and crisis and in urging the church to adapt to the demands of the times, Simon Patten sounds much like the leading—and perhaps most radical—Social Gospel reformer, Walter Rauschenbusch. Four years prior to the publication of Patten's book, Walter Rauschenbusch published *Christianity and the Social Crisis* (1907), which gained a wide reading and an unexpectedly positive public reception. In his explication of the notion of social religion, Rauschenbusch offers a history, a diagnosis, and a cure for the disease of contemporary culture that seems to anticipate Patten's approach. Like Patten, Rauschenbusch understands primitive Christianity—under the "fresh impulse" of Jesus—to be "filled with social forces." But as the church evolved as an institution, Rauschenbusch argues, it developed modes of Christian living that took Christians away from the arena of social concerns. Asceticism, "the law of sacrifice," and individualistic religion may all have been appropriate to an earlier age, writes the Baptist minister, but they are inadequate to the conditions of modern life. Like Patten in *The Social Basis of Christianity*, Rauschenbusch not only urges that social religion is a moral necessity for contemporary society but also maintains that the church itself will lose if it does not take social religion as its path. "This is the stake of the Church in the social crisis," he writes. "If society continues to disintegrate and decay, the Church will go down with it. If the Church can rally such moral forces that injustice will be overcome and fresh red blood will course in a sounder social organism, it will itself rise to higher liberty and life."[34]

Patten and Rauschenbusch see the turn to social religion as being simultaneously good for society and good for the church. Their writings reveal a slight difference of emphasis, however, a difference, perhaps, that bespeaks the distinction between the economist and the theologian or the optimist and the cautious realist. In Patten's view, society will improve—"move toward its utopia"— with or without religion. For Rauschenbusch, society cannot be redeemed without religion, though this religion must constantly "adjust itself" to new social facts in order to be effective.[35] Despite this difference, both writers sound the typical notes of Progressive reformers—concern about crisis, confidence in reform—and both warn that the church will lose if it does not adopt social religion.

While both Patten and Rauschenbusch appeal to the institutions they are trying to reform, Nearing, in his works on social religion, pays more attention to why the church may not be fit at all to respond to the social crises of the day. His intentions are to call Christians to the "true religion" of Christ, whether or not the institution of the church approves. At a speech to the Society of Friends in 1910, Nearing provoked and angered his audience by suggesting that they played a role in furthering the oppression of their neighbors. In *Social Religion* (1913), the book inspired by the occasion of this speech, Nearing adopts a prophetic tone. He warns his comfortable audience: "[If] you could know, if you could secure but an inkling of the real world, perhaps you might look about and see that because you are in the light, you cast a shadow, and that, because you take more than your share of the light, others must be content with darkness."[36] Drawing on the religious imagery of darkness and light, Nearing calls on his privileged audience to look first into the recesses of their own souls and to contemplate the consequences of their actions. Social religion must begin with self-reflection and an understanding of one's own complicity. From self-reflection, it must then turn to action on behalf of the down-trodden and, finally, to reconceptualizing and re-creating society such that it will provide opportunities for people of all classes to enjoy physical, psychological, and spiritual vitality. In what will later become signature phrasing (in terms of his economy of thought and expression), Nearing sums up the practice of social religion as follows: "1. Clean Living. 2. Social Service. 3. Social Justice."[37]

When conveyed by such a bare-bones formula, Nearing's understanding of social religion may seem little different from a secular social program with a call for personal morality thrown in for good measure. Such diction belongs to Nearing the social scientist as well as to Nearing the man of a few well-chosen words. Throughout the text of *Social Religion*, however, the strongest voice is of Nearing the preacher. While Nearing addresses his audience "as an economist, not one versed in theology," he keeps the life of Jesus at the center of his argument, claiming that "if the church wishes to live up to the ideals of its Founder, it must cease dogmatizing and, in pursuance of Jesus' example, it must preach, heal and teach."[38]

Not surprisingly, Nearing organizes his book both scientifically and sermonically. In his social science mode, he lays out the thesis to be proved (that the practice of Jesus' social teachings are urgently needed) as well as the one to be disproved (that America is a land of plenty). He then goes on to give the factual evidence supporting the notion that American society is in a state of crisis.

He systematically addresses the myriad social problems facing the underclass: inadequate diet, motherless children, child labor, tenement housing, overwork, unemployment, job-related injury, and the general physical and psychological destruction of American youth. He concludes by summing up what social religion looks like in both theory and practice and by advising the Christian church of its true, and long ignored, social responsibility.

At the same time that Nearing delivers over two hundred pages of hypothesis, evidence, and conclusion, he also structures his work around the Bible. His texts for the occasion are several, but the most persistent three are the story of Cain and Abel, Jesus' vilification of the scribes and Pharisees, and the parable of the Good Samaritan. Nearing chides his readers for failing to be their "brothers' keeper" abroad and, more important, at home. He quotes Matthew 23 extensively, informing his audience that the scribes and the Pharisees, much like his audience, "had cast aside their obligations to the society of which they had formed an essential part and . . . [had] squandered the substance of the nation on the one hand, and debased its religion on the other."[39] Above all else, he holds up the model of the Good Samaritan and then asks: "Suppose that Jesus should come to America to-night—to one of our great cities. . . . Would he enter the sumptuous churches? . . . Beautiful buildings, exquisite windows, divine singing—but how was that church built?. . . . Did you drop an offering into the collection box? You thought that you were dropping in silver and gold, but it was the bloody sweat of a fellow being, laboring hopelessly beside the roar of the blast furnace—sacrificed on the altar of industrial progress."[40] Nearing accuses his readers of behaving more like the priest and the Levite—or like the scribes and Pharisees—than like the Samaritan, yet he acknowledges that they are blinded by the myth of American prosperity and so first need the scales lifted from their eyes.

As Nearing begins his chapter "Social Religion in Theory," he returns again to the Good Samaritan tale. As his readers might anticipate, he now calls them to take up the Samaritan's role. In retelling the tale, however, he emphasizes that the churchly model of caring for the sick and wounded is inadequate to the task. The Nearing version, betraying the leanings of the soon-to-be socialist, seeks to probe the social forces that made the parable possible: "A man went down from Jerusalem to Jericho and fell among thieves. Who were those thieves? Was their headquarters in the Temple at Jerusalem? Did the leaders among the Scribes and Pharisees hold stock? Were they protected from molestation by the payment of a fat fee to the Roman governor? . . . Why were they thieves? Did they have the opportunity to seek honest employment or was this the slack season in the industrial world?"[41] Nearing's parable of the Good Samaritan goes one step further than Jesus' own. It tells not only the story but also the story behind the story. In so doing, it also prepares for a slightly different lesson. If Nearing's initial message is not enough to cause a stir, the author does not hesitate to drive the point home: Jesus' parable is incomplete; not only is the tale more complicated than it seems, but also the Samaritan is not as "good" as he appears. Nearing continues: "On the following day . . . the Samaritan took out two pence and gave them to the landlord. Where did he get the two pence? Was he a stockholder in a thieving company which was at that moment operating on the roads of Samaria, or did the money represent the exploitation of a hundred slaves toiling endlessly for an exacting master? Was he on his way to collect rents from his unsanitary tenements in Jericho, or was this philanthropist deriving his income from man-destroying industries?"[42] From today's perspective, Nearing's tale almost reads as a parody of Progressive Era social thought, interpreted for a Christian audience. But the original speech had sparked rage and incredulity, thus inciting the author to produce a longer text that could enumerate and footnote the social facts behind the theory.

In the historical moment in which the speech was given, one can only imagine that those not personally threatened by Nearing's attack on their ways of living would have been highly motivated by the reading of the gospel that Nearing gave. Indeed, such readings (though not always so radical) were typical of the Social Gospel movement as a whole and part of its appeal. While Social Gospelers challenged their audiences to reform their lives and work for social change, they also appealed to those audiences by rendering the Christian message in precise, tangible, present-minded terms. Some who supported this movement—regardless of whether they actually became involved in social service—often did so because the Social Gospel was immediately graspable in a way that more traditional, doctrinal Christianity was not. The immense popularity of Charles Sheldon's novel In His Steps: What Would Jesus Do? was indicative of this broad enthusiasm for the updating of Jesus' message.[43] In many ways, Nearing's Social Religion—though hardly fictional—carried with it the same blend of urgency, immediacy, and drama that made Sheldon's novel so gripping. While Sheldon leaned more to the conservative and "personal reform" side of the Social Gospel continuum, he shared with Nearing the ability to portray social problems in terms of individual, three-dimensional cases and to imagine how Jesus would respond to such cases.

What distinguishes Nearing from Sheldon, and even from the more radical Rauschenbusch, however, is that Nearing's social vision led him away from the church and, ultimately, from the use of Christian language altogether. A theological clue to Nearing's emerging dissent from all things Christian can be found in two almost casual refinements of phrase in the theoretical chapter of Social Religion. Referring to Jesus' condemnation of the scribes and Pharisees, Nearing assures his readers that Jesus was not abandoning theology as such and that the content of Jesus' religious theory can be found in the twin exhortations to "Love Thy God" and to "Love Thy Neighbor as thyself." Nearing reformulates these dicta into his theory of social religion, which has two components: "Belief in God and Belief in Men." Explicating his first principle, he writes: "We are to found our lives on God—good—a spirit that must be worshipped in spirit and in truth. We are to believe in God—that is, we are to believe in Good, Truth, Beauty—in all of the great beneficent forces of the universe."[44] For the Christian audience focusing on the lessons of Jesus, Nearing's theological reconstructions might slip by unheeded, but to the careful reader it is clear that in spite of Nearing's Christian language, the traditional Christian notion of God has been changed—by the addition of a second o—to a more universal, ethical one: God as the spiritual representative of the Good, the True, and the Beautiful.

Love of God, Nearing subsequently notes, must first be expressed through love of man, for "if a man cannot love his brother, whom he has seen, how can he love God whom he has not seen?"[45] Nearing's theology, then, begins with a call to believe in humanity and to foster beneficence and beauty among humanity in the present world. The realization of the best of life on earth—through "works" of social service—will serve as an act of faith in God, who is the symbol of the high ideals of Goodness, Truth, and Beauty. Here, in nascent form, is Scott Nearing's recipe for the Good Life. While later in Nearing's life even the use of the term *God* will be largely eliminated—or expansively defined as "All-That-Is"—here God and the Good are rhetorically and conceptually intertwined.[46] The only religion is social religion, and while Christ is retained as hero and exemplar, more evangelical notions of Christian life (as one of personal redemption) and of a Christian God (as a personal force of salvation acting through Jesus) are radically overhauled.

From Social Gospel to "Free Radical": Nearing's Disenchantment

In the early period of Nearing's life—when he was still comfortable with the use of the term *God* (even while redefining it)—the young teacher's greatest concerns with "religion" had to do with the church as an institution. While Nearing would follow Patten and Rauschenbusch in their insistence that Jesus was the proper exemplar for the ideals and actions of social reform, he would not join them in defending the Social Gospel as being "good for the Church." For Nearing, such an argument ultimately constituted needless bowing to an institution inherently bound to the structures of capitalism and therefore determined by capitalist interests.[47] Since true social religion was a form of radicalism, it could progress only so far if promoted within the confines of the church alone. In Nearing's view, the church as an institution could not be capable of true radical action, a position similar to the one held today by Wendell Berry.

Nearing's critique of the church would lead him down several ideological and institutional paths before bringing him, ultimately, to reject all but his own inner promptings about the nature of truth and the responsibility of living rightly. But in reviewing Nearing's journey from the Social Gospel to socialism, communism, and eventually a self-constructed identity as a "free radical," my intent is not to give a biographical overview per se. Instead, I want to point to the particularly religious aspects of Nearing's early life and thinking, which help us to understand his later turn to homesteading as a religious choice.

Well before writing *Social Religion*, Nearing had already parted ways with the conventional church in many respects. He recalls that as a high school student he rejected much Christian theology "because of its discrimination against the 'heathen' who made up the majority of mankind."[48] More important, his early interest in a career in ministry was shattered when his role model for responsible ministry, Russell Conwell, betrayed significant social commitments in a way that struck Nearing to the core. As a young man, Nearing had become heavily involved in Conwell's Grace Baptist Temple. He attended services, taught Sunday school, joined the congregation, and became a leading member of the local Christian Endeavor Society. Nearing was particularly attracted to Conwell's church because of the minister's stated commitments to "preaching, teaching, and healing" in the spirit of Jesus. Conwell had used his personal fortunes to establish a community center at the church as well as Temple College (where Nearing occasionally taught) and Samaritan Hospital, in Philadelphia. In the earliest years of his involvement with the church, Nearing was not yet at the stage at which he would suspect that those "dropping gold" in the offering box were also dropping in "the bloody sweat of the laborer"; nor was Conwell yet preaching his renowned "Acres of Diamonds" sermons, which argued that increased wealth was a positive indicator of God's approval, a formula that delighted Christian businessmen while dismaying progressive reformers.[49] Nearing was attracted to this church and this minister because of the seeming alliance they fostered between following Jesus' message and enacting that message through social service. What Nearing soon discovered, however, was that the social services promoted by Conwell's church came with strings attached.

In 1904, as part of a research project for a political science class at the Wharton School, Nearing began to inquire into the machine politics that were ruling the city of Philadelphia. Among other lessons learned, Nearing discovered that in exchange for the promised political support of one of Philadelphia's most esteemed public figures, the then U.S. senators (Matthew Quay and Boies

Penrose) ensured that institutions such as Conwell's hospital and college received generous portions from the public coffers. While recognizing the worth of Conwell's projects, Nearing could not abide the political process by which they were supported. Young Nearing became involved in reform efforts to clean up Philadelphia politics (particularly the practice of ballot stuffing in the Fifth Ward) and was delighted when Russell Conwell's name appeared on a minister's committee engaged with these reforms. But by the Sunday after Conwell's name was circulated in the newspapers, the machine politics had proved its strength, and the church, its weakness. "I have no idea who saw him or what was said," writes Nearing in his autobiography, "but I was in church when Dr. Conwell . . . withdrew his name from the Committee and said that Philadelphia was one of the best governed cities of its size in the United States. . . . I walked out of Church that morning never to return, and never again to join a religious organization."[50]

For Nearing, this event of personal and social betrayal would be the beginning of the end of any optimism regarding Christianity. While *Social Religion* was an appeal to church members, it placed priority on the life of Jesus and treated the institutional church in a skeptical light. Two years after publishing *Social Religion*, Nearing took his critique to a new level, bringing his questions, concerns, and challenges to the public face and popular icon of evangelical religion, Billy Sunday. Deploying his now well-honed charges against a personalized religion that ignored public duty, Nearing exhorted Sunday to keep the tone of his revivals but change the tune:

> Turn your oratorical brilliancy for a moment against low-wages, over-work, unemployment, monopoly, special privilege and the other forces which grind the faces of the poor. . . . The well-fed people, whose ease and luxury are built upon this poverty . . . sit in your congregations, contribute to your campaign funds, entertain you socially, and invite you to hold prayer meetings in their homes. . . . Before you leave Philadelphia, will you speak these truths? Dare you preach them from your pulpit? . . . While exploitation and social injustice remain, the Kingdom of God never can come on earth and never will.[51]

Sunday's response, reprinted in the *North American* alongside Nearing's letter, was both perfunctory and predictable. "I hold these problems will solve themselves, if capital and labor come to God and accept Jesus Christ as their savior from sin," the evangelist replied. "That's what I'm here for, to preach the atoning blood of Jesus. And I won't permit anyone to get me off that purpose."[52] In the years following the publication of *Social Religion*, public occasions, such as Billy Sunday's visit to Philadelphia, gave Nearing the impetus and the opportunity to develop his earlier skepticism of the church into a carefully considered, but no-holds-barred, criticism.

In 1917, Nearing joined the Socialist Party. In so doing, he left behind the paths laid by his mentors while carrying with him the essential spiritual supplies they had given him. In reflecting on the influence of Simon Patten on his work as a teacher, writer, and activist, Nearing retells a story that sums up his attitude toward the church and, eventually, toward all institutions. Nearing tells the parable of a community located on a cliff whose best and brightest were continually lost by going too near the edge and falling onto the rocks below. Some members of the community raised money to buy an ambulance that would help care for the injured; others argued that building a fence would get at the root of the problem. "Patten was [usually] an ambulance driver . . . ," Nearing notes amid general praise of Patten's tireless labor. "Radicals insisted on a fence. For years I subscribed figuratively, and literally, to the ambulance fund. Gradually I began to turn my thoughts to fence building."[53] For Nearing, fence building meant looking outside existing social institutions in order to solve social problems effectively. The biggest social problem was the problem of capitalism and its attendant control of the distribution of wealth. From the primary evil of unrestrained market competition came a host of evil progeny: crowding in cities, public health crises, prostitution, inadequate nutrition, poverty, and the abuse of the environment. In Nearing's view, the ills created by capitalism were ultimately fatal ones. They ranged from the private anomie that might cost one individual's life, to global warfare, which could cost the lives of multitudes.

It is no surprise that Nearing found in socialism a philosophy and a program for political action that in many ways could replace, and transcend, the role that Russell Conwell's church and Simon Patten's teaching had played in his early life. Like many of his fellow socialists, Nearing carried into his new political identity the longing for a religious life that his sense of social responsibility had forced him to repudiate.[54] In his newly radicalized life, however, Nearing's religious longings would remain submerged, implicit, and only vaguely articulated. The language of God and church was now used only to negative effect.

In 1922, Nearing took up the question "Can the church be radical?" in a public debate with John Haynes Holmes, the Unitarian minister of the liberal Community Church in New York. Nearing's answer to the question was an unabashed, unapologetic no. The church may be beautiful and charitable, Nearing allowed. It may be a source of inspiration and of liberal intentions and actions. "But it is as hard for the Church to be radical as it is for water to be dry . . . ," he maintained. "Every man must be his own radical."[55] Nearing's conclusion was prescriptive for the ills of society and predictive of his own life path. Five years before his debate with Holmes, Nearing lost his professorial position at the University of Toledo for taking a public stance against United States participation in World War I.[56] In 1915, two years before losing his job in Toledo, Nearing had been fired by the University of Pennsylvania for campaigning against child labor. Already, he had been forced to make his way in the world on his own, writing books and giving public lectures. In the ten years after delivering his verdict on the radicalism of the church, Nearing would run for Congress on the Socialist ticket and lose to Fiorello LaGuardia; he would author (or coauthor) sixteen books but would be dropped by the Macmillan Company—again for his antiwar stance—and blacklisted in the publishing world. Finally, he would join the Communist Party, only to be expelled for writing the *Twilight of Empire* (1930), which strayed from party lines, particularly in its pacifism, idealism, and implicit religious dimensions.[57] Nearing's only palpable victory would be his acquittal from charges of disloyalty to the United States, charges for which he was brought to trial after the 1917 publication of his antiwar pamphlet *The Great Madness*.[58]

By 1931, Nearing found himself living in a cold-water flat on the Lower East Side, reconsidering the "problem of living" from a deeply personal standpoint. With the energetic and inspirational Helen Knothe newly at his side, Nearing decided to embark on a new "experiment in living": homesteading in New England. In a strict sense, the problem was economic: how to create a livelihood without professional status and institutional support. But underlying the economic problem of making a living was the religious problem of "right livelihood": how to live in the world in a way that promotes the good, the true, and the beautiful, those values that Nearing had equated with God—and later transformed into "the Good"—when he authored *Social Religion*. The solution of homesteading was clearly an economic one. Homesteading provided a means of subsisting without requiring a paycheck from a capitalist institution to which one had to be ideologically beholden. But as was the case with Nearing's earliest thinking on economics, the economics of homesteading was also always religious.

Making the Earth a Better Place: Homesteading as Postreligious Reform

One can almost predict the path of Nearing's departure from the life of Christian service and to that of a "free radical" when reading his highly original portrayal of the afterlife in *Social Religion*. If indeed there is to be an interview at the pearly gates, Nearing warns, the questions will not be along the lines of the fulfillment of the Ten Commandments; rather, Saint Peter will ask: "From what city did you come? . . . What social conditions prevailed in your city? Were the men, women, children, and boarders crowded into small, inadequate living quarters? Was the school-system reaching the children? Was the death-rate high or low? . . . Did the city councils sell franchises? Was the police department in league with vice?" These questions will come unexpectedly to those accustomed to private acts of devotion, but "make no . . . mistake," Nearing warns, "the questions at the gate of Paradise will be social ones, for St. Peter represents Jesus, and Jesus preached a social gospel."[59]

By the time Nearing approached his own death in 1983, the vision of St. Peter was no longer a viable or effective one, either for Nearing personally or for many in the counterculture to whom he spoke. It was replaced by a personal and social vision that was equally bent on reform but no longer concerned with placing that reform in the context of Christian models or even a Christian vocabulary. The message of the late twentieth century was: "The life people have been living is so far away from the real purpose. We've got to stop fooling around and move toward a new way of life. . . . I'd like to get people into the habit of living physically and mentally in such a way that when they get all through, the earth could be a better place to live in than it was. Sit back and be comfortable? That's no way to be. Sit up. Move forward."[60] The call to follow Jesus was eliminated. The call for progress, however, was as urgent as ever. Significantly, the exhortation to move forward involved two core convictions: that a new way of life was possible and that making the earth a better place was the goal to be achieved. In reflecting on the future of American culture, Nearing was also reflecting on his own past. His choice to homestead had resulted in a rebirth, a new way of life, a way of being in the world that made the earth—and the self—a better place in which to live.

The fifty-one years that Scott Nearing spent homesteading are, in many ways, the most crucial ones to consider, though they were less glamorous, less dramatic, and, until the 1970s, less public than the preceding years had been.[61] In Nearing's years of homesteading—which, it is important to note, were also his years of partnership with Helen Knothe—we see the fulfillment of many of the frustrated dreams and desires that had plagued his earlier life.

Like John Burroughs's earlier choice, Nearing's decision to go back to the land was a personal one that "solved" crucial problems of livelihood and of the life of the spirit. In Burroughs's life on the farm and the writing produced there, we have seen a fascinating example of personal pragmatism and theological creativity. Burroughs embraced science and rejected evangelical religion. He then rejected much of industrial life promoted in the name of science and technology, while infusing nature with the capacity for grace and renewal once reserved only for God. Yet while Burroughs's vision of back-to-the-land was a vision that ultimately urged cultural reform, it was hardly a model of radical dissent, as Nearing's was.

Like Burroughs, Nearing embraced science while resisting many of the consequences of a scientific, technological society. He similarly rejected the church, though more for its neglect of society than for its "superstitious" interest in the supernatural. For a time, socialism seemed the ideal solution. As nature did for Burroughs, socialism enabled Nearing to remain a scientist and reject the church while still leading a spiritually charged life. In Nearing's case, religious life consisted in preaching a social gospel of human kindness through radical reform, a social gospel that now no longer had an explicit Christian content. But just as nature (as represented by Arden) was not enough in Nearing's early life, so political identity and political action (whether as a Socialist or a Communist) was not enough in Nearing's midlife. For Nearing, homesteading became—as it did for Burroughs—an ingenious means of negotiating multiple, and sometimes contradictory, impulses. For Nearing, these were: to escape from society while engaging in cultural reform; to resist capitalism while also resisting other popular "isms" promoted in place of capitalism; to live an intellectual life while engaging in physical labor; to reject the church while maintaining a religious sense of vocation and service.

The portraits of the Nearings' homesteading lives given in earlier chapters have already provided us with some sense of the shape and texture of these negotiations and of the unresolved conflicts at work in the daily practice of homesteading, such as the tension between freedom and control or humility and exceptionalism. But here our task is somewhat different; it is to understand homesteading in the historical context of both a life lived and a culture undergoing profound transformations. The intersection of that life and that culture in the first years of the twentieth century meant that going back to nature was not a meaningful option for Nearing, though certain kinds of back-to-nature activities were extremely popular and increasingly available in the general culture. By 1932, however, much that Nearing had worked for had failed in terms of the broad strokes of history. The president who had promised to keep a nation out of war had brought the nation into war. Widespread optimism regarding the promise of market competition was shattered in the economic crash of 1929 and then by the ensuing Depression. Supporters of the Bolshevik ideal had to come to terms with the grim models of reality emerging in Europe: Stalinism in Russia and fascism in Germany. The optimism of the Social Gospelers was being replaced, by the late 1920s, with the cautious realism (some would say pessimism) of the neoorthodox thinkers, who had turned their attentions to the "God beyond God" and so seemed—to those of Nearing's disposition—even less concerned with social problems and human action than even the evangelicals of an earlier age.[62] It was in this historical and cultural context, as well as the context of his own personal and professional disappointments, that Nearing chose to live off the land. To understand the success of this decision in personal, social, and spiritual terms, we need to investigate Nearing's own words about homesteading more deeply.

Grace and Works: Nearing's Conversion

The rationale for homesteading quoted most frequently by the Nearings was "it is better to be poor in the country than in the city," but this seeming "lesser of two evils" approach to major life choices was, as we know, only part of the story. For Scott Nearing, homesteading may have initially been chosen as a reasonable means to earn a living in the face of the professional stalemate in which he found himself, but as a daily practice it became both art and science or, better, a kind of grand experiment in the fine art of living. For Nearing, giving up a life led predominantly in cities involved "major readjustments," but it also involved a freeing departure from the constraints of academic life in the service of an institution.[63] While Nearing began his homesteading experiment in a state of despair about "Western civilization" and his own role in it, he also found the release from his old life to be a uniquely refreshing and creative opportunity. Writing from the perspective of one who had made homesteading a success, Nearing remembered that the downward professional spiral was also an exhilarating promotion into the "College of Hard Knocks." "I found myself in a new incarnation," he wrote, "enthused by the unaccustomed life and enjoying most of its features. *In a very real sense I felt as if I had been born again.*"[64]

The conversion to a new life of "lecturing, writing, gardening and building" was, in many ways, a return to pieces of his old life (childhood years in Morris Run, early gardening and building projects at Arden) but put together in a new way. Outside the city, Nearing found he could achieve "the linking of vocation and avocation that division of labor, specialization, and automation make all but impossible [in city life]."[65] Here, theory and practice could once again be united, as they had been to some extent at Central Manual Training High School and again at Arden. But now these early educational experiences were no longer separated from the rest of life, as "schooling" or vacation time. They were part and parcel of a means of livelihood that proved to be "educative, interesting, health-giving, exciting and inspiring."[66]

To find a way of life that is personally satisfying may be enough of a struggle—and enough of a reward—for many individuals and, indeed, for many of the homesteaders profiled here. But for Scott Nearing—and in later years, for

Helen as well—personal satisfaction was only a first step. Over the years, the Nearings' work of homesteading was refined from a first-order means of subsistence to a well-articulated example of the Good Life incarnate. The Nearings' own testaments about the value of their work in Vermont and Maine are often, at first blush, humble and modest. They remark, in more than one text, that homesteading "proved to be a means of steadying and stabilizing one household in a teetery world, and of providing the members of that household with an economic base from which they could make their leisure time contribute toward the advancement of the general welfare."[67] But for Scott Nearing especially, homesteading was a social science experiment that, when proven to be worthy, could be systematized and presented to a larger audience so that anyone could do the same." Though written with a sense of urgency, encouragement, and appreciation of detail that made them more compelling reading than some of Nearing's more abstract economic and political texts, the "Good Life" books served, in effect, as extended lab reports on the experiments that the Nearings undertook.

Yet the Nearing approach to homesteading went beyond the idea of experimentation and reporting. It became the basis for a call to "go and do likewise."[68] The point was not simply to prove that a largely self-sufficient life is possible but furthermore to demonstrate that an alternative to the dominant ethos of capitalism and consumerism is desirable on a large, cultural scale. For Nearing the economist, homesteading was an experiment in putting into practice the theoretical values of a use-economy that he believed should become the new norm.

The economic and political goals of homesteading were first articulated by Nearing in Reducing the Cost of Living (1914). The argument laid out here is a fascinating exercise in making distinctions concerning nature and land, distinctions that are revealing, among other things, of the extent to which Nearing's presumed "environmentalism" had yet to be fully developed. Casting back-to-nature urges as synonymous with Rousseauian notions of the noble savage, Nearing warns against those hoping to return to a time before civilization had imposed its deleterious effects. Getting back to nature in a strict sense, writes Nearing, will only put humanity in a state of fear of and dependence on the natural world, with the end result being the "eye for an eye" competition that leads to social disintegration. "Mankind goes in only one direction, forward," he proclaims, using an expression that would become a trademark refrain: "all that the past can hold is less to his advantage than the good works the present and the future can afford." He continues, "No hope lies in getting back to nature. There are no possibilities in the restoration of competition. The welfare of the future depends on man's ability to continue his subjugation of nature." Nearing's vision of the future, in this early articulation, places confidence in a utilitarian approach to nature of which the countercultural fans of the Nearings were seldom aware.[69]

At the same time, however, the title that Nearing gives to this chapter is "The Simple Life," and while extolling the "uses" of nature, he also is prescient in his critique of consumer culture, claiming, "The well-to-do have been led by a will-o'-the-wisp called 'the possession of things.' "[70] His subsequent chapter, "Back to the Land," foresees a solution to rising consumerism that transcends mere economic good sense. "There is salvation in getting back to the land," he writes. "A small part of this salvation lies in a reduction in the cost of living. A great part of it lies in self-service. . . . Back to the land, back to service, means back to a complete life."[71] Like Burroughs, who argues that Adam and Eve ought to do some work around the place, Nearing resists back to nature if it is regressive, fosters dependence and competition, or allows for too many free rewards. Back to nature works only if it is back to the land, where one works for oneself and cooperatively while guarding against turning the farm into another kind of factory.

In *The Making of a Radical*, Nearing revisits these early ideas when reflecting on his purposes in homesteading: "We aimed to be as free as possible from the market and from wagery. Price-profit economy presupposes the exchange of labor-power for cash; the payment of a part of the cash in taxes in exchange for regimentation, and the expenditure of the remainder in the market for food, clothing, gadgets and other commodities. The individual who accepts this formula is at the mercy of the labor market, the commodity market and the State."[72] By reducing their cost of living and spending only one dollar out of every four in the consumption of goods, the Nearings were able to free themselves to a considerable extent from the price-profit economy that they found personally constraining and morally reprehensible.

The gains achieved through the creation of a use-economy began with the direct advantages of moving from the position of a passive consumer at the mercy of the market to a producer-consumer who could remain often (though not always) impervious to market forces.[73] But the Nearings' economic experiment—like other homesteading models discussed here—was one that involved a fully elaborated theory of *oikus*. The benefits of freeing oneself from "a competitive, industrialized social pattern" were not only economic in the strict sense but were also expanded to include the physical, psychological, moral, and spiritual.[74] In the deepest sense, life lived in the context of a reconstructed, nature-centered household was a life of renewed spiritual commitments. These commitments were to both nature and society. They involved the continual process of recognizing the ultimate authority and goodness of nature and simultaneously shaping nature for human good. By living rightly in the natural world, the Nearings argued, one could transform society to function again like community while also restoring the self.[75]

Nature and the Sacred Economy

The commitment the Nearings made in 1932 was a commitment to a life that opposed the sins of society that do harm to the human spirit. The Nearings named four "besetting evils" they felt they had freed themselves from by taking up homesteading: "Greed for things . . . and power to push around our fellow human beings; . . . the hurry and noise connected with the desire to get ahead of other people; . . . the anxiety and fear which are inevitable accompaniments of the struggle for wealth and power; . . . the multiplicity, complexity, and frustrating confusion which result from the crowding of multitudes of people into small areas."[76] The quest for "the good" in living, then, began with a model of how best to resist evil. Indeed, Scott Nearing opens his description of homesteading in *Man's Search* by distinguishing himself and Helen from many of their family and friends "who were more or less dissatisfied with the best that western civilization had to offer" but whose slogan was "sufficient unto the day is the evil thereof." In contrast, writes Nearing, "we were unwilling to accept evil on any terms . . . even if that meant a rather complete estrangement from civilization."[77] For Helen and Scott Nearing, resisting evil and embracing an alternative economic system went hand in hand. While they claimed to be engaged in a modest experiment, clearly they were also engaged in home-based moral and social reform. If homesteading proved effective in one household, it could model alternatives to Western civilization, from which the Nearings had increasingly divested themselves.[78] While recognizing that homesteading was, by nature, a small-scale and often individualized and isolating enterprise, the Nearings felt that family-run homesteads modeled the good society toward which contemporary culture must work. It was not for everybody, they insisted time and again, nor would it be a cure-all for all the ills of modern society. On the other hand, in a turbulent time of "major social changeover from western civilization to a workable alternative," homesteading, in the Nearings' eyes, offered a means of stability and a model for the future. It may well get the "votaries [of an alternative social structure] through the transition period . . . to a new cultural level," Scott proposed.[79] Although homesteading may have been a pragmatic solution to the particular constellation of economic and professional constraints that Scott Nearing faced in 1932, it also became a social program that, in many ways, embodied the aims of the Social Gospel while taking it and one of its most passionate advocates out of the church and out of the city.

Leaving both city and church, Nearing nonetheless reproduced on the homestead those aspects of urban reform and religious work that were most significant to him. If homesteading served for Scott Nearing as a kind of "social gospel of agriculture," it also served for him as a seminary in the woods, in which he and Helen Knothe were first acolytes and then spiritual leaders.[80] The Nearings' stance in regard to nature, as we have already noted, was nothing if not ambivalent. But Nearing himself notes that in summing up the homesteading experience, "it is hardly possible to overemphasize the importance of this relationship with the earth, its rhythms, seasons and cycles."[81]

One sees in Scott Nearing's reflections on his homesteading life that attaining self-sufficiency, actively resisting capitalism, and modeling and advocating alternatives to dominant ways of living are all crucial to his vision and practice of homesteading. Nature, however, is the first foundation of economic viability, political dissent, and social reform. Without recognizing that one is always "in the arms of mother earth," writes Nearing, "man the seeker" will never meet his dreams and goals. But while resource limits may jolt us into recognizing our reliance on nature, resource dependence is not the only kind of relationship with nature that humans experience. In his most philosophical and sometimes mystical moments, Nearing looks to nature as the embodiment of "All-That-Is"; it not only makes a life of homesteading practically possible but also shapes, invigorates, and gives meaning to that life. At a time when he was most dispirited, Scott plunged his hands into the good earth, and doing so, he later wrote, was "the first and most compelling appeal of country living . . . [for] no city or suburban life that I knew gave any real opportunity to contact and deal extensively with nature, with earth, water, sunshine, air, and the changing seasons." This same sentiment was also expressed by Helen, who often documented a sense of emotional and spiritual renewal whenever they returned from New York to Vermont.[82] If life at Arden had been "in a very real sense . . . a good life in miniature," then the return to nature through homesteading was in a very real sense a reclamation of all that was good and true in Scott's earlier life at Arden. And for Nearing, finding and nourishing "the good" was synonymous with what once was a quest for God.

Nearing's emerging theology of nature (a blend of scientific, mystical, and post-Christian perspectives) peeks through much of his writing; but nowhere is it more explicit than in the novel *Freeborn*, which is among the most neglected of Nearing's works. The story focuses on a sharecropper's son (Jim) who finds the promise of a better life through inspirational teachers, the spiritual powers of the natural world, the loving companionship of female kindred spirits, and the political vision of a just, racially integrated future as advanced by the Com-

FIGURE 9.
Scott Nearing at the Vermont homestead in the 1940s. Courtesy of the
Good Life Center and the Thoreau Institute at Walden Woods.

munist Party. As the novel begins, Jim is struggling to understand the forces that
have kept his family poor and oppressed and made it unlikely that they could
improve their social and economic position. Intelligent and energetic, Jim is the
family's best hope for improvement, but he is skeptical about the value of education in a region where black schools are routinely burned down. He is even
more skeptical about his family's devotion to the church and to God, proclaiming, "Ef God done run de world, he sho' must be white!" While Jim dutifully

FIGURE 10.
Helen Nearing at the Vermont
homestead in the 1940s. Courtesy
of the Good Life Center and the
Thoreau Institute at Walden Woods.

goes to school, attends church, and even participates in Sunday school, he longs
for something more, a something he once experienced as a child, playing by the
river and talking with flowers.[83]

One Easter Sunday, Jim finds himself unwilling to go to church and chooses,
instead, to walk into the mountains searching for the source of a familiar brook.
The choice to go to nature in lieu of church proves to be a life-changing one:

> The spongy mold gave under his feet like a thick luscious carpet. All about him
> bare and brown, the round, straight pine trunks mounted toward heaven. Jim

looked up, awestruck. A lump rose in his throat. He felt as he had felt that first Sunday in church, when he wanted to go up and kneel before Parson Jones. . . . Here was . . . a glimpse of that paradise about which Parson Jones talked so much in that stuffy little church in far away Milltown. . . . But here there was no parson, there was only silence, and the long, tapering stems with their feathery branches and far distant tops. How glad he was, now, that he had decided to spend his Easter Sunday adventuring on the hills.[84]

As Nearing describes it, the world that Jim has just entered is everything that the boy had wanted. It is what Jim once thought church could be, but without the "stuffiness," without the hypocrisy, and without the ever-widening gulf between the promise of otherworldly salvation and the reality of this-worldly oppression.

Jim's experience of nature also mirrors the transformation that came over Fred Allen (Nearing's earlier fictional stand-in) when he first contemplates joining the community at Arden. From Will Evans, Allen first hears a theology of the soil, preached from the strawberry bed: "I like to see strawberries grow. . . . Some philosophers will say it is merely gastronomical anticipations, but I do not believe it for an instance. It is something much better and deeper than that—the response of man's soul to the changes which nature works in the world as well as in man. It is his reaction to growth in any of its myriad forms."[85] In claiming there are "sermons in stones" (a borrowing from either Burroughs or Shakespeare), Evans tells Allen, "The earth has her secrets which she imparts only to those very close to her that they may listen." Allen, himself, later declares, "Nature at Arden was beautiful. Men left her so, loving her, meanwhile, for her beauty. . . . Living close to nature, and close to one another's hearts, the Ardenites stood in relation of peculiar beatitude toward mankind and toward life."[86]

As with the fictional Allen in an earlier period, Jim's discovery in the woods evokes the conclusions that Nearing has come to in the course of his own life. Here again (and again, prompted by the muse of a strong woman in his life) the genre of fiction allows Nearing temporarily to shed the skin of the social scientist who must work from hypothesis, to fact gathering, to conclusion. The mood is one of revelation: emotional, ecstatic, and mysterious. Fittingly, these pages—full of longing for nature—were written in the decade before Nearing began his homesteading project in Vermont and published in the year he made the final move.

Unlike John Burroughs's theology of nature, which often contents itself with the individual's solitary experience in the natural world, Nearing's theology, not surprisingly, still maintains a focus on humanity and on social connection within the context of nature. Even the ecstatic reading of nature that Nearing offers in *Freeborn* is ultimately heightened by the creation of a "comrade" with whom Jim can enjoy this "Holy Land." The character of Sara, in fact, has already discovered and laid claim to the "private preserve" that Jim stumbles upon that Easter morning. She too has forsaken church for this sacred grove, and when Jim questions Sara about why she is not celebrating the most sacred day of the year inside the sanctuary, she replies: "Caise dis yar place is more satisfyin' dan de cabin or de church or anything Ah evah done see in mah whole life."[87] For Jim, the mystical experience in nature is matched by the ecstasy of meeting someone who could also understand. The baptism in nature is made more powerful by the presence of another who—while more boisterous and mischievous— shares his deepest thoughts and feelings. Just as Ruth Wade, in "Arden Town," was modeled on Nellie Seeds, so was Sara a reflection of Scott's love for and kinship with Helen.[88]

Jim's ecstatic experience in the mountain glade and his meeting with a soul mate who shared both his dreamlike visions and real-world opinions are a tale of the triumph of the human spirit amid adversity.[89] Such triumphs, writes Nearing, are the most significant aspects of human experience. He maintains that if the "life of the spirit" is "the crowning glory of human existence," then the nurturing of that life must occur in the context of daily labor on nature's ground and on nature's terms. The flowering of "the All," of both "being and becoming," is dependent on connection with the natural world and at the same time goes beyond the relationship with the earth to include "all life forms (including the human) which inhabit the earth." The work with nature and with fellow humans in the context of nature must be done with "faith, hope, love, purpose, creativity, steadfastness, and patience."[90] Thus reads the revised gospel of nature and culture as Nearing came to experience it in the woods of Vermont and on the coastline of Maine.

· · ·

At the beginning of this chapter I asked not only how and why Scott Nearing responded to the technological advances and cultural preoccupations of the Progressive Era in the way that he did but also what legacies of the Progressive Era were actually preserved within Nearing's own acts of dissent. The dominant stance toward nature was that nature is both a force to be controlled and a source of relief from the manifestations of such control, particularly "the city." The prevailing attitude toward progress (though increasingly under fire) was that it is the inevitable, scientific result of the evolution of society and, at the same time, an indication of God's favorable, immanent work in the world, particularly in America.[91] These normative cultural stances toward nature and toward

FIGURE 11.
Helen sugaring in Vermont in 1937. Cour-
tesy of the Good Life Center and the Thoreau
Institute at Walden Woods.

progress are two aspects of the Progressive Era that are latent in Nearing's life
and work, even amid his protest.

Earlier in this study, I have noted the ways in which the Nearings' attitudes
toward nature were often ironically infused with expressions of rigidity and
control in the face of the natural world. Of course, some of the emphasis on discipline and control are matters of personal psychology and temperament and
are also traceable to nineteenth-century notions of character and self-culture,
which were perpetuated in privileged families such as Scott Nearing's. But in

the broader historical context of the events and cultural forces shaping Nearing's early life, these gestures of control become more clear.

While Nearing most consistently defined himself (and was so defined by others) as curious student and dedicated teacher, he must also be understood in light of the sense of vocation that illuminated his external professional identifications. Nearing was always and everywhere both preacher and scientist. In casting Nearing in the light of these vocations, we can see more readily why the work of homesteading was conducted simultaneously as a science experiment and a living sermon. For Nearing, in homesteading, as in all previous projects, it was important to systematize and correct the gathering of data and the making of hypotheses. It was equally important to provide visible and written testament of how he and Helen were able to create a (Protestant ethic) version of Eden on earth. In Scott's view, nature is part of the "web of circumstance" to which humanity must adjust itself. At the same time, human ingenuity should be used to shape and manage those aspects of the natural surround that can be used for human benefit.[92]

In part character and temperament and in part a strong sense of vocation explain the "controlling" aspects of Nearing's response to the natural world, but so also does his position in history. Homesteading was not wilderness preservation but a kind of "control of nature" that, while working against the rampant control of nature celebrated by the owners of railroads and steel factories, still resonated with some of the underlying tones of the ruling culture. While Nearing rejected much of what the cult of progress had to offer, his underlying belief in human ability and in progress itself never flagged. In this sense, his notion of homesteading—however much it was an act of dissent—was also a variation on existing progressive themes of enacting cultural reform through strenuous moral, political, and physical activity aimed at the larger social good.

> By engaging in spiritual practices, the practitioner
> retreats reflectively from the world in order to
> recognize how it is broken and in need of healing;
> then, in recognition that the world is also worthy
> of healing because of its sacral dimensions, the
> practitioner commits energy to the process of
> healing.
>
> Robert Wuthnow, *After Heaven*

Looking Backward

The explorations of chapters 4 and 5 have served to put the work of home-steading—as presented in the first three chapters—into historical perspective. Burroughs's and the Nearings' homesteading efforts (which taken together span a period well over a century) reveal to us the persistence of homesteading as a cultural gesture or performance, by which I mean not that homesteading is "merely" a gesture or "only" a performance but that the practice of home-steading is one way in which a certain group of people have acted on and in the culture in which they find themselves. Experiencing the world, and sometimes themselves, as broken and out of balance, these farmer-writer-activists have used a consciously created daily life of work in nature as a means of perform-ing spiritual and cultural work on themselves and their worlds.

These chapters have also pursued the ways in which homesteading moves in and out of concert with the dominant preoccupations of a particular historical moment. John Burroughs wrote and farmed as a reader of Emerson, Darwin, and Whitman, one wrestling with both the opportunities and the challenges that a post-Transcendentalist, Darwinian view of nature afforded. As the cen-tury turned, Burroughs struggled to write of nature as a scientist, attempting to resist the pathetic fallacy while also revitalizing and transforming earlier notions of nature as a "book" authored by a Christian God. In his writing, Burroughs collapses the traditional distance between nature and God, making nature (rather than the God or Christ of biblical theology) the center of a deeply embodied religious life, a place in which he was truly "at home." Burroughs's turn to nature ultimately speaks to the larger social and spiritual anxieties of the dawning twentieth century, but his practice of farming (and of writing about farming) was first and foremost a means of rescuing and re-creating the self.

Scott Nearing, in contrast, turned to nature as a disenchanted socialist and social scientist, seeking reenchantment in the unity of nature and culture and of the mind and the body. His message is less one of retreat than one of advance. In Nearing's life, homesteading became a logical alternative to what could not be created (despite religious and political reforms) in the city: a model of good living that was healthy, socially just, economically sustainable, and spiritually centered. For Nearing, the practice of homesteading resolved certain core dilemmas of vocation and "calling," but it was also a way of contributing to his own vision of the good society.

As twentieth-century America moved increasingly in the direction of a secular, pluralistic, and scientific culture, Burroughs and Nearing seemed to be leading the way. They both were overtly scientific in their commitments and anti-institutional with respect to religion. But for Burroughs—despite his public protestations against the religious superstitions of his father's generation—the religious was relocated into the natural world. Walks in nature became a new kind of daily devotion, and the knowledge of nature's seasonal cycles brought a new promise of immortality. For Nearing, the persistence of the religious was less recognizably a hair's breadth away from Protestant Christianity. But by tracing the broader pattern of Nearing's life choices, I have shown how Social Gospel ideals gave way to socialist visions, which in turn gave way to the necessity of finding a personal, practical, noninstitutional, and nonideological means of articulating these visions. The return to nature, for Nearing, was a kind of return home to early experiences of harmony and unity as experienced in childhood and at Arden, a return to the All-That-Is. Beyond this return, the daily practice of homesteading became a new practical and spiritual opportunity—an economic choice but also a ritualization—both for the Nearings and for the pilgrims who pursued them. Homesteading promised to rectify the hypocrisy and social inequities perpetuated by social institutions, including religious ones. It was a means to a life of teaching and activism, but it was also an end.

The life stories of Burroughs and Scott Nearing further remind us of the ongoing, complex relationships among nature, self, and society that the practice of homesteading involves. Moreover, we see the persistence of the religious in the work of homesteading. As we have seen with Burroughs, Nearing, and contemporary examples of homesteading, these negotiations are accented differently and in the context of particular cultural legacies. But how do these dynamics of retreat and reform, of nature and self-culture, and of pursuit of a spiritual life outside traditional institutions play themselves out when we consider a broader range of historical examples? While the Nearings liked to portray themselves as innovators and originals, both they and Burroughs are part of a larger story in which the tension between engagement with and retreat from mainstream culture is constantly at work.

Bolton Hall: "The Wild Joys of Living" and Social Reform

"Hard anxious work, with little to show for it in the end, is the portion of the average man," proclaims Bolton Hall in his 1908 treatise, *A Little Land and a Living.* He continues:

> Life is something that was thrust upon him unasked and must be maintained at any cost. It seldom occurs to him that there is anything either beautiful or wonderful in it. He begins to drudge in youth and for years the daily round of rising un-refreshed from sleep under conditions that make rest impossible, to spend hours in a workshop or factory and then return to his cramped, airless quarters, goes on without hope of change. How incomprehensible to him the joyous cry of Browning "Oh, the wild joys of living!" . . . But it was that these wild joys of living might be more generally known that the "Back to the Land" movement was started. It has gathered force so that now nothing can stop it.[1]

While many in environmental circles have heard of Helen and Scott Nearing, few know the name of Bolton Hall, the reformer who preceded both the Nearings and Ralph Borsodi in advocating homesteading as a solution to the personal and cultural ills of modernity. Hall was born in Ireland in 1854 and immigrated with his parents at the age of thirteen. But his was no post–potato famine relocation; rather, he entered an elite religious and cultural world when his father, John Hall, was called to be the new pastor of the Fifth Avenue Presbyterian Church in Manhattan. Hall grew up in New York City and graduated from Princeton in 1875. Eventually, he became a lawyer but also a labor organizer. He founded the American Longshoremen's Union and, under the influence of the writings of Tolstoy and Henry George, founded the New York Tax Reform Association and, later, the Manhattan Single Tax Club in 1887.

Hall agreed with Henry George's assessment that the social problems of the late nineteenth and early twentieth centuries were the result not of private landownership as such but the ability of landowners to gain significant unearned increments based on where the land was located. Particularly in cities, absentee landlords profited by the rise of land values in response to population growth. The accompanying public investment in community facilities in some areas but not others led to an economic arrangement that continued to broaden the gap between rich and poor. The problem of unearned increments, in turn, promoted the crowding of the poor in cities and the neglect of the land in rural areas. The solution, for George, was to apply a single tax on land (which he saw as a form of rent on land that was by nature not private but common to all people). All other sources of taxation, such as real estate and income tax, in George's view, should be abolished. The resources of the land tax would then flow back to the community, making land and community resources (such as roads and good schools) available to all. George hoped to eliminate the over-growth of "the best" neighborhoods that were affordable only for a minority. His model was one of healthy, workable cities and vibrant small communities in rural areas.

George's vision was capitalist with respect to all other market forces but so-cialist when it came to land and natural resources. Moreover, it was a vision in-formed by what historian John Thomas has called a blend of "romantic liberal imagination" and a "millennialist sensibility."[2] This "Social Christian" vision was formulated into a plan that was theologically derived but could also be ex-pressed in the "coolly abstract terms of political economy." As in Nearing's view (who, as we have seen, was sympathetic to the Georgists), George's model for the future was, in its most passionate expressions, a vision of divinely ordained redemption through a return to the land. Thus, George would ask in *Progress and Poverty*: "Have we made the earth that we should determine the rights of those who after us shall tenant in their turn? The Almighty, who created the earth for man and man for the earth, has entailed it upon all generations of the children of men by a decree which no human action can bar." And in describing a more personal vision of what this economically reformed and socially utopian vision would look like, he spoke of his longing to inhabit a pastoral, eighteenth-century-style haven, neighborly and productive on the scale of a village econ-omy. There he could dwell in a hillside retreat, away from the "fierce struggle of our high civilised life," and be gathered together with those he loved.[3]

With George, Bolton Hall came to believe that everyone should have equal opportunity to the resources of the land, and like George's vision, Hall's was a blend of Enlightenment-style "natural rights" logic with a Romantic, liberal, and increasingly "post-Christian" view of nature's redemptive value. Long be-fore the emergence of contemporary theories of "Gaia" as a living system or neopagan interest in the spiritual life force inherent in the land, Hall spoke of "Mother Earth" and argued for democratic means by which all children could have equal access to this nurturing mother. Anticipating contemporary environmental justice movements by almost a century, Hall also argued that the gifts of nature (viable land, pure water, clean air) should be available to all humans. The foundations for his homesteading projects, then, were an interest in self-sufficiency as a way not only to combat the materialism and unhealthiness of modern, urban life but also to address directly inequities in the distribution of wealth.

At the same time, Hall's call to the soil was recognizably located in a blend of Jeffersonian and Transcendentalist ideas. The result of this creative, intellectual fusion was an often unusual and sometimes even amusing discourse that was one part Karl Marx and one part Ralph Waldo Emerson. Drawing on Emerson directly, for instance, Hall wrote: "Everyone instinctively knows that his natural 'job' is on the land. Those who are engaged in other occupations than tilling the soil, as Emerson says, 'are using a makeshift and are only temporarily excused from their real calling.' " Then, as if presiding at the marriage, Hall proclaims, "Land and labor are wed. Whosoever puts them asunder commits sacrilege; for in their union is health, wealth and happiness—in their severance is disease, glut, and hunger, arrogance and misery." Then setting the sermon aside he proclaims, "Therefore, workers, get land."[4]

Bolton Hall took up George's ideas and helped to put them into practice. In 1910, he founded the Free Acres Association, a single-tax community in Berkeley Heights and Watchung, New Jersey, just over thirty miles west of Manhattan. The community was run as a single-tax colony (although not all of its members were "card-carrying" single-taxers). The land was owned in common and rented for a yearly lease, which was renewable unless the occupant failed to pay the lease, harmed the land, or chopped down trees without permission from the community. As one former member described it, "Free Acres was initially a community of summer residences for New York left-wingers, an odd collection of Greenwich Village artists, actors, intellectuals and 'free-thinkers' who cherished a rugged communing with nature . . . and had a special sensitivity toward the environment well before their time."[5] In the 1920s, it became a more permanent community, as more members began to insulate their homes, install plumbing, and settle in throughout the year. Among its better-known members was the actor James Cagney. Emma Goldman, though not a member, was a close friend of Hall and a regular visitor.[6] By the 1930s, radical New York leftists were joined by German and Jewish immigrants who helped improve the community's infrastructure and provided year-round residential stability. These changes, however, eventually led to a move away from the single-tax structure, to the great distress of Hall, who left in 1936.

Before, during, and after his residency at Free Acres, Hall continued his professional life as a lawyer, but his passion was social reform and experiments in living in direct contact with nature, as was the case at Free Acres. Throughout, Hall's vision was one of radically reformed capitalism rather than socialism, which (like George) he feared might lead to a dangerous level of bureaucratic government control at the expense of individualism. Thus, while he shared the lecture circuit with Goldman, John Reed, and others, he remained a supporter of Jeffersonian-style American individualism and certain aspects of the free market. And while Hall poured much energy into the community at Free Acres, he continued to extend his vision of equal access to land beyond the realm of the nature-seeking, free-thinking elites. In founding the Vacant Lot Associations of New York and Philadelphia, he sought to extend benefits of self-sufficiency and semirural experience to those who needed it most, the poor. It is important to note that Hall interpreted this vision not just in economic but also in spiritual terms. In his conclusion to *Things as They Are* (1908), Hall sums up his advocacy of "little lands" for the masses and anticipates the founding of Free Acres with a blend of radicalism and Christian commitment that is echoed today by farmer-visionaries such as Gene Logsdon and Wendell Berry: "There are three stages of moral regeneration: first, to understand that the present state of the world is hell, that is, injustice; second, to realize that there is a kingdom of heaven,—that is, of justice; and third, to believe that we can get there. After that comes the knowledge of the way."[7] For Hall, "the way" had many facets, including pacifism, birth control, antiimperialism, and a tempered version of capitalism. But the way closest to his heart was to advocate for "a little land and a living." The theories were many, but homesteading was his practice.

Hall's little-lands model was a kind of a modified homesteading, one that involved a much greater proximity to the city than Nearing or even Burroughs would ever have allowed. In 1907, Hall published the popular *Three Acres and Liberty*, in which he set out his plan for social and spiritual renewal. Recognizing that humans are, by nature, "social animals," Hall advocated no large-scale retreat to the backwoods or rolling plains but rather encouraged those who wanted a home and livelihood to live on the city's edge, tilling small lots, eating homegrown fruits and vegetables, and nurturing a reliable market for the surplus.[8] Hall's vision was by no means a revolt against the structures of capitalism as such. While he was disdainful of the exploitative practices of most factory owners, railroad companies, and bankers, he encouraged ways for homesteaders to beat the capitalists at their own game rather than change the rules altogether. Thus, while he emphasized the importance of becoming one's own producer, he did not advocate a use-economy to the same extent as the Nearings did.[9]

Self-sufficiency, for Hall, did not mean that the homesteader should "do everything" himself or herself. In the midst of Hall's treatise on homesteading, these strands of elitism show through the cloth of reform. Perhaps anticipating the protestations of his readers, Hall writes: "Those who will read this book can earn more with their heads than their hands. . . . [It] is not necessary, in order to cultivate a little land successfully, that you should work all day on your hands and knees. . . . [When] there is a large job to be done, you can hire Italians or Germans to do it better and cheaper than you can do it yourself."[10] In Hall's view, while there is value in making one's livelihood from the earth (particularly for the poor), it is equally valuable to do so on a part-time basis while pursuing other work and to rely on wage workers to do the unpleasant and monotonous tasks, such as weeding. Unlike some homesteaders, Hall did not seem to feel that the "lowliest" of tasks could be made into artistry, nor was he concerned that in "freeing" some workers from the factory, he might be enslaving still others to wage labor on the farm.[11] In these respects, Scott Nearing and other homesteaders would take issue with Hall. Working out "pure" practices of self-sufficiency, either to develop oneself spiritually or to foster intimacy with nature, is not central to Hall's work.

The historian David Shi has praised Hall for his "vision of a nation of homesteaders liberated from the corporate culture," but he does not seem to account for the problem of Hall's model of middle-class homesteading in terms of its implicit elitism and underlying commitments to the market.[12] Not only did Hall approve of the hiring of (largely immigrant) help, but also he constantly advises his readers on how best to make a profit, how to outcompete neighboring gardeners (by applying fertilizer and harvesting early), and how to corner the market on particular crops.[13] In addition, Hall was not above small-scale land speculation as a means of ultimately acquiring a profitable plot of land on which to build and farm.[14] Finally, Hall seemed only partly concerned with the standard-of-living sacrifices that might come with the acquisition of land. He writes: "[The farmer] can live in a cheap shack [until] he accumulates enough for proper buildings. Many of the successful vacant lot farmers live in a tent or in shanties made of old boxes and the like." While recognizing that improvements in steam, electricity, and telephone communications made it easier for the business class to maintain a job in town and also to cultivate a successful garden at home, Hall did not seem as concerned that his more working-class homesteaders might not have the same amenities.[15] Indeed, Free Acres began with little more than tent platforms, an arrangement that was charmingly rustic for wealthy summer denizens but less so for those who had to live there year-round.

But in noting Hall's comparatively accommodationist stance toward capitalism and consumer culture (relative to the Nearings'), I do not mean to overstate the case. While Hall mixed and matched versions of homesteading such that the costs and benefits did not apply equally to everyone, he did present a carefully researched and tested alternative to the "city squalor versus country drudgery" debates of the time. And while his friend Emma Goldman raised her eyebrows at certain aspects of his elitism ("he had entirely emancipated himself from his highly respectable background except for his . . . frock-coat, high silk hat, gloves and cane"), Hall apparently was aware of his need to negotiate between several worlds. "Don't you see it is my silk hat that gives my speech importance?" was his apparent reply to Goldman.[16] To a greater extent than Nearing, in fact, Hall remained active in promoting homesteading as not only a choice for himself but also a viable social program. In describing his vacant lot efforts at urban reform, Hall provides both compelling anecdotes and hard numbers to argue for the benefits of providing the underclass with the means to produce their own food and, thus, gain some element of control over life and livelihood.[17]

A Return to "the Father's Field"

While Hall did not follow in his father's footsteps professionally, the influence of his formal religious upbringing reverberates throughout his activism and his prose. Like John Burroughs, Hall was ambivalent about traditional Christianity and quickly became impatient with "superstition." Hall eagerly embraced reason as his preferred spiritual path. But, also like Burroughs, his rationalist view of life was infused with religious sensibility and moral earnestness. He was a post-Christian lawyer and moral reformer in the same way that Burroughs was a post-Christian naturalist and Scott Nearing a spiritually motivated, but ultimately anti-institutional, social scientist.

Hall's religious improvisations between his father's professional Presbyterianism and his own more eclectic spiritual vision emerge from a variety of sources. In 1913, for instance, Hall wrote about his own experience with death and loss in a manner that is revealing of his intellectual and spiritual negotiations between the realms of faith and reason. Hall urges his readers neither to "curse God" nor to find "comfort in belief without regard to reason" in the face of death.[18] He advises, instead, a reading of death as "natural" ("a look at the forest or at the garden will show us that it is just as natural for the young and strong or the immature to die"). "If the clouds of bereavement can be made transparent by reason so that the sunshine of love can break through," he writes, "we shall see the way to deal with other griefs and fears." For Hall, even during the most excruciating of life experiences, religion remains "one's theory or view of life as distinguished from mere blind belief," and God is defined as "whatever we may call the Power or Force that brought us up from earth."[19] Physical immortality, Hall argues, is a vain longing that, if it *could* become true on earth, would only result in overpopulation, social disorder, and limitations on spiritual progress. Death, in this reading, is something altogether natural and is to be embraced as a means by which the life force on earth can be renewed continually.[20]

Little is known biographically about the details of Hall's break with formal Presbyterian theology or how this shift may have affected his relationship with his father. The language of his many texts, however, consistently reveals a discomfort with formal Christian doctrine, a welcoming attitude toward open, rationalist, universal language about God, and an engagement with the religious traditions of the East (especially Buddhism). At the same time, Hall's interest was more in broadening and deepening the biblical tradition than in rejecting it entirely. In his time, in fact, Hall's most well-known publication was *The Living Bible* (1928). The drafts of this revision of the King James translation resemble something akin to "the Jefferson Bible"; Hall expurgates and adjusts the text to present it as a rational document emphasizing the positive potential of humanity and the promise of a reformed kingdom of heaven on earth, a vision in keeping with the Social Gospel tradition, but—in Hall's hands—even less distinctly "Christian."[21]

Hall also developed his own version of the Shorter Catechism with the subtitle "Natural Religion," in which he provides his own answers to theological questions together with "proofs" selected from the Christian scriptures. In this reconceived theological dialogue, Hall's unique blend of liberal Christianity, rationalism, and humanism again becomes clear, as when he answers the question of how we may become one with God by suggesting not only meditating on scripture but also turning to "our minds," "the works of nature," and "the Spirit within ourselves."[22]

Hall's moral commitments were Christian in origin but not doctrinal in expression. While his arguments for vacant lot tilling and "commuter homesteading" are based on firm economic principles—particularly the importance of turning consumers and "the consumed" into full- or part-time producers—his thrust is ultimately moral and spiritual. Not surprisingly, then, Hall's "secular," reform-minded books retain the sermonic style and structure in which he was well schooled. He closes one chapter of *A Little Land and a Living*, for instance, by declaiming: "Earth is your Mother; honor her that your days may be long in the land that the Lord thy God giveth, for all the children of men."[23] Similarly, while the majority of *Three Acres* consists of how-tos, Hall's occasional philosophical departures from the problem of means show that his understanding of ends is based on a creative blend of religious sentiment and natural law argument. The practical ideal of homesteading is to find a farm, produce crops, and acquire the leisure time to enjoy the fruits of one's labors. The spiritual ideal is "to live in harmony with . . . Nature's laws and wisdom . . . and in measure comprehend the purposes of nature." The return to the farm may constitute a wise investment in what Hall takes to be the ultimate source of all "capital," but it is also a spiritual return to the garden of human beginnings.[24]

Taken together, Hall's "homesteading" texts—*Three Acres and Liberty* (1907), *A Little Land and a Living* (1908), and *Life, and Love and Peace* (1909)—constitute a series of calls to the homesteading life, calls that, interestingly, trace a pattern from the highly pragmatic to the essentially religious. The philosophical meditations in *Three Acres* are few and far between, for the main thrust of the book is to urge individuals back to the land and to show them how to do it. In *A Little Land*, Hall returns to the promise of homesteading as a program of social reform, this time drawing together numerous exempla of those who have left the city to grow crops in the country and soon found that doctors were superfluous, mental disorders had faded, and they could enjoy "free pleasure" at home rather than "expensive fun" in the city.[25] In *Life, and Love and Peace*, Hall continues to sound the note of social reform but plays it in an even more recognizably religious key. Here he urges urban dwellers to go back to the "great Jocund Earth [where] there will be unlimited scope for endless activity in harmony with Universal Life."[26] Hall's call echoes that of Burroughs in its religious style (we may note a similar affection for capital letters) and its simultaneous revision of prevailing Christian concepts. He makes his position plain when he exhorts his readers to recognize that new times demand new theologies. "We have outgrown creeds, but still cling to them as fixed revelations," he warns on one occasion. "The time has come when it is clear . . . that the idea of renouncing . . . this life for the sake of preparing for a life of one's self beyond is a delusion," he asserts on another.[27] "When the self-conscious, separate-seeming self realizes that humanity is a unity, that there is one Universal Life in which there is joyous activity and harmonious development," Hall writes, "we will abandon the egoistic strife for personal advancement. . . . As soon as we have had enough of this struggle, man will return to his Father's field."[28] Like so many advocates and practitioners of homesteading, Hall—while uneasy with traditional Christian notions of salvation and rebirth—continues to express a commitment to the notion of giving the self over to a higher order of existence (nature) in order to be redeemed.

On the one hand, Hall is critical of the Christian legacies of exceptionalism and otherworldliness. At the same time, he is skeptical of the potential consequences of "science" and wary of social Darwinists.[29] In the end, like both Burroughs and Nearing, Hall treads a middle path between otherworldly salvation-oriented Christians and this-worldly success-oriented materialists. His doctrine is a familiar sounding call for self-sacrifice and a corresponding promise of re-creation and renewal through daily labor in the soil.[30]

The Flight from the City: Ralph Borsodi

Just over a decade after Hall published *Life, and Love and Peace*, Ralph Borsodi, a marketing and economic consultant for Macy's, came to the slow-building realization that life in New York City, whatever the cultural advantages, was characterized by "too much excitement, too much artificial food, too much sedentary work, and too much of the smoke and noise and dust of the city."[31] Ralph's father, William, was a Georgist and a close friend of Hall's, and he had written an effusive introduction to *A Little Land and a Living*. Young Ralph was educated in this climate, fondly remembering his best intellectual experiences at the family table with visiting social radicals, although he also sporadically attended private schools.

Like his father—who had written books on sales techniques before becoming a professional publisher of reform economics tracts—Borsodi first established himself in business and advertising, serving as an economic consultant to Macy's and several marketing firms. His first book, in fact, was *The New Accounting* (1910), on double entry bookkeeping. But also like his father, Ralph's true interests were in social reform. He believed in business serving the needs of the people and in advertising as a forum for communicating information about products (he was among the first to encourage the listing of ingredients on packaging). But as he remained in the growing advertising and marketing world of Manhattan, Borsodi began to see that the dawning culture of consumption was creating "wants" rather than needs and that advertising (on which newspapers were becoming increasingly dependent) was moving from communication to manipulation. Later he would articulate his emergent vision of his own first profession in the bluntest of terms: "No matter how much the customer who can afford to buy may resist," he wrote in *The Distribution Age*, "he must be made to eat more, to wear out more clothes, to take more drugs, to blow out more tires. He must consume, consume, consume so that our industries must produce, produce, produce."[32]

Familiar with Hall's little-lands experiments (Hall was a frequent visitor to the Borsodi household) and swayed by his father's enthusiasm for Hall's projects, Borsodi adopted a similar path. Three dramatic turning points influenced his final conversion: the occasion of hearing a speech by Leo Tolstoy's son on Georgist objections to landownership and the attendant inner-city poverty it produced; a brief, unhappy landowning experiment in Texas, which further solidified his Georgist views; and a conversation with a colleague about the virtues of fasting and the dangers of eating commercially produced food. While his father assented to most of these ideas, Ralph Borsodi was eager to put them into practice. Not unlike the Nearings, however, Borsodi tells the story of his own experiments as if his "flight" were entirely original.

Twelve years before the Nearings would make a similar exodus, Borsodi, his wife, Myrtle Mae, and their two young sons headed to Rockland County, New York, and established a seven-acre homestead (appropriately, if not originally, deemed Seven Acres). Although Ralph Borsodi continued to work in the city for a time, the family was headed in the direction of a primarily home-based economy that would model the virtues of home-based production and present an alternative to the "ugly civilization" of city living, which "[is] polluted, noisy, hectic, over-consuming our natural resources, and murdering time (man's most precious possession), in order to produce more goods[, and] fails to provide a means of living in which people find enjoyment in, and meaning for living."[33] As early as 1921, they were producing and canning all of their fruits and vegetables, making homemade cheese and butter, raising chickens for meat and eggs, and homeschooling their children through the arts and sciences of homesteading life. Four years after their "initial experiment," the Borsodis relocated to a more expansive site called Dogwoods and established a more complex version of their original homestead. By 1936, the Borsodis had created the School of Living at Bayard Lane (near Suffern), forming with friends and like-minded associates a community of sixteen two-acre homesteads surrounding the school.

Like both the Nearings and Hall, the Borsodis understood their decision to be a carefully planned, scientifically controlled "experiment in living," the self-published reports from which would be models of social change. Similarly, they focused on the priority of home-centered production, going beyond food raising to building their homes and outbuildings with their own labor and primarily from stones "picked up on [the] place." Unlike the Nearings, however, the Borsodis consistently cited comfort as an ongoing ideal. In their view, the model was not "pioneering as a way of living in the twentieth century" (the Nearings' phrase) but "a way of living which is neither city life nor farm life, but which is an effort to combine the advantages and to escape the disadvantages of both."[34] Accordingly, the Borsodis welcomed labor-saving devices and electricity and felt no moral qualms about allowing for pleasures beyond the virtuous one of building with stone. A description of Dogwoods reveals the blend of industry and luxury that characterized the Borsodi homestead:

> [In addition to the] things which we produced our first year, we have since added ducks, guineas, and turkeys; bees for honey; pigeons for appearance; and dogs for

company. We have in the past twelve years built three houses and a barn from stones . . . ; we weave suitings, blankets, carpets and draperies; we make some of our own clothing; we do all of our own laundry work; we grind flour, cornmeal and breakfast cereals; we have our own workshops, including a printing plant; and we have a swimming-pool, tennis-court and even a billiard room.[35]

On the one hand, the Borsodi homestead seems opulent when hypothetically viewed from a Nearing perspective. Keeping pigeons for appearances and dogs for company not only goes against the Nearing principle of keeping no animals but also borders on the frivolous, while chicken raising (though also disapproved of) at least has utilitarian purposes. The Nearings would also have had little sympathy for the pleasure principle suggested by the Borsodis' decision to build a swimming pool and a tennis court; for the Nearings, building in stone was their tennis. On the other hand, the Borsodi approach to homesteading is as labor focused as the Nearing method, if not more so. Borsodi not only shares with the Nearings an understanding that work in the garden "has furnished . . . exercise for which we had to pay money in the city," but he also asserts that the majority of urban-based production and labor could be transported to the homestead.[36]

Borsodi placed priority on the extent to which the goods of the city could be reproduced at home. In this respect, the homestead became a site of multiple cottage industries: weaving, sewing, printing, canning, furniture making. Of all of the tools on the homestead, the loom and the sewing machine were heralded as paying the largest dividends on investment and furnishing an important artistic and "creative outlet" for the weaver. Borsodi even noted that the loom was used by occupational therapists as a treatment for nervous disorders and so could be employed in the household as a form of therapy.[37] The next most important tools were the electric mixer and pressure cooker, which "modernized" the Borsodi kitchen and helped to eliminate "drudgery." In both his chapter on food and his chapter on sewing, Borsodi takes his reader through pages of detailed accounting in which the cost of home production is compared with the cost of factory production, and—even after accounting for the imagined "wages" for the producer—the former always comes out the winner. Borsodi consistently (and persuasively) concludes that home production, whether it is the canning of tomato juice or the making of handwoven suits, is cheaper, healthier, more creatively satisfying, and results in higher-quality goods than factory production.

The Nearings would have disapproved of the comparatively grandiose aesthetics of the Borsodi homestead—the praise of labor-saving devices and the presence of a billiard room. Helen noted in 1936, in fact, that she had visited "Borsodi's colony" and deemed it "not exciting."[38] On the other hand, the Nearings did not practice home production nearly to the extent that the Borsodis did. An important aspect of this difference, however, lay not only with the Nearings' austerity ("who *needs* a well-tailored suit or a four-course dinner," they might well have remarked) but also between Helen Nearing's and Myrtle Mae Borsodi's views of domesticity. Helen Nearing often told her visitors that she favored whatever approach would "save work for the housewife" and get her outdoors. Myrtle Mae, by contrast, took obvious pleasure in cooking and in creating coats and frocks that rivaled those of urban boutiques.[39] Notably, neither the Nearing nor the Borsodi homestead operated on a transformed domestic model in which the men spent more time in the kitchen than they did outdoors. The significant issues raised by such gendered aspects of homesteading will be discussed in the next chapter, but it is worth noting here that the variations between the two households were based not only on views of simplicity but also on the extent to which the women in the family chose to follow traditional gender roles.

The Borsodis' intention was not to resist capitalism in toto. In the post–World War II period, in fact, Ralph Borsodi feared that the government was taking a dangerous turn toward socialistic bureaucracy. His goal was to reduce the impact of industrialism and consumerism on the quality of daily living and to offer solutions to the problems of the distribution of wealth. Borsodi's biggest watchwords were *dependence* and *insecurity*, conditions that he saw as inherent results of being "a cog in some part of the complex machinery of our factory-dominated civilization."[40] Like Bolton Hall, Borsodi saw homesteading as a means of returning the production of the essentials of living to the proper hands and interpreted the shift toward production as physically beneficial, morally uplifting, and socially responsible. Borsodi, however, was not raised in the Protestant, Social Gospel atmosphere to which Hall and Nearing are indebted. Borsodi came from a family of liberal Jewish intellectuals and social reformers, observant in their vision of the "repair of the world" but not in a traditional, institutional sense. Correspondingly, Borsodi's use of explicit religious language is comparatively sparse.

When compared with the layers of allusion in Burroughs's and Hall's writings, and even with the Nearings' references to Mother Earth and the All-That-Is, Borsodi's *Flight from the City* is more practical and sociological than it is philosophical or spiritual. Revealingly, when Borsodi *does* call upon the Bible, it is not the Garden of Eden (like Hall) or the pastoral vision of Matthew (like Burroughs) to which he refers. Instead, Borsodi chooses the story of Jacob and Esau and, in the manner of a Scott Nearing, explicates the text as a morality tale about the dependence of one man on another "for the bare necessities of life."[41] No one can afford the sin of dependence, Borsodi warns, and everyone must play a part in resisting the temptation to sell his or her birthright.

But while Borsodi's diction is less obviously biblical, his "method" of argumentation is also the familiar homesteading trope of the conversion narrative. Borsodi places his own *experiences* at the center of his theories, using himself, his wife, and his sons as both proof and testament of how self-sufficient living is more economically stable and more spiritually satisfying than life in the city. What his family is looking for, Borsodi reveals, is the replacement of barrenness with a life "of beauty—the beauty which comes only from contact with nature and from the growth of the soil."[42]

In general, the spiritual and emotional longings for nature are aspects of the homesteading experience that Borsodi tends to play down. Like other homesteaders, Borsodi is anxious about being viewed as a hopeless romantic or a "nuts and berries" convert to natural living.[43] Borsodi defends himself well against potential critics. While preaching against the evils of bleached flour, white sugar, and polished rice with the vehemence of a Helen Nearing—we are "digging our graves with our teeth," he warns—he also goes out of the way to point out that, with respect to vegetarianism, he has "never subscribed to the tenets of this dietetic cult."[44] In discussing the use of pumps and cisterns, he also takes pains to note: "We had no romantic notions about carrying water from a stream. . . . We were not after any such return to nature. . . . There would be enough hard work, we knew, without making a virtue of doing things the hard way."[45] But a closer look at Borsodi's description of his homesteading initiative reveals a subtle though persistent tendency to extol the virtues of vegetarianism (even as a nonbeliever) in the midst of a discussion of meatpacking or to call for a return of the "lost" aesthetics of cooking and weaving in the midst of clamoring for "more chemists in kitchens."[46] Here Borsodi echoes the ambivalence of other nuts-and-berries avoiders, who, despite their protestations to the contrary, reveal a certain longing for the austerities of old and will praise the "spiritual prerequisites" required for eating only corn while it is in season and refusing the lure of store-bought "exotic" goods such as oranges and olive oil.[47] As David Shi points out almost casually in his treatment of Borsodi, what was advocated in this version of homesteading was not only economic reform and a revival of human creativity but also a *"religion of the hearth."*[48]

That Borsodi's principles were never wholly economic was something he made clear to a younger audience when, in an interview with the *Mother Earth News*, he chose to place his final emphasis on the importance of festivals. Community-produced singing, music, dancing, and seasonal observances were an important part of the cultural life of the School of Living in the 1930s (as they also were at Arden). Borsodi argued that regardless of one's how-to knowledge, no sustainable homestead living could proceed without a rich festival life.[49] While thoroughly modern in its use of technology, the Borsodi approach to homesteading still turned on the notion of the redemption of the spirit through the disciplines of gardening and homemaking.

Borsodi's vision of homesteading, then, was both spiritual and social, both a pursuit of private health and well-being and a program for wide-scale resistance to industrialism and consumerism. In later years, his vision of homesteading would be taken up through government programs (in Austin, Minnesota, and Dayton, Ohio) to soothe the sting of the Depression. These eagerly championed projects would eventually founder on bureaucratic inefficiency, debates over local and federal control, and a general resistance to the communal aspects of the homestead plan.[50] But Borsodi's views would regain a hearing in the context of his self-founded institution, the School of Living, and the homesteading and educational projects it continued to support. Borsodi also would go on to found a loosely structured intentional community (of private homes) in Melbourne, Florida, and to serve as chancellor of the experimental University of Melbourne.[51]

In the late 1950s, with Mildred Loomis taking on the role of tireless advocate for Borsodi's views, the Borsodi response to the physical, spiritual, and economic threats of the city gained a new appeal to the emerging counterculture. Today the School of Living still persists and its publishing venture, The Green Revolution, still has an audience. Other community-oriented and reform-minded legacies also remain. The community land trust idea, now common, was the innovation of Bob Swann, an activist alongside Borsodi and a participant in Gandhian forms of community and land management in India. Today's community-supported agriculture (CSA) programs also have their roots in the Borsodi tradition, and the E. F. Schumacher Society continues to foster the outlook of Schumacher, Borsodi, Loomis, and Swann. While the Nearings would be the "cult heroes" of the 1960s back-to-the-landers, the Borsodis and Loomis continue to be minor saints with their own schools of followers.[52]

When we reflect on the homesteading practices of the first three decades of the twentieth century we see a range of expressions of homesteading as "reform"—a reform designed to bring physically and morally strained individuals back to nature and an increasingly fast-paced and industrialized culture back to simplicity and community.

John Burroughs's turn to nature may be interpreted as privatized and accommodationist relative to Scott Nearing's more expansive and radical social vision, but in the preceding pages I have attempted to place Burroughs and Nearing on a continuum rather than in distinctly separate categories. Imagining a continuum between retreat and reform, between "the public" and "the private," is also appropriate for Borsodi and Hall. Both homesteaders addressed the social concerns of their day and saw homesteading as a way to enact gemeinschaft in the midst of gesellschaft. But Hall and Borsodi adopted an approach to homesteading that continued to *reflect* dominant Progressive Era attitudes toward nature and progress, even while they were highly critical of social inequity and prevailing economic structures. They were more political than Burroughs but less sacramental as well. They believed that nature was not so much to be reverenced as to be harnessed and used. Certainly, their uses of nature were more moderate and restrained than those of the dominant culture they were trying to reform, but their work (both homesteading and writing about it) also reflected the prevailing assumptions. Their social programs stayed within certain conventional bounds, representing modified capitalism in Hall's case and reimagined and relocated industrialism in the case of Borsodi.

Here again, a comparison with more traditional religious contexts is illuminating for our analysis. The act of negotiating between retreat and reform, accommodation and resistance, or the public and the private can also be understood as discerning the right path between contemplation and action. As with the religious practitioner, conversion to a radically new way of life is only the first step, the justification, to borrow Protestant terms, that precedes the sanctification. But actually living a holy life (in this case, a life close to nature and against the grain of consumerist, capitalist culture) involves a complex set of choices. A serious Buddhist or Jew may decide a religious life is best lived in retreat from the world, with a focus on daily meditation, prayer, study, and the personal pursuit of a spiritual life (free from attachments or close to God). Another equally serious Buddhist or Jew may take his or her spiritual response to the world as the foundation for practical work for social change in that world. (As we have seen, this was also the case for those involved in the Social Gospel movement.) The "socially engaged" Buddhist might run a soup kitchen or ordain trees that he believes have "Buddha-nature" and should be protected. The Jew might translate her understanding of the divine charge to seek the "repair of the world" (tikkun olam) into a decision to run for office or start a labor union. Others may choose a middle path that blends contemplation and action, either in the course of a day or at various stages of the life cycle. The tension between a life of contemplation (purposely removed from various understandings of worldliness and "sin") and a life of action (active in the world, seeking justice or love) no doubt runs through all manner of human endeavors. But it is no surprise that it should be particularly acute in the realm of the religious life or in the context of the dramatic reorientation of life that is involved in the cultural and spiritual work of homesteading.

We should remember, then, that Hall and Borsodi also speak of the practice of homesteading in a private and contemplative sense—in terms of its effect on them personally, particularly in the interpenetrating spheres of physical, psychological, and spiritual revitalization. These social reformers were clearly personally changed by the intimacy with nature that they experienced through their own labors in the soil. Hall's testaments are voiced in the language of religious renewal (the return to the Garden), while Borsodi speaks primarily of a return to health and well-being in its broadest terms. While both emphasize the reconstruction of society, intimacy with nature and the renewal of the self are never far behind.

The Nearings in the Context of Reform

In contrast to the work of Hall and Borsodi, the Nearings' homesteading projects may seem like a kind of "escape," an intentional retreat from public life. But Scott and Helen Nearings' decision to homestead in Vermont was more complex than the model of "retreatant" allows. As this study has shown, the Nearings' homesteading life, while reclusive by some standards, was a particular iteration of a period of radical social vision that was located in a broader cultural turn to nature (as a moralizing force) that began in the mid-nineteenth century. We see this dynamic clearly in Scott's personal history, where life at Arden and life at the two forest farms serve as bookends to a period of teaching, scholarship, public lecturing, and urban living. While it may not have transpired had academic culture and conservative politics not forced him out of his chosen profession, Scott Nearing's choice to homestead in the 1930s was a choice both to preserve a teaching and scholarly life in the only way he knew how and to recapture the spirit of Arden on his own land.

To the extent that homesteading was a "retreat," it was a retreat from a war-waging government and a price-profit economy but not from a life of teaching, preaching, or research. Significantly, Helen shared in this desire not to be caught up in a spiritual vision of the world that neglected social vision and social change. Her strongest criticism of her first great love, Krishnamurti, was that he would not support "political action and economic reforms," because in his own spiritual metaphysics he thought that all "outer conditions . . . could be surpassed by the mind."[53] In contrast to such private, internal forms of spiritual quest, Helen and Scott founded the nonprofit Social Science Institute as an imprint for their self-published books, because they saw their work as much more than a personal attempt to eke out a meaningful and economically stable existence. Their stated vision was primarily educational and political: "to publish books and hold classes or seminars on social science." In the Nearings' eyes, of course, social science was not simply, as it is today, an umbrella term for a variety of very particular academic disciplines from economics to psychology. They resisted the professionalization of the disciplines, just as Wendell Berry does today.[54] Rather, *social science* was a term that had its roots in broader meanings that were part and parcel of the Social Gospel context from which Scott emerged: an inquiry into the question, "How ought we to live?"

The Nearings hoped that the Social Science Institute could evolve into a large-scale action and research institute for "international peace studies and social sciences," but as homesteading became what was most known and desirable about their work, the house and the nonprofit came to fulfill "other purposes—helping to maintain the farmstead as a modest model of homebuilding, functional independence, of simplicity and right-livelihood on the land. This model includes human, social and natural ecology, organic gardening, and community participation."[55] That model continues today as the Good Life Center, and it is a model that, while straining to "stay small" and "keep to the bare bones," remains directed outward, toward a society that it seeks to reform.[56] As was true about life at Arden, however, the life values that are articulated in the Nearing experiments begin with nature and the soil. Doing good work, for yourself, with and in the earth is seen as the starting foundation for the Good Life. Saving the world begins at home.

One wonders if Hall's, Borsodi's, and the Nearings' visions were the last homesteading experiments belonging to the legacy of Progressive Era social optimism. As we move from their experiences into later homestead texts of the Depression and postwar eras, we see a decipherable shift in motivations, rationales, and even tone. In many cases, homesteading clearly remains a kind of spiritual practice that rebels against both institutional religion and the exponential growth of consumer society while creating a new spiritual and practical economy. But that practice becomes more privatized and personal, less fueled by a religious sensibility for broad cultural reform and more fueled by spiritual longings for what living close to nature can provide for the self. The homesteading of these later decades is performed in the radically new social and historical contexts of economic upheaval, a second world war, and the first (publicly recognized) signs of environmental limits. Yet despite these dramatic differences, the style and significance of homesteading experiments that we see tend to circle back to the where it began, with Thoreau's quest for the self and John Burroughs's desire for the unique blend of labor, leisure, and immanent spirituality that could be found only by proclaiming the Gospel of Nature.

What do we learn, then, from considering a range of homesteading visions from the perspective of more than a century's time? In summing up Ralph Borsodi's contribution to the ethic of simplicity, David Shi remarks that Borsodi "reflects the continuing transformation of the simple life from a societal ethic to a minority ethic." In Shi's analysis, the story of the simple life is, in the broadest sense, a story of declension.[57] Can this be otherwise? It is hard to imagine the simple life as being anything but a minority ethic, given the social and cultural transformations of the twentieth century (and to assume that it was ever dominant may be a nostalgic hope more than an accurate reading). But this does not mean that we should see the *practice* of simple living as a dying art. Nor does it mean that we should interpret the myth of the yeoman farmer as being *only* a myth.[58] If the pursuit of the simple life today is a minority *ethic*, it has also been, in the form of homesteading, a quietly persistent *practice*, one that consistently involves a complex intertwining of inwardly oriented, personal urges toward retreat and private spiritual experience, as well as outwardly oriented impulses toward social reform and the restoration of community values and structures. As we move toward the conclusion of this historical treatment of homesteading and on toward a final analysis of the significance of homesteading as a cultural gesture, it is useful to review these broad themes and to sketch a picture of the forms homesteading has taken from the first experiments of the Borsodis and the Nearings to the ongoing ventures of homesteaders today.

From the Age of Reform to the Age of Affluence: Negotiating Public and Private

Our inquiry into the lives of Burroughs, Nearing, and others in the decades from the Gilded Age to the Depression has shown both the persistence of homesteading's dominant themes—the spiritual quest for nature, self, and new forms of social structure—and the persistence of homesteading itself. One historical lesson that by now should be clear is that the so-called back-to-the-land movement of the late 1960s was not a new cultural gesture, nor was it unique in casting the return to nature in religious terms (whether the religion of personal redemption in nature or of religiously inflected social reform through nature). While performed in a style that was recognizably countercultural and sometimes also socially communal, the homesteading experiments of the 1960s and 1970s had much in common with the ventures that had preceded them.[59] The emphasis on remaking the self on nature's terms, dissenting from materialism, consumerism, and capitalism, and modeling new visions of community—all aspects of the 1960s back-to-nature urge—had already been variously articulated by Burroughs and Nearing, Hall and Borsodi, and a host of others.[60]

Just as important, homesteading was not a gesture that appeared and then disappeared with the growing challenges of second-wave industrialization and the subsequent progressive response to the social problems of the city (i.e., during the period between the 1870s to the 1920s). While the Depression forced many into self-sufficiency for reasons of survival, homesteading as a version of both protest and reform continued to be articulated. Most obviously, Ralph Borsodi's programs received a wider hearing and began to be incorporated into government plans for economic revitalization. But numerous individuals also "took to the woods" and fields and found in so doing that, while America drifted into Depression and war, their own lives were increasingly infused with optimism and peace.[61]

Even the more purposively "ecological" visions of contemporary homesteaders have their precedents in the naturism of Arden and Free Acres. But in the 1930s and 1940s, the idea of homesteading as a practice not only of getting close to nature but also of rescuing and improving a particular ecological habitat emerges with more force. We see this in the work and writings of Aldo Leopold, a part-time homesteader to be sure, but moreover a visionary in understanding his work as not simply science but also ethics.[62] The labor of Louis Bromfield in reclaiming Malabar Farm in Ohio also belongs to this category.[63] Taken together, Leopold and Bromfield (though very different men) represent a kind of link in the chain of public, literary, Jeffersonian-style homesteading, which stretches from Burroughs to Berry. Bromfield is more concerned about chemicals, Leopold fears the cult of the car, but both anticipate 1960s ecological concerns and do so out of their own lived experiments on particular parcels of land.[64]

While homesteading has always involved a criticism of superfluous wealth and often also a concern for the inequities of wealth's distribution, homesteading in the postwar period increasingly became a response to the emerging Age of Affluence. At the same time, however, it was often also implicated in this age. We may remember the story of Brad and Vena Angier, first mentioned in chapter 1. The Angiers led a comfortable literary and theatrical life in Boston, with Brad serving as the New England editor for a theatrical business magazine and Vena producing musicals that played downtown. In 1945, having reread *Walden*, the Angiers decided to re-create Thoreau's experiment one hundred years later. They sold the majority of their possessions, gave themselves a month to depart, and headed northwest. On the Peace River in British Columbia they subsisted on bear meat, bannock, and homegrown vegetables. Not incidentally, they also eventually subsisted on royalties from their articles about how to build log cabins and live off of wild plants. Apparently their hunger for peavine and yarrow was matched by their readership's hunger for practical information and, at least, a vicarious experience of homesteading life.[65]

The Angiers understood their choice to homestead as a reaction against the rush of the city, the pressures of social convention, and the corresponding emphasis on material possessions, all of which they discerned as part of the prevailing postwar atmosphere. At the same time, they expressed their choice not in terms of seeking a life of discipline and asceticism (as some of their predecessors did) but in terms of pursuing a different kind of plenty. This too they saw as a response to the war years. As the Angiers put it: "One reaction crowding the heels of war . . . is a yearning to return to the land . . . where wild foods are free for the gathering, fuel for the cutting, and habitation for the satisfaction of building."[66] Homesteading thus continued to be advanced as a way to leave the rat-race behind and still have it all. Just as Ralph Borsodi had urged his readers that they could go back to the land and still enjoy the comforts of the city, so did others promise a new kind of affluence on the homestead.

A shining example of the blending of the ethic of affluence with the ethic of simplicity—and of enacting resistance in a way that was also accommodation— was a homesteading proposal first introduced by Ed and Carolyn Robinson in an advertisement in 1943. The Robinsons' booklet on self-sufficiency, which became *The Have More Plan*, was certainly a convincing call to leave behind the fast-paced, crowded, and expensive life of the city. The decision was prompted, Ed Robinson claimed, by a taking a trip to a New York City park so that their son, Jackie, could stretch out on the grass. A police officer interrupted this attempt at a pastoral experience by asking Ed how long he thought the grass would last if everybody were allowed to sit and walk on it. The unpleasant park experience tipped the balance for the Robinsons, and their narrative portrays the confidence of new converts to country living who chose never to look back. *The Have More Plan* is also chock-full of practical advice confirming that these authors were not merely paying lip service to the idea. On their two-acre plot in Norwalk, Connecticut (then still a true "country" location), the Robinsons paid the necessary dues of being stung by bees, butted by goats, and occasionally flummoxed by careful plans gone awry.

Yet despite the admitted obstacles, the Robinsons' perky text consistently promises (as the title proclaims) rich rewards, including the security of having "25 broilers in [the] freezer" and "loads of time" in the winter for "parties, dinners or whatnot."[67] The barn-warming party that the Robinsons hosted in May 1943 involved a bevy of New York City guests, who were invited to admire the Robinsons' success in action. Ed particularly hoped his advertising coworker and friend Lyman Wood could be persuaded to publish a magazine, or a least a book, through his business. Wood agreed to the latter and shifted his attentions (revealing, perhaps) from mail-order prayers to mail-order homesteading tips. Eventually, Wood's dual interest in a nonchurchly practical approach to spiritual life and in gardening and homesteading would lead him to found the Garden Way company, which assisted generations of Vermont gardeners and back-to-the-landers.[68]

In Wood's description of the barn party, Carolyn Robinson accidentally made a punch with four times the amount of alcohol given in the recipe, and "a couple of old ladies in high spirits fell off the porch."[69] Certainly, in all respects, this was not a Nearing-inspired vision of frugality and asceticism. Helen Nearing herself apparently commented that the Robinsons had got it wrong. Why the have-more plan, she queried, "What about have-less and be more?"[70]

The very subtitle of their homesteading tract (*A Little Land—a Lot of Living*) emphasizes the extent to which the Robinson vision of homesteading was no bold criticism of capitalism or consumerism. Even while borrowing a phrase from Hall, it was, in some respects a turn *away* from the Hall, Borsodi, and Nearing tradition. Although the intent was to appeal to wartime anxieties about scarcity, it was also to placate these sentiments with promises of abundance and security. The call to "rebuild America" was a call for "decentralized liberty," but it was not an argument for Georgism, pacifism, or socialism. It was an expression, rather, of the hope that every family "could own its own home and a little land."[71] In light of the suburbanization to come, the Robinsons' plan may have been a partial revival of Bolton Hall, but it also contained a hint of Levittown.

But while the Robinsons may not have been on the cutting edge of radical homesteading, their perpetual optimism, their blend of armchair philosophizing and practical advice, and their evangelical can-do tone spoke to a postwar audience in need of practical security and spiritual uplift. In this sense, *The Have More Plan* had much in common with the myriad homesteading texts that both preceded and followed the Robinson experiment. Perhaps it was because of the Robinsons' breezy, confident style and attention to practical details that the *Mother Earth News* picked up the text and reprinted it in full in their second issue in 1970. TMEN's appropriation of *The Have More Plan* is revealing of both the continuities and the continually shifting styles of the practice of homesteading. Here, one of the most conventional and "suburban" of homesteading texts is republished by one of the most prominent engines of the countercultural back-to-the-land movement (in part, one imagines, because the idealists were in great need of the practical details that the Robinsons provided). Of course, the republication of the Robinsons' text was not without an explanatory preface. "You can put down some of the older generation, but not all of it," the editors began. "Some of those who went before were just as interested then as you are now in fresh air, sunshine, green grass and wholesome food," they allowed.[72] While the publishers of TMEN liked to think of themselves as innovators, even they had to admit that their solution to the problems of contemporary culture were not new.

Contemporary Homesteading, Lived Religion, and Reform

When we consider contemporary homesteading efforts, we are reminded of the extent to which today's homesteaders borrow from the whole range of homesteading styles and cultural criticisms that we have seen from John Burroughs to Wendell Berry. At times, the borrowing is explicit and the line of influence is direct. As I briefly mentioned in chapter 1, for instance, Arnold Greenberg's views of homesteading were directly, though not exclusively, shaped by his involvement with the School of Living and the Borsodi-Loomis tradition. Bill Coperthwaite developed his own philosophies of social design through a creative fusing of Scott Nearing's principles and practices, the pacifism of Tolstoy, Gandhi, and Richard Gregg, and his own highly original adaptation of folk traditions from around the world. A member of "the Sauna crowd," Maggie, articulated to me a vision of community that stems from childhood experiences of visiting Arden, where her parents used to live. Dale and Robin, whom we met in chapter 1, consistently turn to the Nearings as their spiritual touchstone, sometimes even sporting Nearing-style Dutch clogs as a symbolic gesture of their attempts to follow in the Nearings' footsteps. At the same time, however, they are departing from the Nearings' practices. Like the Borsodis, they are raising chickens, homeschooling their children, and refraining from some of the more ascetic aspects of the Nearing program.

The homesteading practices of today remain steeped in a variety of traditions, not only particular "homesteading traditions" but also the larger cultural traditions in which homesteading plays a part: the turn to nature as a source of spiritual renewal and the practice of self-sufficiency as an aspect of self-fashioning. Today's homesteaders still long for reform and seek the experience of community and intimacy in the face of threats to stable social structures. But the reform activities they engage in tend to be more home-based (such as the Liberty School) or grounded in personal testaments ("this is what I did") rather than broad social programs ("this is what America ought to do").

Contemporary homesteaders continue to participate in more than a century-old cultural gesture and to express both its dominant themes and its prevailing ambivalences. But in certain respects they seem to have come of age. For instance, the Sauna crowd's resistance to uncritical reverence of the Nearings and to the imposition of "ideologies" of homesteading (such as strict vegetarianism or temperance), while suggesting a certain skittishness with respect to the past, nonetheless models a creative kind of openness and flexibility toward homesteading efforts. These homesteaders refuse to advocate one kind of homesteading as "the answer." While they may resemble Burroughs more than Nearing, Hall, or Borsodi in their privatized approach to homesteading, they also exhibit a certain self-consciousness about the limits of what they do. Perhaps like the neoorthodox theologians who questioned the unbridled optimism of the Social Gospel era, the homesteaders of later periods have a more chastened sense of what is possible and see the virtue of recognizing the limits of their efforts. Something prevents most of them from writing ambitious tracts advocating simple, rural living as a means of national social reform. They are more intent on the *practice* of homesteading than the preaching of it.[73]

Of course, the production of homesteading texts continues into the present, but largely they involve personal stories of individual experiences that make more tentative claims. As early as 1974, for example, John Graves wrote: "The book is concerned with my part of the world insofar as I have a part, and I know a few things about it. . . . The ways in which I accomplish various bucolic purposes, for instance, lack the glow of perfect rightness that shines through in most writings on the soil and country life and related subjects. . . . For the most part, I hope, it is unpolemical and does not seek to grind large axes or to give large answers."[74] Even those who do write of homesteading as cultural reform do so in a new key. Those whose work stands most closely in the tradition of a Burroughs (Berry) or a Nearing (Coperthwaite) still demonstrate a certain complexity, self-reflectiveness, and sophistication that their predecessors could not—and perhaps should not be expected to—attain. Coperthwaite, for instance, combines rather traditional-sounding arguments for homemaking and family preservation with a commitment to yurt building that would strike some as "hippie architecture." Similarly, Berry articulates seemingly liberal "environmentalist" visions but interweaves these with Christian discourse, a defense of the local "tradition" of tobacco farming, and what some would call a prefeminist notion of proper gender roles. Both recognize that they are mixing and matching preconceived notions of how politics, values, and personal style ought to be categorized, and both seem to gain a sense of humor and vitality from engaging in turning these categories upside down and inside out.

Perhaps the best example of the kind of self-awareness and reflexivity that attend some homesteading experiments of the present is the recent work of Linda Tatelbaum. Like Henry and Sal, Tatelbaum understands that the choice to homestead and the practices of homesteading are fluid ones that change as the times change and as the self evolves. In describing the excruciating decision to add electricity to her homestead, Tatelbaum navigates the complex moral and spiritual territory that homesteading so often involves. On the one hand, she is compelled to keep things as they are, to stick to grading papers by Aladdin lamps and to keeping food cool in the root cellar. On the other hand, she recognizes that homesteading is a way of living (and a way of protest) in the modern world, not a full-scale return to a previous era. It soon becomes clear to Tatelbaum that any homesteading decision involves moral ambiguities: "I saw that coming here had been a conscious choice. I had believed that living and writing about this life would be my contribution to change the world. Did I value my principles so little that I would turn my back on my beliefs? How could I write about change while my electric typewriter hummed with splitting atoms? But I also saw how hard I had tried to be consistent without ever questioning 'consistency.' Was it possible, or even desirable that my actions never contradict my beliefs?"[75] In the end, Tatelbaum and her family choose to install photovoltaic solar panels, a choice that gives them electricity while keeping them "off the grid." But Tatelbaum does not fool herself into thinking that such a choice is "morally consistent." She recognizes, rather, that " 'getting power,' gave me power, the power to accept my own changes along with those in the woods and fields around me."[76]

In extolling the virtues of some present-day homesteaders' self-awareness about the nature of their work, I do not mean to suggest that homesteaders of the past were uncritical idealists and homesteaders of the present are thoughtful realists. But I do want to underline the broad pattern of homesteading from Burroughs to the present. The pattern begins and ends with more privatized and individualized versions of homesteading as a solution to personal problems of meaning, while maintaining throughout (especially from the 1910s to the 1970s) peak moments in which homesteading is also advocated—often optimistically and idealistically—as a mode of cultural salvation.

It is easy to embrace the reform-minded work of Hall and Borsodi and to defend the Nearings as advocates of social change more than "escapists." At the same time, however, we recognize that with each evangelist of public reform comes some personal qualities or ethical principles that others find problematic. Hall's elitism, the Borsodis' love of labor-saving devices, the Nearing's unremitting work ethic and vegetarianism, each could fall prey (and sometimes did) to criticism from the other. But when held up against the more privatized versions of homesteading that have also emerged in the late nineteenth and twentieth centuries, these reform models have their appeal: they are more than individual economic experiments and spiritual quests. The net is cast more broadly, with greater risks, perhaps, but also with the potential for greater rewards.

At the same time, it is worth considering even more privatized homestead experiments with attention to the full complexities of what these life choices entail. As I suggested above, while today's homesteaders are perhaps not as ambitious as the reformers of the earlier eras, they also are not necessarily self-satisfied or complacent. In our evaluation of even the more privatized forms of homesteading, then, it is helpful to consider homesteading with attention to the wider cultural gestures of which it is a part. One broader story to which we have given implicit, if not yet explicit, attention throughout this study is the story of antimodernism, the movement (or movements) in American history that have sought to counter such legacies of modernity as industrialism, consumerism, alienation, and, more recently, ecological decline. At first blush, homesteaders certainly may be cast as antimodernists of a kind (although they are likely to protest that they are looking ahead, not going back). But we have learned of some important distinctions between the homesteaders with whom we have become acquainted in these pages and the more familiar antimodernists of the late nineteenth and early twentieth centuries.

In his insightful study of antimodernists, particularly the participants in the Arts and Crafts movement, the historian T. Jackson Lears examines the lives of men and women who, like many homesteaders, have relocated their religious energies (often descending directly from a family tree of religious profession-als) to lives of artistic creativity that celebrate the simple life. Lears's antimod-ernists have much in common with the homesteaders treated in this study. The commonalities can be found in terms of both the protest enacted by the Amer-ican followers of John Ruskin and William Morris ("[against the] deadening ef-fects of rationalization and the desperate need for creative, useful labor") and the historical streams in which Lears places them ("part of a continuing tradi-tion that looked backward to ante-bellum utopias and forward to agrarian com-munities of the New Deal era and the 1960s").[77]

But Lears's argument takes us down an interpretive path that homesteading itself does not necessarily follow. He places his analysis in the context of the alienating effects of America's transition from a producing to a consuming cul-ture. But homesteading, it is important to note, often resists the production/ consumption cultural shift by locating itself firmly in the middle of it. Home-steaders may become producers primarily as a *means* of protest, that is, as a ges-ture of resistance to consumer culture. But the very fact that they are producers and practitioners of self-sufficiency also keeps them somewhat more removed from the cultural developments they are protesting. This relationship between symbolic cultural action and pragmatic economic action may be a circular one, but it is one that keeps homesteaders at a certain distance from those antimod-ernists who traffic mainly in the world of ideas. Moreover, by being engaged in the production of food rather than artifacts, homesteaders, even more than those who have been engaged in the production of crafts, tend to resist the slide into consumer culture that Lears charts as the fate of other dissenting groups.[78]

A related point, and the most important one to my mind, is that while home-steaders are often motivated in their "conversions" by what Lears calls a "quest for authentic experience," this quest does not necessarily finally become an end in itself. In Lears's view, most antimodernists have fallen into the slough of ac-commodation, unable to maintain "religious or communal frameworks of meaning outside the self."[79] Antimodernism, for Lears, performs primarily a therapeutic function.

To call homesteading antimodernism is, if we adopt Lears's analysis, to see it as suspect and self-defeating. While I agree that homesteading, like any cultural gesture (particularly gestures of resistance), ought to be treated with a hermeneutics of suspicion, I am also convinced that the lives studied here demonstrate a sustained (though complicated) resistance to consumerism and a complex understanding of the self that goes beyond Lears's dominant narrative of antimodernists' accommodation to consumerism and retreat into narcissism.

Homesteaders are less apt to fall prey to this narcissistic demise and not only because they are, relative to some antimodernists, less apt to become full-time consumers. Homesteaders' sense of nature as sacred and of maintaining self-sufficiency as a spiritual process mediates—though it certainly does not eliminate—this tendency. While living close to nature and depending on its bounty for livelihood clearly involve the cultivation of the self—and, as we have seen, can even be undermined by the quest for the self—the life of homesteading consistently demands a "larger loyalty" than to the self alone. Moreover, however much the turn to nature may serve therapeutic functions, it is a mistake to understand the multifaceted spirituality of homesteaders as being *merely* therapeutic.

As this study has shown, homesteading clearly locates itself in a cultural and religious tradition of liberal Protestantism and, to a lesser extent, liberal Judaism. While its final form in homesteaders' lives may be explicitly "not religious," the legacies of American religion never fully fade away. These legacies remain in the inner-worldly asceticism that homesteaders exhibit, the commitment to reform that their personal and social programs maintain, and in those practices that call to mind Transcendentalist and Romantic longings for the incarnation of spirit in humanity and in nature. These legacies also contribute to the ironies and ambivalences we see at work in various homesteading projects, but they simultaneously work to foster commitment and connection to a world outside the self alone. In the work of Scott Nearing, references to God may fade, but visions of "the Good" remain; in Henry's progression from hand tools to power tools, contemporary versions of "self-culture" may be a primary theme, but an ongoing commitment to living lightly on a small piece of land for over thirty years is a testament to community and ecological loyalties that extend beyond self-actualization. It is true that homesteaders are not entirely free from the culture of consumption, for, as with broader cultural moves toward simplicity, their actions and words are (ironically) in danger of becoming commodified, whether by products such as *Real Simple* magazine or personalities such as Martha Stewart. Nevertheless, homesteaders' daily lives perform powerful models of resistance.[80]

Whether cast in political terms or in terms of a cultural movement such as antimodernism, homesteading may be seen as involving "retreat," yet its religious dimensions also remind us that it is a retreat of a different kind, not simply an escape or a means of self-development (though such processes themselves certainly have value). In his own study of back-to-the-land efforts, Jeffrey Jacobs has wondered aloud whether today's homesteaders are more complacent than urban-based environmental and political activists. In this study too, I have raised a version of the same question: If homesteading can enable one to be "redeemed" or "chosen" in the midst of the sinful world of modernity, can it become a practice that is oriented more toward the self than toward nature or larger society?[81] On first blush, we might respond that such questions raise the cultural change marker too high, that homesteaders are necessarily bound to their own backyards first and to organizing and campaigning only if spare time and energy allow. But this is merely a logistical reply that does not get to the heart of the matter. The heart of the matter is that homesteading as a way of life is a model and enactment of dissent: a lived politics. Jacobs also finds it odd that homesteaders, while having few religious convictions or communities, feel remarkably satisfied with their way of life despite the many hardships such life entails. Here again he touches on a significant finding but does not probe all the interpretive possibilities: that living out a daily commitment to nature and against consumer culture is a spiritual practice: a lived religion.

Stephen Carter has argued that religious life has the power to embody dissent in a way that political life—based as it is on compromise in the public sphere—can never do.[82] We might say that many homesteaders (at many places on the social change continuum) are reform-minded in this spiritual sense. They live and embody dissent more than they organize and campaign for it. This is the conclusion that Wendell Berry has come to in evaluating the life of Harlan and Anna Hubbard, who, even in "voluntary simplicity" circles, remain comparatively little known. In the conclusion of his portrait of the Hubbards, Berry describes how, in the last years of the Hubbards' lives (the 1980s) Public Service Indiana began to build a nuclear power plant downstream and in plain view of the riverbank at Payne Hollow, where the Hubbards had their cabin. "This plant, like all others," writes Berry, "had been conceived and designed in perfect indifference to the place in which it was to be built." Berry tells us that objections were raised but overruled. Protests were launched but ultimately failed. In the heat of these efforts, Berry wondered why the Hubbards did not take part in the protests, did not campaign with Berry and the others against a project that was "a direct and unignorable affront to all that they had done and stood for." Later, writes Berry, he came to an understanding that had eluded him at the time:

I understood that by the life they led Harlan and Anna had opposed the power plant longer than any of us, and not because they had been or ever would be its "opponents." They were opposed to it because they were opposite to it, because their way of life joined them to everything in the world that was opposite to it. What could be more radically or effectively opposite to a power plant than to live abundantly with no need for electricity? . . . The industrialist's contempt for any life in any place was balanced across the river by a place and two lives joined together in love.[83]

With the Hubbards' balanced and beautiful life as a model, we might find it tempting to say that the problem of retreat versus reform has been resolved. If we consider homesteading as a mode of dissent that is more spiritual than it is political, which begins with "right livelihood" and may or may not move outward, then we might be content with the level of political engagement that we see. If politics and spirituality begin at home, as they do for every homesteader we have considered, they may in many cases stay at home while resisting an "apolitical" stance. Different readers may choose to evaluate homesteaders favorably or not, depending on their own preferences toward the private or the public, retreat or engagement, contemplation or action—but as I have attempted to show here, the "rightness" of one mode over the other is not entirely clear. The many varieties of homesteading are shaped by individual innovation and historical context. Homesteaders' choices in our own time may ring more true to us now, or we may long for a new reformer to take again to the public stage.

What a pity . . . that the kitchen and the housework generally, cannot be left out of our system
altogether! It is odd enough that the kind of labor
which falls to the lot of women is chiefly what
distinguishes artificial life—the life of degenerated
mortals—from the life of Paradise. . . .

[It] was not by necessity, but by choice.
Though we saw fit to drink our tea out of earthen
cups tonight . . . it was at our own option to use
pictured porcelain and handle silver forks again,
tomorrow. . . .

[We] had pleased ourselves with delectable
visions of the spiritualization of labor. It was to be
our form of prayer and ceremonial of worship.

Miles Coverdale in Nathaniel Hawthorne's
Blithedale Romance

It is the ironic nature of religious practice, practice often infused with profound emotional commitment and the sense that one is engaged with the "really real," that ambivalence persists amid these very depths of commitment. For instance: A young man grows up as an evangelical Christian; his life has been transformed by the personal grace of Christ's presence. He is also gay and must contend with his home church's interpretations of the gospel, which condemn who he is and his life with his partner. Yet he refuses to reject the religious experience of Christ's salvation, which has shaped his understanding of the transformative possibilities of love. He remains a committed evangelical Christian and also an openly gay man.

The negotiation of such competing identities (one of religion, one of sexual orientation) is but one particularly dramatic example of the daily negotiations of spiritual life that are enacted everywhere but are perhaps particularly visible in today's religiously creative and eclectic American culture. But there are others.

A woman enters a Catholic church to pray. She genuflects before entering the pew, crosses herself, and says the rosary with her mother's rosary beads in her hands. But is she addressing God in her prayers? Later, she tells someone, she was actually praying to her mother, who died years ago and to whom all of her prayers are directed. We also learn that she is firmly convinced that women should be admitted to the priesthood and that congregations should have the power to decide which priests will serve them. She could leave the church, but she goes to mass every Sunday as well as visiting for prayer when the spirit moves her.

An African-American boy grows up in a Pennsylvania college town. His family has always been Baptist, and it is in the Baptist world of prayer and song that he feels most at home; but he is preparing for college, and the teachers and students he most hopes to emulate are members of the Episcopal church in town. He decides to use some of his savings for new clothes and to spend his Sundays regularly at the Episcopal church. His teachers and older classmates greet him warmly, applauding his decision to join "the most active and important" religious community in town. He wonders if he really belongs there.

A young woman grows up in a politically liberal, nonobservant Jewish home but in her midthirties finds herself becoming a *ba'alat teshuvah*, adopting Orthodox Judaism. Her new religious life includes observing commandments regarding the separation of the sexes at the synagogue and the keeping of ritual purity at home, practices that she used to call superstitions and that her feminist mother had always derided.[1]

These examples of the religious negotiation of identity may seem quite removed from the world of homesteading, where commitment to formal religion has been left behind. But I begin with these to emphasize the continuity rather than the difference between those who have constructed and improvised a spiritual life for themselves close to nature and those who remain active in more traditional religious settings. These, too, are negotiations of cultural identity—religious and otherwise—as when a bookish young man, raised in a nineteenth-century middle-class, liberal Christian household, borrows an axe and creates a life of reading, writing, and hoeing beans, with a pond rather than a church serving as his spiritual dwelling place.

One may suppose that those living on the boundaries of mainstream American society, challenging the dominant culture while also still implicated in it, are *expected* to be ambivalent. Certainly, my examination of the dynamics of "engagement and retreat" reveals the extent to which cultural reform is delicately negotiated by those who also seek to leave that culture behind. At the same time, readers might expect that those who have dramatically converted to a life lived close to nature would *never* stray from this conversion; yet my study has shown that self-culture is always at work in the process of getting close to nature and sometimes interferes with it. Some leave homesteading altogether when the practices of self-sufficiency have taught the necessary lessons. Others who once resisted technology may go on to embrace it in some form. Meanwhile, the ethics and asceticism (such as fasting or vegetarianism) of some homesteaders can seem "unnatural" in terms of other interpretations of the web of life (animals prey on each other; why not eat meat?).

I have also shown that the spiritual promise of nature itself can deemphasize strictly scientific forms of naturalism, as when homesteaders report experiences of what we might call the radical immanence of nature, in which the self is lost in nature or so interconnected with it that "nature's pain" is experienced. Theologies of the soil in which the decay of compost and the flowering of the seed are interpreted as processes in which humans can participate and so gain a kind of immortality are not unscientific, but they are glosses that move beyond a secular understanding of decomposition and photosynthesis and into a realm of human meaning-making that is attentive to nature while also speaking to the spiritual drama of the human condition.

In all of these cases, the construction of "nature" (as with the construction of "religion") is worked out in the context of myriad other ways in which people respond to their personal biographies, their physical place in the world, and their cultural sense of meaningful and ethical living in the world that they inhabit. As with more familiar negotiations of the religious, creating and articulating a homesteading life involve making one's world in the context of multiple and sometimes competing claims. Personal history and the broad sweep of American cultural history work together in forming lives that are well lived but often lived ambivalently. For us to understand this process, it is worth looking at those ambivalent legacies that I have not yet touched on (the legacies of gender and class) before returning to the larger themes of the interplay of religion and nature that have forged the central stories of this book.

Back to the Land or Back to the Kitchen?
Gender Trouble on the Modern Homestead

Staying at home, I have argued, is the central physical and symbolic act of homesteading. It is a particular model for social reform, one in which "the personal is the political." But the emphasis on personal action raises the specter of other ambivalent legacies of homesteading experiments old and new. For the women who made "the personal is the political" the slogan of second-wave feminism, the choice to homestead raises questions about gender that I have only hinted at so far. Of course, a discussion of homesteading and gender could be a book of its own. What we can begin to do here, however, is to isolate and explore what seem to be the most obviously "gendered" issues and consequences of homesteading experience and then place these issues back into the wider context of homesteading as meaning-making work. Let us begin by thinking back to Bill Coperthwaite's reflections on homemaking as the most important and most exciting profession of all. While other homesteaders may be eager to echo such beliefs, the women who have fought to enter the world of work outside the home may hesitate to affirm them. Indeed, an older colleague of mine who had entered professional academic life in the 1960s had just such a response to an early description of my research: "Why would *women* want to do *that*?" she replied with astonishment. "Who would want to regress to all that cooking and canning and laundry?"

If homemaking and a certain return to "tradition" are highly valued in the homesteading world, how do these ideals translate into "real world" negotiations in which homesteading ideals are put into practice by everyday men and women? What is cultural progress and what is "regression"?

An interesting dilemma surfaces immediately when we consider Coperthwaite's situation. He is one of the few homesteaders in my study who do not keep an extensive garden. In fact, he keeps no garden at all, choosing instead to feed himself from an eclectic combination of simple store-bought supplies and the animals that are available in his woods. In answer to my queries about why he did not garden, Bill responded simply that in order to have garden he needed a wife to tend it. He then elaborated a complex theory of gendered homesteading (remarkably resonant with the thought of Wendell Berry), in which he insisted that the ideal homestead depends on shared labor wherein both men and women are responsible for particular circumscribed aspects of homestead living.

Good marriages, in Bill's view, result from a system in which men and women are not only emotionally tied to each other but also physically dependent on each other within the chosen limits of a home-based economy. In this vision, relationships are more stable because they are based on something more than physical and emotional attraction, which might prove to be fleeting over time. In Bill's understanding, one shared by quite a number of homesteaders I interviewed, physical and economic interdependence—as played out in the context of partly self-sufficient living—may serve to strengthen partnerships. In contrast, either the predominant working world of two-career marriages or contemporary versions of "separate spheres" are seen by many homesteaders as being potentially destructive to family life.[2] A certain promotion of "family values"—and conventional socializing—emerges, for instance, when Carolyn Robinson writes her "Letter to Wives," encouraging reluctant women (as we heard earlier) that the Have More Plan promises not only wonderful food and plenty of time to host dinner parties but also a better marriage. "Somehow,"

Robinson muses, "working close to the earth and with nature seems to make the combination of man and wife more important and, I believe, makes marriage a happier success than is possible in sterile city life."[3] In a different vein, Linda Tatelbaum reflects that learning to use a two-person crosscut saw with her husband "almost destroyed, but ultimately improved," her marriage.[4] Like Coperthwaite, Carolyn Robinson and Linda Tatelbaum see stronger marriages emerging from the choice to rely on one's partner not only for affection but also for the necessary work of daily life.

It is also important to note that Coperthwaite's vision does not necessarily include "prescribed" gender roles (men must hunt, cut wood, and do the building projects; women must garden and preserve the food). In general, the roles he chooses to take on as a single homesteader certainly lean in the direction of what has frequently been constructed as "men's work," yet he is also an ace with a pair of knitting needles and values (and re-creates) all kinds of traditional handcrafts. At the same time, however, Coperthwaite has created a living dilemma for himself. By envisioning a homesteading life in which most work is done by hand and in rugged conditions and by including in that vision a system in which men do some things and women do others, Coperthwaite has created a set of expectations that many (including Coperthwaite himself) find challenging to fulfill. Other dilemmas appear on homesteads where partnerships do exist, and "staying home" and "living simply" are similarly valued. How do these ideals translate into lived realities? Does "back to the land" mean "back to the kitchen" for homesteading women and, if so, with what consequences?

One story we see in many countercultural experiments of the 1960s is the story of short-lived attempts at homestead living that quickly fell apart because of unanticipated gendered consequences. There are many straightforward examples of women who experienced the consciousness-raising of the early 1960s and then went back to the land temporarily (often as part of communal experiments with religious or political agendas other than self-sufficiency as such). These women found themselves coerced (or tempted) into doing the majority of the cooking, cleaning, and child raising. Dissatisfied with this state of affairs, they left.[5] But the stories of long-term homesteaders I am telling here are the stories of those who have hung on in one way or another for five to twenty years and who have been actively negotiating (sometimes quite self-consciously wrestling with) what it means to live a "simpler" life close to nature. Practically and symbolically, they have worked out these often gendered meanings in the context of everyday life and in ways both strange and familiar to those outside the homesteading world.

If we imaginatively return to the homestead of Dale and Robin, for instance, we will see a fairly traditional division of labor that echoes, in many ways,

Robin's nostalgia for nineteenth-century ways of life. Dale works on exterior building projects, manages the woodlot, plants fruit trees, and does some of the garden work. Robin, in her own words, has become "almost completely focused on food"; she tends to the majority of the gardening, all of the preserving, and most of the cooking. Child care is shared by both parents but more often falls to Robin, especially in terms of feeding the children, tending to aches and pains, and so on. Dale is more apt to take on odd jobs outside the home for extra income, which also means that more of the homeschooling responsibilities fall to Robin.

Although Dale and Robin often find themselves overloaded in terms of work that needs to be done on the homestead and the need for money that sometimes can only be found off the homestead, they have a happy, solid, functioning marriage and express contentment with the roles they have chosen, even if their everyday life feels somewhat chaotic. Robin's involvement in all aspects of food, for instance, comes from her love and enthusiasm for gardening and cooking, an enthusiasm that sometimes takes her away from the more economically lucrative tasks of making dried wreathes and selling them to local buyers. She exhibits little interest in being involved in wider circles of production other than raising her own food and feeding it to her friends and family, tasks that she finds satisfying and fun as well as ecologically, spiritually, and politically meaningful.[6] The tension on Dale and Robin's homestead seems always to have less to do with gender roles per se and more to do with shared concerns about making ends meet and not spreading oneself too thin.

Yet my early field notes reveal my own surprise in finding a couple of Nearing-inspired radicals who seemed, well, so traditional.[7] One of the early images I found so attractive in my first explorations of homesteading were those of Helen Nearing at age seventy traipsing around in the mud, hauling heavy rocks, and showing callow 1960s youth (mostly male) just how to build a stone house. My "tough as nails" image of Helen Nearing was only confirmed by my own visits with her when she was in her nineties. In contrast, the field notes of my visit to Dale and Robin's homestead reveal my concerns with what I expected homesteading to mean for a thirty-something woman of the 1990s. I often found Robin in the kitchen wearing an apron and tending to her children, not hefting stones à la Helen. Dale and Robin were not intentionally experimenting with sharing particular roles, as were Henry and Jo up the road, who traded cooking and household chores on a rotating, weekly basis. But neither did either one of them seem to be suffering from an urge to escape gender-prescribed boundaries. If there was "gender trouble" on this homestead, it was subtle and relatively benign. The trouble lay more with the ethnographer—me—who had not expected modern homesteading to reflect so closely its earlier precedents.

Nevertheless, Dale and Robin's ideological insistence that homesteading is primarily about both members of the couple "being at home" and "centering your life around home" has led to some unexpected, gendered consequences. Dale and Robin have been so dedicated to producing their own food and staying out of the nine-to-five working world that they frequently have found themselves getting in over their heads in terms of physical labor and economic stress. At one point, they bought a cow and other domestic animals, only later realizing that animal raising, homeschooling, and taking the occasional "outside" job were too much for them. They then had to sell the animals at a loss, and Dale began to take on seasonal work with the Merchant Marine. In this narrative, the ideal model of both members of the couple being home-centered has unintentionally given way to the reality (they hope, temporary) of the man working outside the home (actually being absent for weeks at a time) while the woman takes care of the children, schools them, raises food, and feeds the family.

A more explicitly troubled story emerges in the lives of another homesteading couple, Sal and his wife, Kate. Sal and Kate's homesteading experiment began as an ideal story of shared work. Conscious about wanting to avoid traditional gender roles, both participated in drawing water, cutting wood, keeping the house warm, cooking, and working in the garden. They also followed Nearing-style approaches to dividing the day between them with respect to work and leisure, although there was little leisure in the early years.

But just as this system of work, balanced roles, and a hint of leisure was beginning to be perfected, children entered the picture, and the story turned. "The children just come to me when they are hurt or want something—or just want my attention," said Kate in an interview in the spring of 1994, "and so my role has had to change, with me focusing on the children and [Sal] doing most of the other homestead work."[8] The reality of children, coupled with Sal's role as the unquestionable visionary and theorist of the homesteading project, led to a downward spiral, which ultimately culminated in the demise of the relationship.

The personal story is more complex, of course, but my point here is to note that not only Sal and Kate but also friends and neighbors alike have unfolded this story in highly gendered terms. In the context of this homesteading tale, traditional gender roles (the mother as primary caretaker) became further solidified, in part because of a larger moral vision that was relatively nonnegotiable: a commitment to doing things by hand (such as washing diapers) and a refusal to partake of certain environmental "sins" (such as having a car). Eventually, some of Sal and Kate's initial principles gave way—they bought an old car and started driving forty-five minutes each way into a town that had a laundromat—but much of the emotional cost had already taken its toll. Even after these adjustments, Sal and Kate still heated their home with hand-cut wood, lit it with candles and lamps, and made their living from selling homegrown vegetables and home-baked bread. As Sal increased his bread business, Kate slipped into a growing depression. The story of this marriage and its dissolution is far too multilayered to "blame" solely on the issue of gender, yet the gendered dynamics of homesteading are a persistent and, in this case, an ultimately destructive refrain.

Linda and Kal Tatelbaum have a similar story to tell, but one with a much more salubrious outcome. They also report that their homesteading experiment began with a conscious attempt at sharing roles—roles that became divided along more traditional gendered lines only after their son was born. In an essay revealingly entitled "Used Body Parts," Linda describes her first attempts at homesteading as ventures into "being a boy": "As a very young woman I would inspect myself in the mirror, one feature at a time. . . . [and] wondered, *What's a body for?* To attract? To hide? To sit in a library? To sunbathe on a beach? It was time to take possession, to move in and find out what I could do."[9] Tatelbaum goes on to describe how she placed an ad to do farmwork as a way of getting "an education all over again at age 25." She cut her hair short, donned denim work clothes, and soon learned to lift forty-pound sap buckets. When she was mistaken for a "fella" at the local hardware store, she flashed the embarrassed clerk a "triumphant smile": "I'd made it." From the vantage point of an established homesteader who has perfected the art for twenty-five years and more to come, Tatelbaum reflects on homesteading as a process that both freed her from the dominant (patriarchal) cultural views of a woman's body and allowed her to be truly embodied for the first time:

> It took leaving home to discover the boy within me, the son I wasn't. Without Dad to do it for me, I learned to rig up a bookshelf . . . build a kitchen cabinet with tools like his. . . . I toughed out a New Hampshire winter alone, climbing down a rickety ladder into the awful dirt cellar, in rubber boots and a nightgown, to unclog the flooded sump pump. I learned to thaw frozen pipes, fix stuck doors, re-ignite extinguished pilot lights, chop wood. . . . I'm embarrassed . . . to think a girl becomes a woman without knowing how to be a boy or a man.[10]

Taking pride in her early accomplishments in "boyhood," Tatelbaum worked to maintain her hard-won skills, but (as with Kate and Robin) motherhood changed both the details and the emotional experience of homestead practice. Tatelbaum's memories of this period have a rueful tone:

> [On the homestead] Kal and I were a working unit of one and one. He knew as little as I did about physically creating a life from scratch in the wilderness, luckily. . . . I was free to be a girl-boy-woman acquiring physical skills along-

side my mate. Add a baby into the equation, though, and our one-plus-one partnership shrank to half plus half. . . . Kal was in the garden, the woodshed, the cellar, the truck, and I was in the rocking chair. Overnight, to our shock, the pioneers' story became our story, too. . . . My body wasn't mine anymore, but something to be desired, something to eat, something that bleeds, ceases to bleed, gives birth, gives milk.[11]

Whatever joys motherhood has brought, it has also seemingly brought this young boy-woman back full circle to her early adolescent musings about what in the (American) world a body should be for. Despite the victorious break-throughs of homesteading "boyhood," anatomy once again seems to be destiny. But Tatelbaum's experience of the reduction of her self to a "body" that the self barely owns soon led to a new level of insight. "I rocked in despair until, look-ing into the dark pools of my baby's eyes, I saw myself, an infant like him once, laying down the chapters of my body memory. . . . Feeding a new life does call upon as full a use of body as building a house, I could see that now, watching him grow. My body was still mine, but not only mine."[12]

What is important to focus on in this autobiographical essay is a certain val-uation of the body and the way in which that valuation shifts in the context of both Tatelbaum's initial experiences and her later reflections on them. Initially, she sees herself as having left behind so-called traditional readings of the female body. She is consciously working against what she sees as the dominant patri-archal view that values women primarily for their reproductive capacities, their capacity to give men pleasure, and their capacity to do the domestic labor re-lated to these two functions. She experiences victory in "becoming a boy" and feels defeated and trapped when giving birth seems to reduce her to being little more than a female body. But in the context of a marriage that has supported both her being a boy and being a woman, the crisis of birth and the corre-sponding assumption of traditional roles do not lead to an accompanying cri-sis in the marriage. Instead, Tatelbaum characterizes the dramatic change as one that, correspondingly, needs a shift in vision: "One + one + one = three bod-ies, one family story, something worth building."[13] Significantly also, the vision of homesteading does not harden here into one person's ideal view; rather, it becomes flexible in response to the demands a child brings. This process, in turn, leads Tatelbaum to a sense of flexibility toward homesteading in general, as we can see in her decisions to install solar power and in her unhidden affec-tion for a large leather couch.

In the story Tatelbaum tells, her understanding of her body comes full circle in one sense but resists tradition in another. She ultimately accepts the role of mother, caregiver, cook, and feeder—and gives up some of her outdoor labors that initially attracted her to a homesteading life. But the homesteading life it-self is one that consciously fights against a world of work that both men and "liberated women" are encouraged to do: work outside the home. Much of this work, in her view and in the view of many homesteaders, is work that can be profoundly (and alarmingly) outside nature, disembodied, destructive to home life, and overly bound up in a dominant culture of commercialism, con-sumerism, and greed. While accepting tradition in one sense, Tatelbaum thus also rails against the current status quo, encouraging us to think about both gen-der and homemaking in more complex terms than those normally used in pop-ular debates about feminism and the family.

The negotiation of gender roles is, of course, a negotiation that occurs in every household, but on the homestead—a site of presumed cultural freedom—this negotiation takes particularly complex forms. In Ralph Borsodi's records of the household economy, for instance, we see portraits that are rare for the 1920s and 1930s: Ralph Borsodi weaving his own suits at the hand-loom (an art Har-lan Hubbard also practiced and praised); John Loomis (Mildred Loomis's hus-band) grinding grain for his own breakfast cereal in the kitchen. These pictures dovetail nicely with photographs from the Nearings' self-published *Good Life Album*, in which Helen is photographed with short hair, wearing men's work clothes, and sorting farm tools outside. Such pictures challenged conventional norms and thus helped to fuel the fire of those who sought to portray the Near-ings and the Borsodis as cultural radicals.

While radical in some senses, however, these homesteading experiments of the 1920s through the 1940s also upheld traditional gender roles at a time when women were increasingly entering the American work force.[14] In Ralph Borsodi's narrative of the family homesteading adventure, for instance, Myrtle Mae Borsodi is clearly identified as the housewife, while Ralph portrays himself as the theorist and chief executor of the homesteading project. Although ac-knowledging Myrtle Mae's labor with admiration and gratitude and displaying his willingness to do his own amount of indoor work in terms of weaving and crafts, he clearly leaves the canning and cooking to "Mrs. Borsodi," who seems to welcome these tasks. Indeed, part of the Borsodi "program" was simultane-ously to keep rural men and women "on the farm" and to urge suburban and urban women to reconsider the pursuit of a career. To do this, Myrtle Mae pub-lished numerous articles in magazines suited for domestic and farming audi-ences in which she argued for the professionalization of housewifery, a strat-egy of both accommodation and resistance that goes back to Catherine Beecher's *American Woman's Home* and predicts the sociological diagnosis later de-livered by Betty Friedan.[15]

In an article for *The Silent Hostess* entitled "My Home Is My Career" (1932),

FIGURE 12.
Helen sorts tools (photo by Ralph T. Gardner). As visitors to
the Nearings increased, Helen spent more time receiving and
feeding guests, yet she always preferred outdoor projects and
strived to have "less work for the housewife." Courtesy of the
Good Life Center and the Thoreau Institute at Walden Woods.

Myrtle Mae asks her readers to bring the "true dignity of a career" to homemaking and describes how, in her own life with Ralph Borsodi, she has reconceived "drudgery," by learning to mechanize "nonproductive" work such as
dishwashing, cleaning, and laundry so as to free up time for "productive" ac-
tives that were essential to the homesteading ideal, such as cooking, canning,
sewing, and weaving. While some readers may see these latter activities as also
being drudgery, Myrtle Mae argues that this kind of work requires the same
"vaunted business efficiency" for which she was praised as a New York professional in advertising and publishing. By keeping production at home, she simultaneously battles the "distribution problem" that is at the core of Ralph Borsodi's philosophy, saves money in the midst of the Depression, and finds
meaning in her newfound "professional" role She recalls, "I began to see my
career as a homemaker just as I had considered my career at the office."[16]

The complexity of Myrtle Mae's role in homestead life is further revealed in
an article for Electrical Merchandising, "The Home Laundry Earns Money."[17] Myrtle

THE SILENT HOSTESS

Two dollars grow where one grew before

by

Mrs. Ralph Borsodi

YOU and I know only too well that dollars are harder to earn than they were a few years ago. But we know too that the standards of today have not changed as regards the necessity of education and a "smart" appearance or the desirability of spending-money and travel. The burden of stretching our dollars to cover all the things they did when they were more numerous falls chiefly on us home-makers.

We have to go at the problem in a business-like way. And it was the business man who long ago discovered that one of the easiest ways to make two dollars grow where only one grew before is to buy in large quantity rather than in small quantity, thus obtaining bargain prices.

If you stop to think about it you will realize that we women have for some time past actually been reversing this principle. We have been buying in smaller and smaller quantities — mainly because we were not equipped with proper cold storage or facil-

[10]

FIGURE 13.

In the 1930s, Myrtle Mae Borsodi's articles, such as this one for *The Silent Hostess*, emphasized a professionalization of home-making that sought to bring women back from the workforce. Courtesy of the School of Living, s-o-l.org, and of the Ralph Borsodi Papers, Milne Special Collections, University of New Hampshire Library.

Mae opens her article with a clear indictment of first-wave feminism. "For many years," she begins, "I have claimed that the great woman movement which started with Mary Wollstonecraft and Susan B. Anthony was leading the modern woman into a grotesque abandonment of the only thing that makes life worth living." But a closer examination of her position reveals that her critique (not unlike those articulated by Wendell Berry, Bill Coperthwaite, and others) is not a complaint against feminism as such. The rise of consumer culture is the root object of her concern. Because "millions of dollars have been spent in publicity to induce women left in the home to give up home production," she writes, women are increasingly choosing to "take the commercial products of our factories and mills." Choosing to consume rather than to produce, she argues, leads women into a situation where they are bored, have too much leisure on their hands, and are "hungry to justify their existence." That hunger drives women into "the factory . . . by [which] I mean offices, department stores, art studios and the hundreds of auxiliaries to factory management."

Today's readers might argue with Myrtle Mae Borsodi that her diagnosis of cause and effect is misplaced. Is the drive to "justify one's existence" the only motivation for women who are not driven by economic need to join the workforce? Moreover, is pursuing a career in an art studio really a kind of consignment to "the factory"? And is it not ironic that in one article Myrtle Mae describes doing laundry as nonproductive compared with growing food, weaving, and similar domestic work, but in several other articles laundry doing (albeit mechanized) is at the center of her discussion? Such questions are well worth raising. At the same time, however, it is revealing to consider that however much the Borsodis seemed to exemplify typical gender roles, they also challenged them in various ways: by encouraging a model where not only women but also men stayed at home and by using the home as a base to continue the work of social reform. While Myrtle Mae sometimes represented herself as the housewife and mother par excellence, she was joined by Ralph in many aspects of home production. In some ways, she continued to do the work of her previous career, by serving as an advertiser and publicist, no longer for New York City firms but for the Borsodi homestead vision instead. Knowing that she had to appeal to women to make homesteading viable, Myrtle Mae Borsodi advocated a conventional model of womanhood while subtly subverting some aspects of the conventional work-family structures of the day.

The Borsodis' embrace of a host of labor-saving electric devices (an anathema to many homesteaders) demonstrates the complex dynamics of reverencing nature, reforming consumer culture, and negotiating gender. With all of the "latest" appliances (for the 1930s and 1940s), their model kitchen looked like a suburban show kitchen of the highest order. At the same time, the role the kitchen played at the center of a productive family economy, rather than for show, puts questions of nature and gender in a new light. Although traditionally gendered labor is not turned upside down in this experiment, it is mitigated by a vision of an efficient cottage industry in which both men and women participate. If nature is kept at bay in this vision, this result is more desirable than a form of home economics based on antitechnological perfectionism, an approach that in most cases has burdened women more than men.

Helen Nearing's homesteading roles are also more complex than meets the eye. When she came of age in the 1910s and the 1920s, Helen led a considerably "liberated" life. In training as a concert violinist and actively participating in the international circles of the Theosophist Society, Helen traveled independently throughout Europe and Asia, leading a life she herself called free spirited. In choosing a homesteading life with Scott Nearing, Helen simultaneously took on the role of "housewife," which was previously unknown to her, while also resisting this role in various ways. Helen's aversion to baking bread, for instance, came not only from her philosophical and spiritual allegiances to raw foods but also from her stated desire to have "less work for the housewife."[18] In contrast to the Borsodis, then, she combined a quest for intimacy with nature (seeing raw foods as "more natural") with a means of avoiding excessive amounts of kitchen labor. Helen openly stated that she preferred to work outdoors, loving particularly to build stone structures. On the other hand, she never questioned that the housewife role was hers to fill. She took charge of the cooking, cleaning, and feeding of visitors while Scott would go off to saw wood.

In the early twentieth century, Scott and Nellie Seeds Nearing had argued publicly for the emancipation of women in their jointly authored *Women and Social Progress* (1912).[19] But this argument for the woman's right (and often personal need) to pursue professional work was articulated side by side with older ideas of "woman's sphere." Nellie Seeds obtained a doctorate in 1915, wrote professionally, and went on to become the executive secretary of the Rand School, director of the Manumit School, and a supervisor of adult education for the Works Progress Administration. In concert with Scott's early writing, however, she claimed that motherhood was the most important occupation for a woman to pursue and that women's roles in domestic life were central to the future of American culture. But in time, her marriage with Scott became a troubled one, in part, because of struggles over gender roles (and, in part, because of Scott's hard and fast "simple living" habits, which were an embarrassment to friends and family). In her later writing (particularly an article published in 1922), Nellie rebelled against the confines of motherhood, the customary standards of domestic excellence, and the assumption that woman's place is in the home while men (such as Scott) freely pursue professional, intellectual, and social lives elsewhere.[20] Distancing herself from Scott although never formally divorcing him, Nellie remained a social reformer, but one who embraced capitalism and professionalism, largely because of the personal and intellectual freedoms it afforded her.

Nellie Seeds Nearing was a "homesteader wife" only in the sense of belonging to the summer Arden community and in negotiating with Scott through a series of households in which Scott kept gardens, prepared his own raw food meals, and insisted on using wooden bowls and utensils. But Nellie's own struggle to work out the meaning of "womanhood" side by side with radical politics and a husband whose rules for living were cast in stone is a revealing one and is predictive of the challenges Helen Nearing would face.

Helen's role as the Good Life promoter and publisher was indeed complex. She served as editor and secretary for Scott's projects, a task that was professional on the one hand (Scott often paid her for this work) and that of a helpmate on the other. At the same time, she taught and played violin, wrote her own books (such as the "Simple Foods" cookbook), and increasingly gave her own lectures on homestead living. Yet this professional work was seldom acknowledged by Scott, the public, or even Helen herself. Scott and Nellie Seed's son, Robert, has confirmed that "Helen did the work" of systematizing and publicizing their Good Life projects, although Scott rarely pointed this out. Publicly, Helen deferred to Scott's leadership and vision; and in my own conversations with her, she often diminished her contributions relative to Scott's.[21] In the last decade of Scott's life, however, Helen also visibly came into her own as the main force behind the homesteading projects. And after his death, she increasingly served as a mentor and guide to hundreds of women who approached her through visits and letters, seeking advice from a "strong" female elder, not on homesteading per se, but on marriage, child raising, spirituality, and the many dimensions of living an ethical life as a woman in the late twentieth century.

The "return visits" to now familiar homesteads that I have briefly discussed here all offer complex portraits of how "home" is being interpreted by those who are intentionally crafting lives close to nature and away from consumer culture. In interpreting these lives, I have found it difficult to put them in such easily available categories as liberal or conservative; feminist or traditionalist; essentialist or inessentialist, because indeed, for many of the men and women I have interviewed, these categories of scholarly and popular conversation do not adequately capture the nuances, tensions, and ongoing changes in their lives.

One interpretive approach that has been helpful to me, however, has been to see these modern homesteaders as participating in what Nancy Cott has called (in a different context) a "discourse of domesticity."[22] I do not want to overstate the case by claiming that modern homesteading is just one more iteration of the "cult of domesticity," which emerged in the late eighteenth and early nineteenth centuries, for there are obviously some significant historical contrasts between the worlds that Cott and I have explored. On the other hand, as my attention to Thoreauvian legacies makes clear, modern homesteading contains significant echoes of nineteenth-century, Romantic "quests for authenticity" and cultivations of "original responses to the universe."[23] We also hear echoes of middle-class nineteenth-century (often evangelical) discussions about the value of home as a moral space, "a restorative haven from the anxieties and adversities of public life."[24]

The important difference in this modern "discourse of domesticity," of course, is that the older ideology of "separate spheres" is being actively resisted as men and women commit to being together on the modern homestead. At the same time, however, the division of labor can continue to be gendered in ways that some men and women welcome and others struggle with and resist.[25] For men who grew up in urban or suburban middle-class households, new challenges emerge as they experiment with farming and domestic roles for which they have had few male models or cultural encouragement. For some homesteaders like Craig (who in chapter 2 spoke of "doing things the hard way" as a necessary "pilgrimage"), these vigorous homestead experiments are made possible by a female spouse who works, an arrangement his "old-timer" Vermont neighbors may judge as "unmanly" or odd. And in some cases, the "purity" of some men's vision of what the homestead can and should be does not match the realities of the labor and sacrifice required to put such ideals into practice.

For women, embracing domesticity is no more or less complex, but it involves a different kind of dance with gender roles, both old and new. Friends and family members of some women still see the rigors of house building and farming as "inappropriate for women." At the same time, others read canning a year's supply of tomatoes as a kind of "drudgery" that no "enlightened woman" would choose. For modern homesteading women, making the decision, say, to wash diapers by hand may feel alternatively like entrapment or liberation, depending on which cultural norms (consumer society or "women's sphere") they see themselves working against—and who on the homestead is actually making the decision.

The paradoxes involved in interpreting freely chosen, "homemade" domestic work emerge in a reflection from Fran, a Smith College graduate who lives in rural Massachusetts. Fran's comments on the meaning of baking a cake without electricity evoke the complexities of reimagining "women's role" in the context of back-to-the-land commitments.

Being dependent on power takes power out of our own lives. It removes us from our own power. Think about when you bake a cake. You could just use an electric beater and a mix. But if you don't, you have to do a bit more planning. You have to think about when and how to get the butter to the right consistency. You're using your mind; there's a certain level of skill and of intellect involved. But then you're also using your body. You're using your muscles to beat the batter by hand. And you're using your body in a much more satisfying way because you're really connected to the process of making that cake. And of course, you don't have to deal with the awful noise of the mixer.[26]

This description carries with it a language of domestic work that challenges earlier definitions of what women's work has been. Using one's mind and using one's muscles are celebrated here. Power is the dominant motif. At the same time, we hear the language of revaluing that which is "traditional." Cake baking by hand permits connection to an earlier, simpler time, and for Fran (as she described later), it gives more meaning and value to the food that she gives to her husband and children. This cake baking is not the cake baking of The Feminine Mystique; rather, it is the cake baking of cultural critique. But to say it is not "problematic" (in terms of demanding further inquiry and examination) would be to ignore a long history of homemaking and cake baking that has always been deeply gendered.

Like all cultural work, then, homesteading is gendered work, work that can both challenge and reify competing notions of men's and women's labor. Some "essentialist" distinctions reappear, while others are radically overturned. In every homesteading family, however, decisions about who does what kind of work are not just decisions about gender; they are also decisions about nature and culture. At times, modern homesteaders will emphasize gender difference more than equality, articulating views that some might call prefeminist and others "postfeminist," but views that focus, in either case, on traditional concepts of women's labor as caretaking and mothering. Even homestead experiments that begin with idealized notions of shared labor and child rearing often cash out, in practice, with traditional gender-based labor distinctions: men working outside, women inside; men focusing on whatever "cash crop" is being produced, women focusing on child rearing.

These gendered decisions are not made in isolation, however, but in the service of getting close to nature and resisting certain aspects of mainstream culture. In these moments, again, we find ironic and unintentional resonances with the concepts of proper gender roles articulated, say, by the Christian Right or by Orthodox Jews. Homesteaders, while often in rebellion against traditional religious institutions, share with more traditional religious persons a criticism of modernity and its negative cultural consequences. While most nonreligious homesteaders hold quite liberal views about gender equality in theory, the commitment to homesteading as a practice takes priority, in large part because the practice itself is a spiritual or ethical one. Such practices can look countercultural and, at the same time, deeply traditional.

Class Acts: The Habitus of Homesteading

The Nearings' comment that life is surrounded by a "circumference of choice" reminds us that homesteading is defined by and becomes symbolically significant because it is a choice. It is a choice that has complex implications for concepts of gender and a choice that is made possible and meaningful because of a certain social location. "Voluntary simplicity," "playing at farming," or intentional forms of inner-worldly asceticism of the kind demonstrated by the Nearings all emphasize the extent to which meaning is made by giving up a life of material comfort for a "better way" in more limited circumstances. Homesteading may not be a direct function of financial resources, for certainly some homesteaders I interviewed came from families of limited means. In the majority of cases, however, homesteaders have the power to choose a different life, and that power is often facilitated by economic resources, social formation in groups that presume a level of cultural influence, access to higher education, or some combination of these. The majority of homesteaders I have researched come from middle- and upper-middle-class backgrounds in which opportunities for education, leisure, and self-fashioning abound. This is not surprising and not even typically "American." To phrase the issue as pointedly as it has often been put to me, we cannot conclude a study of homesteading without posing the question, What about class?[27]

One of the more problematic aspects of homesteading is the social context in which it occurs. But I do not mean to suggest that the relatively privileged status of homesteaders is *inherently* problematic. I would argue, however, that social location accounts for some of the ambivalences we see in homesteading. Three aspects of the practice of homesteading that particularly intrigue me pertain to its social and cultural location. They are: the expression of one particular reading of nature, the potential for the commodification of homesteading, and the persistence of the very moral hegemony to which homesteaders object in both traditional religious institutions and in the industrialist and consumerist "cult of progress." I will consider each of these issues in turn.

What readings of nature do we see, and how reflective are they of the possible range of meanings that might be expressed? While homesteaders emphasize their own initiative in converting to their new lives, they are less apt to describe their own role in the *construction* of "nature" or even to consider the extent to which nature is culturally constructed. Of course, it is the scholar's task to make these dynamics of construction clear, as I have attempted to do throughout this study. But we learn something by attending to what I would call a kind of cultivated ignorance toward nature (a stance Thoreau often recommended), which many homesteaders express. In some homesteaders' views, nature comes to have an authority that is indisputable. "Nature" suggests that new structures of time, work, and play are "more appropriate." "Nature" requires vegetarianism (and, for some, Nature requires meat eating). "Nature" dictates that technology is "bad" (or "good") or that certain food, herbs, and physical regimes are "healthy" (because they are "natural"). Not surprisingly, while Nature is presumed to be authoritative, what Nature wants (as, in other settings, what God wants) differs depending on the interpreter of Nature's "truths."

A hint of dogmatism comes to the fore when we examine the language of those homesteaders who insist that nature sets the terms for all human activity and that divergence from nature's rules constitutes a new version of "sin."[28] Such language appears, at times, in the Nearings' testimonies of dietary principles, in manuals praising the virtue and necessity of composting, and in the Total Loss farmers' sense of their lives as being oriented and controlled (as it should be, they imply) by the demands of the garden and Bessie the cow. That we must defer to nature's ecological requirements and limits is an ethical claim that many of us would not hesitate to affirm. It is worth contemplating, however, the range of readings of nature (and the cultural function of those readings) that emerge from those who have made a dramatic commitment to live "on nature's terms."

Some homesteaders offer visions of nature that can be seen, revealingly, as mirror opposites of "Bible-believing" Christians' views (which themselves have been argued in the borrowed language of science, a language of "proof" and "evidence"). In the homesteading context, too, a set of truths (nature's laws) are experienced and interpreted spiritually, supported scientifically, and understood to be the undebatable basis of an all-pervasive, "better" way of living.[29] This new way of living is understood to be spiritually and morally "right," although it may also reap the benefits of improved health, economic independence, and more fluid boundaries between work and play. Finally, nature tends to be viewed primarily as a *benevolent* force, and its aggressive and destructive qualities are often downplayed.

The turn to nature as a source of authority comes out of a particular history of the negotiation between religion and science in the twentieth century. If we recollect John Burroughs's turn from the unshakable Baptist beliefs of his father to his own self-fashioned "Gospel of Nature," it is "culturally logical," as it were, to find—first with Thoreau and Burroughs and later with a host of others—that nature is the new source of Truth, and a particular *vision* of nature (enchanted, benevolent, redeeming) is being propagated. But I have wondered also about the extent to which such a turn to nature also underlines a socially located anxiety about freedom. While homesteaders celebrate their freedom from the dominant culture, their practices of dissent from that culture *reimpose constraint*, which, in turn, rearticulates their initial concerns about the cultural freedoms they have inherited. These include freedom to be among the world's greatest consumers, freedom to harm the natural world, and freedom to dissent from the dominant American view and to remake the self on what appears to be one's own terms. Freedom *itself* is a cultural inheritance that needs to be wrestled with—one with which homesteaders have had to deal both before and during their lives of homesteading.[30]

Amid their anxieties about freedom, then, some homesteaders also enjoy certain kinds of cultural influence that they are reluctant to give up. This becomes clear when we ponder one of the paradoxes of homesteading: the compulsion to write about it. While not all homesteaders are writers, some do seem to produce texts to the same extent as food. Even homesteaders who have been less prolific writers than John Burroughs, Wendell Berry, or Helen and Scott Nearing have been anxious to put their actions into words, in newsletters or minor journals or on the Internet. At the same time, those who have written a great deal and thereby attracted a large following have often done so at the risk of commodifying and overpopularizing their very practices of dissent. "Why risk this?" I have often wondered.

By reminding myself that homesteaders tend to occupy a place in culture where having a good deal of cultural influence is expected and exercising that influence through reading and writing is common, the relationship between homesteading and writing about it makes more sense. Writing homesteading texts is, as I have already mentioned, an economic act. It is also, as I discussed in chapter 1, a logical extension of the experience of conversion to a new way of life. Furthermore, while homesteaders are attempting to throw off old lives that they see as tainted, in part, by commercialization, many of them are eager to spread the word, sometimes at their own peril in terms of privacy and peaceful ways of living.

While homesteaders tend to criticize culture as overemphasizing theoretical or second-hand rather than lived experience, some are unable to stop theorizing about their practices. Some, such as the Nearings, display unrelenting confidence in their ability to create and sustain an appropriate moral vision. (This is what some readers of homesteading texts have more bluntly phrased as "the tendency to take the moral high ground.") Whatever we may call it, I also see this dynamic as an inheritance of the liberal Christian and progressive Jewish tradition in American culture, an inheritance to which most homesteaders are directly connected through family, education, or both. Homesteaders may change the content of their moral vision. They may be eager to take God out of it and put nature at the center. But they do not change their underlying confidence in being able to know what the "right" spiritual or moral vision is, being able to systematize and perfect it in their own lives, and being able to convince others of its essential worth. The desire for dissent from mainstream culture is mitigated by the desire not to give up certain kinds of cultural capital (particularly in the moral sphere) with which homesteaders are all too familiar. The need to create and articulate a moral vision for the self and, in some cases, to "evangelize" this vision with the hope of reforming American culture comes out of homesteaders' particular social and cultural position. To borrow from Max Weber, we can see homesteaders as individuals who seek to reenchant the world of capitalism but who will not give up the cultural traditions of inner-worldly asceticism and the sense of moral authority that helped shape the culture they are trying to reform. To put the situation in Pierre Bourdieu's terms: the habitus of homesteaders does not necessarily go away with a change in habitat.[31]

Nature's Meanings

The themes we have visited so far—the changes in homesteading visions and practices over time, the ongoing tensions between contemplation and action, personal renewal and cultural reform, and the struggle between what we might call "homesteader identity" and the cultural locations of gender and class—remind us again that as much as the experience of getting close to nature is sought by homesteaders, nature remains a moving target.

Nature, however, reverenced and respected in what we might call its own right, remains something that is put to use. It can serve as the backdrop against which the self is constructed and American culture is assessed and found wanting. Nature is also often controlled, not protected in the manner of a wilderness preserve. While homesteaders might agree with environmental ethicists that nature has intrinsic value (and, indeed, they may have more practical experience in nature on which to base this assessment), their own approach to nature is more often utilitarian (attuned to nature's uses) than post-Kantian (valuing nature as an end in itself).[32] The need to "use" nature, not simply to revere it, comes, in part, from the necessity of directly harvesting nature's resources for food, shelter, and some source of income.

Of course, all of us use nature in this way, but often at so many layers of remove from the resources themselves that we encounter nature largely in an aesthetic mode, nature as a source of recreation or contemplation. Homesteaders, by contrast, make a visible impact on nature. They chop down trees, build new homes in the woods (rather than live in existing urban dwellings), and plow the earth in their backyards (rather than support existing farmers and grocers). In the language of the Nearings and Borsodis, homesteads are even referred to as a kind of laboratory for scientific and economic experiments. Some home-steaders make elaborate use of greenhouses to extend the productivity of their gardens into the winter or use their land as testing grounds for solar and wind power stations, projects that certainly control nature and have a visual environ-mental impact. But while putting nature both literally and symbolically "to use," experienced homesteaders also exhibit a deep knowledge of nature that many urban-based wilderness lobbyists do not.[33] In this sense, getting close to nature may mean controlling nature, and seeking intimacy with the natural world may also mean having a direct impact that could otherwise be avoided. Yet while en-gaging in practices that appear more "controlling" than those of the aestheti-cally motivated wilderness hiker, homesteaders also close the distance with na-ture in a way that eludes many "nature-loving" Americans. The ironies and ambiguities of homesteading, then, never fail to double back on themselves.

Scholars of the idea of nature in America are quick to tell us that the classic construction of nature in America is either as a wilderness to be fled or con-quered or as a garden to be enjoyed without human effort.[34] Homesteaders, however, both experience and create a world of nature that occupies a middle ground between these two poles. These gardens are gardens of human effort and impact, not wildernesses to be conquered, as in early periods of American history, or "loved to death," as is more often the case today. Nor are they, how-ever, Edenic retreats where humans are presumed innocent and nature is ex-pected to provide freely. For homesteaders, the garden is both a practical natu-ral resource for getting a living and a symbolic expression of "getting a life." And this symbolic expression, while always a gesture of meaning-making for the self, is also a cultural gesture of lived alternatives to a materialist society. The homestead can serve not only as a call for reform but also as a model for what that reform might look like. In either case, nature is shaped to serve human pur-poses and human desires. But human desires are seldom monolithic, and so it is no surprise that ambivalence toward nature emerges when we consider homesteaders as a group.

Sometimes that ambivalence is expressed when we compare the machine-loving testimonies of Borsodi with the "hand-tools only" ethic of Coperthwaite. If the use of technology in relation to nature is our only criterion for authentic homesteading, then Coperthwaite may be "in" while Borsodi is "out"; yet, would this be a fair judgment of the author of This Ugly Civilization and The Flight from the City? At other times, ambivalence can be discerned when we trace the evolution of homesteaders' lives over time, as with Sal and Henry. Sal's "use" of nature plays a role in his self-construction but ultimately leads him to a life as an entrepreneur in the city. Henry's interpretation of technology changes as his practice of homesteading emerges. On still other occasions, homesteaders, such as the Nearings, have simultaneously expressed a longing for some parts of nature and a resistance to other aspects. Their highly structured approach to time and planning and their dietary scrupulosity are revealing of this resistance. On some homesteads, as we have seen, work is distributed according to a concept of the "natural" divisions of labor that exist between men and women, whose biological differences may suggest the need for gender-divided work. Yet other homesteads flout these "natural" distinctions and experiment with gender-neutral approaches to homestead work, a perhaps ironic stance in its own right for those who are committed to living in step with nature's design. As we consider the varieties of homesteads and homesteaders we have encountered throughout this book, then, we are reminded that a life lived close to nature is often, also, a life lived in a kind of approach-avoidance dance with nature.

Many factors play a role in these approach-avoidance dances, but this ambivalence toward nature persists, in part, because nature serves both practical and symbolic purposes. Getting close to nature "works" as long as psychospiritual needs are being met, as long as homesteading continues to function in terms of either personal remaking or cultural critique, and as long as homesteading is pragmatically possible. But how close to nature one actually gets is worked out in reference to a delicate balance: between practical necessity on the one hand and one's sense of symbolic and ritual work on the other. Different homesteading experiments, then, put nature "to use" for a variety of reasons and to different extents. When we contemplate the symbolic construction of nature and the homemade rituals of living close to it, we are brought back to the question of religion.

"Against" Religion

I have been making the case throughout this book that homesteaders are engaged in a kind of "religion relocated," that they practice a form of spiritual discipline, voluntarily choosing a life of restraint that is personally freeing, spiritually renewing, and ethically demanded in the face of mainstream American culture. While we cannot argue that homesteading is religion, we can see the ways in which these life choices make meaning, spiritually, for those who have left both institutional religion and the culture of consumption behind. We also can see that the spiritual dimensions of homesteading not only are functional (many activities can make meaning) but also derive from a construction of nature as sacred and authoritative, a construction that has a long tradition in American history.

We might say, then, that homesteading is positioned "against" religion, in more than one way. On the one hand, most homesteaders insist that they are "not religious in the formal sense" and indeed are wary of institutional religion. In this sense, homesteaders are against religion in the sense of being *opposed* to it. But the spiritual aspects of homesteading emerge when we consider the resonances with religious life that homesteaders report: a sense of the self as part of a larger force in the world (the experience of the loss, re-creation, or expansion of self) or a sense of life lived close to nature as a kind of penance or redemption from a prior sinful life of materialism and consumption. In these readings, nature is viewed as "enchanted" or "sacred," not limited to strictly scientific explanations or readings, but providing lessons and experiences that shape a spiritually fulfilling, morally appropriate life. Moreover, these readings of nature descend directly from a line of post-Protestant visions of nature that begin with the thought of Thoreau, evolve in the writing of Burroughs, and continue, in a different vein, through the Progressive Era and beyond.

At times, as we have seen, such a reenchantment of the world includes a vision of nature as a source of immortality. This concept of immortality, while less dualistic or transcendent than what we may find in traditional Western religious thought, is nonetheless a cultural legacy of these more traditional religious ideas as well as a legacy of those such as Thoreau and Burroughs, who explicitly began to alternate between God and nature as their sources of authority. Whether as a foundation of ethical virtues, a means of redemption, or an "everyday" context for living a sacred life, nature becomes the immanent source of what was once often sought in concepts of "the transcendent." In relation to this, homesteading is positioned "against" religion in the sense of being culturally located *quite closely* to what we commonly think of as religion.

Needless to say, if homesteading is both opposed to religion and culturally very near it, uneasy negotiations will result. The use of nature spiritually and psychologically can, as we have seen, play a role in keeping at bay certain forms and understanding of nature (for instance, nature as evil, chaotic, threatening, destructive, or simply neutral and "meaningless"). At the same time, anxiety about religion can complicate or even suppress the extent to which homesteading is explicitly talked about in spiritual terms.

Nowhere did this anxiety become more clear to me than on a late September evening when "the Sauna crowd" of Nearing friends and neighbors journeyed to a coastal island to celebrate the fall equinox. As garden-based salads, home-raised chicken, and hand-crafted wine were shared around the fire, talk turned to the word *sacred* and then to Sauna and its meaning. "I think *Sauna* is sacred," declared Matthew, a relatively recent member of the community, "even though this group doesn't think *anything's* sacred." When Matthew made this comment, he struck a chord. Some grumbled at his use of the term; most begrudgingly admitted that he was right. But the conversation leading up to his declaration is an intriguing one. My field notes from that evening tell more than one story:

It all started by someone commenting, "nothing is sacred" after a usual round of conversation in which folks were criticizing one another (lovingly) and getting down on everything from the current crop of political candidates to the infighting at the Co-op over whether or not refined sugar should be off the produce list. After the "nothing is sacred" comment, there were general affirmations. "That's sure the case," "Not even people's mothers," and so on. "That's one thing this group has in common," someone said (and Karl, Henry, and Ernest have said this to me privately as well); "nothing is sacred"—everyone is subject to the same teasing, dismantling, no one ideology is proposed.

Picking up on this, Karl, in his classic iconoclastic and sardonic way concluded: "Nothing is sacred—especially the sacred."

"That's a problem with our group," Emma interceded. "We seem to shy away from the sacred, and sometimes I get the feeling that there's an underlying negativity with us."

"There's not an underlying darkness," Karl replied. "It's just that we don't like dogma."

"Or catma," someone else volunteered.

"Or any other 'ma.' "

"Or running around with blinders on."

"I didn't say deep 'darkness,' " Emma persisted. "I said 'negativity'; we don't want to affirm anything, but then the sacred gets left out."

"Who wants anything to do with the sacred?" Karl proclaimed, revealing some of the reasons behind his objections. "People have been killing each other for millions of years because of the sacred, and I don't want any part of that."

"Maybe it's the wrong word," someone suggested. "Maybe we're talking about spirituality. We don't want dogma, but we do need spirituality in our lives."

"I don't need it," Karl, immovable, remarked.

Some people gave Karl some ribbing for being so convinced that spirituality was absent from life and furthermore to be avoided. Others were more sympathetic.

"You've got to understand," Reed chimed in, "Karl and I are climbing out from under the incredible hypocrisy and ridiculousness of the Lutheran Church. We don't want to live with anything like that again."

"If you think Lutheranism is bad," Henry remarked from his seat on the other side of the fire, "try Catholicism—now that'll kill you."

"I'll say," Jo agreed.

"What about Episcopalianism?" Martha called out, as if trying to win the bidding war. "There you've got Transubstantiation and all that crap."

"What's Transubstantiation?" Ernest asked. . . .

As the conversation ensued, no one made the distinction that I've heard a great deal elsewhere, between religion and spirituality, but "the sacred" seemed too close for comfort for the majority.

When the conversation lulled, I asked: "Do you think there's something spiritual in your lives, even if it's not sacred in the church sense?"

"Oh yes," said Emma instantly. "But we don't want to talk about it."

"But we don't *share* a spirituality," someone remarked.

"Well, maybe we do . . . ," another wondered.

"We're all out here, aren't we?"

A pause.

"And I suppose, we all like the moon."

"But it's the people that are important," Karl added. "I mean most people are shits, but what brings us together is that all of us are decent human beings—well, not all of us," he joked and directed his gaze at some friends. "But most of us. That's what I believe in. I'm a humanist—a secular humanist."

"But what about the natural world?" Emma queried. "I like animals better than most people."

"Yes," Martha added. "Like when the dogs were in the middle [of the circle around the fire], and we were all barking at the moon together. That was the most sacred moment of the evening."

Matthew was standing off on a rock and had been pondering much of this. "What about Sauna?" he asked.[35]

A journey to a coastal island to celebrate the equinox perhaps created the distance needed for the members of this informal group to discuss seriously—for a moment anyway—some of their deeper concerns. While, as a group, the majority seemed relieved to get off of the topic of Sauna's sacredness and to return to joking, storytelling, and carousing, others later told me individually that the discussion that night was an informative reminder of the community's own feelings about itself.

More than one issue was at stake in this discussion around the fire. A reverence for the sacredness of the natural world was implicit in the conversation and explicit in the embodied practices (withdrawal to an island to observe the equinox). At the same time, the obvious anxiety involved in talking about the sacred underlines the community's own sense of itself as a community whose boundaries must remain loose. To be a group held together by a set of rules, an ideology, and, at worst, a shared spirituality strikes almost everybody as "dangerous." But what fears inform this sense of danger, and what do these fears tell us about this collection of homesteaders and their friends?

At first glance, the most obvious concerns expressed are those regarding institutional religion. The bidding war about which religious tradition delivered the most damage to individual psyches was conducted with a sense of humor, but beneath such humor was often a powerful combination of personal pain and intellectual disillusionment. Those Sauna members who have talked to me about their own religious backgrounds sound not unlike Robert Bellah's famous—or infamous—respondent "Sheila," who spoke of having to construct her own religious faith to respond to her particular experience in twentieth-century America, an experience for which traditional religion provided insufficient guidance or meaning.[36] Some members of the Sauna group have rebelled against strict religious upbringing in which religious convictions were wielded by parents as sources of and justifications for "emotional abuse." Others were brought up in more liberal religious environments, where the spirit of inquiry was encouraged. But such inquiry often led to the rejection of mainstream, institutional religion. Ernest, raised as an Episcopalian and active in the church as a small boy, reported going home for the holidays when in his twenties and taunting his parents by demonstrating point by point the ways in which Jesus' message was unabashedly communistic (a position Scott Nearing would have appreciated). Two homesteaders who express the most "organized" religious commitments have been influenced by the teachings of an Indian guru. While they are more likely to openly share a daily spiritual practice (such as meditating and pausing for reflection or a heartfelt om before meals), the nature of that practice is still highly individualized and eclectic.

Not surprisingly, those with the least formal religious education, such Maggie or Emma, are the ones least concerned with discussing spiritual matters directly. Maggie grew up with atheistic scientific parents and some dabbling in the Society of Friends. "My grandmother was concerned that I might not be exposed to anything spiritual," she commented, "and so she took me to meeting from time to time." For Maggie, discussing "the sacred" does not carry with it the emotional danger that it does for Karl, whose father was a radio preacher and relied on him for help with biblical broadcasts.

As I have suggested earlier, we could generalize by saying that this group, in demographic and spiritual terms, belongs to the "generation of seekers" that Wade Clarke Roof and Robert Wuthnow describe and interpret. But placing the Sauna members in the spiritually "seeking" category tells us only so much. They and other homesteaders fall outside the standard definitions of both "seekerism" or Bellah's "Sheilaism" in a number of ways. Exploring these differences is important in offering both an interpretation and an assessment of homesteading practices.

First, as the Sauna crowd's anxiety about the word *sacred* reveals, some home-steaders are resistant to articulate their life choices as explicitly having to do with "the sacred," although in the case of the retreat to an island to celebrate the equinox, actions speak louder than words. Others, such as Wendell Berry, Gene Logsdon, and some of the Total Loss farmers, make a case for a kind of farm-based spiritual practice outside the boundaries of church and synagogue, while using language that emerges from their religious heritages. Still others, such as the Nearings, express reverence for nature and the All-That-Is, while being careful to avoid explicit God-talk.

All of these postures certainly express resistance to institutional religion, but the commitment to living on nature's terms suggests a level of commitment *beyond* that of spiritual self-fulfillment alone. For many homesteaders, a life lived close to nature demonstrates the extent to which the quest for a spiritual life may go "underground" but will not go away. And in a historical context, we can recognize that homesteaders lives today are located in a longer story of the turn to nature as a spiritual and cultural move. But however much this cultural shift "makes sense" in terms of the perspective of American religious history, it is no surprise that continued anxiety about the sacred will persist, for the sacred, wherever it is located and however it is made, resolves some anxieties and ambivalences while reliably reproducing others.

The Virtues of Homesteading

Throughout this text and particularly in my reflections above, I have been intentionally looking at homesteading through a kind of kaleidoscope. I am asking readers to consider what seem to be relatively straightforward—and, indeed, admirable—life choices through the lens of constructions of nature and the self and of religion and spirituality in a particularly American context. With each turn of the interpretive kaleidoscope, we see the same elements emerge in different patterns. For instance, the self is constructed through experiences in nature, but a prior vision of nature (shaped by American history and culture) influences the choice to pursue these experiences. Similarly, a life close to nature is sought as a means to redeem or repair a materialistic culture, and this healing is also experienced as a healing of the self, especially by those who do not find such experiences of redemption in traditional religious contexts.

The analysis I am offering does not intend to be linear, in large part because there is nothing linear about the way in which culture produces our concepts of nature, our concepts of self and culture, and our concepts of the religious and the sacred. It is no surprise that ironies and ambivalences abound in the practice of homesteading or that, with each turn of the analytical lens, new variations on familiar themes come to our attention. But while this study has been primarily sociological and historical in nature, a kind of normative summing up is now in order.

First, it is worth remembering that the writing of history is always inflected with normative claims, regardless of scholars' attempts to resist them. Scholarship works best, however, when the biases of the authors are made explicit. While it has been tempting, at times, to offer "one argument" about what homesteading may mean, I have felt more responsible to the subject matter and to my research collaborators (the homesteaders I have interviewed) when contemplating several sides of the issues at hand. In interpreting homesteading lives and texts, I have offered several different arguments about the religious and cultural work that homesteading performs. I have discussed the ways in which the practice of homesteading both opposes and is located quite close to traditional religious practice, the ways in which homesteading is an act of dissent from dominant American culture, yet still implicated in that culture and, indeed, recognizably "American." It is a practice of both engagement and retreat, of social reform and of individual self-forming, of getting close to nature and yet not too close. I have presented diversity in my analysis because the data demand it. In addition, I have consciously resisted engaging in either a wholesale celebration of homesteading or a critique that attempts to undermine or explain away these life choices.

But in my looking at the past and present, my biases cannot help but be shaped by my sense of the future, a future that, at this writing, continues to be threatened by the ecological consequences of our actions. Our ideas of nature shape our practices on and in it, and these practices, in turn, change nature in ways that shape our ideas. Our ideas and our practices are caught up in the larger story of how, and with what historical precedents, we create meaning in our lives. Making meaning through settlement, the conquering of nature, through technological prowess and unrestrained consumption has been the dominant strand in the American story. Homesteading has been another, less popular, one. As an ongoing practice, homesteading holds promise for our uncertain ecological future while also having certain limits we ought to consider.

In a basic and general way, homesteading is a stance against those unsettling aspects of what Anthony Giddens has called the "juggernaut" of modernity.[37] Homesteaders, as we have seen, often understand nature, not humans, to be ultimately "in control" and often interpret their work to be that of serving nature, recognizing nature's mysteries, or humbling oneself before the expansive power of the natural world. Even those who exhibit a relatively controlling stance toward nature (the Nearings in terms of their rigorous discipline, Wendell Berry in terms of his model of Christian stewardship) still understand nature as setting the terms for human action and understand human ambition and greed (in the form of the misuse of power, money, science, and technology) as posing a threat to the natural world and to life itself.

Although some homesteaders engage in ironic "approach-avoidance" dances with nature, nature remains at the center of their ethical life. The conversion to a life lived close to nature, not unlike a religious person's conversion to life lived "close to God," leads to an intimate knowledge of nature and a life of caring for the natural world, both on the homestead and sometimes beyond it. Such a stance toward nature serves as a counterpoise to the dominant stance of industrialism and consumerism that underlies the modern condition.

While homesteaders seek to reverse the standard equation of the human-nature relationship, they also seek to remake the self. On the one hand, the cultural gesture of going back to the land is rooted in an outlook toward nature that is essentially Thoreauvian and Romantic. Homesteaders stand in the tradition of what M. H. Abrams has called "natural supernaturalism," an intellectual heritage that certainly emphasizes the meaning of nature in terms of what it can do for the self.[38] On the other hand, homesteaders' attention to *practice*, their lived commitment to a daily life of self-imposed "constraints" in nature, mitigates the extent to which knowing and constructing the self may be seen as the only cultural tasks at hand. Homesteaders construct the self within *a self-imposed set of limits*, a set of limits that keep them tied to nature, tied to the "natural" particulars of place and time, and tied to a specific local culture, whose most modern aspects are resisted. Like religious practices in which the devotee voluntarily commits to certain dietary rules, patterns of prayer, devotional practices, and communal rituals, homesteading practices are self-chosen habits of constraint that can keep human hubris in check. There is tremendous ecological and spiritual potential in such a way of living.

What concerns have I raised about homesteading as a cultural gesture? I have asked whether the spiritual benefits of homesteading can keep some homesteaders from working for social change and even lull them into a kind of complacency, one that privileges their own self-fulfillment over broad social concerns. Similarly, if homesteading can enable one to be "redeemed" or "chosen" in the midst of the sinful world of modernity, can it become a practice that is more oriented toward the self than toward nature or the human community?[39] I have also asked what the unintended consequences of homesteading might be, for instance, when we consider the mutually informing influences of gender and class on homesteading or the exceptionalist attitudes that sometimes emerge.

We should remember, however, that such questions are particular versions of persistent, general questions that are often posed of religious individuals or religious movements. Given the religious dimensions of homesteading, it is no surprise that the practice of homesteading poses the same paradoxes of accommodation and resistance, engagement and retreat, self-development and social commitment that we find in more traditional religious contexts. Nor is it a surprise that social class plays a role in this particular style of spiritual engagement or that the spiritual benefits of homesteading might sometimes "trump" contemporary, liberal expectations of gender roles.

Homesteading, then, is a lived spiritual practice that is negotiated in the context of any number of competing tensions: between the threats of secularization and scientism and the constraints of traditional religious life, between living by nature's rules and enjoying the freedom to construct the self, between respecting nature's "intrinsic value" and putting nature to pragmatic and symbolic use, between nostalgia for an early modern simplicity and a desire for late-modern cultural authority that will transform models of dissent into new norms.

Whatever limits, tensions, ironies, and ambivalences persist in homesteading, my accent remains on the promise. The most profound limits upon us, after all, are not the ones placed on us by our religious and cultural history or by our social location and our anxieties about that location. Our American cultural tendency to favor short-term thinking, confidence in technological problem-solving, and "reactive" responses to social problems has clouded our awareness of the extent of the challenge before us, but the real limits placed on us are ultimately ecological ones. For many religious persons, there can be no nature without a divine force that called it into being; however, it is also the case that without a sustainable ecological future, the sacred process of "binding oneself back" to that divine source (one definition of the word *religio*) may be permanently put to rest. The practice of homesteading, when viewed in the most optimistic light, has the potential both to imagine and to model versions of the future that may be more sustaining than our present is.[40] Because of its nature as a *calling* to which one converts and as a *practice* that involves skill, ethical commitment, and a community to nourish it, homesteading may continue in the future as an appealing model of living. While few may become homesteaders, many may take some aspects of homesteading into their daily lives. Indeed, homesteading (and simple living generally), if more integrated into our culture, may prove to be an important counterpoise to "the end of nature" that many of us fear.[41]

The practice of homesteading is important as a call for *restraint*, a call that religious groups, in the face of environmental dangers, are rediscovering in their own traditions. This call is particularly resonant with more conservative religious voices that we might not usually associate with the Nearings and Borsodis of the mid-twentieth century or with the Coperthwaites and Greenbergs of today. If we consider the critique of contemporary culture by such religiously oriented "communitarian" thinkers as Robert Bellah and Alasdair MacIntyre, for instance, we hear an ongoing concern about individualism, lack of commitment to wider social "goods" (e.g., a moral and ethical society), and "weak" forms of community. These authors deplore the triumph of relativistic, "therapeutic" ethics over engaged practice that is enacted in the context of identifiable traditions and communities of memory.[42] These thinkers may see politically liberal, nonchurchgoing "nature lovers" as more of a problem than a solution. But in making my final assessment, I want to explore the underlying, and unexpected, common ground between some communitarians and homesteaders.

Homesteaders and communitarians are strange bedfellows. What binds their work together is the pursuit of a shared notion of the good, a notion that is not limited to self-actualization of an individualistic therapeutic kind, but one that involves a set of ethical commitments beyond the self. The social "goods" pursued by homesteaders, in fact, are those that directly challenge the modernist legacies that communitarians find so troubling. As my discussion of ritualization (in chapter 3) has illustrated, homesteaders are engaged in practices that intentionally further such "goods" as the resistance to materialism and environmental degradation on the one hand and the promotion of the value of home, community, and "place" on the other. As I argued earlier, I do not think that such practices can be explained away as the shared activities of a "lifestyle enclave," as Robert Bellah might hope to describe them. First of all, these practices involve an active resistance to the culture of consumption, while activities in lifestyle enclaves, as Bellah portrays them, are often *defined* by consumption. Moreover, the practices of environmentalists and simplicity advocates emerge out of a commitment to a good that *transcends* the self. This good may not be a life devoted to God, but it is a life devoted to decentering selfish interests and working toward a telos of ecological sustainability for future generations and for the health of the earth itself. The theologian Stanley Hauerwas claims that liberalism has prevented us from posing the foundational Socratic question, "How should one live?"[43] Yet this is *just* the question homesteaders are posing, and they are often doing so within shared, local, community contexts in which particular cultural and biological circumstances set the terms for how that question might be answered.

As my discussion of "homemade ritual" made clear, and as our historical narrative also reveals, homesteaders are ritual experts of a kind who have created for themselves practices of discipline and constraint that nurture a meaningful, spiritual life. Homesteaders seek alternatives to traditional, institutional forms of religious life, but the decision to live according to nature's principles, to stay committed to a life that is more productive than consumptive, to remain place-based through thick and thin, rather than to make life choices on the basis of the best economic opportunity, all suggest a kind of spirituality of "dwelling" that involves a set of commitments to nature and community not prevalent in practices of "seeking" alone. While not articulating the same kind of dwelling that Robert Wuthnow associates with the congregational and denominational stability of the 1950s, homesteading is rooted in what it means to truly dwell in nature, in a particular place and community, and as part of a particular tradition. Like the religious practitioners Wuthnow admires, homesteaders negotiate between dwelling and seeking by engaging in practices, but if anything, these practices bring them back toward a spirituality of dwelling, a dwelling of a different kind. They have chosen to reinhabit particular places in nature and to invest in the local communities, both human and natural, that belong to those places. This also involves an investment in tradition, but a tradition set by biophysical as well as cultural norms.[44]

The importance of place in the exercise of practices and the nurturing of community is not explicitly named by MacIntyre, Hauerwas, or Bellah—perhaps it ought to be—but it is precisely through intentionally dwelling on and in particular landscapes that homesteaders also understand themselves as part of a tradition that precedes and outlasts them. Participation in a tradition that provides a "narrative unity" for one's life is one of the prerequisites for virtuous living in MacIntyre's analysis. Homesteaders participate in a tradition through their investment in local communities and bioregions. These places set the terms for their life narratives and often provide the impetus to write these narratives for a broader audience. Moreover, some homesteaders see themselves as restoring the particular tradition of "self-sufficient farming," which almost has been driven to extinction by agribusiness. While participating in an intellectual tradition nourished by the Romantics and, particularly, Thoreau, homesteaders—in keeping with Bellah, MacIntyre, and Hauerwas—support a Jeffersonian vision for American culture, though for a somewhat different set of reasons.

By committing to a life oriented more toward nature and away from consumer culture, homesteaders (along with such cultural allies as environmentalists and voluntary simplicity advocates) demonstrate ultimate commitments to nature, to place, to tradition, and to a community of others who share their views and their practices. These commitments are not articulations of self-discovery or self-expression that the communitarians deplore. They are, rather, commitments made in reference to what another communitarian thinker, Charles Taylor, has called a "hyper-good," and they involve an explicit turning away from the very "inwardness" that Taylor sees as a regrettable feature of the modern self.[45] In directing their energies to the good of nature, as manifested, in a particular community and bioregion, homesteaders demonstrate and cultivate those virtues that will lead them to a telos in Taylor's sense of the term: the telos of the Good Life.[46]

But the broad claims I am making here somehow seem to take us far away from the world of homesteading itself. I want to close by returning to the texture—the delights, challenges, and ambivalences—of homesteading life with which this study has primarily to do. Let us reenter the world of Harlan Hubbard—a homesteader we have met only briefly in these pages—as he and his wife, Anna, carved it out on the banks of the Ohio River for over thirty years.

Like the Nearings, Harlan and Anna Hubbard enjoyed a partnership of complementary skills and personal styles. They grew their own food, built their own house, kept goats, and cut wood on-site to heat their home. They lived without electricity or running water and had little income beyond what came "dribbling in" through the sale of Harlan's paintings and money supplied by renting out the family home in town. They received many guests who were interested in self-sufficiency but who were not always ready for the seemingly "conservative" values of hard work and plain pleasures that the Hubbards espoused.

In the closing pages of his tale of homesteading on the Ohio River, *Payne Hollow: Life on the Fringe of Society* (1974), Harlan Hubbard reflects on the way of living he has created in his particular nook of Kentucky:

> Today as I swam in the river I looked up with a wild duck's eye into the trees waving as the wind rushed through them, lightly rattling the cottonwood leaves, tossing back the maple branches to reveal their silvery undersides. . . . Suddenly, I felt alone on earth, as I do when lying on the damp ground in spring to see closely the bloodroot raising its leaf sheath through the mold. . . . Even winter—though its cold may snap the thread of my existence—is part of the gentle, soft-edged creation which is wild nature, ever cheerful and friendly, a solace to the spirit of man.[47]

Hubbard uses the term *wild nature*, but the benevolent nature he enjoys is also one he has created and formed. It is made by his hands in the garden and woodlot and by his body and spirit in the ongoing ritualization of an alternative to the culture whose "fringe" is his center. Yet the world that Hubbard has sought to escape lies only just beyond the bend of the river. Hubbard knows this:

> We live on a frontier and a clear vision can see the wilderness extending into the unknown distance. To keep this view ever before us is not easy. Civilization becomes more clamorous and insistent. It is in a way to dominate the earth. Nature already seems to have lost some of its vitality and health. The river is polluted, the very stars are tampered with. Even in Payne Hollow the situation seems almost hopeless on a Sunday afternoon in summer, when the outboards go skittering over the surface of the river and the hellish sounds come from all quarters.

For Hubbard, Sunday ironically threatens to be the most profane day of all. Those who see nature not as "home" but as a place of escape come rushing in for a quick "experience," then dash out again leaving oil slicks and echoes of racing motors in their wake. They are strangers, disrupting the intimacies and calm of the local community, where nature and a few humans live with careful attention to the limits, and the blessings, of a delicately balanced system. For Hubbard, the experience is hellish; the only solution is "to turn within, let the day pass."

But the next day holds new promise: "Then, early Monday morning, when I go down to the shore, the quiet river seems newly created. Mist lifts from the smooth water, creeps up Payne Hollow and rises skyward until it catches the light of the morning sun. My faith is renewed, and I rejoice after my own fashion." Harlan's Monday is his Sunday, a day of sacredness and spiritual renewal. It is a day of labor but also leisure; a day to be bathed in the mists of nature and so, to revitalize the self. Once again, he can enjoy his solitude, away from the desperate crowds, yet he is no longer turned inward as he was the day before. His morning begins with moving outward, descending to the riverbank, whose various denizens, both animal and human, make up his community. Then he will return home, to the house that lets nature in through its windows and handmade furniture and to the patterns of simple domesticity created in concert with Anna.

Hubbard reminds us that however much nature is a cultural construction, it is also very real. In its balanced state, we may take nature's "subjectivity" for granted, but in both its healthy and its damaged forms, it acts on us, sometimes aiding and sometimes threatening our physical and mental well-being.[48] It is a force to be reckoned with, a mystery to be pondered, and sometimes a blessing to be enjoyed. Hubbard also reminds us that while homesteading is a cultural gesture—embedded and implicated in the very culture it resists—it is also always a life lived. It is a spiritual practice and a practical means of living in the world, rich in variety, infused with commitment, and infinite in its complexity. With Hubbard, many homesteaders have left behind the Sundays of social and theological convention, of artificial leisure, of the weekend flight from confined and specialized labor, of the hunger for nature that can never be satisfied. They have remade their Mondays and renewed their lives. They rejoice after their own fashion.

FIGURE 14.

At Helen Nearing's memorial service in October 1995, a
friend posted these reminders of one of the Nearings' favorite
dictums. Another was "Do the best that you can in the place
that you are. And be kind." Both are attributed to Scott, but the
latter was also a favorite of Helen's. Photo by R. K. Gould.

APPENDIX: OF HOES
AND HUCKLEBERRIES

A Note on Method

I have often wondered what Thoreau might have said to me had I sallied up to his cabin with a questionnaire and a tape recorder in hand. Not much. If he welcomed my company at all (which might depend on whether he was drafting his "Visitors" or his "Solitude" chapter that day), he would have liked it best, I imagine, if I had come ambling through the woods with a hoe in hand and an offer to go huckleberrying.

Knowing that the Nearings were more impressed by a willingness to work than by a Harvard degree, I made my first visits to Helen Nearing with this imagined Thoreauvian encounter in mind. I did not bring my tape recorder the first time but spent an early spring weekend helping her to plant peas and gather seaweed. We sat and talked when she was ready, and I left on the timetable that the "Visitors 3–5, Help us live the GOOD LIFE" sign suggested. Other visits followed suit. I came with an extra pair of gloves and sometimes with a book to lend or some ice cream to leave behind. One time I dropped by unannounced (and unseen) and overheard an astrologer friend telling Helen that the stars suggested she needed to protect her own time and energy more. I stayed away for a while afterward, although I am sure that, as with many visitors, I must have intruded even when Helen was too gracious to let on. Later, I certainly felt my own versions of what Helen must have experienced, when Good Life pilgrims arrived at the door late on an August afternoon that already had been brimming with visitors. They wanted to hear my views on "simple living"; I wanted to experience a quiet evening with the crickets.

I have come to think of my methodological approach to this research project as "the hoes and huckleberries" method. Such an approach, many recent ethnographers remind us, is not as unconventional as it might first seem to those more comfortable with double-blind research trials. Scientific "objectivity" possibly may be attained through certain carefully controlled experiments or strategically worded questionnaires. Certain research questions indeed lend themselves to these methods, and I have used them myself. But if the questions pertain to life choices and the embodied practices of living in the context of these choices, other methods are more appropriate. The question here is not one of "objectivity" or "subjectivity" per se but one of authentic approaches to gathering the data we need. This means not assuming that we are "experts" reporting to the world on distant "subjects." Our responsibility as researchers pursuing authentic methodologies is to reflect on who we are as researchers, what we share (and do not share) with our collaborators, and why we think it is important to engage in the study at hand. In most cases, this means probing the questions and issues that are lively (even if challenging) for *all* participants in the research project and then reflecting on and interpreting both the broad themes and the details of data that emerge in these encounters, whether with a person or with a text.

Very early on in my project, it became apparent to me that, even though I was interviewing a population that was quite close to me culturally, cameras, tape recorders, and academic credentials would be off-putting in rural Maine, just as others have found them a hindrance in India or in the South Pacific. Luckily, I never started with these tools of the trade. But because I had experience with outdoor living and was accustomed to composting toilets, I was able to gain what the anthropologists call an entrée into the setting. While I eventually taped a number of interviews, I found that that the most revealing and intriguing comments were made to me when the tape recorder was turned off. Whether I was picking rocks from a potential garden plot, washing dishes in a kitchen, or eating rhubarb pie after a sauna, it was—not surprisingly—in the context of homestead labor (and leisure) that I was most able to learn about what homesteading means to others.

To put my methods in more traditional terms, however, my approach to my research involved several stages and a variety of data-gathering techniques. In 1994, using a snowball sampling technique, I visited and interviewed (often several times) over thirty homesteaders, many of them living within roughly a one-hundred-kilometer radius of the Nearings and others scattered more widely throughout rural New England and beyond. Many of those I initially interviewed became my neighbors when I began living on the Nearing homestead in 1996. Some interviews were taped; others were captured in my field notes immediately following. Events, conversations, observations, and the like were recorded in field notes or written directly into early draftings of this manuscript. (In the notes, more formal interviews are listed as "interviews," while comments made in participant-observation settings are usually noted as "conversations." In each case, I have given the month and the year in which these interviews and conversations took place.)

In transferring notes to text, I have given the majority of my interviewees pseudonyms but have preserved the actual names of those (such as Helen Nearing) who were part of the historical story, or those (such as Bill Coperthwaite) who have published homesteading-related material under their own names. In some cases, I have used code names when discussing details of the lives of homesteaders who have authored books and actual names when citing their writing, again for the purposes of masking identities. I have constructed no "composite" portraits, although in the cases of two quotations, I have changed enough details to protect the anonymity of those whom I quoted. Within the tightly knit community of those living near the Good Life Center, individuals will recognize themselves and perhaps one another, but I trust that such recognition will not emanate far beyond this circle. More important, I have taken pains not to share personal information (gathered in conversations and interviews) other than that which seems important to the analysis I am giving here. Certain details about personal lives, interpersonal grudges, and other matters, whether in reference to the Nearings or others, I have simply kept to myself. In addition, I have made an earlier version of this manuscript available for consultation at the Good Life Center and have solicited feedback from those I have written about as well as from those who knew the Nearings and other community members well. While I have sought to correct misquotations or misattributions along the way, I take responsibility for any errors that remain.

The ethnographic approach and methods described here, however, represent only one part of the larger study. The other sources for this work are clearly historical and literary. Preparation for this study also involved the analysis of over sixty homesteading texts, primarily first-person narratives of American back-to-the-land experiments from the 1880s to the present. In addition, I gained access to contemporary homesteading discussions and narratives by engaging in content analysis of homesteading magazines such as the *Mother Earth News, Back Home Magazine, Countryside,* and the *Green Revolution,* as well as smaller magazines, journals, and newsletters. A sampling of articles from these periodicals are listed in the bibliography. I also subscribed to two Internet discussion lists on homesteading for over three years. As a member of the Good Life Center, first on the board of directors and later as a participant in the larger "group of stewards," I have participated actively in conversations about the Nearing legacy and the meaning of the good life in these turbulent, religiously pluralistic, and ecologically fragile times. These compelling conversations have greatly influenced my work and are, themselves, part of homesteading history.

The interpretive work I offer here is, of course, my own. While I trust I have represented their words and actions fairly, not every homesteader I have written about would necessarily see his or her own story as part of a broader story of religion and nature in American culture. This is my own reading of their work, and an important one, but it is not the only reading one might give. Nevertheless, each homesteader should find something of himself or herself in this text. I have raised some important cautions and criticisms along the way, and I have subjected some very pragmatically oriented people to a kind of intellectual analysis that may appear to some of them to be a less "applicable" reading than one finds in a seed catalog. Nevertheless, my hope is that my research collaborators will recognize how much I have learned from them. The homesteaders of today, and those predecessors whose lives I have come to know through texts alone, have been a wonderful set of teachers who have influenced my own teaching and scholarship. Their visions of a sustainable future are rarely enacted, but they are ones from which all of us can learn.

. . .

A large body of literature has influenced my understanding of effective and ethical fieldwork and of the proper relationship between the practice of fieldwork and the intellectual questions being pursued (an understanding that begins with self-awareness but, one hopes, avoids unnecessary bouts of narcissism).

Some texts that go beyond normal "textbook" treatment include: John Lofland and Lyn H. Lofland, *Analyzing Social Settings: A Guide to Qualitative Observation and Analysis*, 2nd ed. (Belmont, CA: Wadsworth Publishing, 1984); Danny L. Jorgensen, *Participant Observation: A Methodology for Human Studies*, Applied Social Research Methods Series, vol. 15 (London: Sage Publications, 1989); and David M. Fetterman, *Ethnography Step by Step*, Applied Social Research Methods Series, vol. 17 (London: Sage Publications, 1989).

Some important interpretations of the cultural significance (and accompanying dangers) of ethnographic work are offered by James Clifford, *The Predicament of Culture: Twentieth-Century Ethnography, Literature and Art* (Cambridge, MA: Harvard University Press, 1988); James Clifford and George Marcus, eds., *Writing Culture: The Poetics and Politics of Ethnography* (Berkeley: University of California Press, 1986); Alison James, Jenny Hockey, and Andrew Dawson, eds., *After Writing Culture: Epistemology and Praxis in Contemporary Anthropology* (New York: Routledge, 1997); Renato Rosaldo, *Culture and Truth: The Remaking of Social Analysis* (Boston: Beacon Press, 1989); George E. Marcus and Michael M. J. Fischer, *Anthropology as Cultural*

Critique: An Experimental Moment in the Human Sciences (Chicago: University of Chicago Press, 1986); and the essays appearing in Women in the Field: Anthropological Experiences, ed. Peggy Golde, 2nd ed. (Berkeley: University of California Press, 1986).

I have found several monographs—largely concerned with religion and ritual—to be useful as models (particularly in their attention to the complex, reflexive relationships between author and "subject"). See Steven Feld, Sound and Sentiment: Birds, Weeping, Poetics, and Song in Kaluli Expression, revised 2nd ed., Publications of the American Folklore Society, ed. Marta Weigle (Philadelphia: University of Pennsylvania Press, 1990); René Devisch, Weaving the Threads of Life: The Khita Gyn-Eco-Logical Healing Cult among the Yaka (Chicago: University of Chicago Press, 1993); Gananath Obeyesekere, Medusa's Hair: An Essay on Personal Symbols and Religious Experience (Chicago: University of Chicago Press, 1981; paperback reprint, 1984); Margaret Trawick, Notes on Love in a Tamil Family (Berkeley: University of California Press, 1990; paperback reprint, 1992); and the work of Tanya Luhrman.

Closer to home with respect to the study of American religion are the case studies offered by Nancy Tatom Ammerman, Bible Believers: Fundamentalists in the Modern World (New Brunswick, NJ: Rutgers University Press, 1987); Meredith McGuire (with Debra Kantor), Ritual Healing in Suburban America (New Brunswick, NJ: Rutgers University Press, 1988; paperback reprint, 1991); R. Marie Griffith, God's Daughters: Evangelical Women and the Power of Submission (Berkeley: University of California Press, 1997); and Robert Orsi, Thank You, St. Jude Women's Devotion to the Patron Saint of Hopeless Causes (New Haven, CT: Yale University Press, 1996).

Finally, two publications have captured the essence of what I take to be the methodological issues before us, particularly in the realm of religious studies: James Spickard, J. Shawn Landres, and Meredith McGuire, Personal Knowledge and Beyond: Reshaping the Ethnography of Religion (New York: New York University Press, 2002); and Robert Anthony Orsi, "Snakes Alive," in In the Face of the Facts, ed. Richard Wightman Fox and Robert B. Westbrook (Washington, DC: Woodrow Wilson Center Press; and Cambridge: Cambridge University Press, 1998).

NOTES

Abbreviations

The following abbreviations of publication titles are used throughout the notes.

CB I	*The Life and Letters of John Burroughs*, vol. 1, by Clara Barrus
CB II	*The Life and Letters of John Burroughs*, vol. 2, by Clara Barrus
CGL	*Continuing the Good Life*, by Scott and Helen Nearing
FLIGHT	*The Flight from the City*, by Ralph Borsodi
GL	*Living the Good Life*, by Scott and Helen Nearing
HC	*Home Comfort*, ed. Richard Wizansky
JOURNALS	*The Heart of Burroughs's Journals*, by John Burroughs
LL	*Loving and Leaving the Good Life*, by Helen Nearing
LLP	*Life, and Love and Peace*, by Bolton Hall
MR	*The Making of a Radical*, by Scott Nearing
MS	*Man's Search for the Good Life*, by Scott Nearing
TAL	*Three Acres and Liberty*, by Bolton Hall
TALKS	*John Burroughs Talks*, ed. Clifton Johnson
WPF	*What Are People For?* by Wendell Berry

Preface

Epigraph: Helen Knothe Nearing, *Loving and Leaving the Good Life* (Post Mills, VT: Chelsea Green, 1992), 102. Hereafter *Loving and Leaving the Good Life* is cited as LL.

1. It is important to point out from the outset that "homesteader" was not Scott Nearing's primary identity. He saw himself first as a teacher, scholar, and activist who advocated a socialist society that could avert the evils of both capitalism and totalitarian communism. At the same time, however, homesteading became for him not only a means to an end when he could no longer teach professionally (because he had been blacklisted for his socialist convictions) but also a way of bringing to fruition his earlier experiences in social reform and simple living.

2. The dates given here are the ones the Nearings publicized, although they did not live year-round in Vermont until 1935. Throughout their homesteading lives they often left for portions of the winter for research, lecturing, and travel and did not give up their apartment in New York City until 1940.

The Nearings' most well-known "Good Life" book is *Living the Good Life*, first published by the Social Science Institute (the Nearings' own press) in 1954. It was republished by Schocken in 1970 to an enthusiastic reception. *Continuing the Good Life* (New York: Schocken, 1979) was also quite popular. The two texts have been republished in one volume, *The Good Life* (New York: Schocken, 1989). So that the reader may know which of the two texts is being cited, *Living the Good Life* is hereafter cited as GL, and *Continuing the Good Life* is cited as CGL, but with pagination given from the combined 1989 edition.

3. Letter to the author from the Bontas, dated January 1, 1997. Cited with permission.

Contemporary interest in homesteading appears to be growing. One source of evidence for growth can be found in the circulation health of various magazines on homesteading and rural life (*Mother Earth News, Harrowsmith, Countryside and Small Stock Journal, Back Home Magazine*, and *Backwoods Home Magazine*) as well as an increasing number of books, Web sites, and Internet discussion groups on home-based ecology and self-sufficiency.

This "build your own house and grow your own food" literature also belongs to a wider context of growing cultural urges toward slowing the pace of life, protecting the environment, pursuing simplicity, and practicing alternative health care. Representative popular texts include Cecile Andrews, *The Circle of Simplicity* (New York: Perennial Books, 1999); Duane Elgin, *Voluntary Simplicity: Towards a Life That Is Inwardly Simple, Outwardly Rich* (New York: William Morrow, 1981); Thomas Moore, *The Re-enchantment of Everyday Life* (New York: HarperCollins, 1996); Jim Nollman, *Why We Garden: Cultivating a Sense of Place* (New York: Henry Holt, 1994); Vicki Robin and Joe Dominguez, *Your Money or Your Life* (New York: Viking, 1992); E. F. Schumacher, *Small Is Beautiful* (London: Blond and Briggs, 1973); and Jerome Segal, *Graceful Simplicity* (Berkeley: University of California Press, 1999).

For analytical commentary on the social and historical forces behind some of these developments, see Meredith McGuire, *Ritual Healing in Suburban America* (New Brunswick, NJ: Rutgers University Press, 1988; paperback reprint, 1991); Catherine L. Albanese, "Fisher Kings and Public Places: The Old New Age in the 1990s," in *Religion in the Nineties*, ed. Wade Clark Roof, *Annals of the American Academy of Political and Social Science* 527 (May 1993): 131–43; Juliette B. Schor, *The Overworked American: The Unexpected Decline of Leisure* (New York: Basic Books, 1991), especially 139–65; and Schor, *The Overspent American* (New York: Basic Books, 1998).

4. Clifford Geertz, *The Interpretation of Cultures* (New York: Basic Books, 1970; paperback reprint, 1973), 100–101.

5. My interviews and correspondence with Helen Knothe Nearing began in the winter of 1994. On September 17, 1995, Helen Nearing was killed in a car accident near her home. A month before the accident, Helen had filed her will in Hancock County, which included a gift agreement with the Trust for Public Land, temporarily donating her land and buildings to the trust with the intention of creating the nonprofit Good Life Center on her property. As part of the emerging programs of the Good Life Center, I was offered the opportunity to live at Forest Farm as a caretaker and steward.

The complex negotiations of the Good Life Center concerning the Nearings' cultural legacy have been informative for this study. Thoughtful attention to the birth of this organization has been paid by Kate Gunness Williams in "The Good Life Center: From Individual Lives to Organizational Context, the Story of a Moment of Creation," master's thesis, Sloan School of Management, Massachusetts Institute of Technology, 1997.

6. Helen Nearing reported in texts and numerous interviews that the number of summer visitors was once up to twenty-three hundred (LL, 120). The number of visitors to Forest Farm in the summer continued to be between one thousand and two thousand.

Questions about whether the Nearings really built their homes themselves point to the complex relationship between truth and myth that often plagues the Nearings' legacy. The stone house in Maine (and many Vermont buildings) was constructed with a great deal of help from summer visitors and skilled neighbors, yet Helen often referred to it as a "one woman, one man house." Similarly, the Nearings were not candid about the financial resources (substantial gifts from friends) that supported their land acquisition and house-building projects. Scott also inherited stocks from his family (a subject he did not like to talk about), although we do not know if he collected on them. My research has confirmed the extent to which the Nearings did not acknowledge the assistance (of labor and money) that they were given in their homesteading years, a practice of silence that disappointed many would-be homesteaders. On the other hand, the Nearings' decision to make homesteading "look easy" was, in part, an expression of their evangelical enthusiasm for the ways of life they had chosen. Furthermore, much of the day-to-day operations of the homestead *were* funded largely by what the Nearings produced themselves: maple sugar, blueberries, lectures, and books.

The question of truth and myth pertains not only to self-sufficiency. The nature of Scott's death by conscious fasting, for instance, was not as gentle or as freely chosen as Helen portrayed it in *Loving and Leaving the Good Life* (for Scott's death was already imminent when he chose to fast). Similarly, Helen's attitude toward her own passing was ambivalent. While she publicly announced that she planned to go by fasting, as Scott did, she mentioned to me and to others that she would prefer a sudden death. When Helen Nearing *did* die suddenly in a car accident, knowledge of her private wishes was a source of comfort for those who knew her best. In contrast, the press and the public tended to stress the radical incongruity between her ways of living and her way of dying. In matters of diet and health, the Nearings indeed presented a "purer" portrait in their published works than was the case in their daily life. Finally, Scott's marriages to both Nellie Seeds and Helen Knothe were, again, more complex in reality than either Scott or Helen ever acknowledged publicly.

Although I think it is crucial to explore the complexity of the Nearings' legacy, my purpose in this study is not to write an exposé; thus I mention inconsistencies and true stories when they illuminate my larger arguments, but I do not share personal details when they are not relevant. I am indebted to many of Helen Nearing's friends and neighbors (who shall remain anonymous) for shedding light on the issues I refer to throughout this study. Several illuminating works by others have spelled out some of the discrepancies between the public and the private Nearing stories. Among these are: Ellen LaConte, "The Nearing Good Life: A Perspective on Its Principles and Practices," *Maine Organic Farmer and Gardener*, March/April 1989, 11–12, and LaConte's self-published books *On Light Alone: A Guru Meditation on the Good Death of Helen Nearing* (Stockton Springs, ME: Loose Leaf Press, 1996) and *Free Radical: A Reconsideration of the Good Death of Scott Nearing* (Stockton Springs, ME: Loose Leaf Press, 1997); Greg Joly, "Epilogue: The Publication of *The Maple Sugar Book*" in the Nearings' reissued *The Maple Sugar Book*, Fiftieth Anniversary Edition (White River Junction, VT: Chelsea Green Publishing Company and Good Life Center, 2000); and Jean Hay Bright in her self-published memoir, *Meanwhile, Next Door to the Good Life* (Dixmont, ME: Brightberry Press, 2003). All three authors had quite different relationships to the Nearings, and each does an excellent job in bringing to light some hidden details about the Nearings' lives. Each also demonstrates deep gratitude and respect for the Nearings, even while hoping to correct their story.

7.   Helen gave a portion of these files to me, and they remain in my possession. The majority of the letters are currently archived as part of the Helen and Scott Nearing Papers, Thoreau Institute, Lincoln, Massachusetts.

8.   Perry Miller, *Nature's Nation* (Cambridge, MA: Harvard University Press, Belknap Press, 1967).

9. Two important challenges to the assumption that Christian life in early America was a monolithic and stable cultural force can be found in David Hall, *Worlds of Wonder, Days of Judgement* (Cambridge, MA: Harvard University Press, 1990), and Jon Butler, *Awash in a Sea of Faith* (Cambridge, MA: Harvard University Press, 1990).

10. Some helpful studies of these broad changes include: James Turner, *Without God, Without Creed: The Origins of Unbelief in America*, New Studies in American Intellectual and Cultural History, ed. Thomas Bender (Baltimore, MD: Johns Hopkins University Press, 1985; reprint, Johns Hopkins Paperbacks, 1986); Thomas Tweed, *The American Encounter with Buddhism, 1844–1912: Victorian Culture and the Limits of Dissent*, Religion in North America, ed. Catherine L. Albanese and Stephen J. Stein (Bloomington: Indiana University Press, 1992); and Ronald Numbers, *Darwinism Comes to America* (Cambridge, MA: Harvard University Press, 1998).

Introduction

Epigraphs: Emily Dickinson, *Poems by Emily Dickinson: Edited by Two of Her Friends*, Mabel Loomis and T. W. Higginson, 4th ed. (Boston: Roberts Brothers, 1891), 74; and GL, 190.

1. Ralph Borsodi, *Seventeen Problems of Man and Society* (Anand, India: Charotar Book Stall, 1968), 2.

2. Interview with "Robin," August 2000. All interview collaborators in this project have been given pseudonyms unless they have also published works from which I have quoted or have otherwise agreed to be identified. See the Appendix.

3. Linda Tatelbaum, *Carrying Water as a Way of Life* (Appleton, ME: About Time Press, 1997), 21.

4. For just two representative examples of this kind of argument, see, on the construction of "nature," William Cronon, ed., *Uncommon Ground: Toward Reinventing Nature* (New York: W. W. Norton, 1995), and, on the making of "religion," Talal Asad, *Genealogies of Religion* (Baltimore, MD: Johns Hopkins University Press, 1993).

5. Wade Clark Roof, *A Generation of Seekers: The Spiritual Journeys of the Baby Boom Generation* (San Francisco: HarperCollins, 1993); Robert Wuthnow, *After Heaven: Spirituality in America since the 1950s* (Berkeley: University of California Press, 1998).

6. Here I am borrowing language from Christian theologians Gordon Kaufman and Paul Tillich.

7. Samuel Ogden in *The New England Vegetable Garden* (Woodstock, VT: Countryman Press, 1957), as quoted by Shepherd Ogden (his grandson) in his revision of his grandfather's work, *Step by Step Organic Vegetable Gardening* (New York: HarperCollins, 1992), xv–xvi.

8. Paul Corey, *Buy an Acre* (New York: Dial Press, 1944), 140–41.

9. Gladys Dimock, *Home Ground* (Woodstock, VT: Countryman Press, 1985), 64–65.

10. Viewing nature as "the sacred" or as the source of sacred experience fits into one definition of religion provided by Nancy T. Ammerman. I share her view that, "substantively, religious activity is recognized as such not because of its function (cohesion, meaning-making, and the like), but because it has something to do with things that are 'sacred,' transcendent, or beyond the ordinary." Nancy T. Ammerman, "Religious Practice in Everyday Life," paper presented to the Society for the Scientific Study of Religion, November 2002. While Ammerman's definition attends to those who report that "God" or divine forces are at work in their lives, this definition could be expanded to include other examples of "sacred" experience (such as experiences in nature), even those that are, in contrast to Ammerman's adjectives, less transcendent and more immanent and seemingly "ordinary" when compared with traditional religious rituals. My point here, then, is that homesteading is not simply about "making meaning" but also about constructing and responding to nature in particular ways.

11. On the other hand, to argue as Chidester and Linenthal do, that sacred space is sacred only if it is "contested," may lead to the exclusion of certain spaces—such as the homesteads I have visited—which are undoubtedly "constructed" but are seldom sites of public contestation. The literature on sacred space is voluminous, but see the helpful review essay by Peter W. Williams, "Sacred Space in North America," *Journal of the American Academy of Religion* 70, no. 3 (September 2002): 593–609. Other important texts include David Chidester and Edward T. Linenthal, *American Sacred Space*, Religion in North America, ed. Catherine L. Albanese and Stephen J. Stein (Bloomington: Indiana University Press, 1995), and Belden Lane, *Landscapes of the Sacred: Geography and Narrative in American Spirituality*, Isaac Hecker Studies in Religion and American Culture, ed. John Coleman (New York: Paulist Press, 1988).

12. Robert Orsi, "Everyday Miracles: The Study of Lived Religion," in *Lived Religion in America: Toward a History of Practice*, ed. David D. Hall (Princeton, NJ: Princeton University Press, 1997), 3–21, quotations from 7 and 12; Rebecca Kneale Gould, "Getting (Not Too) Close to Nature: Modern Homesteading as Lived Religion in America," in *Lived Religion in America*, ed. Hall, 215–42. For David Chidester's definitions of religion, see Chidester, *Patterns of Action: Religion and Ethics in Comparative Perspective* (Belmont, CA: Wadsworth, 1987), 4.

13. The religious language of contemporary homesteaders resembles that of the liberal "baby boomers" described by Wade Clark Roof in *A Generation of Seekers*. Roof (76 and passim) summarizes the distinctions usually made between "religious" and "spiritual." The term *religious* often refers to institutional structures (churches or denominations), to rituals and practices (often perceived by boomers as "empty"), and to traditional forms of religiosity (such as those practiced by parents, grandparents, etc.). *Spiritual* tends to be defined as noninstitutional, involving self-selected and self-motivated moral ideas and practices, supporting general attitudes of reverence for life, and playing a role in the psy-

chospiritual processes of self-actualization. As Roof importantly notes, concepts of spirituality are not only the province of the religiously liberal but today also tend to infuse the ideas and practices of those who call themselves conservative or evangelical. Roof (76) also makes the significant remark that almost everyone who was interviewed for his book "had an opinion about the difference between being 'religious' and being 'spiritual.' While they did not always agree as to what that difference was, they were sure that there was one."

For a quantitative survey analysis of these distinctions, see also Brian J. Zinnbauer and Kenneth I. Pargament, "Religiousness and Spirituality: Unfuzzying the Fuzzy," *Journal for the Scientific Study of Religion* 36, no. 4 (December 1997): 549–64. A broad discussion of noninstitutional religion in America can be found in Robert C. Fuller's *Spiritual, but Not Religious: Understanding Unchurched America* (Oxford: Oxford University Press, 2002).

14. It is worth pointing out that *spirituality* is a term that often refers to rituals and concepts developed *within* traditional religious institutions. "Christian spirituality" and "Jewish spirituality," for instance, are debated, taught, and ritualized with particular reference to contemplative practice (such as prayer and meditation), forms of mysticism, spiritual formation, and so on. The long history of institutional claims on spirituality within a religious context is just one example of the problems that ensue if we unhesitatingly accept contemporary, popular definitional distinctions.

In the academic study of religion, a different set of conundrums appears. Scholars are increasingly pointing out the limits of the field itself in its historical attention to "the spiritual" (by which is generally meant cognitive, conceptual, ahistorical, and theological) dimensions of religion to the neglect of other aspects. Robert Orsi, in particular, has pointed out that these limits have led to a bias in the field toward the texts and concepts of elites as opposed to embodied practices played out in diverse cultural fields. Orsi, "Introduction to the Second Edition," *The Madonna of 115th Street* (New Haven, CT: Yale University Press, 1985; 2nd ed., 2002), ix–xxxviii.

15. To put these comments more theoretically, we might say that this work is informed by the contributions of Mircea Eliade, Mary Douglas, Victor Turner, and Clifford Geertz, while leaning toward the corrections and illuminations brought to this older literature by the writing of Peter Berger, Pierre Bourdieu, Robert Wuthnow, Robert Orsi, and Catherine Bell, among others.

In describing my intellectual orientation as partly Weberian, I am, again, not doing so in the service of strictly functional definitions of religion so much as I am sharing his goal of *verstehen* in investigating the lives of others. The religious dimensions of homesteading come to the fore in this study not *because* homesteading "makes meaning" but because it makes meaning in a particular *way*, which has to do with the history of how religion, nature, and the self all have been constructed in American culture from the nineteenth century to the present.

16. In this respect, I depart from the work of Geertz.

17. A history of homesteading has yet to be written, although this study intends to correct that gap. Several older studies, however, shed light on the cultural gestures of which homesteading is a part. These include: Peter Schmitt, *Back to Nature* (Oxford: Oxford University Press, 1969); David Shi, *The Simple Life: Plain Living and High Thinking in American Culture* (Oxford: Oxford University Press, 1985; paperback reprint, 1986); and a study of parallel trends in England by Peter Gould, *Early Green Politics: Back to Nature, Back to the Land and Socialism in Britain, 1880–1900* (New York: St. Martin's Press, 1988). See also the illuminating sociological study by Jeffrey Jacob, *New Pioneers: The Back-to-the-Land Movement and the Search for a Sustainable Future* (University Park, PA: Pennsylvania State University Press, 1997). Jacob's work was not available when I began this study. It provides a welcome addition of survey data to my own analysis.

The literature of Schmitt, Shi, and others produces some confusions about the back-to-the-land movement, which accounts, in part, for the reason I prefer the term *homesteading*. Some treat back-to-the-land impulses as only a post-1960s phenomenon (Jacob), while others (Schmitt) characterize it as a social reform movement of the early twentieth century. Some make distinctions between back-to-nature and back-to-the-land (Schmitt), while others conflate the two (Shi, Jacob). Also, by characterizing the turn to nature as a movement, the complexity and variety of the lives and practices involved are often overlooked. In chapter 1, I elaborate on the definitions of homesteading I have already offered in this introduction, but I want to emphasize here that the word *homesteading*—in addition to being the term most preferred by the practitioners themselves—puts an important emphasis on the daily practices involved (it is a practice more than a movement) and appropriately underlines the significance of "home" for those who engage in it.

Finally, let me clearly state the parameters of this study. While there are rural experimenters (e.g., libertarian survivalists and rural fundamentalist Christians) who share some "family resemblances" to homesteaders, they are not a part of this study. This book is also not primarily concerned with intentional communities, except when considering the thought of Ralph Borsodi and Mildred Loomis.

18. Catherine Albanese, *Nature Religion in America*, Chicago History of American Religion, ed. Martin Marty (Chicago: University of Chicago Press, 1990).

1. Conversion

Epigraph: Scott Nearing, *The Making of a Radical* (New York: Harper and Row, 1972; paperback reprint, Harborside, ME: Social Science Institute, 1974), 211. Hereafter *The Making of a Radical* is cited as MR.

1. The following portrait of "Dale and Robin's" homestead is based on my first visit there in October 1995. This description and the other portraits below

are also informed by later, ongoing visits, conversations, and follow-up interviews through 2002.

2. Eric Schlosser persuasively argues in *Fast Food Nation* (New York: Perennial, 2002) that most Americans do not know the origins of their food.

3. This portrait of Bill Coperthwaite's homestead is based on my first visit, in October 1995.

4. William Coperthwaite, "Society by Design," *Manas* 36, no. 50 (December 1983): 2. Some of Coperthwaite's previously unpublished essays are now available in William S. Coperthwaite, *A Handmade Life* (White River Junction, VT: Chelsea Green, 2003).

5. Coperthwaite, "Society by Design," 2.

6. Ibid., 7.

7. Ibid., 7.

8. Ibid., 1.

9. Ibid., 7–8. This focus on maturity is an ongoing theme. The prevailing notion seems to be either that homesteading assists the development of the "mature" self or that it is a social ideal for a mature society (or both). John Burroughs and Ralph Borsodi articulate similar sentiments, as I shall discuss in ensuing chapters.

10. Interviews with Bill Coperthwaite, October 1995 and October 1996.

11. The portrait of Arnold Greenberg in his "café-homestead" is based on my first meetings with him in October 1995.

12. Arnold founded this school at a farm, which was one of several outposts of the School of Living (first established in Suffern, New York, in the winter of 1934–35) initiated by Ralph Borsodi and continued by his protégé, Mildred Loomis. Arnold set forth his initial vision for a homesteading school quite unaware of the Borsodi-Loomis efforts. He then began to dovetail his own ideas with the long-standing Borsodi-Loomis tradition. Mildred Loomis herself, then in her eighties, participated in the work of the school while also editing *Green Revolution*. See Arnold Greenberg's original proposal for the Deep Run School of Homesteading, "Searching for Alternatives in Education: The Homestead School," *Green Revolution* 35, no. 5 (June 1978): 19–21. Greenberg describes the Deep Run experiment in "Homesteading: Stepping Back towards the Future," *Adventures on Arnold's Island* (Blue Hill, ME: Left Bank Press, 1994), 163–87. Today (in the first decade of the twenty-first century), Arnold's vision is up and running as the fully accredited Liberty School.

13. Greenberg, *Adventures on Arnold's Island*, 184–85.

14. Gary Snyder, *The Practice of the Wild* (San Francisco: North Point Press, 1990), 24.

15. Wendell Berry, *Sex, Economy, Freedom, and Community* (New York: Pantheon Books, 1992), 133 and 148–49. Philosopher Edward S. Casey makes a similar argument in *Getting Back into Place* (Bloomington: Indiana University Press, 1993).

16. MR, 210.

17. Jodi Summit and Marshall Helmberger, reporting in "Avoiding the Rat Race," in *The Harrowsmith Country Life Reader*, ed. Michael Webster, Thomas Rawls, and Karen Davis Cutler, with an introduction by James Lawrence (Charlotte, VT: Camden House Publishing, 1990), 23. This anthology draws together numerous articles originally published in the magazine *Harrowsmith* (now *Harrowsmith Country Life*) since the 1970s.

18. Elizabeth and Charles Long, reporting in "Life in the Clearings: Is the Back to the Land Movement Dead?" *The Harrowsmith Country Life Reader*, 29.

19. See Janet Chadwick, *How to Live on Almost Nothing and Have Plenty* (New York: Knopf, 1979), especially 4–14.

20. See the profiles of Hauserman and Dwinell in *The Harrowsmith Country Life Reader*, 18–21.

In his sociological survey of back-to-the-land movements, Jeffrey Jacob includes a broader range of back-to-the-landers than I do here. He includes, for instance, "weekenders" with full-time employment away from the home and "pensioners" making country living a form of retirement. Nevertheless, Jacob points out that even those furthest from the "purist" category often evaluate their life choices and daily labors with reference to the Nearings as a model. Jacob, *New Pioneers*, especially 45–81.

21. Catherine Mills profile, *The Harrowsmith Country Life Reader*, 24.

22. Interview with "Reed," November 1996.

23. M. G. Kains, *Five Acres and Independence* (New York: Greenberg Publishers, 1935); Bolton Hall, *Three Acres and Liberty*, 1st ed. (New York: Macmillan, 1907). Hereafter *Three Acres and Liberty* is cited as *TAL*. For a testament of suburban homesteading (which draws inspiration from the Nearings), see Judith Moffett, *Homestead Year: Back to the Land in Suburbia* (New York: Lyons and Burford, 1995).

24. Taking agrarianism seriously as part of environmentalism is a relatively recent development. Some representative recent texts (beyond the prolific contributions of Wendell Berry) in this area are: Eric Freyfogle, ed., *The New Agrarianism* (Washington, DC: Island Press, 2001); Brian Donahue, *Reclaiming the Commons: Community Farms and Forests in a New England Town* (New Haven, CT: Yale University Press, 1999); and Richard W. Judd, *Common Lands, Common People: The Origins of Conservation in Northern New England* (Cambridge, MA: Harvard University Press, 1997).

25. Interviews with Bill Coperthwaite, October 1995.

26. J. G., himself referring to a number of similar, previous statements, in an online homesteading discussion list, August 2, 1996; C. Q., ibid., March 20, 1996. This discussion list no longer exists, but a similar one can be found at www.homestead.org.

27. Jd and Diane Belanger, editors, *Countryside and Small Stock Journal*. The full quo-

tation can be found under the heading "Our Philosophy" on the masthead page of each edition. Jeffrey Jacob also cites this statement as a key to understanding back-to-the-land mentality.

28. One visitor to Forest Farm remarked that perhaps the best way to narrow the fuzzy line between homesteaders and "gentleman farmers" is by paying attention to how people manage human waste. But even on this matter homesteaders disagree. The Nearing's last homestead was outfitted with an outhouse and a composting toilet, and many neighbors have followed suit. As "Karl" remarked: "In the old days we used to eat in and shit out, now we shit in and eat out. I'm trying to reverse that process by growing my own food and using an outhouse." But "Ernest" replied: "If I were somewhere else, I might have a composting toilet, but there's plenty of water around here, so I flush."

29. Duane Elgin tracks broad versions of the voluntary simplicity trend in his popular book, *Voluntary Simplicity: Towards a Life That Is Inwardly Simple, Outwardly Rich* (New York: William Morrow, 1981). A more strictly philosophical treatment was first offered by Richard Gregg, a student of Gandhi's work, in 1936. See Gregg, *The Value of Voluntary Simplicity*, Pendle Hill Essays, vol. 3 (Wallingford, PA: Pendle Hill, 1936).

30. Scott Nearing, *Man's Search for the Good Life*, 2nd ed. (1954; Harborside, ME: Social Science Institute, 1974), 142. Hereafter *Man's Search for the Good Life* is cited as *MS*.

31. This carrot then sat on my computer for the months it took to complete my doctorate and thus took on a new symbolic life of its own. For this, I thank its maker!

32. Henry David Thoreau, *Walden*, Norton Critical edition, ed. William Rossi (1854; New York: W. W. Norton, 1992), 1.

33. A. H., Homestead List, Internet, April 18, 1997.

34. Harlan Hubbard, *Payne Hollow: Life on the Fringe of Society* (New York: Eakins Press, 1974), 8; Louise Dickinson Rich, *We Took to the Woods* (Philadelphia: Lippincott, 1942), 29.

35. Rich, *We Took to the Woods*, 28; Bradford and Vena Angier, *At Home in the Woods* (New York: Sheridan House, 1951), 168.

36. Gene Logsdon, *You Can Go Home Again* (Bloomington: Indiana University Press, 1998), 57.

37. Ralph Borsodi, *Flight from the City*, 1st ed. (New York: Harper and Brothers, 1933), 2.

38. *TAL*, 20.

39. William Duryee, *A Living from the Land* (New York: World Publishing Company, 1934), 6.

40. Wendell Berry, "The Long-Legged House," reprinted in Berry, *Recollected Essays, 1965–1980* (San Francisco: North Point Press, 1981), 51–52.

41. Interview with "Ernest," October 1995.

42. William James, *The Varieties of Religious Experience*, Modern Library Edition (1902; New York: Random House, 1936), 158.

43. Raymond Mungo, *Total Loss Farm: A Year in the Life* (New York: E. P. Dutton, 1970), 151.

44. Wendell Berry, *Home Economics: Fourteen Essays by Wendell Berry* (San Francisco: North Point Press, 1987), especially "Two Economies," 54–59.

45. Wendell Berry, *The Unsettling of America: Culture and Agriculture* (San Francisco: Sierra Club Books, 1977), 138.

46. For his critique of "organized" Christianity, see Berry's essay "God and Country," in *What Are People For?* (New York: North Point Press, Farrar, Straus and Giroux, 1990), 95–102. Hereafter, *What Are People For?* is cited as *WPF*.

47. Gene Logsdon, *The Contrary Farmer*, Real Goods Independent Living Series (White River Junction, VT: Chelsea Green, 1994), xiv.

48. In addition to my own use of this term, see the innovative work of Bron Taylor in "Earth and Nature-Based Spirituality (Part I): From Deep Ecology to Radical Environmentalism," *Religion* 31 (2001): 175–93, and "Earth and Nature-Based Spirituality (Part II): From Earth First! and Bioregionalism to Scientific Paganism and the New Age," *Religion* 31 (2001): 225–45.

49. In the study of religion, such a stance is as troublesome as assuming or denying the divinity of Christ, the presence of Elijah at the Passover table, or the role of Corn Woman in renewing the Hopi agricultural season. The approach I am taking is akin to that suggested by Robert Wuthnow, who writes, "It is entirely possible to talk about the sacred's being dependent on human institutions [language, social contexts, psychological orientations] without staking out theological claims that would either deny or affirm the possibility of the sacred's acting independently of (or upon) these institutions." Robert Wuthnow, *Producing the Sacred: An Essay on Public Religion*, Public Expressions of Religion in America, ed. Conrad Cherry (Urbana: University of Illinois Press, 1994), 3.

50. For the use of this term, I am indebted to David D. Hall, who, in his lectures at Harvard Divinity School on liberalism in nineteenth-century American religion, spoke of the uses of (nonsacred) literature in this regard. The turn to literature as a source of spiritual guidance and of meaning in its own right, in fact, goes hand in hand with the turn toward nature in the liberalizing of religion in the late nineteenth century.

51. The literature here is vast, but a few representative works may be cited:

In an illuminating article on secularization theory, Jeffrey Hadden summarizes a wide range of quantitative studies and covers both aspects of twentieth-century American religious development, particularly in the last forty years. He reviews the stability of both the belief in God and practices such as prayer and church attendance (though the last has come under dispute since

Hadden's article). At the same time, Hadden confirms the decline in membership and influence of "mainline churches" as well as the decline in belief in heaven and in literalist interpretations of the Bible. In summing up, Hadden argues that the data, while always subject to multiple readings and reconfigurations, generally cannot confirm "the historical process predicted by secularization theory." He compellingly argues, rather, that "secularization" is more often a doctrine of certain segments of society (and of the positivist tradition) than a social fact. See Jeffrey K. Hadden, "Desacralizing Secularization Theory," *Secularization and Fundamentalism Reconsidered*, Religion and the Political Order, vol. 3, ed. Jeffrey K. Hadden and Anson Shupe (New York: Paragon House, 1989), 3–26. See also Karl Dobbelaere, "The Secularization of Society? Some Methodological Observations," ibid., 27–44; and, more recently, William H. Swatos Jr. and Daniel V. A. Olson, eds., *The Secularization Debate* (Lanham, MD: Rowman and Littlefield, 2000).

Popular magazines such as *Time* and *Newsweek* have also tended to support these arguments, emphasizing, for instance, the persistence of Americans' belief in God and the effectiveness of prayer but the declining belief in biblical literalism and the existence of a physical heaven. See *Time*'s cover story, "Whatever Became of Heaven?" *Time*, 24 March 1997. (Similar observations, however, were made by the Lynds as early as 1929. Robert S. Lynd and Helen Merrell Lynd, *Middletown: A Study in Contemporary American Culture* [New York: Harcourt Brace, 1929] especially, 322–31.)

The argument for the decline of traditional religious values and practices setting the terms for American culture generally has been popularized by Stephen L. Carter in *The Culture of Disbelief: How American Law and Politics Trivialize Religious Devotion*, rev. ed. (New York: Anchor Books, 1994), although at this writing, some countervailing trends have reemerged.

The important argument that religious change (both toward and away from secularization) is less a result of "psychic shifts" in American culture than a result of a change in what religious options are available in the culture has been made by Roger Finke and Laurence Iannaccone in "Supply-Side Explanations for Religious Change," *Religion in the Nineties*, ed. Wade Clark Roof, *Annals of the American Academy of Political and Social Science*, 527 (May 1993): 27–39. See also Finke and Stark, *The Churching of America: Winners and Losers in Our Religious Economy* (New Brunswick, NJ: Rutgers University Press, 1992); and Wuthnow, *Producing the Sacred*,

52. Wade Clark Roof briefly speaks to both conservative and liberal baby boomers' increased emphasis on the sacredness of nature and the body (*A Generation of Seekers*, 144–48).

53. In addition to the work of Wade Clark Roof, see R. Laurence Moore, *Selling God: American Religion in the Marketplace of Culture* (New York: Oxford University Press, 1994); Finke and Stark, *The Churching of America, 1776–1990*; and Richard Cimino and Don Lattin, *Shopping for Faith* (San Francisco: Jossey-Bass, 1998). Peter Berger

hypothesized quite early on that the religious public would increasingly become consumers, and religious institutions and religious "content" would increasingly become subject to market forces. Peter Berger, *The Sacred Canopy* (Garden City, NY: Doubleday, 1966; reprint, Anchor Books, 1969), 145–53.

54. While none seem to make the argument as pointedly as I do here, it is certainly suggested by Roof, *A Generation of Seekers*, and Steven Tipton, *Getting Saved from the Sixties* (Berkeley: University of California Press, 1982; paperback reprint, 1984), as well as by Meredith McGuire (with Debra Kantor), *Ritual Healing in Suburban America* (New Brunswick, NJ: Rutgers University Press, 1988; paperback reprint, 1991), and, more recently, by Wuthnow, *After Heaven*.

Another form of protest and reconstruction worth mentioning is what I call *ritual mirroring*. Some homesteaders take up practices that are consciously intended as acts of dissent, as reversals of rituals common in contemporary American culture. Some, for instance, choose to fast on Thanksgiving, to resist shopping for gifts at Christmas, to observe the natural markings of the winter solstice as opposed to the calendrical New Year. Such choices, however, are not choices "against" ritual so much as choices to engage in rituals *of reversal*, like the very reversals that are at work *within* established rituals such as Mardi Gras and the Hindu festival of Holi.

55. See Rosabeth Moss Kanter, *Commitment and Community: Communes and Utopias in Sociological Perspective* (Cambridge, MA: Harvard University Press, 1972); Robert Houriet, *Getting Back Together* (New York: Coward, McCann and Geoghegan, 1971); and Laurence Veysey, *The Communal Experience* (New York: Harper and Row, 1973; paperback reprint, Chicago: University of Chicago Press, 1978).

56. Note that both Verandah and Alicia have assumed names, the first emphasizing leisure, the second emphasizing nature. Those Total Loss Farmers who went on to author books include: Pete Gould, *Burnt Toast*; Verandah Porche, *The Body's Symmetry*; Marty Jezer, *The Food Garden*; Alicia Bay Laurel, *Living on Earth*; and Raymond Mungo, *Famous Long Ago* and *Total Loss Farm*.

57. Richard Wizansky, ed., *Home Comfort* (New York: Saturday Review Press, 1973). Hereafter *Home Comfort* is cited as *HC*. The title is taken from the brand name of the wood stove that the authors found in the farmstead kitchen upon purchasing the farm (in 1968, for five thousand dollars). The title also reflects the shared conviction that Total Loss Farm was a comfortable and successful homestead and, for many, a truer home than they had ever formerly known.

58. Wizansky, "Who's in Charge," *HC*, 75–76.

59. Porche, "The Making of a Culture Counter," *HC*, 81. Porche is spoofing Theodore Rozak's *The Making of a Counter Culture* (Garden City, NY: Doubleday, 1969).

60. Mungo, *Total Loss Farm*. Mungo eventually leaves the farm before the others and in letters back discusses his need to wander but also reveals a longing for the farm, which he describes as his authentic spiritual and familial home.

61. Ibid., 22.

62. Ibid., 17.

63. Interview with "Kate," July 1994.

64. Although Fran's group is more balanced than most ("50 percent white, 50 percent native or mixed blood," according to Fran), the existence of Native American spirituality groups dominated by nonnative peoples is a prominent feature of contemporary spirituality, as Catherine Albanese (155–63) points out. Such groups can offer readings of native traditions that are inaccurate or insensitive or that tend to ignore tribal differences. Having studied comparative religion, Fran speaks with more awareness than many of the complexity of "borrowing" from other traditions. See Catherine Albanese, Nature Religion in America, Chicago History of American Religion, ed. Martin Marty (Chicago: University of Chicago Press, 1990).

65. Interviews with "Fran," October 1996.

66. For wider treatments of these tendencies, see Albanese, Nature Religion in America, and also Robert Ellwood, The Sixties Spiritual Awakening: American Religion Moving from Modern to Postmodern (New Brunswick, NJ: Rutgers University Press, 1994).

67. Peter Gay, The Enlightenment: An Interpretation—the Birth of Modern Paganism (New York: Knopf, 1966). An intellectual "companion volume" of sorts can be found in M. H. Abrams's treatment of Romanticism in Natural Supernaturalism (New York: W. W. Norton, 1971; paperback reprint, 1973). Both texts provide a long-range view of intellectual currents that reveal the roots of the turn to nature that I am describing here.

2. Getting (Not Too) Close to Nature

Epigraph: John Burroughs, The Heart of Burroughs's Journals, ed. Clara Barrus (Boston: Houghton Mifflin, 1928; reprint, Port Washington, NY: Kennikat Press, 1967), 71–72.

1. In the 1980s, Helen wrote a well-researched and witty discussion of the reception of Walden by Thoreau's contemporaries, in which her unflagging admiration for him is obvious. Helen Nearing, "Thoreau, Judged in His Own Time," Helen and Scott Nearing Papers, the Thoreau Institute, Lincoln, MA.

2. Lawrence Buell also makes note of what we might call the imitatio Walden tradition in The Environmental Imagination: Thoreau, Nature Writing and American Culture (Cambridge, MA: Harvard University Press, Belknap Press, 1995), especially 145–56.

3. Henry David Thoreau, Walden, Norton Critical Edition, ed. William Rossi (1854; New York: W. W. Norton, 1992), 75.

4. Jeffrey Jacob mistakenly takes the Nearings' description of the value of

leisure at face value, without interpreting their "purism" as also involving a critique of leisure (particularly the pursuit of leisure by those unused to hard physical labor). See Jacob, *New Pioneers*, 56.

5. Conversation with "Simon," June 2001, as well as ongoing communication from 1995 to the present.

6. Interview with "Joshua," July 2001.

7. *Walden*, 138.

8. Ibid., 104–10.

9. For the best treatment of the Emersonian idea of self-culture, see David Robinson, *Apostle of Culture* (Philadelphia: University of Pennsylvania Press, 1982). A broader examination of the development of ideas of the self in nineteenth-century American culture can be found in Daniel Walker Howe, *Making the American Self* (Cambridge, MA: Harvard University Press, 1997).

10. The descriptions given here are based on my first visits to Helen Nearing and to "Sal" in the spring and summer of 1994 but are obviously informed by my later, lengthier stays.

11. The Nearings' original homestead and garden in Maine (and the successor to the first "Forest Farm" in Vermont) were sold to Stan Joseph in 1980 and remained in use until his death in 1995. It is this original garden and wall to which the Nearings refer in their writings.

For the story of the transformation of Helen and Scott's original farmhouse and garden, see Stanley Joseph and Lynn Karlin, *Maine Farm: A Year of Country Life* (New York: Random House, 1991). Helen Nearing's cautious foreword to this text hints at the significant differences in "homesteading style" between these two neighbors and the tensions such stylistic differences produced.

12. See Helen Nearing and Scott Nearing, *Our Home Made of Stone* (Camden, ME: DownEast Books, 1983), and "We Build a Stone House" (55–89), in GL.

13. Nearing and Nearing, "We Build a Stone House," GL, 57–58.

14. Ibid., 78.

15. CGL, 383.

16. While Sal's garden is highly original, no-till gardening itself is not his invention but enjoys popularity among many who are interested in alternative farming.

17. Interviews with "Sal," July 1994. All subsequent quotations in this discussion are from these interviews.

18. Wendell Berry, "The Agricultural Crisis as a Crisis of Culture," *The Unsettling of America*, 47.

19. Many homesteaders have followed the Nearings' model of careful planning before embarking on their own adventures. But some have also poked fun at their rigidity. Guy and Laura Waterman, for instance, counted the Nearings as

a major influence in their own project in East Corinth, Vermont. In Nearing style, they drew up a ten-point set of principles in 1971, when they had purchased their land but had not yet settled it. The last principle, however, included both a wink at and a nod to the Nearings: "10. Be dogmatic in nothing. If it's desirable to make an exception from any of these principles, do so." Guy and Laura Waterman, Appendix I, "Barra: An Operator's Manual," unpublished MS, 1998. My gratitude goes to Laura Waterman for loaning me this manuscript and for her keen insights into her own and others' homesteading ventures.

20. Helen Nearing did have a more "mystical" side to her, however, which was rooted in her upbringing as a Theosophist. She maintained an interest in dowsing, astrology, Spiritualism, UFOs, automatic writing, and related esoteric practices. Scott shared these interests, from at least the early twentieth century, but he was less vocal about them.

21. Here it is helpful to remember that in the context of the study of religion the use of the word *symbolic* is rarely meant to suggest "not real"; it is most often meant to convey that which is both real and more than real, that is, reflective of one's larger convictions about the nature and mysteries of existence.

In this sense, homesteaders' actions are little different from those who commit their lives to Christ and then express this commitment by wearing the cross. Wearing the cross may be "merely" a symbolic act, but if—as Paul Tillich has written—"symbols participate in the reality to which they point," then wearing the cross is both a symbolic gesture and a "real," daily rededication to a life lived in Christ. In the same vein, homesteaders who daily saw wood by hand to heat their homes are both responding to the "real" necessity of using a cheap, readily available, and renewable natural resource and symbolically articulating the depth of their commitment to living in a natural environment that they believe deserves care and respect. See Paul Tillich, "The Nature of Religious Language," in *Theology of Culture*, ed. Robert Kimball (Oxford: Oxford University Press, 1959), 54–55.

22. LL, 2. Here, as elsewhere, the Nearings' affirmation of the cyclical nature of life is in tension with their desire to live on in the memory of others. They both do and do not want to be immortalized.

23. Interviews with "Henry," October 1995.

24. See "Visitors and Helpers," in GL, 358–65.

25. Linda Tatelbaum, *Carrying Water as a Way of Life* (Appelton, ME: About Time Press, 1997), 4.

26. Conversation with "Craig," July 2004.

27. Interviews with "Sal," October 1995.

28. See Peter Berger, *The Sacred Canopy* (New York: Doubleday, 1967).

29. Raymond Williams, *The Country and the City* (Oxford: Oxford University Press, 1973; paperback reprint, 1975).

30. *Walden*, 140. Thoreau did actually eat woodchuck on at least one occasion and regretted it.

31. Other examples would be Thoreau's descriptions of taking daily baths or of drinking from Walden as if from the Ganges.

32. *Walden*, 140.

33. For guidance in my reading of *Walden*, I am indebted to many illuminating conversations with Lawrence Buell. For Buell's treatment of *Walden* and of Thoreauvian nature writing in general, see *The Environmental Imagination*. For Buell's discussion of Thoreau's "religiocentrism" and simultaneous resistance to it, see 230–31 and 403–5.

34. Annie Dillard relates the weasel story in *Teaching a Stone to Talk* (New York: Harper and Row, 1982), 14–15.

35. Ibid., 15–16.

36. Buell (*The Environmental Imagination*, 74, 237–46) treats the Dillard-Thoreau connection at several junctures in his book. He reminds us that Dillard not only wrote her master's thesis about *Walden* but also consciously constructed her more celebrated *Pilgrim at Tinker Creek* (New York: Harper and Row, 1974) to mirror the structure of *Walden*. Buell's evidence with respect to *Pilgrim* and my own reading of *Teaching a Stone to Talk* suggest more than a circumstantial similarity between Thoreau's woodchuck encounter and Dillard's meeting of minds with the weasel.

3. Homemade Ritual

Epigraph: Jonathan Z. Smith, *To Take Place: Toward Theory in Ritual* (Chicago: University of Chicago Press, 1987; paperback reprint, 1992), 109.

1. I am speaking of ritual, here, in its rich, dynamic, symbolic, and potentially transformational sense (as it is often discussed in the study of religion), not as primarily "empty" or "routinized" behavior, as the term *ritual* is sometimes used in everyday conversation.

2. Linda Tatelbaum, *Carrying Water as a Way of Life* (Appleton, ME: About Time Press, 1997), 3.

3. Catherine Bell, *Ritual Theory, Ritual Practice* (Oxford: Oxford University Press, 1992), 67–93.

4. Robert Payne, "Hemorrhoids in Paradise," in *HC*, 192–93.

5. Marty Jezer, "Psychic Farming: The Organic Method," in *HC*, 127–28.

6. Marty Jezer, "Maple Sugaring: Our Finest Hour," in *HC*, 213–17. See Helen Nearing and Scott Nearing, *The Maple Sugar Book* (New York: John Day Company, 1950; paperback reprint, New York: Schocken, 1970). This was the first comprehensive book on the history and practice of maple sugaring yet to be published.

7.   The Nearings also disapproved of maple cream on the grounds of health and an implied morality. They wrote: "Maple cream is a typical product for an age that savors and relishes cream puffs. No laborious chewing or biting is required. The stuff slides down with one easy gulp." See Nearing and Nearing, *The Maple Sugar Book*, 186.

8.   Ibid., 117–18.

9.   Jezer, "Maple Sugaring," HC, 216.

10.   Ibid., 216.

11.   Even without the sugarhouse, Jezer admits, "[we will have] enough maple syrup to stuff ourselves with pancakes for a month or two and get good and fat before starting to build that illusive sugarhouse again." But the opportunity for such "decadence" is not created by a sudden trip to the store. The farmers still earn these pleasures by assisting their neighbors in sugaring and with their own practices of setting "sixty or seventy buckets" close to the house and making syrup over a wood fire in the front yard "a slow, tedious process that produces a thick, dark liquid somewhere between grade Y and Z." Ibid., 217.

12.   Drawing on Foucault's claim that "nothing is fundamental. . . . There are only reciprocal relations, and the perpetual gap between intentions in relation to one another," Bell makes clear to her readers her conviction that theoretical claims regarding ritual as "fundamental," an "essence" or a "key" to human experience, are mythical and misleading. Michel Foucault in "Space, Knowledge and Power," an interview with Michel Foucault in *The Foucault Reader*, ed. Paul Rabinow (New York: Pantheon, 1984), cited and discussed by Bell, *Ritual Theory, Ritual Practice*, 37.

I would add that while I find Jonathan Z. Smith's perspective on ritual illuminating in terms of interpreting the performative work produced by homesteaders (hence the use of Smith in the epigraph), I also share Bell's concerns that ritual not be seen simply as a set of balanced contrasts or binary oppositions.

13.   See, for instance, Jack Goody, "Against 'Ritual': Loosely Structured Thoughts on a Loosely Defined Topic," in *Secular Ritual*, ed. Sally F. Moore and Barbara G. Myerhoff (Amsterdam: Van Gorcum, 1977), 25–35.

14.   Bell's critique of Geertz's description of ritual "failure" (*Ritual Theory, Ritual Practice*, 32–35) is particularly illuminating in this regard.

15.   Ibid., 74.

16.   David D. Hall's analysis of "the uses of ritual" (though pertaining to a quite different historical context) is illuminating for this discussion. See David D. Hall, *Worlds of Wonder, Days of Judgment: Popular Religious Belief in Early New England* (Cambridge, MA: Harvard University Press, 1990), chapter 4.

17.   Hubbard, *Payne Hollow*, 94–95.

18.   LL, 151–52.

19. Harlan Hubbard, in a journal passage of 1958 or 1959, as quoted by Wendell Berry in *Harlan Hubbard: Life and Work* (New York: Pantheon Books, 1990), 37 and 105 n. 1. In his biography of Hubbard, Berry glosses Hubbard's reflections on faith with a more traditional theological reading than I would give. He implicitly compares Hubbard's life with his own and makes more explicit biblical connections than Hubbard's journal and writings themselves reveal. While I lean away from Berry's "Christianizing" of Hubbard, I also find it revealing of the broader continuum we see in homesteading literature, one that moves from Berry's radical Christian (earth focused, critical of the church) stance to those who place nature at the center of their values and practices without the need of any religious referents. Thanks to Jonathan Greene for a conversation on these matters.

20. Sal's newsletter (title omitted to protect anonymity), 2–3.

21. Letter to me from Laura Waterman, October 14, 2002.

22. Logsdon, *The Contrary Farmer*, 141.

23. Arne Naess, *Ecology, Community and Lifestyle*, trans. David Rothenberg (Cambridge: Cambridge University Press, 1989; paperback reprint, 1990).

24. Tatelbaum, *Carrying Water*, 16.

25. Ibid., 17.

26. Mungo, *Total Loss Farm*, 164.

27. Ibid., 128.

28. Pierre Bourdieu, *Distinction: A Social Critique of the Judgement of Taste*, trans. Richard Nice (Cambridge, MA: Harvard University Press, 1984), 179.

For provocative analyses of the practice of eating as a means of establishing particular racial, cultural, and religious identities, see Margaret Vesser, *Much Depends on Dinner* (New York: Grove Press, 1987); Kathy Neustadt, *Clambake: A History and Celebration of an American Tradition*, Publications of the American Folklore Society (Amherst: University of Massachusetts Press, 1992); Deane Curtin and Lisa Heldke, eds., *Cooking, Eating, Thinking: Transformative Philosophies of Food* (Bloomington: Indiana University Press, 1992); and Jualynne E. Dodson and Cheryl Townsend Gilkes, "There's Nothing Like Church Food," *Journal of the American Academy of Religion*, 63, no. 3 (Fall 1995): 519–38. Volume 63 of the *JAAR* is thematically dedicated to the topic of religion and food.

29. Bourdieu asserts that the development of "taste" for certain kinds of foods is a means of creating and maintaining social and cultural distinctions. He probes the complexities of this process in chapter 3 of *Distinction*, "The Habitus and Space of Life-Style" (177–200). Here he argues persuasively against the theory that patterns of consumption are simply a function of income.

30. Richard Wizansky, "Rituals," in *HC*, 278.

31. Examples of such rituals include the farm's "Ali Baba" nights, the making and wearing of Moroccan hooded capes and the telling of the mythic tale of Ka-

jamunya, which served as the grounding "reality" behind the farm, particularly in the farm's shaky first year. See Jezer, "Psychic Farming," HC, 129.

32. In this use of the word *formalize*, I am referring not to social conventions of "formality" but to ritual behavior as being attentive to form.

The practice of eating from wooden bowls is not restricted to the Nearings but is shared also by those who seek to emulate the Nearings as well as by some members of the "Sauna crowd" who got into the habit, even if their relationship with the Nearings is marked both by admiration and dissent. Henry and his partner, Jo, for instance, always bring their own wooden bowls to Sauna.

33. Snyder writes: "What a big potlatch we are all members of! To acknowledge that each of us at the table will eventually be part of the meal is not just being 'realistic.' It is allowing the sacred to enter and accepting the sacramental aspect of our shaky temporary personal being." Gary Snyder, *The Practice of the Wild* (San Francisco: North Point Press, 1990), 19.

34. In this section I am referring to the Nearings' chapter "What We Eat and Why," in CGL, 368–74.

The claim that Helen and Scott never visited a doctor (CGL, 379) was not wholly accurate. Helen and Scott both infrequently consulted medical professionals in their later years. As with other "myth" versus "reality" distinctions, however, the Nearings were generally (if not exclusively) true to their principles.

35. See the chapter entitled "We Practice Health," in CGL, 378–84.

36. GL, 119.

37. LL, 24–30.

38. Ibid., 11.

39. Helen Nearing reports that in 1917 Scott noted four changes that marked a turning point in his life (ibid., 19–20; also 14–22):

1. I become a socialist, a pacifist, a vegetarian.
2. I give up dancing and dress clothes as symbols of the life I am leaving.
3. I abandon the role of a successful and popular lecturer [i.e. he continues to lecture, but vows no longer to attempt to please or entertain his audience, but rather to simply 'tell the truth']. . . .
4. I dedicate myself to promote the general welfare, the commonweal, the common good.

40. MR, 225.

41. On Nearing's early involvement in the fitness movement and vegetarianism as part of the Progressive Era generally, see John Saltmarsh, *Scott Nearing: An Intellectual Biography* (Philadelphia: Temple University Press, 1991), 50–57.

For a discerning inquiry into the relationship among religion, health, and masculine ideologies of control in this period (with special attention to Macfadden), see R. Marie Griffith, "Apostles of Abstinence: Fasting and Masculinity during the Progressive Era," *American Quarterly* 52, no. 4 (December 2000): 599–638.

An earlier treatment of the fitness craze and Macfadden in Progressive Era America can be found in James C. Wharton, *Crusaders for Fitness: The History of American Health Reformers* (Princeton, NJ: Princeton University Press, 1982), 270–303. See also Colin Spencer, *The Heretic's Feast: A History of Vegetarianism* (London: Fourth Estate, 1994), and Janet Barkas, *A History of the Vegetarian State of Mind* (London: Routledge and Kegan Paul, 1975).

A more thorough assessment of Scott Nearing's early life appears in chapter 6, where I describe the ways in which his impulses toward "living close to nature" were both nurtured and deferred in the Progressive Era until finally brought to realization in the life of homesteading in the 1930s.

42. GL, 144.

43. CGL, 371.

44. GL, 144.

45. CGL, 373.

46. Ibid.

47. GL, 106.

48. Henry David Thoreau, journal entry, December 5, 1856, as cited in GL, 106.

49. GL, 106. In contrast (as noted above), the Total Loss farmers rejoiced in the prospect of eating eggplant out of season, provided they grow and preserve it themselves.

50. Ibid., 105.

51. Helen Nearing gives a revealing account of the dynamics of freedom and discipline in her life with Scott by quoting from a series of letters between the two of them in the early period of their relationship.

During a stay in Europe in 1929, a year into their relationship, Helen writes to Scott celebrating the feeling of being "free as a bird," resisting the pull of responsibilities and social expectations. Scott's reply to Helen—characteristically divided into three sections (I: "Theoretical Comment," II: "Certain Applications of These Theoretical Points," and III: "Free for What?"), each with subsections separated by letter and number—constitutes a call for her to investigate seriously the question of freedom, to recognize the extent of her duties and responsibilities in a world where others are poor and oppressed, to acquire a skill that will make her economically independent, and to "build a higher life through meditation, study, thought . . . [so as] to develop the great talents that are in keeping" of her. Though these letters are by no means absent of love and affection, they demonstrate Scott's characteristic rigor and firm-mindedness as well as his concern for the flights of fancy and pleasure seeking that Helen indulged in while in Europe. LL, 86–88.

Helen's writing about her own attitude toward discipline, then, is curiously mixed. She describes herself as one who "enjoys cold when others are close to the fire" (interviews, May 1994), and her public attitudes toward food are particularly ascetic, yet she portrays herself as having learned discipline through Scott.

52. GL, 142.

53. Ibid.

54. Ibid., 141–42.

55. Jeffrey Jacob also comments on the Nearings' approach as "purist" but does so without attention to the realities behind the texts or to the ambivalence that can be detected within them. Since his approach to the Nearings is an intentionally short overview for the purposes of developing a typology of back-to-the-landers, his surface treatment is understandable but not wholly accurate. Jacob, New Pioneers, 54–57.

56. Quoted by Berry in The Unsettling of America, 139.

57. Ibid., 138. Here Berry's language resonates remarkably with psychologist Robert J. Lifton's assessments of the crisis of the late twentieth century. See Lifton, The Broken Connection (New York: Basic Books, 1979). In a certain sense, Berry and Lifton are making the same argument, that the social and natural world needs to be "symbolized differently" in order for the broken connections to be restored.

58. Berry, "The Pleasures of Eating," WPF, 152.

59. While I hesitate to give a portrait of the Nearings that is unfairly harsh, the following anecdote from Helen not only indicates the extremes to which "rigor" could be taken but also further suggests that Helen rebelled against Scott's rigidity: " 'What do you do for fun?' we were often asked. 'Everything we do is recreation, is enjoyable, otherwise we wouldn't do it,' we answered. As for 'fun,' it was not a word Scott used. At one time I said I was working on a book of my own, 'I'm having a lot of fun with it, whether anyone else likes it or not.' Scott remarked, not unkindly, 'That's too bad you're having fun with it. Life is not about fun. Do a serious job at it.' It was only a cookbook, so it hardly got very serious." LL, 165.

A glance at the finished product to which Helen refers here—the cookbook, Simple Food for the Good Life (New York: Dell, 1980; reprint, Delta/Eleanor Freide Paperback, 1982)—reveals an interesting mix. The text is full of her characteristic wit and charm. Clearly, she did have fun with it. But her comments on vegetarianism and the evils of meat eating are without compromise. In this sense, it was, as Scott would say, "a serious job."

60. WPF, 151. In discussing the virtues of homemade cheese, Pete Gould makes a similar remark: "The memory of spring and summer grass was in that food; for me the cow's milk had been transfigured into a substance that had a myste-

rious physical presence, soft as a breast." Gould, "Cheese Making on the Small Farm," in *HC*, 89.

61. *WPF*, 150. For a more elaborate discussion of the way in which working with animals is both practically useful and pleasurable for farmers and animals alike, see Berry's essays, "Looking Back—or Ahead—to Horses," in *The Gift of Good Land* (San Francisco: North Point Press, 1981), 189–95, and "Getting Along with Nature," in *Home Economics*, 6–20.

62. On the keeping of domestic animals, the Nearings write: "Widespread and unwarranted exploitation of domestic animals includes robbing them of their milk or eggs as well as harnessing them to labor for man. Domestic animals, whether cows, horses, goats or chickens, dogs or cats are slaves. Humans have the power of life or death over them. Domestic pets kill and drive away wild creatures, whose independent, self-respecting lives seem far more admirable than those of docile, dish-fed retainers . . . although some of our best friends in Vermont have been canine and feline neighbors." *GL*, 36.

Again, actual practices depart somewhat from stated principles. The Nearings used horses in their first year of sugaring in Vermont, though Helen was loathe to comment on this when I pressed the point in interviews (May 1994). In Maine, Helen was "adopted" by several cats, one of whom was particularly dear to her. Helen felt no need to hide this fact, however, and published several pictures of herself and "Pusso" in *The Good Life Album of Helen and Scott Nearing* (New York: E. P. Dutton, 1974).

63. *GL*, 167. For a much more comprehensive and equally uncompromising treatment of the problem of flesh eating, see Helen Nearing's chapter "To Kill or Not to Kill: Flesh Foods versus Plants," in *Simple Food for the Good Life*, 37–57.

64. My thanks to Greg Joly for sharing his own impressions with me on the views of the Nearings in the eyes of their Vermont neighbors. My research in Maine confirmed a similar history of uncomfortable sentiment.

65. Berry probes the moral complexities of tobacco farming but sides, ultimately, with the tobacco farmers, admitting that much of his position is shaped by childhood memories of growing up in "tobacco country." He writes, "Our nationality was more or less American. Our religion was nominally and sometimes approximately Christian. But our culture was largely determined by tobacco, just as the culture of the Plains Indians was determined by the horse." See Berry, "The Problem of Tobacco," *Sex, Economy, Freedom and Community* (New York: Pantheon Books, 1992), 54.

66. Interview with Helen Nearing, July 6, 1994. I later sent Helen a copy of Wendell Berry's *What Are People For?* both as a thank you for the interview and in hopes of having a more detailed discussion of Berry's work. Helen died before such a discussion took place. While living at the Nearing homestead, however, I found the book that I had sent her and had the pleasure of reading Helen's

marginalia. Her notations characteristically show both a respect and admiration for Berry's work and her need to distinguish the "Nearing way." Not only did Helen object to Berry's carnivorous practices, but also she objected to his use of machine-powered tools. In response to a story Berry tells of having a pond dug on his land, Helen wrote in the margins, "Scott dug his by hand!"

West Virginia homesteader and sheep farmer Donald McCaig sought the advice and inspiration of both Wendell Berry and Helen Nearing and profiles each in his *An American Homeplace* (New York: Crown Publishers, 1992). McCaig offers no sustained analysis or comparative treatment but does capture nicely what a visit with Helen Nearing is like. The early section of the book is a homestead narrative in itself, which resembles many other homesteading texts in its "how I left Greenwich Village and took up sheep farming, without knowing what I was getting myself into" narrative structure.

67. Mary Douglas, *Purity and Danger* (London: Routledge and Kegan Paul, 1966), 36.

68. See Douglas's discussion of holiness, ibid., 49–57.

69. See Wharton's chapter, "The Kingdom of Health," *Crusaders for Fitness*, 3–12, and also, Albanese, *Nature Religion in America*, especially chapter 4, "Physical Religion: Natural Sin and Healing Grace in the Nineteenth Century."

70. Saltmarsh, *Scott Nearing*, 56.

71. Wharton tends to separate the "self" and "other" orientations historically, contrasting the "altruistic" tendencies of late nineteenth- and early twentieth-century vegetarians with the self-oriented nature of the "running craze" of the late twentieth century. Wharton comments that there has been "a steady drift of reform emphasis from the society to the individual" in the last half century. While Wharton's comment seems generally true in terms of the late twentieth-century emphasis on "self-actualization," he belies the complexity of his own earlier discussions of vegetarianism (on which Saltmarsh draws) in making this summary statement. Certainly, in the case of the Nearings and in the broader context of "muscular Christianity" in which Scott Nearing came of age, the understanding of the body as a temple and of the self as capable of being purified and improved through bodily discipline is clearly in evidence. Such notions seem little different from the "I am in the Kingdom and the Kingdom is in me" interpretations of the spirituality of running that Wharton quotes. See Wharton's chapter 7, "Muscular Vegetarianism," 201–38, and his final chapter, "A Modern Conspectus," 331–49 in *Crusaders for Fitness*.

72. Nearing and Nearing, *The Good Life Album*, 84–86.

73. See *Conscious Living, Conscious Dying*, a documentary directed and produced by Andrea Sarris and Polly Benell, which investigates Helen Nearing's life and approach to death and dying.

For Helen Nearing's own meditations on the "naturalness" of death, see her foreword to her book *Light on Aging and Dying* (Gardiner, ME: Tilbury House,

1995), vii–xii. One of several strange coincidences surrounding Helen's own death was that the first box of these books from the publisher arrived at Helen's door on the day after her passing. For a moving personal meditation on Helen's passing, which also reveals more of Helen's own thinking on the issue of human mortality, see Ellen LaConte, *On Light Alone: A Guru Meditation on the Good Death of Helen Nearing* (Stockton Springs, ME: Loose Leaf Press, 1996).

74. Helen's parents thought their daughter was a reincarnation of a Theosophist leader. Helen, in turn, liked to say that she had "chosen" to be born to particularly good and appropriate parents. Author interviews with Helen Nearing, May 1994.

75. H. Nearing, *Simple Food for the Good Life*, 54.

76. See LaConte, *On Light Alone*, 85–96.

77. H. Nearing, *Simple Food for the Good Life*, 54. In one interview (July 8, 1994), Helen spoke to me with considerable admiration of a man she knew who lived only on leaves of lettuce.

78. Lawrence Buell's interpretation of Berry's work also considers the issue of Berry's occasional anthropocentric—and androcentric—stance toward nature. See Buell, *The Environmental Imagination*, 161. Although my particular focus here is not on anthropocentrism per se, questions of anthropocentrism are obviously in play in the complex dynamics of human intimacy and distance with respect to the natural world.

79. Berry directly promotes this model of stewardship, a model that is both Christian and ecological, in "God and Country," *WPF*, 95–102, and in "Christianity and the Survival of Creation," *Sex, Economy, Freedom and Community*, 93–116.

80. Wendell Berry, *Farming: A Handbook* (New York: Harcourt Brace, 1970), 3.

81. Louis Bromfield, *Pleasant Valley* (New York: Harper Brothers, 1945), 275–6.

82. Thomas Jefferson's words almost two hundred years earlier: "Those who labour in the earth are the chosen people of God, if ever he had a chosen people, whose breasts he has made his peculiar deposit for substantial and genuine virtue." Jefferson, *Notes on the State of Virginia* (1787), ed. William Peden (New York: W. W. Norton, 1972), 165.

83. Raymond Mungo, *Total Loss Farm* (New York: E. P. Dutton, 1970), 164.

84. Ibid., 169.

85. Interviews with "Sal," July 1994.

86. The very notion of becoming a living book captures what I am describing here. It also articulates the quest for immortality in recognizably "post-Christian" terms.

87. Sal was raised as a Catholic, and his way of articulating an incarnational view of nature has struck me as post-Catholic in the same vein that the Nearings' preference for asceticism and rigor can be interpreted as post-Protestant.

88. It is important to note, however, that a Sauna meal would never consist entirely of store-bought items. Store-bought foods are usually accoutrements (appetizers, condiments, or dessert), not centerpiece items.

89. Conversation with a member of the Sauna crowd, September 1996.

90. A similar comment about Sauna was made by Noah Adams in *Piano Lessons: Music, Love and True Adventures* (New York: Delacorte Press, 1996).

91. Conversation with "Henry," June 1996.

92. Interview with "Maggie," October 13, 1996.

93. Robert Bellah et al., *Habits of the Heart*, updated ed. (Berkeley: University of California Press, 1996), 234–35.

94. Wuthnow, *After Heaven*, 129; Roof, *A Generation of Seekers*, 38, 203. In a somewhat different vein, Charles Taylor also identifies the intellectual turn to nature as an individualistic and "expressivist" phenomenon rather than considering the possibility that nature-oriented practice may transcend such leanings toward individualistic and inward moral sources. Taylor, *Sources of the Self: The Making of Modern Identity* (Cambridge, MA: Harvard University Press, 1989).

95. Bellah et al., *Habits of the Heart*, 71–75, 335.

96. Ibid., 335.

97. Levy as quoted by Bellah et al., ibid., 137. The interview was probably conducted by Steven Tipton.

98. Ibid., 137.

99. The distinction between community and lifestyle enclave is described in Bellah's glossary, ibid., 333–36, and more fully on 153–54.

100. Wizansky, "Who's in Charge," in HC, 76.

101. This vision of nature is, of course, part reality (the perception of the limits that nature sets) and part cultural construction (the perception of nature as a largely beneficent force establishing restraints that are good for humans). Such readings are variations on a theme that is firmly established in the writings of Henry David Thoreau.

102. See Bellah et al., *Habits of the Heart*, especially 32–35, 55–84, and 142–63.

103. Wuthnow, *After Heaven*. On the shift from "dwelling" to "seeking," see especially 3–18; on seeking and the limits of freedom, 72–84. Wuthnow captures the limits of the quest for discipline (particularly 1980s versions) when he writes: "There was little evidence of people engaging in spiritual disciplines that called them to sacrifice the standard of living to which they had grown accustomed or even to devote significant portions of their week to seeking a deeper relationship with God. Pursuing a disciplined spiritual life meant, at most, rediscovering the soft technology of saying a brief prayer before going to bed. . . . [Spiritual discipline] . . . amounted to little more than keeping one's feelings in check and having faith that one's institutions were right" (113).

My own use of the term *discipline* with respect to homesteading, especially in this chapter, is more in keeping with what Wuthnow calls "practice." That is, I am most often discussing self-conscious choices in daily life that are means of constraining freedom in the service of deepening one's knowledge of the self, one's relationship to nature, and one's sense of moral obligation to local communities and bioregions. This process is obviously distinct from the "soft technology" character of discipline as Wuthnow describes it. Nevertheless, I use the term *discipline* as a complement to the term *practice* as a way of emphasizing the "aesthetics of rigor" as well as the approach-avoidance relationship with nature that is sometimes at work in homesteading.

Interlude

Epigraph: Woody Allen, as cited by Eric Lax, *Woody Allen: A Biography* (New York: Knopf, 1991), 39.

1. See Jonathan Z. Smith, *To Take Place: Towards Theory in Ritual*, Chicago Studies in the History of Judaism, ed. Jacob Neusner et al. (Chicago: University of Chicago Press, 1987; paperback reprint, 1992), 109.

2. For this definition of culture, see Mary Douglas, *Purity and Danger* (London: Routledge and Kegan Paul, 1966), 12.

3. Here I am thinking not only of the relationship between homesteading and the many liberal, Protestant valuations and "uses" of nature (about which more in chapters 5 and 6) but also of the American Catholic turn to nature, as seen, for example in the Catholic Worker–inspired "Peter Maurin Farms." The contemporary growth of "eco-Judaism" (with attention to vegetarian models of keeping kosher) also bears some family resemblances to homesteading.

4. These are all elements that Williams explores as well, though he casts them somewhat differently. See Raymond Williams, *The Country and the City* (Oxford: Oxford University Press, 1973; paperback reprint, 1975), especially "Knowable Communities," 165–81.

5. Pierre Bourdieu, *The Logic of Practice*, trans. Richard Nice (Stanford, CA: Stanford University Press, 1990).

4. The Reenchantment of the Farm

Epigraph: John Burroughs, "Phases of Farm Life," in *Signs and Seasons* (1886), *The Writings of John Burroughs*. (See note 7 for a full explanation of the multivolume publication of *The Writings of John Burroughs*.)

1. Edward J. Renehan Jr., *John Burroughs: An American Naturalist* (Post Mills, VT: Chelsea Green, 1992), 95. Renehan's text is the first comprehensive, scholarly biography of Burroughs and is particularly successful in charting Burroughs's many literary friendships and illuminating his difficult relationship with Ursula. The bi-

ography makes excellent use of archival sources but follows much of the same chronological narrative (and sometimes also interpretive stance) as Clara Barrus's more celebratory biographical treatments follow.

2.   It was at the urging of Ursula that Burroughs pursued a few unlikely schemes for acquiring instant financial success. One of these was an investment in a new version of a buckle on a horse harness. Burroughs dropped everything for this project, only to learn later that a patent for a similar buckle had already been registered. Clara Barrus (Burroughs's authorized biographer and long-term companion) tells this story in John Burroughs: Boy and Man (Garden City, NY: Doubleday, Page, 1920), 185–87.

Just how close a companion Barrus was for Burroughs is a matter of debate. Renehan describes a romantic affair between them, while Edward Kanze argues that this was not the case. See Kanze, The World of John Burroughs (San Francisco: Sierra Club Books, 1996), and, more particularly, Kanze's "The Truth about Santa Claus (John Burroughs)," also titled, "A Study in Biography: The Secret Life of John Burroughs," unpublished MS, undated.

3.   See Renehan, John Burroughs: An American Naturalist, 93; and Barrus, John Burroughs: Boy and Man, 259.

4.   Barrus reports that the flow of pilgrims began around 1896. The high tide of visitors came in the first decade of the twentieth century. Clara Barrus, The Life and Letters of John Burroughs, vol. 1 (Boston: Houghton Mifflin, 1925), 358. Hereafter, volume 1 of The Life and Letters of John Burroughs will be cited as CB I.

5.   See Schmitt, Back to Nature; and, more generally, Shi, The Simple Life, especially 198–201.

6.   Barrus points out that the sluggish pace of work in the early years of the Treasury's existence enabled Burroughs to get a significant amount of writing done at his desk there. During the time he worked at the Treasury, Burroughs completed Notes on Walt Whitman as Poet and Person (1867), Wake-Robin (1871), and many of the essays that would appear in Winter Sunshine. See Barrus, John Burroughs: Boy and Man, 231–32.

7.   John Burroughs, "Winter Sunshine," in Winter Sunshine (1875), The Writings of John Burroughs, 2:2–3. Most of the Burroughs volumes cited here belong to The Writings of John Burroughs, 1st ed. (Riverside Edition) (Boston: Houghton Mifflin, Riverside Press, 1895). Volumes published after 1895 belong to the 23-volume Riverby Edition (Boston: Houghton Mifflin, Riverside Press, 1904–23) and are cited as such. The volume number is given for each text of either edition. In each case, the original date of publication will be given at first mention in the notes or text so that the reader may follow Burroughs's personal and literary development chronologically.

8.   Renehan (John Burroughs: An American Naturalist, 92) paradoxically writes that when Burroughs acquired his Treasury job, "from that time on he always put financial security ahead of literature," though he later acknowledges that Bur-

roughs "wanted to be able to define himself solely via the creative processes through which he found his most vital link to the past: the processes of farming and writing" (121). Barrus mentions that Burroughs turned to farming not to "brag to his neighbors of his economy," like Thoreau, but "to support himself and family comfortably, send his son to college, and make enough from his fruit farm so that he might write when and what he pleased" (Barrus, *John Burroughs: Boy and Man*, 282).

Renehan and Barrus are certainly accurate in their comments, but I would place the emphasis differently. While Barrus is always eager to distinguish Burroughs from the curmudgeonly Thoreau, she misses the point of connection between them. For Burroughs, farming was a spiritual imperative, an opportunity for intimacy with the natural world that could be gained in no other way. While Burroughs remarked to fellow nature writer Clifton Johnson that he "farmed for the money there was in it," he also named the numerous obstacles that plagued the farmer and discussed the anxiety he felt: "[I made] only a few hundred dollars a year for a while, and that didn't take account of the interest on my investment." John Burroughs, *John Burroughs Talks*, ed. Clifton Johnson (Boston: Houghton Mifflin, 1922), 139. Hereafter *John Burroughs Talks* will be cited as *Talks*.

Certainly, Burroughs was aware of both the financial opportunities and financial risks of farming, and he initially chose to remain in the world of banking (part-time) because he "hesitated to depend on farming for a living" (*Talks*, 130).

Burroughs's account of how he came to choose his farm site reveals the deeper concerns and motivations that were influencing him in this period: "I had a curious feeling, when I stepped on the dock (at what later became West Park) that the place was to be my home. It was a very distinct occult premonition. . . . The stars may play a much greater part than we have any idea they do. . . . Yes, much is inexplicable from the viewpoint of our present knowledge. But a mental and spiritual evolution is going on, and depths beneath depths will open in the course of time. . . . I felt, when I arrived here, that I had reached the end of my quest" (*Talks*, 131).

9. By 1888, Burroughs had increased his landholdings to twenty acres and was growing grapes (Concords, Campbell's Early, Moore's Early, Delwares, and Niagaras) on a large scale. According to Barrus, he was actively cultivating twenty-four hundred grape vines, twenty-six hundred currant bushes, and two thousand "hills" of raspberries. Barrus, *John Burroughs: Boy and Man*, 281.

Burroughs's crops suffered heavy damage twice, once from a drought, the second time from a hail storm. A bigger problem, for Burroughs, was the growing popularity of Champion grapes. Burroughs deemed them to be "a boarding-house grape [that] looks well and smells good . . . but hogs can't eat it" (*Talks*, 147). Burroughs refused to grow grapes that were tasteless and took pride in keeping his crop on the vine until it was truly ripe. Such decisions underline the extent to which Burroughs understood farming to be an art and a source of personal satisfaction more than a business. A comment in Burroughs's journal (July 24, 1888) about potatoes also reflects this prevailing attitude: "Digging our potatoes for market; prices high ($3.75) but yield poor, owing to dry weather. May get back the expense, and a little more, in which case the fun of the thing will not have cost me anything." John Burroughs, *The Heart of Burroughs's Journals*, ed. Clara Barrus (Boston: Houghton Mifflin, 1928; reprint, Port Washington, NY: Kennikat Press, 1967), 151. Hereafter *The Heart of Burroughs's Journals* will be cited as *Journals*.

10. The phrase "exhilarations of the road" alludes to Burroughs's essay by that name, published in *Winter Sunshine*, 2:23–39.

11. Burroughs's devotion to self-culture was strongly influenced by his reading of Emerson, as will be discussed below. For the effect of Emerson on Burroughs's personal and intellectual development, see CB I, and Clara Barrus, *The Life and Letters of John Burroughs*, vol. 2 (Boston: Houghton Mifflin, 1925), 3. Hereafter, volume 2 of *The Life and Letters of John Burroughs* will be cited as CB II.

For the development of the idea of self-culture in the nineteenth century, particularly with respect to Emerson, see David Robinson, *Apostle of Culture* (Philadelphia: University of Pennsylvania Press, 1982), especially 7–35 and 85–94.

12. Burroughs, "Phases of Farm Life," in *Signs and Seasons* (1886), *The Writings of John Burroughs*, 7:244.

13. For general treatments of the cultural shifts of this period (particularly related to patterns of work, domesticity, and changing notions of the self), see Herbert G. Gutman, *Work, Culture and Society in Industrializing America: Essays in American Working-Class and Social History* (New York: Knopf, 1976); Colleen McDannell, *The Christian Home in Victorian America, 1840–1900* (Bloomington: Indiana University Press, 1986); Katherine Kish Sklar, *Catherine Beecher: A Study in American Domesticity* (New Haven, CT: Yale University Press, 1973); and the essays in Richard Fox and T. J. Jackson Lears, eds., *The Culture of Consumption: Critical Essays in American History, 1880–1980* (New York: Pantheon Books, 1983).

14. For Burroughs's praise of stone walls, see "Phases of Farm Life" and "Roof-Tree" in *Signs and Seasons*. For his paean to the cow, see "Our Rural Divinity" in *Birds and Poets* (1877), *The Writings of John Burroughs*, vol. 3.

15. For one example of this growing cultural concern, see David I. Macleod, *Building Character in the American Boy: The Boy Scouts, YMCA and Their Forerunners, 1870–1920* (Madison: University of Wisconsin Press, 1983). The threat to "character" that was perceived in the early twentieth century is made clear by Warren Sussman in his study of the emergence of the competing (and ultimately victorious) concept of "personality." It is worth observing that Burroughs's own life and reception attests to this shift, for while Burroughs consistently preached the virtues of character, he became, by the early twentieth

century, a personality in the wider cultural sphere. See Warren I. Sussman, "Personality and Twentieth-Century Culture," *Culture as History* (New York: Pantheon Books, 1984), 271–85.

16. Burroughs, *Signs and Seasons*, 7:245.

17. Ibid..

18. The three other books that were written in this period are *Birds and Poets* (1877), *Pepacton* (1881), and *Fresh Fields* (1884).

19. For John Burroughs's appeal as a "true man of the soil," see Shi, *The Simple Life*, 198.

20. Burroughs, "A March Chronicle," *Winter Sunshine*, 2:91.

21. Renehan, *John Burroughs: An American Naturalist*, 14.

22. Ibid., 14. Renehan writes that Burroughs spoke these words to a friend, although the date and the person spoken to are not mentioned.

23. Burroughs's "anxiety of influence" in regard to Thoreau's work is too complicated a diversion to engage in here, except to say that any careful reading of "The Exhilarations of the Road" and "The Apple" (also in *Winter Sunshine*) reveals that Burroughs borrowed heavily from Thoreau, whether consciously or otherwise. Burroughs's eagerness to criticize Thoreau in both journal entries and public essays also underlines his need to reassure both his readers and himself that he and Thoreau occupied different literary, moral, and aesthetic terrain. Still, according to Barrus, Burroughs denied that Thoreau had any major influence: "To Thoreau Burroughs felt less indebted (as compared to Emerson), although it is to Thoreau that he has been so often compared. He greatly admired the 'Week on the Concord and Merrimack Rivers,' and 'Walden' . . . but disclaimed deriving any conspicuous formative influences from them" (CB II, 3).

24. Burroughs, "The Exhilarations of the Road," *Winter Sunshine*, 2:26, 25.

25. Ibid., 30–31.

26. Ibid., 38.

27. Barrus, *John Burroughs: Boy and Man*, 273. Burroughs's hunger for gravel is also indicated in "The Exhilarations of the Road." He writes: "I sing of the sweetness of gravel, good sharp quartz-grit. It is the proper condiment for the sterner seasons, and many a human gizzard would be cured of half its ills by a suitable daily allowance of it" (*Winter Sunshine*, 2:39).

28. Burroughs, "The Pastoral Bees," in *Locusts and Wild Honey, The Writings of John Burroughs*, 4:25.

29. Burroughs, "Sharp Eyes," ibid., 4:28.

30. In his chapter "Immersion in the Local," Renehan (*John Burroughs: An American Naturalist*, 124) similarly remarks on the relationship between Burroughs's new life on the farm and the texts he produced. He notes: "As an artist interpreting nature, [Burroughs] had charged himself to become immersed in its

local occurrences, investing his personality and love into the landscape of his own region as had Thoreau, and using his native terrain as a local lens through which to view things that were universal in scope."

Renehan's emphasis here, however, is more literary than spiritual. His portrait of the artist shows Burroughs going to nature in order to write about it with more immediacy and effectiveness, although Burroughs himself liked to deny that he walked or farmed in order to write. While not entirely disagreeing with Renehan (or taking Burroughs's comments only at face value), my own sense of Burroughs's experience is weighted differently. I see his writing in this period as being more a response to the spiritual imperative of returning to the natural world than it was an aesthetic choice to be closer to the source of his literary material. Renehan *does* give some consideration of Burroughs's spiritual reading of nature in his prologue, "John the Baptist," referring especially to the theological essays that appeared after the turn of the century. One of my intentions here, however, is to explore the spiritual developments Burroughs experienced prior to writing these later essays; for the farming and writing Burroughs engaged in between 1872 and 1900 enabled him to reach the theological refinements that we see later. See Renehan, *John Burroughs: An American Naturalist*, 1–6 and 125–36.

31. May 9, 1880, *Journals*, 80.

32. Burroughs, "A Sharp Lookout," *Signs and Seasons*, 7:3.

33. Ibid., 5. In these words we hear echoes of the same themes of intimacy and sacrifice that Sal expressed when describing the process of building his house.

34. Burroughs, "A Sharp Lookout," *Signs and Seasons*, 7:4.

35. Burroughs, of course, had his own concerns about the uses and abuses of the pathetic fallacy. They were given voice in a 1903 article entitled "Real and Sham in Natural History," published in the *Atlantic Monthly*. The articles sparked a controversy (in which President Theodore Roosevelt eventually got involved) between Burroughs and such alleged "Nature Fakers" as Ernest Thompson Seton and Rev. William J. Long. See Renehan's chapter "The Nature Fakers and Roosevelt" (*John Burroughs: An American Naturalist*, 229–50). For a book-length study that places the controversy in broader historical and cultural perspective, see Ralph Lutts, *The Nature Fakers: Wildlife, Science and Sentiment* (Golden, CO: Fulcrum, 1990).

In his introduction to *The Ways of Nature* (1905), Burroughs informs his readers that the essays to follow are "the outcome of the currents of thought and inquiry that [the Nature Faker debate] set going in my mind." Burroughs makes clear to his readers that he has not been able to fully persuade himself "that the lower animals ever show anything more than a faint gleam of what we call thought and reflection." At the same time, he admits that in his own writings he has sometimes found himself "giving the wild creatures credit for more 'sense' than they really possessed." Burroughs's introduction is revealing of his underlying ambivalence with respect to "reading" the natural world. As a naturalist, he is cautious about imputing intelligence where there is only instinct.

As a writer, philosopher, and preacher of the "gospel of nature," he is concerned with how he writes himself onto the landscape and how the land "answers" his questions and reflects his sentiments. See *Ways of Nature, The Writings of John Burroughs* (Riverby Edition), vol. 12:v–vii.

Lawrence Buell also notes that the "older, consoling notion of kindred sensibility . . . competed in Burroughs's mind with a newer materialist evolutionism." Buell, *The Environmental Imagination*, 191–92.

In terms of Burroughs's preference for the "garden" over the wilderness (relative, say, to his contemporary John Muir), it is worth noting that his aesthetic leanings in no way indicate a lack of environmental concern on his part. In his essay "A Spray of Pine," Burroughs sounds a call for the protection of old-growth forests that is eerily prescient. Of old-growth pine, he writes: "This aboriginal tree is fast disappearing from the country. Its second growth seems to be a degenerate race. . . . All the large tracts and provinces of the original tree have been invaded and ravished by the lumbermen, so that only isolated bands and struggling remnants of a defeated and disorganized army, are now found scattered up and down the country" (*Signs and Seasons*, 7:45). For a thoughtful comparison of Burroughs and Muir, see Buell, *The Environmental Imagination*, 192–200.

36. Burroughs's essay "The Gospel of Nature" appears in *Time and Change* (1908), *The Writings of John Burroughs* (Riverby Edition), vol. 19.

37. CB I, 41.

38. *Talks*, 177.

39. 1857, *Journals*, 4–5.

40. Ralph Waldo Emerson, *Nature*, intro. Jaroslav Pelican, facsimile of the 1st ed. (1836; Boston: Beacon Press, 1985), 32–33.

41. CB I, 53; and *Talks*, 178. There is a subtle difference between Emerson's *Nature* and Burroughs's "Expression" that is worth mentioning here. In *Nature*, the poet is enjoined to go to nature for inspiration and for the cleansing of perception. The structural logic of the essay is also outward, representing a kind of upward spiral toward the realm of idealism. In Burroughs's essay, by contrast, nature "comes down" to earth and "forms" the poet. This slight difference may be predictive of Burroughs's departure from Emersonian idealism to the more "grounded" (though still idealistic) essays, the foundations of which are the how-tos of farming, woods walking, and bird watching.

42. John Burroughs, "An Egotistical Chapter," *Indoor Studies* (1889), 8:247–48.

43. In 1862, Burroughs's himself proposed to write a book of essays that would conclude with a meditation on self-culture, but he was dissuaded by a mentor who thought his work not yet sufficiently mature. See *Journals*, 34.

44. Robinson, *Apostle of Culture*, 9–10.

45. Burroughs, "Expression," as quoted by Barrus, CB I, 54.

46. Burroughs, "Spring Jottings," *Riverby* (1894), *The Writings of John Burroughs*, 9:167.

47. April 12 and 13, 1890, *Journals*, 156–57.

48. Burroughs, "Spring Jottings," *Riverby*, 9:167–68.

49. Burroughs, "Lovers of Nature," ibid., 9:205.

50. Renehan, *John Burroughs: An American Naturalist*, 170.

51. Renehan takes his cue from Burroughs's own comment to Benton: "I do no literary work, though I have plenty of calls. . . . The theological seems to be the last state of man, after that barrenness." Burroughs to Myron Benton, October 4, 1891, as quoted by Renehan, ibid., 170.

This is a curious remark. Burroughs acknowledges his shift to a more theological identity and at the same time expresses his concern that his literary-naturalist role may be correspondingly at risk. Yet Burroughs seems extremely happy in the period when he forsakes pen for plow, as the letters he writes to Whitman and Benton (below) reveal. Barrus likewise testifies that the 1880s and 1890s were a time of renewed vigor and delight for the farmer (Barrus, *John Burroughs: Boy and Man*, 281–82). It is not until 1891 that Burroughs mentions "barrenness," and this comment seems to refer to a period of emotional uncertainty between 1891 and 1895 (which Renehan terms a "mid-life crises"), made more acute by Whitman's death in March 1892. In my view, the years in which Burroughs was primarily devoted to farming provided him with experiential access into the spiritual dimensions of farming. Burroughs then gives a theological rendering of these experiences in his later texts, particularly in *The Light of Day* (1900), *The Breath of Life* (1915), and *Accepting the Universe* (1920).

52. December 30, 1880, *Journals*, 81.

53. Burroughs to Myron Benton, April 23, 1888; Burroughs to Walt Whitman, April 23, 1888; as cited by Renehan, *John Burroughs: An American Naturalist*, 171, 330.

54. April 27 and May 22, 1888, *Journals*, 149.

55. Whitman commenting on Burroughs to Horace Traubel, as quoted by Renehan (but with no precise citation), 171.

56. CB I, 10; January 21, 1884 (shortly after his father's death), *Journals*, 106.

57. John Burroughs, *The Light of Day: Religious Discussions and Criticisms from a Naturalist's Point of View* (Boston: Houghton Mifflin, Riverside Press, 1900), 4.

58. See the chapters "Christianity Confused" and "The Intellectual Crisis of Belief" in Turner, *Without God, Without Creed*, 141–67 and 171–202. While Burroughs's religious views seemed unorthodox to some, they certainly were in keeping with the growing liberal critique of Christianity that thrived in this period.

59. Burroughs, *The Light of Day*, 2; Renehan, *John Burroughs: An American Naturalist*, 17; CB I, 9.

60. *Talks*, 232–34. Burroughs gives a somewhat more expansive, but conceptually consistent, definition of God in his journal: "Let me define God in my

own terms, as the active vital principle of the universe, without which nothing is, or can be, then I agree with the God-makers. Everything is of God, and for God, and by God. Not a sparrow falls, or can fall, to the ground without his cognizance, not a bud unfolds or a seed sprouts without his ordering. You and I are a part of God in a literal sense." October 20, 1904, *Journals*, 240.

61. Burroughs's comments on Christian Science show his characteristic impatience with those who try to mix and match science and religion. He remarked: "Anybody who thinks at all can't help but see the folly of Christian Science. Really, though, the other religions are not free from folly either. They're all preposterous" (*Talks*, 236). The frank language Burroughs uses with Clifton Johnson rarely makes it into his essays. Barrus also consistently tries to put Burroughs's impatience with views of formal religion in a gentle light.

For a useful treatment of the intricate relationship between religion and science in the period before Darwin, see Herbert Hovenkamp, *Science and Religion in America*, 1800–1860 (Philadelphia: University of Pennsylvania Press, 1978).

62. Burroughs, *The Breath of Life*, *The Writings of John Burroughs* (Riverby Edition), 18:vi–vii.

63. Barrus, introduction to *Journals*, vii.

64. August 17, 1883, *Journals*, 98. Burroughs's emphasis on beneficence here is revealing. The "cruelty" of nature was one of nature's mysteries that persistently bothered Burroughs and that he never fully resolved.

65. Burroughs elaborates on his reading of Darwin in "The Divine Soil," *Leaf and Tendril* (1908), *The Writings of John Burroughs* (Riverby Edition), vol. 13.

On liberal theologians' responses to Darwin, see Sydney Ahlstrom, *A Religious History of the American People* (New Haven, CT: Yale University Press, 1972), 766–72; and for a more comprehensive treatment, James Moore, *The Post-Darwinian Controversies* (Cambridge: Cambridge University Press, 1979). On evangelical uses of evolutionary theory (but opposition to natural selection), both before and after Darwin, see Moore and also David Livingstone, *Darwin's Forgotten Defenders: The Encounter between Evangelical Theology and Evolutionary Thought* (Grand Rapids, MI: William B. Eerdmans, 1987). For concise and informative overviews of the response to Darwin (by both religious and scientific communities) in America, see Edward J. Pfeifer, "United States," and Michele L. Aldrich, "United States: Bibliographic Essay," in *The Comparative Reception of Darwinism*, 2nd ed., ed. Thomas F. Glick (Chicago: University of Chicago Press, 1988), 168–226.

66. November 5, 1886, *Journals*, 134–35.

67. Burroughs, *The Breath of Life*, 18:vi–vii.

68. For a midcentury assessment of Burroughs's "Gospel of Nature," see Clifford Hazeldine Osborne, *The Religion of John Burroughs* (Boston: Houghton Mifflin, Riverside Press, 1930). The author seeks to redeem Burroughs from charges of atheism, charges that Osborne is disturbed to see still circulating in the cultural air of the 1930s. Osborne admits that Burroughs "frequently wandered into the

cathedral of organized Christianity without wiping from his shoes the delicious but disconcerting mud which they had collected in [the] terrestrial garden," but he argues that Burroughs's religion "drew him further into the recesses of the world of the spirit than orthodoxy is doing at the present time" (vii–viii). From our vantage point, we can see that the need for religious liberals to defend Burroughs theologically would be especially strong in this period when neoorthodoxy is beginning to make its entrance on the cultural stage. It should also be noted that this defense of Burroughs is published by the same press that published almost all of Burroughs's books.

69. February 16, 1878, *Journals*, 73.

70. CB I, 39.

71. Berry, "Two Economies," in *Home Economics*, 54–75.

72. Burroughs, *Light of Day*, 169, 184, 185.

73. Ibid., 170.

74. January 17, 1866, *Journals*, 45–47.

75. Burroughs, *The Breath of Life*, 18:vi.

76. *Talks*, 202.

77. Biographical treatments before Renehan are largely celebrations of Burroughs as a public figure and tend to whitewash his own contribution to the troubled marriage. Barrus, for obvious reasons, gives only scant attention to Ursula.

78. *Talks*, 197.

79. Renehan, *John Burroughs: An American Naturalist*, 115. Burroughs's decision to do the majority of his writing in a hand-built outbuilding (known as the Bark Study), rather than in the indoor study, was the first step in his removal from the main house.

80. Burroughs, "Roof-Tree," *Signs and Seasons*, 7:247–63.

81. Ibid., 7:256.

82. GL, 56–66.

83. Burroughs, "Roof-Tree," *Signs and Seasons*, 7:256–57.

84. *Talks*, 205–7.

85. Breakfast at Slabsides (as described by Clifton Johnson) was—with the exception of bacon and eggs on the menu—reminiscent of the style of luncheons the Nearings provided their guests: "Besides the corn [cooked into a breakfast mush by Burroughs], we had oatmeal, eggs, milk, tea, honey, bread, and fried bacon; and there were tomatoes and cucumbers, and peaches, which were handed around in their skins for each one to deal with as he chose. There was no ceremony about our eating. We sat at the table in our shirt-sleeves, helped ourselves to what was within our reach, and each went to the fireplace to get an egg when he was ready for it. The butter was in a tin pail, whence we extracted

it with our knives to suit our individual needs." Clifton Johnson, introductory remarks to his interview with Burroughs in "Rustic Housekeeping," chapter 9, *Talks*, 156.

86. The rabbit story is repeated in Shi, *The Simple Life*, 199.

87. CB II, 320. Barrus does not note whether this comment was made in a letter, a journal entry, or to her directly.

88. *Talks*, 150.

89. Ibid., 200.

90. See my discussion in note 35, above.

91. The most famous visitor to Slabsides was President Theodore Roosevelt, in July 1903.

92. The societies were sponsored by the publishers at Houghton Mifflin, both as a response to Burroughs's growing popularity and as a marketing tool of their own. See Renehan, *John Burroughs: An American Naturalist*, 256–57.

93. Ursula (playing Scott to John's Helen) accused her husband of being "two-faced" with regard to visitors, cordially welcoming them upon arrival and sighing loudly after they departed. She would rather not let them in at all, unless they were well-known. John, on the other hand, felt that it was his public duty to receive all visitors, both the interesting and the dull. See CB II, 290.

94. Renehan, *John Burroughs: An American Naturalist*, 191–93.

95. Barrus points out that Burroughs was, in 1919, still fuming about the *Century's* decision not to follow his advice. CB II, 372.

96. As Renehan indicates (*John Burroughs: An American Naturalist*, 23), Ford's gift to Burroughs (shortly after his criticisms of the automobile were published) was "at once a sincere gesture from a genuine admirer and a brilliant publicity gimmick." Burroughs's debt to Ford was further sealed when Ford provided him with the financial assistance necessary to buy the old family farm in Roxbury.

97. Ibid., 4.

98. Burroughs as quoted by Renehan, ibid., 21.

99. Burroughs, "Phases of Farm Life," *Signs and Seasons*, 7:219.

100. A crackle was used in the breaking of hemp; the swingling knife served as a scraper to clean flax or hemp before spinning. Burroughs elegiac comment "The quill-wheel, and the spinning-wheel, and the loom are heard no more among us" (231) seems to echo the wistful remarks made by Horace Bushnell several decades earlier in his "Secular Sermon," delivered at the Centennial Celebration of Litchfield County. "If our sons and daughters should assemble a hundred years hence . . . everything that was most distinctive of the old home-spun mode of life shall then have passed away. The spinning-wheels of wool and flax, that used to buzz so familiarly in the childish ears of some of us, will be heard no more for ever." Here we see that American longings for a simpler

agrarian past can be traced through infinite regressions. Bushnell, "The Age of Homespun," *Work and Play* (London: Alexander Stahan and Co., 1864), 39–76. My thanks to both Lawrence Buell and Laurel Thatcher Ulrich for bringing this essay to my attention.

101. Burroughs, "Phases of Farm Life," *Signs and Seasons*, 7:232–42.

102. Ibid., 245.

103. Burroughs, "An Outlook upon Life," in *Leaf and Tendril*, 13:261. Shi mentions the article's popularity and includes a slightly different excerpt (*The Simple Life*, 199–200). See also CB II, 89.

104. On Burroughs's attitude toward work, his son Julian remarked: "So whether the life of John Burroughs was one long life of happiness and lazy play, or whether it was one of hard work, depends, like so many other things, on the point of view. I like to think of his long and happy life as one in which he turned all work to play, and in so doing he accomplished mightily." Julian Burroughs, *Recollections of John Burroughs*, ed. Elizabeth Burroughs Kelley (West Park, NY: Riverby Books, 1991), 40.

105. Burroughs maintained a friendship and correspondence with Edward Carpenter, who first visited him in 1877 (Renehan, *John Burroughs: An American Naturalist*, 131). For treatments of the back-to-the-land movement in Britain and its relationship to socialist movements see, Fiona MacCarthy, *The Simple Life: C. R. Ashbee in the Cotswolds* (Berkeley: University of California Press, 1981); and Peter C. Gould, *Early Green Politics: Back to Nature, Back to the Land, and Socialism in Britain, 1880–1900* (New York: Saint Martin's Press, 1988). A typical text coming out of these movements was Harold E. Moore's *Back to the Land* (London: Methuen, 1893).

A treatment of Bolton Hall's reform-oriented and religious view of homesteading appears in chapter 6.

5. Scott Nearing and the Social Gospel of Agriculture

Epigraph: Helen Nearing, *Loving and Leaving the Good Life* (Post Mills, VT: Chelsea Green, 1992), 102.

1. A discussion of the single-tax movement occurs in chapter 6, when I describe Nearing's predecessors in back-to-the-land reform, Bolton Hall and Ralph Borsodi.

2. MS, 10. Nearing also describes his time at Arden in his autobiography, *The Making of a Radical*, 40–41.

3. Although there are several Burroughs books at the Nearing homestead in Maine (*Winter Sunshine*, *Indoor Studies*, and *Signs and Seasons*), the marks in the books are in Helen's hand.

4. Nearing's articles began to appear in the *Independent* as early as 1907. Like Burroughs, Nearing also wrote articles (often coauthored with his first wife, Nellie Seeds) for Edward Bok's *Ladies' Home Journal*. Publication in both of these venues placed Nearing increasingly in the public eye. By the time Nearing was fired from his post at the Wharton School (1915) for his refusal to compromise his arguments against child labor, he was sufficiently well-known to elicit outraged articles about his dismissal in the *New York Evening Post*, the *Chicago Herald*, the *Philadelphia North American*, and the August issue of the *Metropolitan*. This early entry on the public stage was soon followed by public debates with the likes of Clarence Darrow (1917) and Bertrand Russell (1924).

After Nearing retired from public lecturing and began to lose offers of publication because of his antiwar views, he sensed that his days of public influence were over. It is ironic, in retrospect, to read the words Nearing wrote in 1972: "Those who will listen to my voice or read my writings are fewer than they were" (MR, 208), for this was just after the republication of *Living the Good Life* (1970) and immediately preceding his corresponding rediscovery by a new generation. For the response to Nearing's dismissal from the Wharton School, see Steve Sherman's introduction to *A Scott Nearing Reader*, ed. Steve Sherman (Metuchen, NJ: Scarecrow Press, 1989).

5. "Temporarily" is worth noting here, for comparatively little work was published on Burroughs between the mid-1930s and the 1970s. Since the 1970s (probably because of growing environmental concerns) interest in Burroughs has enjoyed something of a revival. In terms of mainstream recognition, however, the Nearings are likely to lag behind. It is difficult to imagine, for instance, that "Helen and Scott Nearing societies" would ever be a common feature of our nation's public school system.

6. European Romanticism and New England Transcendentalism, of course, provide early cultural models for this transition, but what we are discussing here is a much more popular middle-class reading of nature, one that also developed in a post-Darwinian and increasingly industrialized American context.

For examples of earlier views of nature as stage for the spiritual drama, see Perry Miller, *Errand into the Wilderness* (Cambridge, MA: Harvard University Press, Belknap Press, 1956) and *Nature's Nation* (Cambridge, MA: Harvard University Press, Belknap Press, 1967); for the new (Progressive Era) understanding of nature as a source of moral uplift and cleansing, which deserves protection for future use, see Samuel P. Hayes, *Conservation and the Gospel of Efficiency: The Progressive Conservation Movement, 1890–1920* (Cambridge, MA: Harvard University Press, 1959). For broader portraits of these changes, see Catherine Albanese, *Nature Religion in America*, Chicago History of American Religion, ed. Martin Marty (Chicago: University of Chicago Press, 1990); and Roderick Nash, *Wilderness and the American Mind*, 3rd ed. (New Haven, CT: Yale University Press, 1972).

7. On Bok, see Shi, *The Simple Life*, 181–85; on Seton and related groups, see ibid., 206–11.

8. Ralph Borsodi drew on reports of the U.S. Census and the Bureau of Agriculture Economics to conclude that the high point of movement from the country to the city occurred in 1922, with a net movement of 1,137,000 individuals from farms to the cities. By 1931, in response to the Depression, the trend began to reverse itself, although not for long. Ralph Borsodi, *The Flight from the City* (New York: Harper and Brothers, 1933), xii.

9. William Cronon, "The Trouble with Wilderness, or Getting Back to the Wrong Nature," in *Uncommon Ground*, ed. Cronon, 69–90.

10. Peter Schmitt, *Back to Nature* (New York: Oxford University Press, 1969), 144. See also Earl Amos Brooks, *A Handbook of the Outdoors* (New York, 1925) and "Back to Nature," *Outlook* 74, (June 6, 1903), as cited in Schmitt, *Back to Nature*, 143 and note, 214. Schmitt also notes other examples, such as Bishop William Quayle's vision of Jesus as the sine qua non of outdoorsmen and Rev. Charles W. Gordon's twenty-two novels of outdoor life intended to inspire the development of Christian manhood in his readers.

On the Boy Scouts, in addition to David Mcleod's *Building Character in the American Boy* (Madison: University of Wisconsin Press, 1983), see Jeffrey P. Hantover, "Sex Role, Sexuality and Social Status: The Early Years of the Boy Scouts of America," PhD dissertation, University of Chicago, 1976. Hantover points out that more than half of the eighty boys and mixed youth groups (most of them camping and outdoor oriented) that came into being between 1893 and 1919 listed "religious" as their main purpose. Hantover as cited by Martin Marty in *Modern American Religion*, vol. 1: *The Irony of It All*, 1893–1919 (Chicago: University of Chicago Press, 1986), 358, notes 12 and 18. See also Leigh Eric Schmidt, "From Arbor Day to the Environmental Sabbath: Nature, Liturgy and American Protestantism," *Harvard Theological Review* 84, no. 3 (1991): 299–323.

11. In addition to the literature cited in previous chapters, see R. Laurence Moore, "Secularization: Religion and the Social Sciences," in *Between the Times: The Travail of the Protestant Establishment in America*, 1900–1960, ed. William R. Hutchison, Cambridge Studies in Religion and American Public Life, ed. Robin W. Lovin (Cambridge: Cambridge University Press, 1989; paperback reprint, 1990), 233–52.

12. See Catherine Albanese's treatment of Muir in her *Nature Religion in America*, 100.

Steve Holmes makes the compelling argument that Muir's "instant conversion" in the Sierras was not as radical or spontaneous as the texts make it appear. Even with the important interpretive contribution that Holmes adds, however, we know that Muir's public expressions of his religion of nature were still less palatable to his contemporary audience than they are today. Interestingly, the reception of Burroughs has shifted in the other direction; while there has been a revival of interest in Burroughs, it is much less extensive than the revival of interest in Muir. See Steven J. Holmes, "Blessed Home: Nature, Religion, Science and Human Relationship in the Early Life of John Muir," PhD dissertation,

Harvard University, 1996, and *The Young John Muir: An Environmental Biography* (Madison: University of Wisconsin Press, 1999).

13. One example among many of such "absorbed" challenges is the Harriman expedition to Alaska in 1899. The expedition was sponsored by a railway magnate and had among its members several oil and land speculators. But the trip was popularized and its purpose softened by Burroughs's presence as an invited guest.

14. MS, 3.

15. For an excellent treatment of Henry George, see John L. Thomas, *Alternative America: Henry George, Edward Bellamy, Henry Demarest Lloyd and the Adversary Tradition* (Cambridge, MA: Harvard University Press, Belknap Press, 1983). Thomas pays close attention to the relationship between George's liberal religious views and his cooperative agrarian vision, a vision expressed in the abstract language of economics on some occasions and with millennialist "Kingdom of God on earth" fervor at others. Thomas also clearly describes (191–92) the middle ground between capitalism and socialism that George advocates. Surprisingly, however, Thomas focuses on George's literary production and does not even mention Arden. For a discussion of George's followers as being essentially religious converts, see Ronald Yanosky, " 'Seeing the Cat': The Georgist Conversion Experience," paper presented to the American Colloquium of the Harvard Divinity School, October 18, 1994.

16. MR, 210; and MS, 2–10.

17. John Saltmarsh, *Scott Nearing: An Intellectual Biography* (Philadelphia: Temple University Press, 1991), 57–58. For Scott Nearing's pursuit of "the strenuous life," see 50–64.

18. MS, 1.

19. Ibid., 10.

20. Nearing in debate with Percy Ward, "Would the Practice of Christ's Teachings Make for Social Progress?" 1920, as quoted by Saltmarsh, *Scott Nearing*, 4, 45, and 276 note 64.

21. Scott Nearing, "Arden Town," unpublished MS (written under the pseudonym "Max Worth"), 1913, 7. My debts of gratitude for this text go in several directions: first to the archivists at Arden, who made it available to John Saltmarsh, and then to John, who turned it over to me.

Nearing's decision to use the example fire-escape "cover up" to show Allen's mistaken preference for "the bottom line" over workers' rights is likely a reference to the Triangle Shirtwaist Factory fire in New York City in 1911. In this fire on the Lower East Side, 146 people (mostly female workers) died largely because of fire code violations that made it impossible for them to escape from the burning building. Nearing's audience at the time likely would have made this connection.

22. Ibid., 206.

23. Ibid., 209.

24. Scott and Nellie Seeds were married in 1908.

25. Scott Nearing and Nellie Seeds Nearing, *Women and Social Progress* (New York: Macmillan, 1912).

26. Here I am borrowing the phrase from John Thomas.

27. The very language of social crises, William Hutchison notes, became an emergent and then dominant mode in the liberal theological literature after 1900. Hutchison attributes the literature of crisis to particular domestic and international events that aroused social concern, but he also acknowledges that "the sheer passage from the nineteenth to the twentieth century or [the] revulsion against the self-congratulatory publicity surrounding that event" might have played a role. William R. Hutchison, *The Modernist Impulse* (Durham, NC: Duke University Press, 1992), 145 and note 1.

28. Marty, *The Irony of It All*, 286 and 362 note 10, places the origin of the term *Social Gospel* with an Iowa Congregationalist minister who apparently used the phrase in reference to—interestingly enough—Henry George's *Progress and Poverty*. Marty's tale of origins draws on the initial sleuthing of Ronald C. White Jr. and C. Howard Hopkins, *The Social Gospel: Religion and Reform in Changing America* (Philadelphia: Temple University Press, 1976), 167 note 13.

29. Hutchison, *The Modernist Impulse*, 165 note 36, clarifies much confusion over "who's in and who's out" of the Social Gospel movement by making this important distinction between emphases on social and personal salvation. Hutchison also provides a list of those cultural leaders who, while liberal, "lacked interest" in the Social Gospel.

30. Henry May broadens the discussion to include conservative, progressive, and radical expressions of "Social Christianity." Under this umbrella, May restricts the term *Social Gospel* to those of the moderate, progressive school. For May, the representative man of the Social Gospel is Washington Gladden. See May's *Protestant Churches and Industrial America* (New York: Harper and Row, 1949). While theologians and ministers are the first candidates for "membership," economists such as Richard Ely and John Commons as well as Simon Patten should be considered "lay" participants. See also Robert M. Crunden, *Ministers of Reform: The Progressive's Achievement in American Civilization, 1889–1920* (New York: Basic Books, 1982).

31. Simon Patten, *The Social Basis of Religion* (New York: Macmillan, 1911), v.

32. Ibid., 195.

33. Ibid., 204.

34. Walter Rauschenbusch, *Christianity and the Social Crisis* (New York: Macmillan, 1910), 341.

35. Rauschenbusch, while recognizing that this is "not the highest line of ap-

peal" (288), addresses the church's concern about its own economic vitality; see his chapter 6, "The Stake of the Church in the Social Movement," 287–342. Rauschenbusch (341) also provides a much more detailed program for social reform than Patten does, one that has much in common with Nearing's program. Among Rauschenbusch's suggestions: that humanity's dependence on the land be more fully recognized and that "the simple life become the fashion."

36. Scott Nearing, *Social Religion* (New York: Macmillan, 1913; reprint, 1916), 22. The book originated as a speech in 1910.

37. Ibid., 197.

38. Ibid., xiii. Interestingly, this same phrase is one that Nearing elsewhere remembers as being used by his early mentor, Russell Conwell (MR, 32). Nearing's eventual disenchantment with Conwell is discussed below.

39. S. Nearing, *Social Religion*, 7.

40. Ibid., 12.

41. Ibid., 185–86.

42. Ibid., 187–88.

43. Charles Sheldon, *In His Steps: What Would Jesus Do?* (New York: Grosset and Dunlap, 1897). Alice Payne Hackett notes that *In His Steps* was the number-one best-selling novel for sixty years, selling over eight million copies and still occupying a healthy fifth place as late as 1967. See Alice Payne Hackett, *70 Years of Best Sellers: 1895–1965* (New York: R. R. Bowker, 1967), 12.

44. S. Nearing, *Social Religion*, 194.

45. Ibid., 194.

46. Helen Nearing tells the story of one of Scott's definitions of God in *Loving and Leaving the Good Life* (LL). Nearing was asked by Jeremy Rifkin (posing as a small boy) to state whether or not he believed in God. Nearing, characteristically, promptly wrote back asking Rifkin to define his terms. Following Rifkin's expansive definition of God as "the energy spirit that connects us all," Scott Nearing replied: "I accept it with a slight change. Omit 'us'. . . . Taking out 'us' makes it easier to include animals, flowers, rocks, trees, and other aspects of the All." Helen approved of Scott's response and also suggested "the All-Being" or "The Great Entirety" as alternatives to "God." LL, 158–59.

Helen herself was fond of saying that she was a "Unit-arian," believing that all things in this world and beyond together formed a sacred unity.

47. Nearing, however, was not openly critical of Rauschenbusch but, rather, praised *Christianity and the Social Crisis* as a model of criticism for how "the church has failed to fulfill its mission." S. Nearing, *Social Religion*, xi. Rauschenbusch, in turn, credited Nearing's early writings in his *Christianizing the Social Order* (New York: Macmillan, 1912). See Saltmarsh, *Scott Nearing*, 275 note 53. Paul Minus also notes that Rauschenbusch was particularly pleased to receive Nearing's highly favorable review of *Christianizing the Social Order*. Apparently Rauschenbusch

found it reassuring that a trained economist would support his views and corresponded with Nearing to that effect. See Paul H. Minus, *Walter Rauschenbusch: American Reformer* (New York: Macmillan, 1988), 172.

48. MR, 23.

49. Russell Conwell, *Acres of Diamonds* (New York: Harper and Brothers, 1915).

50. MR, 34.

51. Scott Nearing's letter to Billy Sunday, as quoted by Nearing in MR, 78. See also "A Religious Lesson for Billy Sunday," *Public*, February 12, 1915, 155.

52. Billy Sunday's reply, as quoted by Nearing in MR, 79.

53. MR, 24.

54. In his study of the Left, John Patrick Diggins remarks that many American socialists and communists (and other members of the "Lyrical Left") found in their new political commitments a kind of Christianity without Christ. Although I disagree with Diggins's critique of the Left more broadly, I share his sense that the liberal intellectuals of the early twentieth century carried with them "the heritage against which they had rebelled" (as we see with many homesteaders in this study). John Patrick Diggins, *The Rise and Fall of the American Left* (New York: Harcourt Brace Jovanovich, 1973; reprint, Norton Paperbacks, 1992), 97.

55. Scott Nearing, "Can the Church Be Radical?" in *A Scott Nearing Reader*, ed. Sherman, 119.

56. Scott Nearing's official positions at the University of Toledo were professor of social science and dean of the College of Arts and Sciences. The objections to Nearing's views were based not only on his stance against war generally but particularly on his contention that capitalist interests were the main reasons for U.S. entry into war. While Nearing was acquitted from government charges of insubordination (tied to the Espionage Act), most other radicals who objected to the war did not fair nearly as well, as both Sherman (*A Scott Nearing Reader*, 10) and Diggins (*The Rise and Fall of the American Left*, 102–6) point out.

57. Nearing ultimately left both the Communist and Socialist parties for some of the same reasons that he left the Christian church: "After my disillusioning adventure into the labyrinth that linked politics with Christian believers and tied the professing Christians to the coattails of monopolistic capitalism, I did not want to commit myself to any set of authoritarian beliefs" (MR, 145). His political views, however, remained generally socialist in orientation throughout his life. On the Communist Party's critique of Nearing's inability to reject "faith" and idealism for science and a strict Marxist position, see Saltmarsh, *Scott Nearing*, 238–42.

58. For a rich and eloquent treatment of Scott Nearing's political and intellectual life in this period, see Saltmarsh, *Scott Nearing*.

59. S. Nearing, *Social Religion*, 219–20.

60. Scott Nearing as quoted by Helen Nearing in LL, 183.

61. They are also generally neglected. Shi (*The Simple Life*) gives Nearing only superficial treatment, and while Saltmarsh (*Scott Nearing*) importantly makes up for Shi's light touch, the bulk of his work is on the years before the Nearings took up homesteading.

62. See Sydney Ahlstrom, *A Religious History of the American People* (New Haven, CT: Yale University Press, 1972), 937–48. Ahlstrom argues that "despite all," neoorthodoxy was still a hopeful intellectual movement, one that "because it did not rest its ultimate faith in human arrangements . . . could bear—or even advocate—the shaking of cultural foundations" while upholding an "eschatological sense of hope" (946). Despite the sympathetic attention paid by neoorthodox writers to contemporary developments in the arts, science, sociology, history, and biblical criticism, the renewal of interest in doctrine and ecclesiology exhibited by the these thinkers (especially Tillich and the Niebuhrs) was of little interest to those reformers, such as Nearing, who had already felt betrayed by the traditionalism and thinly veiled capitalism of the institutional church.

63. MR, 211.

64. Ibid., 137 (emphasis added).

65. Here, Nearing's comments resemble much of Wendell Berry's writings against specialization in both daily living and in intellectual pursuits. John Burroughs also often claimed that he was not "a particularist" and therefore better off in the farming-writing vocation he had chosen.

Nearing also compares the daily life of homesteading with patterns of living he experienced in Morris Run as a child (MR, 219).

66. MS, 13. It should be noted that Nearing attended Central Manual School as part of a conscious choice to gain an education that was practical as well as theoretical. Most youth of similar academic ability were encouraged to attend the other, "better" public school in town.

67. Ibid., 13. Similar comments are made throughout *Living the Good Life*, *Continuing the Good Life*, and *The Maple Sugar Book*.

68. MR, 232.

69. Scott Nearing, *Reducing the Cost of Living* (Philadelphia: G. W. Jacobs, 1914), 209–12.

70. Ibid., 209.

71. Ibid., 227.

72. MR, 213.

73. It should be remembered, however, that the Nearings' maple sugar business was, indeed, a business, relying on advertising, market forces, and the early "selling" of the Vermont image.

74. Quoted phrase from MR, 214.

75. A model for the Nearings' views of community was the vision of Arthur E. Morgan. Morgan was director of the Tennessee Valley Authority and unsuccessfully attempted to create a model town (Norris) that would blend republican agrarian and socialist cooperative models of the good society. Eventually, Morgan was fired by Roosevelt from his position because of both the federal government's uneasiness with Morgan's semisocialist views and the local resistance to being culturally "managed" by a northern intellectual. See Arthur Morgan, *The Small Community* (New York: Harper and Brothers, 1942). Shi gives a brief treatment of Morgan in *The Simple Life*, 235–38, as do Arthur A. Ekirch Jr., *Ideologies and Utopias: The Impact of the New Deal on American Thought* (Chicago: Quadrangle Books, 1969; paperback reprint, 1971), 118–21; and Roy Talbert Jr., *FDR's Utopian: Arthur Morgan of the TVA* (Jackson: University of Mississippi Press, 1987).

76. MR, 214. In this comment we can hear echoes of Burroughs's pointed remark (quoted in chapter 4): "When I depart [from the simple life] evil results follow."

77. MS, 11.

78. For Nearing's final acts of departure, see "I Part Company with Western Civilization," MR, 193–206.

79. Ibid., 229.

80. Bill Coperthwaite remarked to me once that "if Scott had lived in another age he would have been a monk." This comment underlined Coperthwaite's sense of Nearing's underlying religiousness, though correspondingly downplayed Nearing's commitment to social change. Conversation with Bill Coperthwaite, October 1995.

81. Nearing and Nearing, *The Maple Sugar Book*, 245.

82. MR, 210–11. Helen's five-year diary (1936–1940) is replete with examples of the palpable relief she felt when returning from research and errands in New York to homestead activities in Vermont (a pattern that the Nearings actively maintained through the 1940s and continued on some level throughout their public life). While Helen maintained an active social life of visiting friends and family, keeping up with Theosophical Society networks, and enjoying lunches out and movies, she sometimes expressed regret for these activities when back in Vermont and, moreover, records a consistent rise in spirits when engaged in outdoor seasonal labor or in marking the annual arrival of sparrows, flowers, and berries. Helen Knothe's diary, the Helen and Scott Nearing Papers, the Thoreau Institute, Lincoln, Massachusetts.

83. Jim tells his mother, " 'De flowahs allus tells me stories. . . . Ah tell dem stories an' dey tells me stories. Hain't yo' nevah heerd no flowahs a-talkin'?' " (Scott Nearing, *Freeborn* [New York: Urquhart Press, 1932], 10). Nearing subtitled this book "An Unpublishable Novel" and found a noncommercial press to print it after receiving numerous rejections from commercial publishers who dared not support its politics.

Nearing's use of dialect has a patronizing ring to twenty-first-century readers but was typical of novels of this period and earlier. In this connection, it is worth noting that the structure, plot, and tone of this book read something like a 1930s version of *Uncle Tom's Cabin*, with communism ultimately playing the role that evangelical Christianity played in Stowe's text.

84. Ibid., 82.

85. S. Nearing, "Arden Town," 175–76.

86. Ibid., 202.

87. S. Nearing, *Freeborn*, 85.

88. Helen Nearing informed John Saltmarsh (who, in turn, informed me) that the female protagonists in Nearing's novel were modeled on her. Anyone who has spent time with Helen would likely make the connection upon reading this passage from *Freeborn*: "She was quick, vivacious, over-flowing and sparkling with life" (83).

Saltmarsh (*Scott Nearing*, 231–35) also gives a reading of *Freeborn* in his biography of Nearing but treats, instead, the latter half of the book, paying attention to its uses as proletarian fiction.

89. In the course of the novel, however, this triumph is only temporary. After Jim joins the Communist Party, he is jailed on trumped-up charges, put on trial for his political beliefs, and found guilty. The story calls to mind how the Scott Nearing trial might have ended and also reflects Nearing's own feelings at the time: that working for peace and justice results in banishment from society.

90. MS, 21–22.

91. See generally Hutchison's *The Modernist Impulse*; Henry May, *The End of American Innocence: A Study of the First Years of Our Own Time* (New York: Knopf, 1959); Richard Hofstadter, *The Age of Reform* (New York: Random House, 1955; reprint, Vintage Books, 1960), 174–214; and Christopher Lasch, *The True and Only Heaven: Progress and Its Critics* (New York: W. W. Norton, 1991), 329–68.

92. MS, 52. While Nearing here acknowledges that humans are always "in the arms of mother nature, and subject to her all-pervasive forces and powers," he continues also to celebrate the human ability to harness natural forces for the benefit of civilization.

John Saltmarsh has pointed out that in these later texts (*Man's Search for the Good Life* and *The Making of a Radical*) the language of the "control of nature" is much less apparent and that Nearing has distanced himself from an earlier stance of perfectionism (conversation with John Saltmarsh, July 1997). I agree with Saltmarsh in general, but my own shading of the issue is slightly different. In my reading, the explicit language of perfectionism does fade (with a corresponding rise in more "mystical" readings of nature) but is still persistent. Moreover, the *practices* and "style" of homesteading (as discussed in chapters 2 and 3) continue to suggest a perfectionist and controlling stance, even amid public utterances emphasizing harmony and humility.

6. The Dynamics of Engagement and Retreat

Epigraph: Robert Wuthnow, *After Heaven* (Berkeley: University of California Press, 1998), 197.

1. Bolton Hall, *A Little Land and a Living*, 3rd ed. (New York: Arcadia Press, 1908), 247–48.

2. John Thomas, *Alternative Americas* (Cambridge, MA: Harvard University Press, Belknap Press, 1983), 119.

3. For both quotations from George I am indebted first to Thomas's *Alternative Americas*, 119–20. See Henry George, *Progress and Poverty* (New York: Modern Library, n.d.), 339. Helpful background on the relationships among the Protestant Social Gospel and related socialist reform movements can be found in Ronald C. White and C. Howard Hopkins, *The Social Gospel, Reform and Religion in Changing America* (Philadelphia: Temple University Press, 1976), especially the sections on socialism and Christian socialism, 26–31 and 129–95.

4. Hall, *A Little Land*, 248–49.

5. Linus Yamane, "Free Acres," unpublished MS, 1997, 3. The author is not only a former member of the colony but also a professor of economics.

6. Martin Bierbaum, "Free Acres: Bolton Hall's Single-Tax Experimental Community," *New Jersey History* 102, no. 1–2 (Spring/Summer 1984): 37–63. See also Mark Sullivan's introduction, "Bolton Hall and the Third Tradition," in Bolton Hall, *Selections from Free America and Other Works*, ed. Mark Sullivan (Port Townsend, WA: Loompanics Unlimited, 1987), 1–12.

7. Bolton Hall, *Things as They Are*, as excerpted in *Selections from Free America*, 197.

8. Hall did not believe that cities, in themselves, were a social problem. One "earns more and learns more in crowds," he claimed. On the other hand, the "needless want and misery" of the cities was something that could be avoided if the poor denizens of the city could move to surrounding communities and live as producers rather than consumers. This way of living was preferable, both for the poor, who would otherwise become exploited wards of the state, and for the wealthier classes, whose lives, lived "tied to a desk," put them far away from the "natural condition of living" by direct labor in the earth. *TAL*, v, 4–5.

9. Ibid., 8. The Nearings, in turn, did not totally exempt themselves from the capitalist system, as their investments, land purchasing and sales practices, and sugaring business make clear. Their ideal vision, however, was a combination of limited markets, socialism, and small-scale agrarianism.

10. Ibid., 72.

11. Note, too, that Hall's attitude toward cows is that they are efficient "machinery"—again a contrast to the Nearings' "non-slavery of animals" policy. Ibid., 9–10.

12. Shi, *The Simple Life*, 204.

13. See the chapter "Advantages from Capital" in TAL, 154–83.

14. TAL, 36. While Hall did not disapprove of small-scale land speculation as part of the process of acquiring financial stability and reliable real-estate, he was quite critical of large-scale land speculation, to which he attributed the degenerate state of country life in the West. See his chapter "Present Conditions," in TAL, 21–32.

15. TAL, 8.

16. Emma Goldman, Living My Life, vol. 1 (New York: Alfred Knopf, 1931; paperback reprint, New York: Dover, 1970), 348–49.

17. Hall notes that over the course of ten years the Philadelphia Vacant Lot Cultivation Association helped more than forty-four hundred families gain partial self-sufficiency through cultivating urban lots.

18. Bolton Hall, The Halo of Grief (1913), edited and reissued with an introduction by Ellen LaConte and Dorothy Hatfield (Stockton Springs, ME: Loose Leaf Press, 1997), 1. In an interesting case of "homesteading intertextuality," LaConte and Hatfield, good friends of Helen Nearing, republished this book by Hall partly in response to their own experiences of grieving Helen Nearing's death.

19. Ibid., quotations from 40, 2, 11, and 111, respectively.

20. Ibid., 139–45. This view of death is very similar to the one that Helen Nearing often expressed.

21. Draft MS of The Living Bible, Bolton Hall Papers, Box 8, Archives and Manuscripts Division, New York Public Library. In the draft of his "Explanation to the Publisher," Hall explicitly argues against advancing a particular doctrinal or sectarian stance, adding, "Bible stories should be acceptable both to Jew and Gentile: both to sinner and saint. His version he likened to "Kingsley's Greek Heroes." Bolton Hall Papers, Box 8. The published version (dedicated to his mother and his minister father) turns out to be more traditional, but Hall does make a point of excising "repetitions" (such as the majority of Chronicles), "ceremonial details," genealogies, geographic descriptions, and so on, focusing on "the presentation of the idea . . . of each writer" of the various books. Bolton Hall, ed., The Living Bible (New York: Knopf, 1928).

22. "The New Shorter Chatechism: Natural Religion, the Chatechism [sic] with Scripture Proof," unpublished MS (drafted and revised between 1913 and 1923), 2. Bolton Hall Papers, Box 8. Hall apparently sent this material for publication and received approval but not suggestions for changes. His own notes suggest that he was considering turning the work into an article but that he was not certain it was worth the effort. His writing on the cover page is revealing: "The idea is good; but those who would need it would not read it" (emphasis in the original).

23. Hall, A Little Land, 84.

24. *TAL*. Hall was also connected to the broader country life movement (headed up by Liberty Hyde Bailey), which emerged in this same period and was an aspect of the Social Gospel impulse. See Merwin Swanson, "The Country Life Movement and the American Churches," in *Protestantism and Social Christianity*, ed. Martin Marty, Modern American Protestantism and Its World, vol. 6, ed. Martin Marty (Munich: K. G. Sauer, 1992), 297–312; and William L. Bowers, *The Country Life Movement in America*, 1900–1920, National University Publications Series in American Studies, ed. James Shenton (Port Washington, NY: Kennikat Press, 1974).

25. Hall, *A Little Land*, 239, 242, 259, 267.

26. Bolton Hall, *Life, and Love and Peace* (New York: Arcadia Press, 1909), 58–59. Hereafter *Life, and Love and Peace* is cited as LLP.

27. Ibid., 56, 51.

28. Ibid., 55–56, 58–59.

29. While Burroughs, Nearing, Hall, and Borsodi were all concerned, to varying degrees, about social injustice (especially the uneven distribution of wealth) and the potential consequences of unbridled social Darwinism, they also all shared a certain belief in the inborn superiority of some humans with respect to others and advocated for the special responsibilities of the privileged to guide society. We have already noted the hints of elitism in Hall's *Three Acres*. Burroughs's reluctance to criticize such magnates as Ford and Gould emerged, in part, from his sense that their success had more to do with powers and virtues disposed by nature than by the misuse of power in the social context. He even went so far as to say, on one occasion, "The millionaires add to the positive health and well-being of all." As Renehan notes, the message was "sugarcoated" but Spencerian underneath. See Renehan, *John Burroughs: An American Naturalist*, 198–200.

Both Nearing and Borsodi were caught up in the growing enthusiasm for eugenics, understanding it as an opportunity for individuals actively to shape American society rather than passively to accept the potential social problems arising from the natural forces of hereditary determinism. Nearing argues the case in *The Super Race: An American Problem* (New York: B. W. Huebsch, 1912), but, as Saltmarsh notes (*Scott Nearing*, 68), his interest in eugenics seemed to wane after 1916. On Borsodi, see Shi, *The Simple Life*, 228.

30. Like the early Nearing, Hall is skeptical about evangelical Christianity but often cites the Gospels and the example of Jesus to support his moral arguments. Like Burroughs, he is just as likely to deploy such statements as "This is the light that Walt Whitman came to show." LLP, 50, 142–43.

In his *Back to Nature*, Peter Schmitt provides a curious treatment of Hall that is worth reviewing more closely. In his effort to portray getting back to nature as an urban impulse, Schmitt makes a fundamental distinction between back-to-nature and back-to-the-land movements, defining the latter primarily in terms of Hall's and other reformers' efforts to relocate the urban poor on garden patches that would bring them self-sufficiency. Schmitt then goes on to disinvite Hall from his primary (back-to-nature) category of analysis by remarking that Hall's attitude toward getting back to nature was alarmingly democratic ("any dunce could raise a crop of onions on an acre of land") in contrast to the prevailing cast of mind, which saw the return to nature as a moral quest for the leisure classes. Schmitt also sees Hall's industrial metaphors—"the cow was merely a 'ruminating machine for producing milk' "— as being as "disconcerting to nature lovers as Hall's 'little lots well-tilled' were foreign to working farmers." See Schmitt's extensive footnote in *Back to Nature: The Arcadian Myth in Urban America* (Oxford: Oxford University Press, 1969), xvii note 4.

Before Schmitt even embarks on his interpretation of back-to-nature movements, he thus neatly dismisses the source of many early twentieth-century experiments in nature on the basis that the philosophy is "too industrial" and at the same time too rooted in the practical realities of farm labor. Shi (*The Simple Life*, 203–4), on the other hand, rightly emphasizes that Hall shared with other Progressive Era reformers an understanding of nature as a moral category, one that offered therapeutic benefits as well as the opportunity for economic advancement. If we focus on Hall's moral sense of nature—and his belief that "three acres of liberty" will help him and his peers as much as the poor—we see that Hall is clearly in sympathy with Schmitt's "literary commuters" and fresh-air enthusiasts. That these spiritual sympathies are nestled within a larger social program of self-sufficiency through homesteading should draw us toward him, not away from him. See Schmitt, *Back to Nature*, xvii note 4.

31. Ralph Borsodi, *The Flight from the City*, 2. Hereafter *The Flight from the City* is cited as *Flight*. His preceding book—less a personal tale than a diatribe, but also based on conclusions arrived at through homesteading—was *This Ugly Civilization: A Study of the Quest for Comfort* (New York: Harper and Brothers, 1929).

32. Ralph Borsodi, *The Distribution Age* (New York: D. Appleton, 1927), 3–4. The history of Borsodi's life I am sketching here is drawn primarily from the following sources: Mildred Loomis, *Decentralism: Where It Came from and Where Is It Going?* (York, PA: School of Living Press, 1980), especially "Ralph Borsodi: Decentralist Supreme," 63–71; Richard Patrick Norris, "Back to the Land: The Post-Industrial Agrarianism of Ralph Borsodi and Austin Tappan Wright," PhD diss., University of Minnesota, 1976; David B. Danbom, "Romantic Agrarianism in the Twentieth-Century," *Agricultural History* 65 (1991): 1–12; William H. Issel, "Ralph Borsodi and the Agrarian Response to Industrial America," *Agricultural History* 41 (1967): 55–66; biographical profiles by Borsodi followers printed periodically in the *Green Revolution*; and the Ralph Borsodi Papers, University of New Hampshire, Milne Special Collections and Archives. For the growth of the culture of consumption in this period, see Roland Marchand, *Advertising the American Dream: Making Way for Modernity, 1920–1940* (Berkeley: University of California Press, 1985; paperback reprint, 1986).

33. Borsodi, *This Ugly Civilization*, preface.

34. *Flight*, 4–8, xiii.

35. Ibid., 6.

36. Ibid., 40.

37. Ibid., 56–60.

38. Helen Knothe's diary (1936–1940), entry of November 29, 1936, Helen and Scott Nearing Papers, Thoreau Institute. The Nearings generally distanced themselves from the Borsodis and stressed their own innovations and approach. At a 1972 gathering of the School of Living, however, the Nearings, Ralph Borsodi, and Mildred Loomis all shared the stage. See R. Bruce Allison, ed., *Humanizing Our Future: Some Imaginative Alternatives*, Complete Proceedings of the NE School of Living Conference, Conway, New Hampshire, June 23–25, 1972.

39. See Borsodi, *Flight*, especially his chapter "The Loom and the Sewing Machine," 56–60.

40. *Flight*, 122. Borsodi notes that industrialism, consumerism, and the dependence of the worker are problems of the farm industry as well. His homesteading vision is not a call for city dwellers to take up current farming practices; it is a call to reform the economics and daily practices of both city and country.

41. Ibid., 147.

42. Ibid., 2.

43. Henry Tetlow is another Depression Era homesteader who claims to have nothing to do with the "nuts and berries school" of living, whose proponents advocate "a return—rather, a regression—to pioneer if not primordial conditions." Henry Tetlow, *We Farm for a Hobby and Make It Pay* (New York: William and Morrow, 1938), 11.

44. *Flight*, 38.

45. Ibid., 72.

46. See particularly Borsodi's chapters "Capital" and "Food, Pure Food and Fresh Food" in *Flight*, 96–111 and 20–47, respectively. Borsodi sounds a particularly nostalgic note when, in his discussion of weaving, he muses back to the days of his grandmother, when "the music of the spinning wheel and the rhythm of the loom filled the land" (50).

47. See Tetlow, *We Farm for a Hobby*, 29; and *Flight*, 103.

48. Shi, *The Simple Life*, 229.

49. "Interview with Ralph Borsodi" (Interview by Carolyn Kimsey), "The Plowboy Interview," *Mother Earth News*, no. 26, March/April 1974, 13.

50. Shi, *The Simple Life*, 238–42.

51. See Richard Crepeau, *Melbourne Village: The First Twenty-five Years, 1946–1971* (Gainesville: University Press of Florida, 1997).

52. Like Burroughs and the Nearings, Borsodi enjoyed his share of admirers.

Consider this letter written by a young homesteader-to-be living in a small college town. Addressing Borsodi as a kindred spirit, the young man writes: "As a librarian . . . located in a hopelessly conventional and very religious college community, you may be able to imagine the inhibitions and morbid mental confinement of my existence." In the language of a convert, the young man then describes how he fell by chance upon Borsodi's This Ugly Civilization in the library and decided to change his life: "Having the sweet companionship of your book in such an iron-clad environment of bondage is comparable to the Mormon conception of Joseph Smith finding the golden tablets." Anonymous letter, as quoted by Borsodi, Flight, 128; see also additional letters, 126–31.

The reasons that countercultural homesteaders tended to prefer the Nearings' example over the Borsodis' is not entirely clear, although the Nearings' comparatively radical politics may be one reason. Laurence Veysey suggests that resistance to formalistic Georgist principles and land trust ideas may have played a role, while Shi (drawing on Mildred Loomis's remarks) notes that many couples—despite early communalist tendencies—were ultimately more interested in establishing privately owned, family-based homesteads. See Laurence Veysey, The Communal Experience: Anarchist and Mystical Communities in Twentieth-Century America (Chicago: University of Chicago Press, 1973; reprint, Phoenix Books, 1978), 38; and Shi, The Simple Life, 259.

53. LL, 56.

54. See, for instance, Berry's essay "An Argument for Diversity," in WPF, 109–22.

55. LL, 140.

56. Here I am quoting from persistent comments made at Good Life Center board meetings by neighbors and board members seeking to balance the vision of social change with maintaining the simple, small-scale model of the homestead itself.

57. Shi, The Simple Life, 229. Shi qualifies his general reading in his conclusion by adding that while the simple life "is destined to be a minority ethic" that find its most sustained expression in times of national emergency (such as world wars, depression, and energy crises), it also can be "more than an anachronism or an eccentricity" (280). Shi notes that, rather than cultural pressure or social planning, individual personal will is important in the success of the simple life. He mentions the "thousands who practice the homesteading ideal" today as being among those who are responsible for keeping "the simple life" on the cultural playing field (278).

58. Richard Hofstadter makes a compelling case for the transformation in agriculture: that as early as 1815 in some states and by 1860 in the majority of America, yeoman farming had given way to "the relentless advance of commercial agriculture" (The Age of Reform, 38). Hofstadter makes this point in service to a particular argument (that populism was a product not of the frontier

but of entrepreneurial radicalism), but he does seem to overlook the reintro-duction of *actual* yeoman farming in the context of Progressive Era reforms. See ibid., 23–59.

59. For treatment of 1960s communal back-to-the-land movements (which had living close to nature as a conscious goal), see, in addition to works already cited in chapter 3, Albert Bates and Timothy Miller, "The Evolution of Hippie Communal Spirituality: The Farm and Other Hippies Who Didn't Give Up," in *America's Alternative Religions*, ed. Timothy Miller, SUNY Series in Religious Studies, ed. Harold Coward (Albany: State University of New York Press, 1995), 371–77; Andrew Kopkind, "Up the Country: Five Communes in Vermont," *Working Papers* (Spring 1973): 44–49; and Joseph P. Kahn, "Where It Survived (in Brattleboro the Sixties Never Left—They Just Got More Conventional)," *New England Monthly*, March 1988, 43–45, 98.

60. In this sense, while I find nothing out of turn in Wade Clark Roof's char-acterization of "the generation of seekers," I do think that continuities must be weighed against uniqueness. Roof's emphasis on baby boomers' pragmatism, religious eclecticism, emphasis on the self, and turn toward nature as a source of the spiritual is accurate but is certainly not limited to boomers only. Bur-roughs, Nearing, Hall, and Borsodi can all be said to have made spiritually eclec-tic and pragmatic choices, largely through sacralizing nature and attempting to reform self and society according to nature's beneficence and limits. See Roof, *A Generation of Seekers*. In stressing continuities amid innovation, I am also sharing portions of Robert S. Ellwood's appraisal of the 1960s in his book *The Sixties Spir-itual Awakening*, especially 326–36.

61. See Duryee, *A Living from the Land*; Kains, *Five Acres and Independence*; Tetlow, *We Farm for a Hobby and Make It Pay*; Rich, *We Took to the Woods*; Corey, *Buy an Acre*; and Hay-den Pearson, *Success on the Small Farm* (New York: McGraw-Hill, 1946).

62. Aldo Leopold's most well-known work is *A Sand County Almanac* (Oxford: Ox-ford University Press, 1949). A good treatment of the intellectual traditions in which Leopold's work can be placed is offered by Roderick Nash in "Aldo Leopold's Intellectual Heritage," in *Companion to "A Sand County Almanac*," ed. J. Baird Callicott (Madison: University of Wisconsin Press, 1987), 63–88. Nash rightly points out that Leopold's land ethic, while admirable, was not as groundbreak-ing or original as it appeared to be. While Leopold was not a homesteader in terms of the definitions I have set out here, his weekend sojourns to "the shack" did involve many of the same rituals of domesticity and husbandry that home-steaders perform. The everyday life of Leopold on his prairie farm (a farm that grew food for wildlife more than for people) is treated well by Susan Flader in her "Aldo Leopold's Sand County," ibid., 40–62.

63. In terms of expansiveness and hired labor, neither does Bromfield's exper-iment quite qualify as a homestead, but the project also belongs on the home-steading continuum, and Bromfield's works remain inspirational to many home-

steaders. See Louis Bromfield's autobiographical treatments in *Pleasant Valley* (New York: Harper and Brothers, 1945), *Malabar Farm* (New York: Harper and Brothers, 1947), and *From My Experience: The Pleasures and Miseries of Life on a Farm* (New York: Harper and Brothers, 1955). No sustained biography of Bromfield is available, although a literary biography in the Twayne series is a beginning. See David Anderson, *Louis Bromfield*, Twayne Series, vol. 55 (New York: Twayne, 1964).

Interestingly, both Leopold and Bromfield describe their choices to live intimately with the natural world in terms of *conversion*. Leopold experienced his after shooting a wolf and staring into its eyes; Bromfield (after a preview in France), immediately upon seeing the farmland in Ohio that later became his home.

Both Bromfield and Ralph Borsodi became actively involved in Friends of the Land ("a non-profit, non-partisan society for the conservation of soil, rain, and man") in the 1940s. A typical issue of the association's journal, the *Land* (6, no. 4 [Winter 1947–48]), contains an article by Ralph Borsodi against "Big Farming" and an article by Bromfield on "Loafing Sheds," and it reveals the extent to which these reformers were in conversation with each other.

64. For a trenchant, and prescient, critique of the Motor Tourist, see Leopold's essay, "The River of the Mother of God," in *"The River of the Mother of God" and Other Essays by Aldo Leopold*, edited by Susan L. Flader and J. Baird Callicott (Madison: University of Wisconsin Press, 1991).

65. Bradford and Vena Angier, *At Home in the Woods* (New York: Sheridan House, 1951). In addition to this homesteading narrative, Bradford Angier has authored numerous how-to books on cabin building, edible wild plants, and wilderness survival. Vena Angier offers her own perspective in *Wilderness Wife* (Radnor, PA: Chilton Books, 1976).

66. Angier and Angier, *At Home in the Woods*, 165–66.

67. "A Letter to Wives from Mrs. Robinson," in Carolyn Robinson and Ed Robinson, *The Have More Plan: A Little Land—a Lot of Living*, reprinted in *Mother Earth News* 1, no. 2, March 1970, 13. The *Mother Earth News* reports the original publication of *The Have More Plan* as being 1947, but other sources (such as Lyman Wood, below) suggest a more accurate date of 1944, with republication in 1947.

68. My thanks to Lyman Wood's daughter, Nancy, for adding her insights on her father's role in supporting homesteading projects. Much of Lyman's approach to life, she noted, was rooted in his role in the Life Study Fellowship and his commitment to his own "five keys to a happier life." Gardening was a big part of his simple, pragmatic approach to faith, as was his business approach (before *socially responsible business* was a term) of "doing well by doing good."

69. The Robinsons' story is told by Roger Griffith and Lyman Wood in *What a Way to Live and Make a Living: The Lyman Wood Story* (Charlotte, VT: In Brief Press, 1994), 41–60. Some members of the Good Life Center knew the Robinsons

personally and have helped to fill in the details. Lyman Wood, who went on to found the Garden Way company in Vermont (which supplied many home-steaders and "wannabes" with farm tools), got his start from working with the Robinsons. See also Richard Thruelsen, "Pioneers on the 5:15," *Saturday Evening Post*, March 29, 1947, 28–29, 146.

70. My thanks to Eliot Coleman for sharing this story and for being such a warm and hospitable neighbor.

71. Griffith and Wood, *What a Way to Live*, 50.

72. *Mother Earth News* 1, no. 2, March 1970, 9.

73. Only two whom I know of in the Sauna group have published books, and these are primarily practical texts on gardening.

74. John Graves, *Hard Scrabble: Observations on a Patch of Land*, 2nd ed. (New York: Knopf, 1980), 5.

75. Tatelbaum, *Carrying Water as a Way of Life*, 32.

76. Ibid., 33.

77. T. J. Jackson Lears, *No Place of Grace: Antimodernism and the Transformation of American Culture, 1880–1920* (New York: Pantheon Books, 1981; reprint, Chicago: University of Chicago Press, 1994), 65. See also Lears's preface, in which he concisely lays out his ultimate assessment of the majority of antimodernists (xv–xx) and his treatment of the simple life (74–83). Lears does acknowledge that there are occasional exceptions to his interpretive rule. If we are to characterize homesteaders primarily as antimodernists, we must do so then in the sense that they are exceptions of the kind that Lears notes.

78. On the other hand, some homesteaders are engaged in the production and consumption of homesteading *texts*, texts that homesteaders and nonhome-steaders alike consume. If we pursue this phenomenon, the Lears thesis rears its head once more and is, with respect to homesteaders, an appropriate criticism to deliver.

79. Lears, *No Place of Grace*, 65.

80. The drive toward self-fulfillment through self-sufficiency can produce strange bedfellows, as when Martha Stewart advocates "self-reliance" and "how-to" (while selling her magazine to millions), and "authorities" on simple living are praising the virtues of Lean Cuisine frozen dinners.

For example, Martha Stewart emphasized her commitment to producing her own food and household decor in an editorial in her then hugely popular magazine, *Martha Stewart Living*. She writes: "To me, the most important change (over the past few decades) . . . has been that self-reliance and 'how-to' are worthwhile and above all, acceptable." "A Letter from Martha," *Martha Stewart's Living*, June 1997, 8. Her remarks, of course, reveal that her commitments to simplicity, however laudable, are ultimately conventional.

It is intriguing, though not wholly surprising, that a Nearing–Martha Stewart connection actually exists. Several visitors to the Nearing homestead informed me that Stewart credited the Nearings for inspiring her to buy a Connecticut farmhouse and grow her own food, a credit that the Nearings would not necessarily have appreciated! See Martha Stewart, "Remembering: The Good Life," *Martha Stewart's Living*, April 1996, 148. My thanks to Laura Rotolo for providing me with this article.

For the comment on the "simplicity" of Lean Cuisine, see Elaine St. James, *Living the Simple Life: A Guide to Scaling Down and Enjoying More* (New York: Hyperion, 1996), 238. However well-intentioned they may be, the writings of St. James and Stewart do epitomize the danger of the commodification of "simplicity" and "natural living" in the 1990s.

81. Several studies speak to the potential complacency and privatism of homesteading, though none make the precise argument (based on the religious aspects of homesteading) that I am suggesting here. In a broad survey of Canadian and American homesteaders (and homesteading enthusiasts), Jeffrey Jacob found that while the majority expressed "strong environmental values," they were surprisingly "conventional," "capitalistic," and "apolitical." Jacob supports his conclusions, however, by analyzing his respondents' relative lack of interest in community organizing and rural activism, without considering (as I have been suggesting throughout) the ways in which the act of homesteading itself can be a political act. Furthermore, my own fieldwork has demonstrated (in a way less available to those relying on survey results) the extent to which the life of homesteading, perhaps ironically, keeps participants so busy with their own work of self-sufficiency that "activism," in the way that Jacob describes it, is difficult except on a seasonal basis. See Jeffrey C. Jacob, "The North American Back-to-the-Land Movement," *Community Development Journal* 31, no. 3 (July 1996): 241–49, and *New Pioneers*, 100–103 and 169–211.

Danièle Hervieu-Legér, in a study of "neo-rural" French youth, has demonstrated identifiable change over time. Early anarchistic, countercultural groups had, by 1979, made various concessions to the mainstream, particularly in terms of privatism, capitalism, hierarchical authority, and the work ethic. Hervieu-Léger's story is not just one of decline, however, for she identifies an essential "ethical continuity" between early and late versions of "practical neo-ruralism." See Danièle Hervieu-Léger, "Communautés rurales en France, aprés 1968—'Vivre sans règle,'" *Recherches sociologiques* 10, no. 1 (January 1979): 7–22, and, more generally, *Le retour à la nature: "Au fond de la forêt, l'état"* (Paris: Seuil, 1979).

82. Carter, *The Culture of Disbelief*.

83. Berry, *Harlan Hubbard*, 97–98. My thanks to Peter Forbes for the gift of the book and to John Saltmarsh for reminding me of this particular passage.

7. Gender, Class, Nature, and Religion

Epigraph: Nathaniel Hawthorne, *Blithedale Romance* (1852), Penguin Classics Edition (New York: Penguin Books, 1986), 16, 24 and 65.

1. These portraits of religious ambivalence are drawn from a range of textual sources on American religion, as well as from fieldwork. Some are drawn particularly from the ethnographic work of contributing authors in James Spickard, J. Shawn Landres, and Meredith McGuire, *Personal Knowledge and Beyond* (New York: New York University Press, 2002).

2. My research has tended to confirm more than deny the existence of a "traditional pattern" of gender roles on the homestead. While there are some notable exceptions among the homesteaders I interviewed (particularly in the case of gardening, which is sometimes shared by homesteading couples and often the primary domain of *either* the man or the woman), it is more often the case that women—in heterosexual relationships—spend more time cooking, cleaning, sewing, and child rearing than they spend chopping wood, doing carpentry, digging wells, and tending to the grounds.

Jeffrey Jacob's questionnaire results (N = 565, with variation in responses to particular questions) confirm my findings. He found that in the categories of traditional "woman's work," homestead chores were performed "usually by the wife" (meals, 76 percent; dishwashing, 74 percent; and housecleaning, 80 percent), gardening and animal care, by contrast, tended to be shared by both men and women, with women doing slightly more of the labor. "Repair work," however, was reported by 79 percent as being performed "usually by the husband." See Jacob, *New Pioneers*.

Tension around such gender divisions arose among Wendell Berry's readership when those who admired him for his seemingly left-leaning ecological principles also chastised him for being the high-profile writer and farmer while his wife, Tanya, typed his manuscripts and cooked the meals. Berry responded to his critics in "Why I Am Not Going to Use a Computer" and "Feminism, the Body and the Machine," in *WPF*, 170–96. In these essays, Berry reveals that his resistance to technology (and his attention to the details of ecologically sound farming) is made possible only by the willingness of his wife to fulfill the role of typist, and he also argues persuasively (not unlike Bill Coperthwaite) for a gendered division of labor. Also like Bill, Berry argues that the dominant world of middle-class labor (going out to an office to work for someone else, usually at some cost to long-term social or environmental health) is a practice both men and women should resist.

3. "A Letter to Wives from Mrs. Robinson" in Robinson and Robinson, *The Have-More Plan*, 13. Robinson's letter also reveals a nervous insistence that doing tough work such as beheading chickens and mucking out stalls will not make you any less of a good wife or a good hostess.

4. Tatelbaum, *Carrying Water as a Way of Life*, 4.

5.   Emily Culpepper describes this situation as normative in many of the "new religious movements" of the 1960s and 1970s. In these religious experiments what seemed "alternative" to men was experienced as all too traditional for women. Culpepper writes: " Most contemporary 'new' religious movements (for example, Baba Lovers, Hare Krishnas, Maharaji Ji followers, independent charismatic Christian groups—to name a few) offer only pseudo-newness for women. The roles for women within such movements are heavily traditional, patriarchal ones—usually urging a norm of hetero-sexist, reproductive, nuclear family goals. The theology is frequently explicitly or implicitly woman-hating." See Culpepper in Jacob Needleman and George Baker, eds., *Understanding the New Religions* (New York: Seabury Press, 1978), 220. Similarly, Zsuzanna Budapest reflects on her personal experiences in the not-so-New Age movement: "When you looked at how these new-age gurus ran their businesses, you could see the women in the kitchen peeling organic potatoes with babies strapped to their saris and men teaching yoga and running the show. This kind of new age was actually the proverbial 'old hat.' " See Budapest "Teaching Women's Spirituality Rituals," in *The Goddess Celebrates*, ed. Diane Stein (Freedom, CA: Crossing Press, 1991), 14. My thanks to Sarah McFarland Taylor for pointing me to these sources. The work of Vivien Rose (see note 14, below) pointed me to similar moments of dismay among those in the 1970s for whom homesteading was the primary goal. One author she cites recalls: "In my head, I wanted to be the perfect homestead wife and us to be that perfect homestead family, [but I] built a monument to the nuclear family that became a coffin." Harriet Bye, "Memoirs of an Ex-Homesteader's Wife," *Country Women* 1, March 1973, 19–20.

6.   These comments are based on interviews with Dale and Robin in October 1995 and ongoing contact since.

7.   In this connection, it is worth making the obvious, but nonetheless often overlooked, query about the ethnographer's—or historian's—role. If what we are looking at makes us uncomfortable, how often does this discomfort have to do with the expectations we may bring to the texts and lives we are studying? Here I have found helpful Nancy Cott's comments on the ways in which twentieth-century assumptions have unduly influenced women historians' various interpretations of the "cult of domesticity," "the cult of true womanhood," and "the doctrine of separate spheres." As Cott sees it, "The intrusion of mid-twentieth century assumptions entails a particular distortion of this subject because women of the past centuries rarely perceived, as many modern feminists do, an antithesis between women's obligations in the domestic realm and their general progress." The same might be said of ethnographic bias. See Nancy Cott, *The Bonds of Womanhood*, 2nd ed. (New Haven, CT: Yale University Press, 1997), 199.

8.   Interviews with "Kate," July 1994.

9.   Linda Tatelbaum, *Writer on the Rocks: Moving the Impossible* (Appleton, ME: About Time Press, 2000), 58.

10. Ibid., 59.

11. Ibid., 60–61.

12. Ibid., 61. Sal, in writing for a local newsletter about what it means to build a house from scratch, makes the comparison in the opposite direction, equating house building explicitly with the labors of giving birth.

13. Tatelbaum, *Writer on the Rocks*, 61.

14. The dissertation research of Vivien Rose ("Homesteading as Social Protest: Gender and Continuity in the Back-to-the Land Movement in the United States, 1890–1980," PhD diss., State University of New York, Binghamton, 1997) is an excellent addition to the literature on homesteading, one that was not available to me in the early draftings of this manuscript. While Rose's aims are different from my own, she shares some of my thinking on a number of issues. Most important, she treats questions of gender throughout her study, a welcome approach.

15. On the Beechers' professionalization of homemaking and its link to Christian virtue, see Colleen McDannell, *The Christian Home in Victorian America, 1840–1900* (Bloomington: Indiana University Press, 1986).

16. Myrtle Mae Borsodi, "My Home Is My Career," *Silent Hostess* 4, no. 3, 1932, 10–11, 23.

17. Mrs. Ralph [Myrtle Mae] Borsodi, "The Home Laundry Earns Money," *Electrical Merchandising* 45, February 1931, 30–33.

18. Helen commented on eating simply as a means of saving oneself from excessive kitchen work, especially in her cookbook, *Simple Food for the Good Life*, as well as in personal conversation with the author.

19. See also Scott and Nellie Seeds Nearing, "When a Girl Is Asked to Marry," *Ladies' Home Journal*, March 1912, 7, and "Four Great Things a Woman Does at Home," *Ladies' Home Journal*, May 1912, 12. If the titles are any indication, apparently it is marriage and domestic life that turn a girl into a woman.

20. John Saltmarsh assesses both Scott and Nellie's early commitment to the concept of the home as woman's sphere and also Nellie's later struggles with this concept. See Saltmarsh, *Scott Nearing*, 42–43, 197–99. The article from which Saltmarsh quotes extensively is Nellie Marguerite Seeds, "Why Martha," *Call Magazine*, May 7, 1922.

21. "Remarks by Robert Nearing," at "Helen and Scott Nearing: The Vermont Experiment," Stratton Mountain Foundation, June 22–23, 2002. Scott's dedication to Helen in his *Making of a Radical* is also revealing in this light. The published dedication reads "To Helen, who did half the work." In Helen's privately inscribed copy, however, Scott writes, "To Helen, who did *more* than half the work" (emphasis mine), thus indicating a disjunction (again) between public and private representations of their life together.

Helen's tendency to praise Scott's work to interviewers while downplaying her own contributions was not only my experience but that of several others as well. Vivien Rose tells a familiar story when, in the midst of an interview in 1988, she got up to fetch something for Helen, and while the tape recorder was rolling Helen leaned into it and remarked, "While she's gone, what I have to say is, why bother about my opinion about anything ha ha ha"; Rose, "Homesteading as Social Protest," 5. Self-deprecating in some ways, Helen never failed to be mischievous and to have the last laugh in others.

22. Cott, drawing on the work of Aileen Kraditor and others, introduces the concept of the discourse of domesticity as a more flexible, post-Foucauldian concept for talking about idealizations of "the domestic" and of "women's sphere" in late eighteenth-century New England and beyond. See Cott, preface to The Bonds of Womanhood, xvi–xvii. Kraditor's original coining of the phrase "the cult of domesticity" appeared in her introduction to Up from the Pedestal: Selected Writings in the History of American Feminism (Chicago: Quadrangle Books, 1968).

23. Here I am borrowing language eclectically from Peter Gay and Ralph Waldo Emerson.

24. Cott, The Bonds of Womanhood, xvii.

25. The situation on the modern homestead, then, intriguingly resembles both the Victorian idealizations of the moral meaning of home, which Cott discusses, as well as the more cooperative, dual-gendered small farming life that Nancy Osterud, in a rejoinder to Cott, describes. Nancy Grey Osterud, The Bonds of Community (Ithaca, NY: Cornell University Press, 1991).

The historical argument concerning separate spheres in the eighteenth and nineteenth centuries has itself been challenged by more recent scholarship. Some representative texts include: Leonore Davidoff and Catherine Hall, Family Fortunes: Men and Women of the English Middle Class, 1780–1850 (Chicago: University of Chicago press, 1987); and Jeanne Boydston, Home and Work: Housework, Wages and the Ideology of Labor in the Early Republic (New York: Oxford University Press, 1990). See also Cott, The Bonds of Womanhood, xx footnote 15; and Ann Douglas, The Feminization of American Culture, 2nd ed. (New York: Noonday Press, 1998).

26. Interview with "Fran," October 1996.

27. Jeffrey Jacob's survey of 565 readers of Countryside produced statistics that correspond with my qualitative findings. In terms of education, 58 percent of his respondents had college experience, and 18 percent had done graduate-level work. While homesteaders' incomes were modest when compared with incomes they were capable of receiving (54 percent reported incomes between twenty thousand and fifty thousand dollars), these incomes, Jacobs notes, were often seen as "affluent" in the context of the rural areas in which the respondents lived. In Jacobs's survey the educational backgrounds of the parents of homesteaders were less strong (with roughly 25 percent of the parents having received college education), while the homesteaders I interviewed tended to have more highly educated parents. In both cases, however,

the lives most people led before going back to the land were shaped by middle- and upper-middle-class education and professional goals, which, if not achieved by the parents, were made available and "desirable" for the children. Thus, these homesteaders' educational levels were quite high, with 58 percent of Jacobs's respondents reporting some undergraduate study or more, 33 percent of these having attained a bachelor's degree and 18 percent having been involved in graduate study. See Jacobs, *New Pioneers*, 38–40 and 77–79.

Linda Breen Pierce's simplicity study (N = 211) includes a broader range of "simplicity" practitioners than homesteaders per se but reveals demographic data similar to mine and Jacobs's. Of her respondents, 34 percent reported an annual income over fifty-one thousand dollars, and 74 percent reported educational levels of having reached a college degree or beyond, with 54 percent of the total having done some postgraduate work. That high education levels correlate more positively with "simplicity" than income does is not surprising, since many simplicity advocates have consciously chosen to reduce their income and have reported it on the basis of current, rather than previous, earnings. See Pierce, *Choosing Simplicity* (Carmel, CA: Gallagher Press, 2000).

For European examples of back-to-the-land impulses, see Hervieu-Léger, *Le retour à la nature*; Jan Marsh, *Back to the Land: The Pastoral Impulse in England, from 1880 to 1914* (London: Quartet Books, 1982); Fiona McCarthy, *The Simple Life: C. R. Ashbee in the Cotswolds* (Berkeley: University of California Press, 1981); and Peter C. Gould, *Early Green Politics: Back to Nature, Back to the Land, and Socialism in Britain, 1880–1900* (New York: St. Martin's Press, 1988).

We might also ask, "What about race?"—an equally important question, the answer to which may correlate with class but likely is not determined by it. The Nearings report that in their many visits with aspiring homesteaders, they never encountered an African American person who voluntarily chose to establish (or return to) a life of small farming and self-sufficiency. That they should even raise the issue puts them ahead of some commentators and is not surprising given their long-standing interest in questions of race (Scott authored *Black America* in 1929). Neither Jacob nor Pierce reports on African American or Latina/Latino homesteaders, and homesteading magazines feature white faces in their stories and advertisements. This is not to say that racial diversity in homesteading does not exist, but it is not prominent.

28. For instance, Liberty Hyde Bailey, using language that seems prescient today, speaks of practices that defile the "Holy Earth" in the borrowed Christian language of sin and salvation. He calls humans who have "fallen away" from the earth to recognize that the true creation in not man-centered (or God-centered) but "biocentric." Recognizing "biocentrism" as the true model for living enables both personal and cultural redemption. Liberty Hyde Bailey, *The Holy Earth*, in *This Incomparable Lande: A Book of American Nature Writing*, ed. Thomas J. Lyon (New York: Penguin, 1991), 254.

29. For a sympathetic, scholarly portrait of Christian fundamentalism as it is

lived in modern America, see Nancy Tatom Ammerman, *Bible Believers* (New Brunswick, NJ: Rutgers University Press, 1987). Ammerman's excellent discussion of fundamentalist readings of scripture, uses of science, and responses to modernity is particularly useful in terms of the comparative reflections I am offering here. See also George Marsden's treatment of fundamentalist "uses" of science in *Understanding Fundamentalism and Evangelicalism* (Grand Rapids, MI: William B. Eerdmans, 1991).

30. John Saltmarsh begins his study of Scott Nearing, in fact, with a meditation on Nearing's own complex notion of the "terrible freedom" (the phrase is Emerson's) he has inherited. See Saltmarsh, *Scott Nearing*, 1–4.

31. See Bourdieu's treatment of the concept of habitus in *Outline for a Theory of Practice*, trans. Richard Nice, Cambridge Studies in Social and Cultural Anthropology, vol. 16, ed. Ernest Gellner (Cambridge: Cambridge University Press, 1977), 78–87. See also Bourdieu, *The Logic of Practice*, trans. Richard Nice (Stanford, CA: Stanford University Press, 1990), 80–97.

32. It should be pointed out here that Immanuel Kant was no "nature lover," and he clearly argued against viewing animals as moral beings. But his ethics established one approach for future environmental ethicists: the viewing of nature not only as a "means" for human use but also as an "end" of its own.

33. A critique of nature-loving wilderness advocates whose knowledge of nature is not necessarily intimate can be found in Richard White, " 'Are You an Environmentalist or Do You Work for a Living?': Work and Nature," in *Uncommon Ground*, ed. Cronon, 171–85.

34. For two classics that express this common view, see Leo Marx, *The Machine in the Garden* (Oxford: Oxford University Press, 1964); and Roderick Nash, *Wilderness and the American Mind*, 3rd ed. (New Haven, CT: Yale University Press, 1972).

35. Field notes, September 1996.

36. "Sheilaism" is the classic example of (loosely) Christian religious individualism in contemporary America that Bellah cites. See Robert Bellah et al., *Habits of the Heart, Heart*, updated ed. (Berkeley: University of California Press, 1996), 221 and 235–37.

37. See Anthony Giddens, *The Consequences of Modernity* (Stanford, CA: Stanford University Press, 1990), 55–62 and 139.

38. M. H. Abrams, *Natural Supernaturalism: Tradition and Revolution in Romantic Literature* (New York: W. W. Norton, 1971).

39. Tension around this issue—though not necessarily interpreted in this way—has surfaced numerous times with respect to the legacy of the Nearings. Those who see the Nearings' greatest contribution as being to social justice or environmental preservation are often irritated by what they see as New Age interest in the Nearings as spiritual exemplars.

40. This is argued by Wendell Berry in numerous essays and by Gene Logsdon

in "Pastoral Economics" and "The Garden is the Proving Ground for the Farm," in *The Contrary Farmer*, 16–37, 38–52. See also Logsdon, *At Nature's Pace: Farming and the American Dream* (New York: Pantheon Books, 1994).

41. Bill McKibben, *The End of Nature* (New York: Random House, 1989; paperback reprint, New York: Doubleday, 1990).

42. See Bellah et al., *Habits of the Heart*; Stanley Hauerwas and Charles Pinches, *Christians among the Virtues* (Notre Dame, IN: University of Notre Dame Press, 1997); and Alasdair MacIntyre, *After Virtue*, 2nd ed. (Notre Dame, IN: University of Notre Dame Press, 1984).

43. Hauwerwas and Pinches, *Christians among the Virtues*, 56–57.

44. *Reinhabitation* is a term often used by bioregionalists. Bioregionalists themselves represent one portion of a broader cultural interest in reinvesting in "place" as both a moral and physical source of stability in the face of modernity. Much literature of place exhibits the same interest in structure, limits, self-discipline, and daily sacramentalism as I have argued is at the heart of homesteading. See, for instance, Casey, *Getting Back into Place*; Tony Hiss, *The Experience of Place* (New York: Knopf, 1990); Thomas H. Rawls, *Small Places: In Search of a Vanishing America* (Boston: Little, Brown, 1990); and Chidester and Linenthal, eds., *American Sacred Space*.

It is interesting to note in this connection that Robert Bellah himself mentions Wendell Berry as a positive exemplar, thus suggesting the link I am arguing for here, an important (if unintentional) connection between homesteading (and broader environmental and simplicity movements) and communitarian understandings of virtuous living. See Bellah et al., *Habits of the Heart*, xviii and 278.

45. Charles Taylor, *Sources of the Self: The Making of Modern Identity* (Cambridge, MA: Harvard University Press, 1989), 63–73 and 100–106.

46. It is interesting to note that Will Kymlicka attempts to close the distance between liberals and communitarians by insisting that liberalism is also invested in the Good Life. See Kymlicka, *Liberalism, Community and Culture* (Oxford: Oxford University Press, 1989; paperback reprint, Clarendon, 1991), 9–25, 36–43. My thanks to Heidi Grasswick for introducing me to his work.

47. This and the two excerpts that follow are from Hubbard, *Payne Hollow*, 166–67.

48. Provocative critiques of the environmental dangers of seeing nature only as a "cultural construct" are offered in Michael Soulé and Gary Lease, eds., *Reinventing Nature? Responses to Postmodern Deconstruction* (Washington, DC: Island Press, 1995), and in Cronon, ed., *Uncommon Ground*.

Laurel Kearns also persuasively argues for the "subjectivity" of nature (particularly nature that has been altered by humans) in her "Greening Ethnography and the Study of Religion," in *Personal Knowledge and Beyond: Reshaping the Ethnography of Religion*, ed. James Spickard, J. Shawn Landres, and Meredith McGuire (New York: New York University Press, 2002).

SELECTED BIBLIOGRAPHY

Manuscript Collections

Abernathy Library and Special Collections, Middlebury College Library, Middlebury, VT

Borsodi, Ralph. Papers. Milne Special Collections and Archives, University of New Hampshire Library, Durham, NH.

Hall, Bolton. Papers. Archives and Manuscripts Division, the New York Public Library, New York, NY.

Johnson, Clifton. Papers. Jones Library, Amherst, MA.

Nearing, Helen and Scott. Papers. The Thoreau Institute at Walden Woods, Lincoln, MA.

Special Collections, Bailey Howe Library, University of Vermont, Burlington, VT.

Magazines

Back Home Magazine

Backwoods Home Magazine

Countryside and Small Stock Journal (now Countryside)

Farmstead

Green Revolution

Harrowsmith

Land and Liberty

Manas

Mother Earth News

Homesteading Books, Magazine Articles, and Related Texts

Allen, Mel. "Helen's Garden." *Yankee Magazine*, October 1987, 203–7.

Allison, R. Bruce, ed. *Humanizing Our Future: Some Imaginative Alternatives.* Complete Proceedings of the NE School of Living Conference, Conway, NH, June 23–25, 1972.

Anderson, Clifton. "Nostalgia Not the Only Reason for 'Back-to-the-Land' Movement." *AgWorld* 5, no. 2 (1979): 7.

Andrews, Cecile. *The Circle of Simplicity.* New York: Perennial Books, 1999.

Angier, Bradford, and Vena Angier. *At Home in the Woods.* New York: Sheridan House, 1951.

Angier, Vena. *Wilderness Wife.* Radnor, PA: Chilton Books, 1976.

Austin, Phyllis. "The Wilderness Way: For the Conovers and the Watermans, Making a Life and a Living Deep in the Northern Forest Comes Naturally." *Maine Times,* June 20, 1995, 2.

Berry, Wendell. *Collected Poems.* San Francisco: North Point Press, 1984.

———. *Farming: A Handbook.* New York: Harcourt, Brace, 1970.

———. *The Gift of Good Land.* San Francisco: North Point Press, 1981.

———. *Harlan Hubbard: Life and Work.* New York: Pantheon Books, 1990.

———. *Home Economics: Fourteen Essays by Wendell Berry.* San Francisco: North Point Press, 1987.

———. *Recollected Essays: 1965–1980.* San Francisco: North Point Press, 1981.

———. *Sex, Economy, Freedom and Community.* New York: Pantheon Books, 1992.

———. *The Unsettling of America: Culture and Agriculture.* San Francisco: Sierra Club Books, 1977.

———. *What Are People For?* New York: North Point Press, Farrar, Straus and Giroux, 1990.

Borland, Hal. *Hill Country Harvest.* Philadelphia: Lippincott, 1967.

Borsodi, Mrs. Ralph [Myrtle Mae]. "The Home Laundry Earns Money." *Electrical Merchandising* 45, February 1931, 30–33.

Borsodi, Myrtle Mae. "My Home Is My Career." *Silent Hostess* 4, no. 3, 1932, 10–11, 23.

Borsodi, Ralph. *The Distribution Age.* New York: D. Appleton, 1927.

————. *The Flight from the City*. 1st ed. New York: Harper and Brothers, 1933.

————. "Interview with Ralph Borsodi." Interview by Carolyn Kimsey. "The Plowboy Interview," *Mother Earth News*, no. 26, March/April 1974, 6–13.

————. *Seventeen Problems of Man and Society*. Anand, India: Charotar Book Stall, 1968.

————. *This Ugly Civilization: A Study of the Quest for Comfort*. New York: Harper and Brothers, 1929.

Bright, Jean Hay. *Meanwhile, Next Door to the Good Life*. Dixmont, ME: Brightberry Press, 2003.

Bromfield, Louis. *From My Experience: The Pleasures and Miseries of Life on a Farm*. New York: Harper, 1955.

————. *Malabar Farm*. New York: Harper and Brothers, 1948. Reprint, New York: Aeonian Press, 1978.

————. *Pleasant Valley*. New York: Harper and Brothers, 1945.

Burn, June. *Living High: An Unconventional Autobiography*. New York: Duell, Sloan and Pearce, 1941.

Burroughs, John. *The Heart of Burroughs's Journals*. Edited by Clara Barrus. Boston: Houghton Mifflin, 1928. Reprint, Port Washington, NY: Kennikat Press, 1967.

————. *John Burroughs Talks: His Reminiscences and Comments*. Edited by Clifton Johnson. Boston: Houghton Mifflin, 1922.

————. *The Writings of John Burroughs*. 1st ed. Riverside Edition. Boston: Houghton Mifflin, Riverside Press, 1885.

————. *The Writings of John Burroughs*. Riverby Edition, 23 vols. Boston: Houghton Mifflin, Riverside Press, 1904–23.

Chadwick, Janet. *How to Live on Almost Nothing and Have Plenty*. New York: Knopf, 1979.

Cole, John N. "Scott Nearing's Ninety-Three-Year Plan." *Horticulture*, November 1976, 23–30.

Colfax, David, and Miki Colfax. *Hardtimes in Paradise: An American Family's Struggle to Carve Out a Homestead in California's Redwood Mountains*. New York: Warner Books, 1992.

Coperthwaite, William. "Beauty" (13 pages). "Nurture" (30 pages). "Simple Living" (15 pages). "Simplicity" (23 pages). Typewritten manuscripts, undated, signed, provided to the author by William Coperthwaite.

————. *A Handmade Life*. White River Junction, VT: Chelsea Green, 2003.

————. "Interview with Bill Coperthwaite." Interview by Bruce Williamson. "The Plowboy Interview," *Mother Earth News*, no. 9, January 1973, 6–12.

————. "Society by Design." *Manas* 36, no. 50 (1983): 1.

————. "Society by Design, Part II: 'Bread Labor.'" *Manas* 37, no. 37 (1984): 1.

———. "Wealth, Riches, Treasure." *Manas* 61, no. 5 (1988): 1.

Corey, Paul. *Buy an Acre*. New York: Dial Press, 1944.

Damon, Bertha. *A Sense of Humus*. New York: Simon and Schuster, 1943.

Deming, Alison Hawthorne. *Temporary Homelands*. San Francisco: Mercury House, 1994.

Dimmock, Gladys. *Home Ground*. Woodstock, VT: Countryman Press, 1985.

Duryee, William B. *A Living from the Land*. New York: McGraw-Hill, 1934. Reprint, New York: World Publishing Company, 1941.

Elgin, Duane. *Voluntary Simplicity: Towards a Life That Is Inwardly Simple, Outwardly Rich*. New York: William Morrow, 1981.

Fritts, Frank, and Ralph W. Guinn. *Fifth Avenue to Farm*. New York: Harper and Brothers, 1938.

Graves, John. *Hard Scrabble*. New York: Knopf, 1974. Reprint, Knopf, 1980.

Grayson, David [Ray Stannard Baker]. *Adventures in Contentment*. Edited by James Stannard Baker et al. 1907. Reprint, Fredrick, CO: Renaissance Publishing House, 1987.

Greenberg, Arnold. *Adventures on Arnold's Island*. Blue Hill, ME: Left Bank Press, 1994.

Gregg, Richard. *The Value of Voluntary Simplicity*, Pendle Hill Essays, vol. 3. Wallingford, PA: Pendle Hill, 1936.

Gumpert, David. "Eliot and Sue Coleman Find 'Homesteading' Is a Satisfying Way of Life." *Mother Earth News*, no. 11, September 1971, 38–41.

Gussow, Joan. *This Organic Life: Confessions of a Suburban Homesteader*. Real Goods Solar Living Books. White River Junction, VT: Chelsea Green, 2001.

Hall, Bolton. *Life, and Love and Peace*. New York: Arcadia Press, 1909.

———. *A Little Land and a Living*. 3rd ed. New York: Arcadia Press, 1908.

———. *Three Acres and Liberty*. 1st ed. New York: Macmillan, 1907.

Hoover, Helen. *A Place in the Woods*. New York: Knopf, 1967.

Hubbard, Harlan. *Journals, 1929–1944*. Edited by Vincent Kohler and David F. Ward. Lexington: University Press of Kentucky, 1987.

———. *Payne Hollow: Life on the Fringe of Society*. New York: Eakins Press, 1974.

Jackson, Wes. *New Roots for Agriculture*. San Francisco: Friends of the Earth and the Land Institute, 1980.

Joseph, Stanley, and Lynn Karlin. *Maine Farm: A Year of Country Life*. New York: Random House, 1991.

Kains, M. G. *Five Acres and Independence*. New York: Greenberg Publishers, 1935.

Kimber, Robert. *Upcountry*. New York: Lyons and Burford, 1984.

Kotzsch, Ronald. "The Indomitable Scott Nearing." *East-West Journal* (February 1981).

———. "The Irrepressible Helen Nearing." *East-West Journal* (June 1981).

Krizmanic, Judy. "Inch by Inch, Inspirations from Organic Gardeners with Styles All Their Own." *Vegetarian Times*, March 1989, 46.

LaBastille, Anne. *Beyond Black Bear Lake: Life at the Edge of Wilderness*. New York: W. W. Norton, 1987.

LaConte, Ellen. *Free Radical: A Reconsideration of the Good Death of Scott Nearing*. Stockton Springs, ME: Loose Leaf Press, 1997.

———. "The Nearing Good Life: A Perspective on Its Principles and Practices." *Maine Organic Farmer and Gardener*, March/April 1989, 11–12.

———. *On Light Alone: A Guru Meditation on the Good Death of Helen Nearing*. Stockton Springs, ME: Loose Leaf Press, 1996.

———. "The Wind Was with Her: A Biographer Looks at the Life of Helen Nearing." *Convergence* 9, no. 4 (1996): 20.

Lemley, Brad. "Coveting the Good Life." *New Age Journal*, July 1994, 35–38.

Leopold, Aldo. *"The River of the Mother of God" and Other Essays*. Edited by Susan Flader and J. Baird Callicott. Madison: University of Wisconsin Press, 1991.

———. *A Sand County Almanac*. New York: Oxford University Press, 1949.

Levering, Frank, and Wanda Urbanska. *Simple Living*. New York: Penguin, 1992.

Logsdon, Gene. *At Nature's Pace: Farming and the American Dream*. New York: Pantheon Books, 1994.

———. *The Contrary Farmer*. The Real Goods Independent Living Series. White River Junction, VT: Chelsea Green, 1994.

———. *Homesteading: How to Find New Independence on the Land*. Emmaus, PA: Rodale Press, 1973.

———. *You Can Go Home Again*. Bloomington: Indiana University Press, 1998.

Loomis, Mildred. *Decentralism: Where It Came from and Where Is It Going?* York, PA: School of Living Press, 1980.

———. "The Decentralist Answer." *Christian Century* 45, April 30, 1947, 557, 559.

———. "Ralph Borsodi's Principles for Homesteaders." *Land and Liberty* (November/December 1978): 85–87.

———. "The Return of the Productive Home." *Christian Century* 39, November 26, 1941, 1468–70.

———. "What Is a Free Society?" *Christian Century* 44, September 4, 1946, 1060–61.

Martin, Lawrence. *The Homesteaders' Handbook*. New York: Mayflower Books, 1979.

Matson, Peter H. *A Place in the Country*. New York: Harcourt Brace Jovanovich, 1977.

McCaig, Donald. *An American Homeplace*. New York: Crown Publishers, 1992.

Mitchell, Don. *Moving UpCountry*. Dublin, NH: Yankee Publishing, 1984.

Moffett, Judith. *Homestead Year: Back to the Land in Suburbia*. New York: Lyons and Burford, 1995.

Moore, Thomas. *The Re-enchantment of Everyday Life*. New York: HarperCollins, 1996.

Morrill, George P. *Snow, Stars, and Wild Honey*. Philadelphia: Lippincott, 1975.

Mungo, Raymond. *Total Loss Farm*. New York: E. P. Dutton, 1970.

Nearing, Helen. "A Conversation with Helen Nearing." Interview by Larry and Ellen Becker. *Journal of Family Life* 1, no. 2 (1995): 26–32.

———. "Interview with Helen Nearing." Interview by Matthew Scanlon. *Mother Earth News*, no. 144, June/July 1994, 70–77.

———. *Light on Aging and Dying*. Gardiner, ME: Tilbury House, 1995.

———. *Loving and Leaving the Good Life*. Post Mills, VT: Chelsea Green Publishers, 1992. Reprint, Chelsea Green, 1993.

———. *Simple Food for the Good Life*. New York: Dell, 1980. Reprint, Delta/Eleanor Freide, 1982.

Nearing, Nellie Seeds, and Scott Nearing. *Women and Social Progress*. New York: Macmillan, 1912.

Nearing, Scott. "Arden Town." Unpublished MS (written under the pseudonym Max Worth). 1913. Arden Archives, Arden, DE.

———. *Black America*. New York: Vanguard, 1929.

———. *The Conscience of a Radical*. Harborside, ME: Social Science Institute, 1965.

———. *Freeborn*. New York: Urquhart Press, 1932.

———. *The Making of a Radical*. New York: Harper and Row 1972. Reprint, Harborside, ME: Social Science Institute, 1976.

———. *Man's Search for the Good Life*. Harborside, ME: Social Science Institute, 1954. Rev. ed., Harborside, ME: Social Science Institute, 1974.

———. *Reducing the Cost of Living*. Philadelphia: G. W. Jacobs, 1914.

———. *Social Religion*. New York: Macmillan, 1913. Reprint, 1916.

Nearing, Scott, and Helen Nearing. *Continuing the Good Life*. New York: Schocken, 1979.

———. *The Good Life*. Reprint of *"Living the Good Life"* and *"Continuing the Good Life,"* with a foreword by Helen Nearing. New York: Schocken, 1989.

———. *The Good Life Album of Helen and Scott Nearing*. New York: E. P. Dutton, 1974.

———. "Interview with Helen and Scott Nearing." Interview by Hal Smith. "The Plowboy Interview," *Mother Earth News*, no. 11, September 1971, 6–15.

———. *Living the Good Life*. Harborside, ME: Social Science Institute, 1954. Reprinted with a foreword by Paul Goodman. New York: Schocken, 1970.

———. *The Maple Sugar Book*. New York: John Day Company, 1950. Reprint, New York: Schocken, 1970.

Nollman, Jim. *Why We Garden: Cultivating a Sense of Place.* New York: Henry Holt, 1994.

Ogden, Samuel. *The New England Vegetable Garden.* Woodstock, VT: Countryman Press, 1957.

Pearson, Hayden S. *Success on the Small Farm.* New York: McGraw-Hill, 1946.

Proko, Barbara, and Tim Spotted Wolf. "Negotiating the Simple Life: An Interview with Bob and Sheila Lipham." *Inner Guide,* August 1996, 2–5.

Rich, Louise Dickinson. *We Took to the Woods.* Philadelphia: Lippincott, 1942.

Robin, Vicki, and George Dominguez. *Your Money or Your Life.* New York: Viking, 1992.

Robinson, Carolyn, and Ed Robinson. *The Have More Plan: A Little Land—a Lot of Living.* 1944. Reprinted in *Mother Earth News* 1, no. 2, March 1970, 9–77.

Schumacher, E. F. *Small Is Beautiful.* London: Blond and Briggs, 1973.

Seymour, John. *The Fat of the Land.* London: Country Book Club, 1963.

Smith, Keith, and Irene Smith. *The Essential Earth Garden.* Melbourne: Thomas Nelson Australia, 1982.

Snyder, Gary. *The Practice of the Wild.* San Francisco: North Point Press, 1990.

———. *The Real Work: Interviews and Talks, 1964–1979.* Edited by Scott McLean. New York: New Directions, 1980.

Tatelbaum, Linda. *Carrying Water as a Way of Life.* Appleton, ME: About Time Press, 1997.

———. *Writer on the Rocks: Moving the Impossible.* Appleton, ME: About Time Press, 2000.

Tetlow, Henry. *We Farm for a Hobby and Make It Pay.* New York: William Morrow, 1938.

Thoreau, Henry David. *Walden.* 1854. Norton Critical Edition. Edited by William Rossi. New York: W. W. Norton, 1992.

Thruelsen, Richard. "Pioneers on the 5:15." *Saturday Evening Post,* March 29, 1947, 28–29, 146.

Thurston, Ellie. "They Took to the Woods Long Ago." *Berkshire Sampler,* Sunday, December 19, 1976.

Unger, Tom. *Far Out Isn't Far Enough.* London: Methuen, 1984.

Waterman, Laura, and Guy Waterman. *Wilderness Ethics.* Woodstock, VT: Countryman Press, 1993.

Wizansky, Robert, ed. *Home Comfort.* New York: Saturday Review Press, 1973.

Doctoral Dissertations

Coles, Gerald Stuart. "Political Economy and Education in Progressivism and Socialism, 1905–1932: Scott Nearing." PhD diss., State University of New York at Buffalo, 1974.

Gould, Rebecca Kneale. "At Home in Nature: The Religious and Cultural Work of Homesteading in Twentieth Century America." PhD diss., Harvard University, 1997.

Holmes, Steven J. "Blessed Home: Nature, Religion, Science and Human Relationship in the Early Life of John Muir." PhD diss., Harvard University, 1996.

Norris, Richard Patrick. "Back to the Land: The Post-industrial Agrarianism of Ralph Borsodi and Austin Tappan Wright." PhD diss., University of Minnesota, 1976.

Rose, Vivien. "Homesteading as Social Protest: Gender and Continuity in the Back-to-the Land Movement in the United States, 1890–1980." PhD diss., State University of New York at Binghamton, 1997.

Saltmarsh, John. "The Terrible Freedom: An Intellectual Biography of Scott Nearing." PhD diss., Boston University, 1989.

Whitefield, Stephen. "Scott Nearing and the Ambiguity of American Radicalism." PhD diss., Brandeis University, 1972.

Scholarly Articles, Book Chapters, and Manuscripts

Anderson, Clifford B. "The Metamorphosis of American Agrarian Idealism in the 1920s and 1930s." *Agricultural History* 25 (October 1961): 182–88.

Bartowski, John P., and W. Scott Swearingen. "God Meets Gaia in Austin Texas: A Case Study of Environmentalism as Implicit Religion." *Review of Religious Research* 38, no. 4 (1997): 308–24.

Bierbaum, Martin. "Free Acres: Bolton Hall's Single-Tax Experimental Community." *New Jersey History* 102, no. 1–2 (Spring/Summer 1984): 37–63.

Brinkerhoff, Merlin B. "Quasi-Religious Meaning Systems, Official Religion, and Quality of Life in an Alternative Lifestyle: A Survey from the Back-to-the-Land Movement." *Journal for the Scientific Study of Religion* 26, no. 1 (1987): 63–80.

Brinkerhoff, Merlin B., and Jeffrey C. Jacob. "Alternative Technology and Part Time, Semi-subsistence Agriculture: A Survey from the Back to the Land Movement." *Rural Sociology* 51, no. 1 (1986): 43–59.

Danbom, David B. "Romantic Agrarianism in the Twentieth-Century." *Agricultural History* 65 (1991): 1–12.

Dobbelaere, Karl. "The Secularization of Society? Some Methodological Observations." In *Secularization and Fundamentalism Reconsidered*, Religion and the Political Order, vol. 3, ed. Jeffrey K. Hadden and Anson Shupe, 27–44. New York: Paragon House, 1989.

Dodson, Jualynne E., and Cheryl Townsend Gilkes. "There's Nothing Like Church Food." *Journal of the American Academy of Religion* 63, no. 3 (Fall 1995): 519–38.

Douglas, Mary. "The Idea of a Home: A Kind of Space." *Social Research* 58, no. 1 (1991): 287–307.

Finke, Roger, and Laurence Iannaccone. "Supply-Side Explanations for Religious Change." In *Religion in the Nineties*, ed. Wade Clark Roof. *Annals of the American Academy of Political and Social Science* 527 (May 1993): 27–39.

Fleming, Donald. "The Roots of the New Conservation Movement." *Perspectives in American History* 6 (1972): 7–91.

Fox, Richard. "The Culture of Liberal Protestant Progressivism, 1875–1925." *Journal of Interdisciplinary History* 23, no. 3 (1993): 639–60.

Gould, Rebecca Kneale. "Getting (Not Too) Close to Nature: Homesteading as Lived Religion in America." In *Lived Religion in America*, ed. David D. Hall, 217–42. Princeton, NJ: Princeton University Press, 1997.

———. "Making the Self at Home: John Burroughs, Wendell Berry and the Sacred Economy." In *Sharp Eyes: John Burroughs and American Nature Writing*, ed. Charlotte Zoe Walker. Syracuse, NY: Syracuse University Press, 2001.

———. "Modern Homesteading in America: Negotiating Religion, Nature and Modernity." *Worldviews: Environment, Culture, Religion* 3, no. 3 (1999): 183–212.

———. "Modern Homesteading in America: Religious Quests and the Restraints of Religion." *Social Compass* 44, no. 3 (1997): 157–70.

Hadden, Jeffrey K. "Desacralizing Secularization Theory." In *Secularization and Fundamentalism Reconsidered*, Religion and the Political Order, vol. 3, ed. Jeffrey K. Hadden and Anson Shupe, 3–26. New York: Paragon House, 1989.

Hervieu-Léger, Danièle. "Communautés rurales en France, aprés 1968—'Vivre sans règle.'" *Recherches sociologiques* 10, no. 1 (1979): 7–22.

Issel, William. "Ralph Borsodi and the Agrarian Response to Industrial America." *Agricultural History* 41 (1967): 55–66.

Jackson, W. Charles. "Quest for the Good Life: Helen and Scott Nearing and the Ecological Imperative." Master's thesis, University of Maine, 1993.

Jacob, Jeffrey C. "The North American Back-to-the-Land Movement." *Community Development Journal* 31, no. 3 (1996): 241–49.

Kaufman, Maynard. "The New Homesteading Movement: From Utopia to Eutopia." In *The Family, Communes and Utopian Societies*, ed. Sallie TeSelle, 63–82. New York: Harper Torchbooks, 1971.

Naess, Arne. "The Shallow and the Deep, Long Range Ecology Movements." *Inquiry* 16 (1973): 95–100.

Orsi, Robert A. "Everyday Miracles: The Study of Lived Religion." In *Lived Religion in America: Toward a History of Practice*, ed. David D. Hall, 7–13. Princeton, NJ: Princeton University Press, 1997.

———. "Introduction to the Second Edition." *The Madonna of 115th Street*, ix–xxxviii. New Haven, CT: Yale University Press, 1985. 2nd ed., 2002.

Putnam, Robert. "Bowling Alone: America's Declining Social Capital." *Journal of Democracy* 6 (January 1995): 65–78.

Schmidt, Leigh Eric. "From Arbor Day to the Environmental Sabbath: Nature, Liturgy and American Protestantism." *Harvard Theological Review* 84, no. 3 (1991): 299–323.

Swanson, Merwin. "The Country Life Movement and the American Churches." In *Protestantism and Social Christianity*, ed. Martin Marty, 297–312. Modern American Protestantism and Its World, vol. 6, ed. Martin Marty. Munich: K. G. Sauer, 1992.

Taylor, Bron. "Earth and Nature-Based Spirituality (Part I): From Deep Ecology to Radical Environmentalism." *Religion* 31 (2001): 175–93.

———. "Earth and Nature-Based Spirituality (Part II): From Earth First! and Bioregionalism to Scientific Paganism and the New Age." *Religion* 31 (2001): 225–45.

White, Lynn. "The Historical Roots of Our Ecological Crises." *Science* 155 (1967): 1203–7.

Williams, Peter W. "Sacred Space in North America." *Journal of the American Academy of Religion* 70, no. 3 (September 2002): 593–609.

Zinnbauer, Brian J., and Kenneth I. Pargament. "Religiousness and Spirituality: Unfuzzying the Fuzzy." *Journal for the Scientific Study of Religion* 36, no. 4 (December 1997): 549–64.

Scholarly Books

Adams, Carole, ed. *Ecofeminism and the Sacred*. New York: Continuum Press, 1993.

Albanese, Catherine. *Nature Religion in America*. Chicago History of American Religion, ed. Martin Marty. Chicago: University of Chicago Press, 1990.

Ammerman, Nancy Tatom. *Bible Believers: Fundamentalists in the Modern World*. New Brunswick, NJ: Rutgers University Press, 1987.

Asad, Talal. *Genealogies of Religion*. Baltimore, MD: Johns Hopkins University Press, 1993.

Barkas, Janet. *The Vegetable Passion: A History of the Vegetarian State of Mind*. London: Routledge and Kegan Paul, 1975.

Barrus, Clara. *John Burroughs: Boy and Man*. Garden City, NY: Doubleday, Page, 1920.

———. *The Life and Letters of John Burroughs*. 2 vols. Boston: Houghton Mifflin, 1925.

Berger, Bennett M. *The Survival of a Counterculture*. Berkeley: University of California Press, 1981.

Berger, Peter. *The Sacred Canopy: Elements of a Sociological Theory of Religion*. Garden City, NY: Doubleday, 1966. Reprint, Anchor Books, 1969.

Bestor, Arthur E., Jr. *Backwoods Utopias*. Philadelphia: University of Pennsylvania Press, 1950.

Bourdieu, Pierre. *Distinction: A Social Critique of the Judgement of Taste*. Translated by Richard Nice. Cambridge, MA: Harvard University Press, 1984.

———. *The Logic of Practice*. Translated by Richard Nice. Stanford, CA: Stanford University Press, 1980.

———. *Outline for a Theory of Practice*. Translated by Richard Nice. Cambridge Studies in Social and Cultural Anthropology, vol. 16, ed. Ernest Gellner. Cambridge: Cambridge University Press, 1977.

Buell, Lawrence. *The Environmental Imagination: Thoreau, Nature Writing and American Culture*. Cambridge, MA: Harvard University Press, Belknap Press, 1995.

Burroughs, Julian. *Recollections of John Burroughs*. Edited by Elizabeth Burroughs Kelley. New York: Riverby Books, 1991.

Canclini, Néstor García. *Hybrid Cultures: Strategies for Entering and Leaving Modernity*. Translated by Christopher L. Chiappari and Silvia L. López. Minneapolis: University of Minnesota Press, 1995.

Carter, Paul. *The Spiritual Crisis of the Gilded Age*. Dekalb: Northern Illinois University Press, 1971.

Carter, Stephen L. *The Culture of Disbelief: How American Law and Politics Trivialize Religious Devotion*. Rev. ed. New York: Anchor Books, 1994.

Casey, Edward S. *Getting Back into Place*. Bloomington: Indiana University Press, 1993.

Chidester, David. *Patterns of Action: Religion and Ethics in Comparative Perspective* Belmont, CA: Wadsworth, 1987.

Chidester, David, and Edward T. Linenthal, eds. *American Sacred Space*. Religion in North America, ed. Catherine L. Albanese and Stephen J. Stein. Bloomington: Indiana University Press, 1995.

Cimino, Richard, and Don Lattin. *Shopping for Faith*. San Francisco: Jossey-Bass, 1998.

Clifford, James. *The Predicament of Culture*. Cambridge, MA: Harvard University Press, 1988.

Clifford, James, and George Marcus, eds. *Writing Culture: The Poetics and Politics of Ethnography*. Berkeley: University of California Press, 1986.

Crepeau, Richard C. *Melbourne Village: The First Twenty-five Years (1946–1971)*. Gainesville: University Press of Florida, 1988.

Cronon, William, ed. *Uncommon Ground: Rethinking the Human Place in Nature*. New York: W. W. Norton, 1995.

Crunden, Robert M. *Ministers of Reform: The Progressive's Achievement in American Civilization, 1889–1920.* New York: Basic Books, 1982.

Curtin, Deane W., and Lisa M. Heldke, eds. *Cooking, Eating, Thinking: Transformative Philosophies of Food.* Bloomington: Indiana University Press, 1992.

Curtis, Susan. *A Consuming Faith: The Social Gospel and Modern American Culture.* New Studies in American Intellectual and Cultural History, ed. Thomas Bender. Baltimore, MD: Johns Hopkins University Press, 1991.

Cushman, Philip. *Constructing the Self, Constructing America: A Cultural History of Psychotherapy.* New York: Addison-Wesley, 1995.

Cutler, Donald R., ed. *The Religious Situation: 1968.* Boston: Beacon Press, 1968.

de Certeau, Michel. *The Practice of Everyday Life.* Translated by Steven Rendell. Berkeley: University of California Press, 1984.

Devall, Bill, and George Sessions. *Deep Ecology.* Salt Lake City: Gibbs Smith, 1985.

Diggins, John Patrick. *The Rise and Fall of the American Left.* New York: W. W. Norton, 1992.

Donahue, Brian. *Reclaiming the Commons: Community Farms and Forests in a New England Town.* New Haven: Yale University Press, 1999.

Douglas, Mary. *Implicit Meanings.* London: Routledge and Kegan Paul, 1978.

Douglas, Mary, and Steven Tipton, eds. *Religion and America: Spirituality in a Secular Age.* Boston: Beacon Press, 1983.

Douglas, Mary, and Aaron Wildavsky. *Risk and Culture: An Essay on the Selection of Technological and Environmental Dangers.* Berkeley: University of California Press, 1982.

Edgell, Stephen, Kevin Hetherington, and Alan Warde, eds. *Consumption Matters.* Oxford: Blackwell, 1996.

Elder, John C., and Steven C. Rockefeller. *Spirit and Nature: Why the Environment Is a Religious Issue.* Boston: Beacon Press, 1992.

Ellwood, Robert. *The Sixties Spiritual Awakening: American Religion Moving from Modern to Postmodern.* New Brunswick, NJ: Rutgers University Press, 1994.

Evernden, Neil. *Natural Alien.* 2nd ed. Toronto: University of Toronto Press, 1993.

Finke, Roger, and Rodney Stark. *The Churching of America, 1776–1990: Winners and Losers in Our Religious Economy.* New Brunswick, NJ: Rutgers University Press, 1992.

Fox, Richard, and T. J. Jackson Lears, eds. *The Culture of Consumption: Critical Essays in American History, 1880–1980,* New York: Pantheon Books, 1983.

Fox, Warwick. *Towards a Transpersonal Ecology.* Boston: Shambhala Books, 1990.

Freyfogle, Eric, ed. *The New Agrarianism.* Washington, DC: Island Press, 2001.

Fuller, Robert C. *Spiritual, but Not Religious: Understanding Unchurched America.* Oxford: Oxford University Press, 2002.

Geertz, Clifford. *The Interpretation of Cultures*. New York: Basic Books, 1970. Reprint, 1973.

Giddens, Anthony. *The Consequences of Modernity*. Stanford, CA: Stanford University Press, 1990.

Gittlin, Todd. *The Sixties: Years of Hope, Days of Rage*. New York: Bantam, 1987.

Golde, Peggy, ed. *Women in the Field: Anthropological Experiences*. 2nd ed. Berkeley: University of California Press, 1986.

Gottlieb, Roger S. *This Sacred Earth: Religion, Nature, Environment*. London: Routledge, 1996.

Gould, Peter. *Early Green Politics: Back to Nature, Back to the Land and Socialism in Britain, 1880–1900*. New York: St. Martin's Press, 1988.

Guarneri, Carl J. *The Utopian Alternative: Fourierism in Nineteenth-Century America*. Ithaca: Cornell University Press, 1991. Reprint, Cornell Paperbacks, 1994.

Hall, David D. *Worlds of Wonder, Days of Judgment: Popular Religious Belief in Early New England*. Cambridge, MA: Harvard University Press, 1990.

Hammond, Phillip, ed. *The Sacred in a Secular Age*. Berkeley: University of California Press, 1985.

Hayes, Samuel P. *Conservation and the Gospel of Efficiency: The Progressive Conservation Movement, 1890–1920*. Cambridge, MA: Harvard University Press, 1959.

Hervieu-Léger, Danièle. *Le retour à la nature: "Au fond de la forêt, l'état."* Paris: Seuil, 1979.

Hessel, Dieter, ed. *After Nature's Revolt: Eco-justice and Theology*. Philadelphia: Fortress Press, 1992.

Hofstadter, Richard. *The Age of Reform*. New York: Random House, 1955. Reprint, Vintage Books, 1961.

Holmes, Steven J. *The Young John Muir: An Environmental Biography*. Madison: University of Wisconsin Press, 1999.

Houriet, Robert. *Getting Back Together*. New York: Coward, McCann and Geoghegan, 1971.

Hovenkamp, Herbert. *Science and Religion in America, 1800–1860*. Philadelphia: University of Pennsylvania Press, 1978.

Hutchison, William R., ed. *Between the Times: The Travail of the Protestant Establishment in America, 1900–1960*. Cambridge: Cambridge University Press, 1989. Reprint, 1990.

———. *The Modernist Impulse*. Durham, NC: Duke University Press, 1992.

Jacob, Jeffrey. *New Pioneers: The Back-to-the-Land Movement and the Search for a Sustainable Future*. University Park: Pennsylvania State University Press, 1997.

James, Alison, Jenny Hockey, and Andrew Dawson, eds. *After Writing Culture: Epistemology and Praxis in Contemporary Anthropology*. New York: Routledge, 1997.

James, William. *The Varieties of Religious Experience*. Modern Library Edition. New York: Random House, 1936.

Judd, Richard W. *Common Lands, Common People: The Origins of Conservation in Northern New England*. Cambridge, MA: Harvard University Press, 1997.

Kanter, Rosabeth Moss. *Commitment and Community: Communes and Utopias in Sociological Perspective*. Cambridge, MA: Harvard University Press, 1972.

Kanze, Edward. *The World of John Burroughs*. San Francisco: Sierra Club Books, 1996.

Kolodny, Annette. *The Land before Her: Fantasy and Experience of the American Frontiers, 1630–1860*. Chapel Hill: University of North Carolina, 1984.

Kramer, Mark. *Three Farms: Making Milk, Meat and Money from the American Soil*. Cambridge, MA: Harvard University Press, 1987.

Lane, Belden. *Landscapes of the Sacred: Geography and Narrative in American Spirituality*. Isaac Hecker Studies in Religion and American Culture, ed. John A. Coleman. New York: Paulist Press, 1988.

Lasch, Christopher. *The Culture of Narcissism*. New York: W. W. Norton, 1978.

———. *The True and Only Heaven: Progress and Its Critics*. New York: W. W. Norton, 1991.

Lears, T. J. Jackson. *No Place of Grace: Antimodernism and the Transformation of American Culture 1880–1920*. New York: Pantheon Books, 1981. Reprint, Chicago: University of Chicago Press, 1994.

Lutts, Ralph. *The Nature Fakers: Wildlife, Science and Sentiment*. Golden, CO: Fulcrum Press, 1990.

Lynd, Robert S., and Helen Merrell Lynd. *Middletown: A Study in Contemporary American Culture*. New York: Harcourt, Brace and Co., 1929.

Lyon, Thomas. *This Incomperable Lande: A Book of American Nature Writing*. New York: Penguin, 1991.

Marcuse, George, and Michael Fischer. *Anthropology as Cultural Critique*. Chicago: University of Chicago Press, 1986.

Marsden, George. *Understanding Fundamentalism and Evangelicalism*. Grand Rapids, MI: William B. Eerdmans, 1991.

Marsh, George Perkins. *Man and Nature*. New York: Scribner's, 1864. Reprint, Cambridge, MA: Harvard University Press, 1965.

Marsh, Jan. *Back to the Land: The Pastoral Impulse in England, from 1880 to 1914*. London: Quartet Books, 1982.

Marty, Martin. *Modern American Protestantism and Its World*. Vol. 6, *Protestantism and Social Christianity*. Munich: K. G. Saur, 1992.

———. *Modern American Religion*. Vol. 1, *The Irony of It All, 1893–1919*. Chicago: University of Chicago Press, 1986.

Marx, Leo. *The Machine in the Garden: Technology and the Pastoral Ideal in America.* New York: Oxford University Press, 1964.

May, Henry. *The End of American Innocence: A Study of the First Years of Our Own Time.* New York: Knopf, 1959.

McCaig, Donald. *The American Homeplace.* New York: Crown Publishers, 1992.

McCarthy, Fiona. *The Simple Life: C. R. Ashbee in the Cotswolds.* Berkeley: University of California Press, 1981.

McDannell, Colleen. *The Christian Home in Victorian America, 1840–1900.* Bloomington: Indiana University Press, 1986.

McFague, Sallie. *The Body of God.* Minneapolis: Fortress Press, 1993.

———. *Models of God.* Philadelphia: Fortress Press, 1987.

McGuire, Meredith B., with Debra Kantor. *Ritual Healing in Suburban America.* New Brunswick, NJ: Rutgers University Press, 1988. Reprint, 1991.

Melville, Keith. *Communes in the Counter Culture.* New York: William Morrow, 1972.

Merchant, Carolyn. *Radical Ecology.* New York: Routledge, 1992.

Miller, James. *Democracy Is in the Streets: From Port Huron to the Siege of Chicago.* 2nd ed. Cambridge, MA: Harvard University Press, 1994.

Miller, Timothy, ed. *America's Alternative Religions.* SUNY Series in Religious Studies, ed. Harold Coward. Albany: State University of New York Press, 1995.

Miller, Perry. *Nature's Nation.* Cambridge, MA: Harvard University Press, Belknap Press, 1967.

Minus, Paul. *Walter Rauschenbusch: American Reformer.* New York: Macmillan, 1988.

Moore, James. *The Post-Darwinian Controversies.* Cambridge: Cambridge University Press, 1979.

Moore, R. Laurence. *Selling God: American Religion in the Marketplace of Culture.* New York: Oxford University Press, 1994.

Mullin, Bruce, and Russell Richey, eds. *Reimagining Denominationalism: Interpretive Essays.* New York: Oxford University Press, 1994.

Naess, Arne. *Ecology, Community and Lifestyle.* Translated by David Rothenburg. Cambridge: Cambridge University Press, 1989.

Nash, Roderick. *The Rights of Nature: A History of Environmental Ethics.* Madison: University of Wisconsin Press, 1989.

———. *Wilderness and the American Mind.* 3rd ed. New Haven, CT: Yale University Press, 1972.

Norwood, Vera. *Made from This Earth: American Woman and Nature.* Chapel Hill: University of North Carolina Press, 1993.

Numbers, Ronald. *Darwinism Comes to America.* Cambridge, MA: Harvard University Press, 1998.

Obeyesekere, Gananath. *Medusa's Hair: An Essay on Personal Symbols and Religious Experience*. Chicago: University of Chicago Press, 1981. Reprint, 1984.

Oelschlaeger, Max, ed. *The Wilderness Condition: Essays on Environment and Civilization*. Washington, DC: Island Press, 1992.

Orsi, Robert. *The Madonna of 115th Street*. New Haven, CT: Yale University Press, 1985.

Osborne, Clifford Hazeldine. *The Religion of John Burroughs*. Boston: Houghton Mifflin, Riverside Press, 1930.

Patten, Simon. *The Social Basis of Religion*. New York: Macmillan, 1911.

Pells, Richard H. *Radical Visions and American Dreams: Culture and Social Thought in the Depression Years*. Middletown, CT: Wesleyan University Press, 1984.

Pierce, Linda Breen. *Choosing Simplicity*. Carmel, CA: Gallagher Press, 2000.

Prothero, Stephen. *The White Buddhist: The Asian Odyssey of Henry Steel Olcott*. Religion in North America, ed. Catherine Albanese and Stephen J. Stein. Bloomington: Indiana University Press, 1996.

Rauschenbusch, Walter. *Christianity and the Social Crisis*. New York: Macmillan, 1910.

Renehan, Edward, Jr. *John Burroughs: An American Naturalist*. Post Mills, VT: Chelsea Green Publishers, 1992.

Reuther, Rosemary Radford. *Gaia and God: An Ecofeminist Theology of Earth Healing*. San Francisco: HarperCollins, 1992.

Robinson, David. *Apostle of Culture*. Philadelphia: University of Pennsylvania Press, 1982.

Roof, Wade Clark. *A Generation of Seekers: The Spiritual Journeys of the Baby Boom Generation*. San Francisco: HarperCollins, 1993.

Rosaldo, Renato. *Culture and Truth: The Remaking of Social Analysis*. Boston: Beacon Press, 1989.

Rozak, Theodore. *The Making of a Counter Culture*. Garden City, NY: Doubleday, 1969.

Sale, Kirkpatrick. *The Green Revolution: The American Environmental Movement, 1962–1992*. New York: Hill and Wang, 1993.

Saltmarsh, John. *Scott Nearing: An Intellectual Biography*. Philadelphia: Temple University Press, 1991.

Schama, Simon. *Landscape and Memory*. New York: Knopf, 1995.

Scheffer, Victor. *The Shaping of Environmentalism in America*. Seattle: University of Washington Press, 1991.

Schmidt, Leigh Eric. *Consumer Rites: The Buying and Selling of American Holidays*. Princeton, NJ: Princeton University Press, 1995.

Schmitt, Peter J. *Back to Nature: The Arcadian Myth in Urban America*. Oxford: Oxford University Press, 1969.

Schor, Juliette B. *The Overspent American*. New York: Basic Books, 1998.

——————. *The Overworked American: The Unexpected Decline of Leisure*. New York: Basic Books, 1991.

Segal, Jerome. *Graceful Simplicity*. Berkeley: University of California Press, 1999.

Shabecoff, Philip. *A Fierce Green Fire: The American Environmental Movement*. New York: Hill and Wang, 1993.

Sherman, Steve, ed. *A Scott Nearing Reader*. Metuchen, NJ: Scarecrow Press, 1989.

Shi, David. *The Simple Life: Plain Living and High Thinking in American Culture*. Oxford: Oxford University Press, 1985. Reprint, 1986.

Smith, Jonathan Z. *To Take Place: Towards Theory in Ritual*. Chicago Studies in the History of Judaism, ed. Jacob Neusner et al. Chicago: University of Chicago Press, 1987. Reprint, 1992.

Soulé, Michael, and Gary Lease. *Reinventing Nature? Responses to Postmodern Deconstruction*. Washington, DC: Island Press, 1995.

Spencer, Colin. *The Heretic's Feast: A History of Vegetarianism*. London: Fourth Estate, 1994.

Spickard, James, J. Shawn Landres, and Meredith McGuire, eds. *Personal Knowledge and Beyond: Reshaping the Ethnography of Religion*. New York: New York University Press, 2002.

Swatos, William, and Daniel V. A. Olson, eds. *The Secularization Debate*. Lanham, MD: Rowman and Littlefield, 2000.

Thomas, John L. *Alternative America: Henry George, Edward Bellamy, Henry Demarest Lloyd and the Adversary Tradition*. Cambridge, MA: Harvard University Press, Belknap Press, 1983.

Thomas, Keith. *Man and the Natural World: Changing Attitudes in England, 1500–1800*. London: Allen Lane, 1983. Reprint, Oxford: Oxford University Press, 1996.

Tipton, Steven. *Getting Saved from the Sixties*. Berkeley: University of California Press, 1982. Reprint, 1984.

Tuan, Yi Fu. *Topophilia: A Study of Environmental Perception, Attitudes, and Values*. Englewood Cliffs, NJ: Prentice-Hall, 1974.

Turner, James. *Without God, Without Creed: The Origins of Unbelief in America*. New Studies in American Intellectual and Cultural History, ed. Thomas Bender. Baltimore, MD: Johns Hopkins University Press, 1985. Reprint, Johns Hopkins Paperbacks, 1986.

Turner, Victor. *The Ritual Process*. Ithaca, NY: Cornell University Press, 1969. Reprint, Cornell Paperbacks, 1977.

Tweed, Thomas. *The American Encounter with Buddhism, 1844–1912: Victorian Culture and the Limits of Dissent*. Religion in North America, ed. Catherine L. Albanese and Stephen J. Stein. Bloomington: Indiana University Press, 1992.

Veysey, Laurence. *The Communal Experience: Anarchist and Mystical Communities in Twentieth-Century America*. New York: Harper and Row, 1973. Reprint, Chicago: University of Chicago Press, 1978.

Walker, Charlotte Zoe. *Sharp Eyes: John Burroughs and American Nature Writing*. Syracuse, NY: Syracuse University Press, 2000.

Wharton, James. *Crusaders for Fitness: The History of American Health Reformers*. Princeton, NJ: Princeton University Press, 1982.

White, Ronald C., and C. Howard Hopkins. *The Social Gospel, Reform and Religion in Changing America*. Philadelphia: Temple University Press, 1976.

Williams, Raymond. *The Country and the City*. Oxford: Oxford University Press, 1973. Reprint, 1975.

Wilson, Bryan. *Religion in Sociological Perspective*. Oxford: Oxford University Press, 1982.

Worster, Donald. *Nature's Economy: A History of Ecological Ideas*. 2nd ed. Studies in Environment and History, ed. Donald Worster and Alfred Crosby. Cambridge: Cambridge University Press, 1985.

————. *The Wealth of Nature: Environmental History and the Ecological Imagination*. New York: Oxford University Press, 1993.

Wuthnow, Robert. *Acts of Compassion: Caring for Others and Helping Ourselves*. Princeton, NJ: Princeton University Press, 1991.

————. *After Heaven: Spirituality in America since the 1950s*. Berkeley: University of California Press, 1998.

————. *Producing the Sacred: An Essay on Public Religion*. Public Expressions of Religion in America, ed. Conrad Cherry. Urbana: University of Illinois Press, 1994.

————. *Sharing the Journey: Small Groups and America's New Quest for Community*. New York: Free Press, 1994.

————, ed. *"I Come Away Stronger": How Small Groups Are Shaping American Religion*. Grand Rapids, MI: William B. Eerdmans, 1994.

INDEX

Writers are referred to by surname. (In subentries, Scott and Helen Nearing are referred to by first name.)

ambivalence (*continued*)
homesteaders, 61–62; as resistant
to culture and culturally determined, 9, 92–93, 105–7; of social
reform, 173–78, 188–90; of technology juxtaposed to homesteading, 181–88; varieties of,
228–29
Ammerman, Nancy T., 248n10, 305–
6n29
Angier, Bradford, 25, 191–92, 298n65
Angier, Vena, 25, 191–92, 298n65
Anthony, Susan B., 213
anthropocentrism: Berry's, 88–89,
268n78; Burroughs's, 118, 137,
275–76n35
antimodernism movements, 196–99,
299n77
Arden (Del.) community: goals of,
144–45; homesteading as reclaiming best of, 164, 172, 188; legacy
of, 191, 194; limits of, 146–47;
Nearings at, 10, 79, 139–40, 215;
Scott's novella (*Arden Town*) about,
145–46, 167
art and creativity: Arts and Crafts movement and, 197; cabinetmaking as,
52–53; nature in tension with, 43–
44; relocating religion in, 197
asceticism: adjustments to, 194; ambiguities of, 203; emphasis on, 28,
196, 214–15, 237; and food, 78–
81; limits of, 149; meaning-
making in, 218; persistent practice
of, 198; pleasure vs., 45, 54, 88.
See also self-discipline
Ashbee, C. R., 137
Asian religious traditions: Bolton Hall's
interest in, 179; contemplation/ac-
tion continuum in, 187–88; current interests in, xiv; Nearings' interests in, xiii, 88; walking garden
and, 46
Atlantic Monthly, 119, 275–76n35
authorship. *See* narratives and texts of
homesteading; writing
automobiles, 134, 191, 280n96

back-to-nature movement: advocacy of,
139–40; Back-to-the-Land distinguished from, 162, 293–94n30;
Burroughs and, 109, 111, 133–38;
continuum of, 144–45; democratic
view of, 174–75, 176, 294n30;
historical context of, 112–13, 190;
popularity of, 159–60; process in,
110; Scott's cautions about, 161–
62; Slabsides as symbol of, 133–
38; as solution to social problems,
141–44; turn-of-the-century interests in, 111–12, 140–44
Back-to-the-Land movement: back-to-
nature distinguished from, 162,
293–94n30; confusions about,
250n17; emergence of, 173; Nearings as model for, xiv, 252n20;
questions about, 104–5; as radical
dissent, 158–60; social and historical contexts of, 8–9; "spiritual"
readings of nature in, 34
Bailey, Liberty Hyde, 293n24, 305n28
Baptists, 202
Barrus, Clara: on Burroughs, 116, 123,
124–25, 134, 271nn1,6, 272n8,
277n51, 279n77; Burroughs's relationship with, 271n2; on Emerson
and Burroughs, 119; on pilgrims,
271n4; on Thoreau and Burroughs,
274n23
Beecher, Catherine, 210
being vs. seeing, 57–59
Belanger, Diane, 23
Belanger, Jd, 23
Bell, Catherine, 65, 68–69, 249n15,
261n12
Bellah, Robert: on Berry, 307n44; as
communitarian, 232, 233; on
community, 97, 101; on concern
for nature as expressive individualism, 97; on individualism and
community, 97–99; on lifestyle enclaves, 232–33; on practices, 98;
ideal model of, 98–99; on
Sheilaism, 227, 306n36
Bentham, Jeremy, 81

Benton, Myron, 116, 120, 121

Berger, Peter, 59, 249n15, 255–56n53

Berkowitz, Nancy, xix

Berry, Tanya, 301n2

Berry, Wendell: anthropocentrism of, 88–89, 268n78; Bolton Hall as precursor to, 176; Burroughs as precursor to, 112, 116, 126; choices of, 1; on church as institution, 154; conversion to homesteading, 27; Coperthwaite compared with, 204; on culture and agriculture, 47; eating rituals of, 81–83, 84–85, 265n57; as exemplar, 307n44; on farming, 30, 35; on gender, 195, 301n2; Helen on, 84–85, 266–67n66; on home, 20; on Hubbards, 199–200, 262n19; on professionalization, 188; radical Christian stance of, 262n19; religious terminology of, 104; self-awareness and reflexivity of, 195; on specialization, 288n65; spiritual materialism of, 90; on spiritual practice, 228; on tobacco farming, 266n65; works: *Farming: A Handbook*, 89; *What Are People For?*, 266–67n66

biblical references: Bolton Hall's, 179–80, 292–94n30; Borsodi's, 184; Burroughs's, 117, 122–23, 135, 136; Scott's, 151–53

biocentrism, 305n28

bioregionalism, 307n44

body: cultural views of, 207, 208–10; embracing of, 87; knowledge of, 91; as sacred, 255n52; sauna tradition as habit of, 92; self-culture as activity of, 121; as temple, 267n71; as vessel for self, 88

Bok, Edward, 141, 282n4

Borsodi, Myrtle Mae: gender roles and, 210–14; homesteading of, 182–84

Borsodi, Ralph: background of, 26, 181, 184; Bolton Hall compared with, 186–87; Burroughs compared with, 112, 187; choices of, 1; conversion to homesteading, 181–82,

185; Coperthwaite compared with, 222–23; on dependence, 184; eugenics and, 293n29; on farm industry, 295n40; gender roles and, 210–14; homesteading of, 182–84; as influence, 194, 295–96n52; on land issues, 174–75, 176, 186, 190–91; on maturity, 251n9; nostalgia of, 295n46; organizational activities of, 298n63; on personal revitalization, 187–88; principles of, 184–86, 192; progressivism and, 189; on ritual, 185; School of Living and, 18, 182, 185–86, 251n12; simplicity ethic and, 189–90, 296n57; tools used by, 182–83, 185, 196, 211, 213–14, 295n46; on urban development, 283n8; works: *Distribution Age, The*, 181; *Flight from the City, The*, 181–88; *New Accounting, The*, 181; *This Ugly Civilization*, 182, 296n52

Borsodi, William, 181, 182

Bostic, James, Jr., 81

Bourdieu, Pierre, 76, 221, 249n15, 262n29

Boy Scouts, 142–43, 283n10

breadmaking: emphasis on, 208; Helen's aversion to, 214; meaning-making and, 55–59

Bromfield, Louis, 89–90, 191, 297–98n63

Brooks, Earl Amos, 142–43

Buck, Pearl, 38

Buddhism, 187–88

Buell, Lawrence, 257n2, 260nn33,36, 268n78, 276n35

Burroughs, Chauncey, 122–23

Burroughs, Hiram, 110

Burroughs, John: ambivalence of, 106; anthropocentrism of, 118, 137, 275–76n35; biographies of, 270–71n1; Bolton Hall compared with, 176, 178, 187, 293–94n30; Borsodi compared with, 187; character and personality of, 273–74n15; contradictions and tensions

52; symbols of, 37, 259n21. *See also* institutional religion; religion; religious language and concepts

Christian Science, 278n61

city: Burroughs on, 134–35; call to reform economics of, 295n40; country distinguished from, 106, 134–35; growth of, 142, 283n8; Hall on, 291n8; landownership in, 173–74, 181–82; nature as relief from, 111–12; as testing ground, 134–35; as ugly civilization, 182. *See also* country; rural life

class: expectations based in, 220–21; of homesteaders, 218–20; as influence, 230–31

comfort. *See* pleasure

commercialism and commodification: of do-it-yourself pragmatics, 299–300n80; of homesteading, 198–99, 218, 220; retreat from, 129–30; struggles against, 2. *See also* capitalism; consumer culture

communism: as religion without God, 287n54, 290n83

Communist Party: racial integration and, 164–65; Scott's disenchantment with, 287n57; Scott's involvement in, 140, 157

communitarians, 232–34, 307n46

community: boundaries of, 95–96; centrality of, 18–19, 20; commitments to, 232–34; eating practices and, 75, 76, 84; festivals' role in, 185; fostering of, 28; institutional religion and, 98–99; intentional, 186; interdependence of, 97–101; loss/recovery of, 29–30; redefinition of, 84; single-tax movement and, 10, 79, 139–40, 144, 175; vision of, 194. *See also* Arden (Del.) community; Sauna crowd

community land trust (concept), 186

compost bins, 42, 51, 54

Conscious Living, Conscious Dying (documentary), 267n73

consumer culture: accommodation to, 177–78, 179, 192–93; advertising's role in, 181; alternative to, 161; critique of, 49, 162, 213; difficulties of rejecting, xiv–xv, 11–12; homesteading as dissent from, 137–38; individual choice in, 75; persistence of, 218; reducing impact of, 184, 186; rejection of/resistance to, 2, 22, 28, 189–90, 197–98, 218, 232; religion in, 255–56n53. *See also* capitalism; commercialism and commodification; materialism

consumption and communion theme, 120–21

conversion: of Berry to homesteading, 27; of Borsodi to homesteading, 181–82, 185; of Bromfield and Leopold, 298n63; of Burroughs to homesteading, 116, 271–72n8; complications of, 105–6; as first step, 187; nature's role in, 230; quest for authentic experience in, 197; in religious traditions, 123, 143; sauna tradition as embodiment of, 96–97; of Scott to homesteading, 160–63; turn to farming and land as, 112–13, 117–18, 136; writing as extension of, 24–27, 220

Conwell, Russell, 154–55, 156, 286n38

Coperthwaite, Bill: on attitudes toward nature, 23; Borsodi compared with, 222–23; Burroughs as precursor to, 112; choices of, 17–18; eating rituals of, 76, 204; on family farm, 16–17; on gender, 301n2; on homemaking, 15–16, 204, 205; homestead of, 13–15; influences on, 194; on Scott, 289n80; self-awareness and reflexivity of, 195

Corey, Paul, 5

Cosmopolitan (magazine), 135

Cott, Nancy, 215–16, 302n7, 304nn22,25

cottage industry. *See* home-based production

countercultural homesteaders, 34–36, 67, 99; concessions of, 300n81; gender roles and, 205, 302n5; historical context of, 190; preferences of, 296n52; themes of, 190–91

country: call to reform economics of, 295n40; city distinguished from, 106; as cultural category, 59. *See also* city; rural life

country life movement, 293n24

Countryside and Small Stock Journal, 23, 252–53n27, 304–5n27

Cromwell, Cassie, 97

Cronon, William, 142

cultivated ignorance (concept), 58, 219

cult of domesticity, 216, 304n22

cult of nature, 63

cult of progress, 218

cultural critique: Burroughs on, 133–34; homemaking as, 216–17; homesteading as, 4, 137–38; Nearing model of, 48; particular commitments in, 98; search for truth and light in, 47–48

cultural gestures: concept of, 250n17; context of, 196–97; gardening as, 222; home-based production as, 197–98; theorizing and, 220–21. *See also* homesteading

cultural reform: baking as, 216–17; escape from society juxtaposed to, 159; hopes for, xvii; nature's role in, 8; negotiations of, 202–3; space for thinking about, 15; turn to farming and land as, 112; writing of homesteading as, 195. *See also* social change

cultural work: as culturally determined, 105–7; daily life of homesteading as, 171–73; eating as, 75, 77

culture: agrarianism linked to, 47; anxieties about Christianity and secularization in, 126; crisis of, 81–82; embodied practice as alternative to, 135–36; engagement with and re-treat from, 4, 173, 200, 202–3, 229; food and eating as drudgery in, 82; homesteading as resistant to and determined by, 9, 92–93, 105–7, 111–12; Jeffersonianism in, 175, 233; keeping distance from, 13; literature on, 240–41; meaning of nature in, xx, 3, 9–10, 221; as not having grown up, 81; religion and spirituality in, xx, 9–10; ritualizations in response to, 83–84; short-term thinking of, 231; as stage for work of homesteading, 103; strengths/limits of, 140; symbolic commentaries on, 28

daily lived experience: of ambivalences, 104; approach to, 7–10; authenticity in, 237–40; balance in, 112; Burroughs's improvisations in, 129–32; commitment to, 230; concept of, 6–7; conflicts in, 159–60; grace and works in, 160–63; integrated activities of, 11; of living close to nature, 100–101; nature as sacred in, 32–37; Nearings' four-four-four pattern of, 39, 207; negotiations and compromise in, 54, 205–18; religious concepts for, 4, 9; ritualization of, 65, 68–69, 72–73, 100, 135–36; as sacred, 58–59; sanctification in, 28; scholarship and real life linked in, xix, xxi; search for truth and light in, 47–48; as spiritual and cultural work, 171–73. *See also* living close to nature ideal; ritual

dairy products, 79, 81, 265–66n60

Darrow, Clarence, xiii, 282n4

Darwin, Charles, 112, 124–25, 137, 171

death: grieving of, 178, 292n18; naturalness of, 31, 87–88, 91, 178–79, 267–68n73. *See also* immortality and afterlife

Deep Ecology theory, 72, 118

environment: limits of, 231–32; Scott's hopes for improving, 158–60; protection of, 276n35. *See also* Mother Earth; nature

environmentalism: agrarianism as part of, 22–23, 252n24; Christian discourse and, 195; commitment to, 23; Leopold and Bromfield as anticipating, 191; precursors to, 175; as social good that transcends self in, 232–34; utilitarianism vs., 221

environmental problems: meaning-making and, 229, 231; nature craze as response to, 142; rejection of, 28

Episcopalians, 202

equality: in access to land and nature, 174–75, 176; gender difference vs., 217–18

ethics: ambiguities of, 203; differences in, 48–50; engaged practice vs., 232; Leopold's land, 297n62; of pleasure, 82–83; of sauna tradition, 94–95; science linked to, 191; vegetarianism as ritualization of, 78. *See also* simple living ethic

ethnographic bias, 302n7

Eucharist, 77

eugenics, 293n29

evangelicalism: rejection of, 158–59; of Sauna crowd, 95–96; skepticism about, 293–94n30

evil: resistance to, 163

exceptionalism: Burroughs on, 127–28; in immortality ideal, 87–88; as influence, 230; of living close to nature, 88–89; of Nearings, 87; of Sauna crowd, 96; sectarian, 9–10; skepticism about, 180–81

expressive individualism (concept), 97, 232

factory production, 183–84, 213

farming life: appeal of, 114–16; as dissent, 89; as fostering knowledge of nature, 118; gardening compared with, 5; hiring labor for, 177–78; lament for, 16–17; "playing" at,

65–74, 218; religious aspects of, 34–35, 122–23; as ritual action, 30, 35, 65–74; self-culture linked to, 120–22; as sign of maturity, 134–35; theological terms for, 35, 86–91, 268n82; Thoreau on, 41; as vocation, 110–13, 116, 136

fascism, 159

fasting: Borsodi's interest in, 182; encouragement of, 78; experiments with, 79; as expression of belief in spiritual continuity, 88; Macfadden on, 78, 263n41; Nearings' interest in, 78–80; Sal's interest in, 83; shaving head compared with, 87; as symbolic commentary, 28

feminists and feminism, 17, 26, 203, 205, 213. *See also* gender roles

festivals, 185. *See also* ritual

Finke, Roger, 255n51

folk arts and techniques, 17–18, 194, 205

food: Berry's views of, 81–85; Borsodi's views of, 182, 185; dairy products, 79, 81, 265–66n60; Helen on, 214, 265n59, 303n18; as locus of health, 78; meaning-making and, 216–17; Nearings' views of, 74–81. *See also* eating; vegan diet; vegetarianism

food preparation: with/without electricity, 183, 216–17; simple, for less work, 214, 303n18. *See also* breadmaking

food production: of Borsodi family, 182; fruit, 167, 272–73n9; lack of knowledge about, 251n2; as means of protest, 197–98; self-sufficiency in, 12, 21–22; Stewart's commitment to, 299–300n80. *See also* farming life; gardening

Ford, Henry, 133, 134, 280n96, 293n29

Forest Farm, xv; animals at, 266n62; cultural critique emanating from, 133; current caretaking of, xiii, xvii–xix, 10, 245n5; educational role of, xiv–xv; four-four-four pattern of activity at, 39, 207; garden of, xix; human waste treatment at, 253n28; nature and art juxtaposed at, 43–44; stone house at, xix, 54, 245–46n6; visitors to, xvi–xvii, xix, 50–51, 237, 245–46n6. *See also* Good Life Center

Forest Lodge, 139, 147 fig.

Foucault, Michel, 261n12

France: neo-rural youth in, 300n81

Free Acres Association, 175–76, 177, 191

Freeborn (S. Nearing): characters in, 168, 290n88; description of, 164–68; publication of, 289–90n83; trial in, 290n89

freedom: anxieties about, 220; from institutions, 160; meanings of, 66; Nearing's/Emerson's "terrible," 306n30; ritual as ordering, 99; self-discipline and, 264–65n51

Friedan, Betty, 210

Friends of the Land, 298n63

fruit crops, 167, 272–73n9

Gandhi, Mohandas, 15, 194

garden: as construction of nature, 42; of Forest Farm, xix; human health linked to, 47; nature vs., 118, 276n35; order vs. disorder in, 42–50; as practical natural resource, 222; preserving produce of, 51–52; religious terminology for, 26, 30, 36; sacralization of, 73–74; stone wall around, 42–44

gardening: alternative style of, 44–49; centrality of, 12–13; competition in, 177; eating rituals linked to, 75–76; farming compared with, 5; gender roles and, 204, 301n2; no-till, 45–49, 258n16; as pragmatic approach to faith, 298n68; religion relocated in, 36; as ritual act, 30, 73–74; spiritual benefits of, 5; symbol of, 24

Garden Way publishing, 192, 298–99n69

Gay, Peter, 37

Geertz, Clifford, xvii, 249n15, 261n14

gender roles: Berry on, 195, 301n2; children's arrival and, 207, 208–10; Coperthwaite on, 204–5; in domestic models, 184; as influence, 230–31; meanings of nature and, 223; mitigation of, 213–14; reimagining of, 216–18; separate spheres ideology and, 216, 304n25; traditional, 205–8, 210–14, 301n2, 302n5, 303n20. *See also* domesticity and homemaking, public/private dynamic

George, Henry: capitalism and socialism of, 174–75, 176, 284n15; as influence, 181; outlook of, 284n15; reference to, 285n28; single tax concept of, 144, 173–74; works: *Progress and Poverty*, 174, 285n28

Giddens, Anthony, 229

Gilded Age, 116, 141. *See also* progressivism

Gladden, Washington, 285n30

God: as authority, 224; Bolton Hall's definition of, 178–79; Burroughs's definition of, 123–24, 127, 277–78n60; Scott's definition of, 153, 286n46; socialism and communism as religion without, 287n54, 290n83. *See also* All-That-Is concept

Goldman, Emma, 175, 176, 178

Good Life (concept): as beyond subsistence, 161; characterizations of, 23–24; discourse on, 239–40; foundation of, 189; liberalism and, 307n46; miniature version of, 139, 144, 164; quest for, 145, 198; reflections on, 101; telos of, 233; values of, 153, 163, 172

Good Life Album of Helen and Scott Nearing, The, 210, 266n62

Good Life Center: community surrounding, 239–40; creation of, xviii, 245n5; garden at, 42–43; goals of, 189; Helen's role in, 215; pilgrims to, 237. *See also* Forest Farm; Sauna crowd

industrialism and industrialization: critique of, 49, 134; language of, 294n30; nature craze as response to, 142; persistence of and resistance to, 218; reducing impact of, 184, 186; rejection of, 28, 158–59; relocation of, 182–85, 187; struggles against, 2; ways of living threatened by, 111

institutional religion: ambivalence about, xx–xxi; capitalism linked to, 153–55, 287n57; critique of, 115–16, 126–27, 153–55; decline of, 32, 255n51; economics and, 285–86n35; everyday vs. ritual practices in, 77; moral hegemony of, 218; nature and, 37; participating in, 98–100; radicalism of (or not), 156–57; rejection of, 30–37, 87, 189, 224, 225–27; religion of service vs., 148–50; resistance to, 228; self-construction in, 97, 101; spirituality in context of, 249n14

Israel: kibbutz in, 40

Jacob, Jeffrey: on back-to-the-land movement, 199, 250n17, 252n20, 252–53n27, 300n81; on home-making and gender, 301n2; on homesteaders' backgrounds, 304–5n27; on leisure, 257–58n4; on Nearings' eating rituals, 265n55

James, William, 59, 78–79; typologies of religious experience, 29–30

Jefferson, Thomas, 175, 233, 268n82. See also yeoman farmer myth

Jezer, Marty, 34, 66–67, 261n11

John Burroughs societies, 133, 280n92

Johnson, Clifton, 278n61, 279–80n85

John the Baptist, 117

Joseph, Stanley, 258n11

Judaism: contemplation/action continuum in, 187–88; as influence, 198, 220–21; practice of, 202; relocation of expressions of, 32–33; return to source in, 29–30; symbolic legacy of, 37; terminology of, 31; turn to nature in, 270n3

Kant, Immanuel, 221, 306n32

Kanz, Edward, 271n2

Kearns, Laurel, 307n48

Knothe, Frank, 78, 268n74

Knothe, Helen. See Nearing, Helen

Knothe, Maria, 78, 268n74

Kraditor, Aileen, 304n22

Krishnamurti (teacher), xiv, 38, 188

Kymlicka, Will, 307n46

labor. See work

LaConte, Ellen, 292n18

Ladies' Home Journal, 141, 282n4

LaGuardia, Fiorello, xiii, 157

land: Borsodi's impact on, 186, 190–91; equal access to, 174–75, 176; farmer's relationship with, 89–90; grounding self in, 52–54, 88–91; human beings as dependent on, 286n35; Leopold's ethic for, 297n62; ownership of, 173–74, 181–82; purchased from Nearings, 50–51; speculation in, 177, 292n14

Laurel, Alicia Bay, 34

Lears, T. J. Jackson, 197–98, 299nn77–78

leisure: Burroughs on, 129, 131, 132; critique of, 257–58n4; Hall on, 294n30; Nearings on, 39, 257–58n4; self-determination in, 129; work balanced with, 136–37, 281n104. See also pleasure

Leopold, Aldo, 191, 297n62, 298n63

Levy, Ruth, 98–99

Liberty School, 251n12

Life Study Fellowship, 298n68

Lifton, Robert J., 265n57

Linenthal, Edward T., 248n11

literature: on Arden community, 145–46, 167; country and city distinguished in, 106; of crisis, 285n27; how-to, 192–93; and nature religion in Scott's fiction, 164–68; on outdoor life, 283n10; of place, 307n44; as source of spiritual guidance, 254n50; on wilderness, 191, 298n65

lived religion (concept), 6–7. *See also* daily lived experience

living close to nature ideal: ambivalence about, 41, 43–44, 49–50, 58–62; balance in, 223; daily lived experience of, 100–101; exceptionalism of, 88–89; gendered decisions about, 217–18; historical context of, 112–13, 137–38; knowledge gained in, 91; meanings of, 222–23; nature's limits/rules for, 99; negotiations in, 205–18; possibilities in, 59–62; redefinition of, 55–59; redemption through, 224, 228, 230; search for, xx, 4, 8, 20, 22–23, 28; self-construction juxtaposed to, 8, 104–5, 198; as solution to social problems, 141–44; subordinated to self-cultivation, 57–59; theological and vocational training in, 117–18, 127; Walden as model for, 40–41. *See also* ambivalence; daily lived experience

Living the Good Life (Nearing and Nearing): as affirmation, 50; on guiding principles, 79; as lab report, 161; popularity of, 55, 244n2; publication of, xiv; republication of, 282n4; *Walden* compared with, 39

Lloyd, Henry Demarest, 134, 136

Logsdon, Gene, 25, 30, 72, 176, 228

Long, William J., 275–76n35

Loomis, John, 210

Loomis, Mildred, 18, 186, 194, 251n12

Lowell, James Russell, 119

Macfadden, Bernarr, 78

Macmillan Company, 157

Manhattan Single Tax Club, 173

Manumit School, 214

Maple Sugar Book, The (Nearing and Near-

ing): description of, 261nn7,11; publication of, 260n6; readers of, xiv; spoof of, 66–67

maple sugaring, 114, 135, 169 fig., 288n73

marriages and partnerships: economic strains on, 206, 207; interdependence in, 204–5; traditional roles in, 203–4, 209

Marty, Martin, 285n28

Marx, Karl, 175

materialism, 29–30, 90–91. *See also* consumer culture

maturity: concept of, 251n9; eating right tied to, 81, 83; farming life as sign of, 134–35; spirituality linked to, 57

May, Henry, 285n30

McCaig, Donald, 267n66

McIntyre, Alasdair, 232, 233

Mcleod, David, 283n10

meat eating: appropriate/inappropriate type of, 85–86; condemnation of, 81; dependence on, 84; moderation and awareness in, 91; nature as authority on, 219; pleasures of, 82–83

meditation, 40

Melbourne (Fla.): intentional community at, 186

men: identity negotiations of, 216. *See also* gender roles

methodology: interviews, 11, 32, 40–41, 237–40; literature utilized, 240–41; personal views and biases, 229, 302n7

Metropolitan, 282n4

Miller, Perry, xx

Mills, Catherine, 22

Minus, Paul H., 286–87n47

models of homesteading: before and after in, 19–20, 24–27; community in, 18–19; continuum of, 186–88, 200, 297–98n63; cultivating self vs. sacralizing nature in, 57–62; definitions in, 20–24; differences in, 48–50; Hall's little-

models of homesteading (*continued*)
lands as, 176–78; living close to
nature in, 20, 22–23; as model alternatives, 163; of Nearings vs.
Burroughs, 106; removal from
dominant society in, 11–13; self-
sufficiency in, 12, 21–22; societal
reform in, 13–18; themes in, 191
modernity: ambivalence about, 124;
homesteading as stance against,
229–30; movements against, 196–
99, 299n77; Thoreau as preface to
critique of, 63–64
mono-diets, 79
morality: ambiguities of, 195–96; of institutional religion, 218; nature as
foundation of, 127, 294n30; stages
of, 176; value of home in, 16,
216. *See also* norms
Morgan, Arthur E., 289n75
Morris, William, 197
mortality. *See* death; immortality and afterlife
Mother Earth: definitions of, 26, 179,
184; equal access to, 174–75, 176;
mural of, 58; use of term, 26, 164,
174
Mother Earth News, 185, 193
Muir, John, 22, 143, 276n35, 283–
84n12
Mungo, Raymond: Burroughs as precursor to, 112; departure of, 256n60;
on gardening, 73–74; spiritual materialism of, 90–91; on spiritual renewal, 36; as Total Loss Farm member, 34; on "truly material," 29–30
muscular Christianity, 78–79, 267n71

Naess, Arne, 72
narratives and texts of homesteading:
approach to, 239–40; compulsion
to write, 220; consumption of,
299n78; as conversion narratives,
24–30; as mini-*Waldens*, 64; production of, 195; sacralization of
nature in, 30–37; uncertain beginnings in, 51–54; *Walden* as, 38–40,

257n1; whites in, 305n27; "why"
in, 8
Nash, Roderick, 297n62
Native American practices: borrowing
from, 257n64; as nature-oriented,
36–37; walking garden reflective
of, 46
"natural": definitions of, 23, 125–26;
loss/recovery of, 29–30
natural rights, 174–75
natural supernaturalism (concept), 230
nature: ambivalence about, 10, 41–44,
49–50, 58–62, 90–91, 164, 221–
23, 230; authority of, 99–101,
219, 224, 229–30; benevolence/
cruelty of, 125, 219, 234, 278n64;
centrality of, 30–37, 101; commitments to, 23, 97–98, 232–34; construction of, xxi, 3, 48, 50, 140–
44, 203, 219, 222, 269n101,
307n48; contemplation of, 118–
19; creativity in tension with, 43–
44; cultivation of, 110, 118, 168–
70 (*see also* farming life); cult of, 63;
development of Burroughs's views
on, 114–16; as divine, 124, 277–
78n60; embracing of, 87; end of,
231; equal access to, 174–75, 176;
experience of self in, 60–62; food
as connected to, 76–77, 263n33;
garden as construction of, 42;
homesteaders as lost/found in, 74;
human control of, 9–10, 161–63,
168–70, 187, 290n92; human impact on, 22–23; human response
to, 49–50; human uses of, 221–23;
incarnational experience of, 60–62;
life values based in, 189; limits of,
231–32; living in vs. visiting, 70–
72; meanings of, 218–19, 221–23;
models of, 48–49; possibilities in,
xvii; questions about nature of,
104; radical immanence of, 203;
religious language for, 4–6, 9; relocating religion in, 7, 32–33, 35–
37; reverence for and resistance to,
88–89; ritualizations in response

to, 83–84; as sacred, 30–37, 50, 248n10, 255n52; self-construction juxtaposed to, 55–59, 106–7, 221–23; as shape-shifting, 59–60; social and historical contexts of, 3; spiritual commitment to, 162–63; spiritual renewal in, 142–43, 158–59, 194; subjectivity of, 235, 307n48; theological and vocational training in, 117–18, 127; transformational experience of, 69–70; turn-of-the-century interests in, 111–12, 140–44; vicarious experience of, 136–37. *See also* gospel of nature; living close to nature ideal; sacralization of nature; theologies; wild nature

nature craze, 133–36, 141–44

Nature Faker debate, 124, 133, 137, 275–76n35

nature religion/spirituality: concept of, 9; daily practices in, 120–21; Hall's treatise on, 179, 292n22; health reform in, 85–86; novel about, 164–68; self-construction in, 97, 101

Nearing, Helen: approach to, 10; asceticism of, 28, 196; author's visits to, 237; background of, xiv; on Berry, 84–85, 266–67n66; Borsodi family compared with, 183, 295n38; Burroughs as precursor to, 112, 130; character modeled on, 168, 290n88; as cultural radical, 210; on death, 292n20; death of, xvii, 245n5, 246n6, 268n73, 292n18; distinguishing self from, 52–54; documentary on, 267n73; domestic views of, 184; early relationship with Scott, 157, 158; eating rituals/discipline of, 76, 77–81, 83–86, 88, 99, 131, 263n32, 265n55; on eating simply for less work, 214, 303n18; fasting of, 87; finances of, 245–46n6, 291n9; on fun, 265n59; health of, 77, 263n34; historical context of, 106; as hostess, 133; as influence, xiv, xv, 194, 252n20, 300n80,

306n39; legacy building of, 259n22; letters to, xix–xx; marriage of, 246n6; on New York vs. Vermont, 164, 289n82; others' ambivalence about, 92, 95–96, 104, 194; "Pay as you go" dictum of, 236 fig.; professional roles of, xvi, 215, 303–4n21; public vs. private, 53, 245–46n6, 303–4n21; in reform context, 188–90; on Robinsons, 193; spiritualism of, xiii, 48, 78, 259n20, 286n46; stonework of, 206; on *Walden*, 38–39, 257n1; work preferences of, 214; works: *Continuing the Good Life* (with Scott), 39, 79, 161, 244n2; *Good Life Album of Helen and Scott Nearing, The*, 210, 266n62; *Light on Aging and Dying*, 267–68n73; *Loving and Leaving the Good Life*, 286n46; *Simple Food for the Good Life*, 214, 265n59, 303n18. *See also* Forest Farm; *Living the Good Life* (Nearing and Nearing)

Nearing, Nellie Seeds, 147 fig.; background of, 214; character modeled on, 168; gender roles and, 303n20; homestead role of, 215; marriage of, 246n6; writing of, 146, 214–15, 282n4

Nearing, Robert, 215

Nearing, Scott: antiwar views of, 156–57, 282n4, 287n56; approach to, 10; asceticism and work ethic of, 28, 196, 214–15, 237; background of, xiii, 30, 154, 160, 188, 288n66; Borsodi family compared with, 183; Burroughs compared with, 112, 130, 137–38, 141, 167, 186; career plans of, 140, 145; choices of, 1, 154, 157–60; conversion to homesteading, 160–63; death of, xvi, 158; distinguishing self from, 52–54; eating rituals/discipline of, 76, 77–81, 83–86, 99, 263n32, 265n55; eugenics and, 293n29; on evil, 163; fasting of, 87; fi-

Pierce, Linda Breen, 305n27

pilgrims and pilgrimages: Bontas as, xvi–xvii; to Bromfield's farm, 89; to Burroughs's cabin, 109, 133–36, 140, 271n4, 280n93; Helen as mentor to, 215; to Nearings' farm, xvi–xvii, 140; number of, xix; purity and, 55; questions of, xix–xx; race of, 305n27

place: belonging to, 27; bioregionalists on, 307n44; commitments to, 62, 232–34; meanings of being in, 20; responsibilities to, 70; walking and observation of, 117–18. See also home and homestead; sacred space

plants: desire to live as, 88

play: concept of, 65–66; farming life and, 65–74, 218; nature as authority on, 219

pleasure: aesthetics of, 92; asceticism vs., 45, 54, 88; of eating, 81–86; emphasis on, 182–83; of farming, 89; of maple cream, 261n7; writing as, 265n59. See also leisure

plenty: search for, 191–93

poets and poetry, 89, 118–20

politics: of countercultural homesteaders, 296n52; gender roles and, 217–18; home and, 16; influences in, 154–55; retreat/engagement dynamic and, 199–200

poor people: Hall's vision for, 176–78, 291n8, 294n30; land issues and, 173–74, 181–82

Porche, Verandah, 34, 35

power plants, 199–200, 222

practice: commitment to, 230; discipline as complement term for, 269–70n103; embodied, as alternative to culture, 135–36; history of, 3–4; in nature spirituality, 120–21; of simple living, 190; of spirituality, 100–101; theorizing about, 220–21; writing vs., 194–95. See also daily lived experience; ritual action; spiritual practice; theory/practice dynamic

Presbyterianism, 178, 179

problem of meaning. See search for meaning

professionalization: embrace of, 215; of homemaking, 210–13; resistance to, 188–89

progress: cult of, 218; definitions of, 106; embrace of/resistance to, 90–91; optimism for, 158, 168–69

progressivism: Arden community in context of, 144–45; Coperthwaite's vision and, 17; health reforms and, 85–86; homesteading experiments belonging to, 189; as influence, 224; nature and progress in, 141, 168–70, 187, 294n30; self-culture and, 79. See also science; Social Gospel movement

public/private dynamic: in age of affluence, 191–93; choices of, 200; in Nearings' lives, 53, 245–46n6, 303–4n21

purity: danger and, 85–86; eating right tied to, 81, 265n55; quest for, 58–59; relaxing demands for, 53–55, 58–59; self as capable of, 267n71. See also asceticism

Quakers (Society of Friends), 150, 227

Quay, Matthew, 154–55

Quayle, William, 283n10

race and racial integration, 164–68, 305n27

Rand School, 214

Rauschenbusch, Walter: on economics and church, 285–86n35; Scott on, 286–87n47; Social Gospel of, 149–50, 152–53

Real Simple magazine, 198

reason and rationalization, 178–79, 197

redemption: Christian view of, 29–30; of living close to nature, 224, 228, 230; of spirit through homesteading, 185–86, 230. See also salvation

Reed, John, xiii, 176

reform: contemporary homesteading as, 193–200; economic, 295n40; home-based efforts in, 194; homesteading as, 186–88; Nearings in context of, 188–90; school movements for, 141. *See also* cultural reform; social change

reinhabitation (concept), 307n44

religion: studies of religion, 249n14, 259n21

religion and religious traditions: approach to, 4–7; choices in, 2–4, 255n51; contemplation/action continuum in, xviii, 187–88, 200; conversion in, 123, 143; critique of, 115–16, 143; decline of, 32, 255n51; definitions of, 6, 33, 248n10; distanced from church, 136–37; of hearth, 185; homesteading as, 193–200; homesteading as dissent from, 137–38, 224–28; "hygienic," 85–86; improvisations of, 178–81; legacies of, 198; literature on, 241; market forces and, 255–56n53; negotiating between science and, 219–20; new movements in, 302n5; reason infused with, 178–79; rebellion against and revitalization of, 34; rejection of, 158–59; relocations of, 7, 32–33, 35–37, 197, 223–28; self-loss and -recovery in, 74; of service, 148–50, 153; spirituality as distinguished from (or not), 7, 248–49n13; stability of, 254–55n51. *See also* Asian religious traditions; Christianity; institutional religion; Judaism

religious language and concepts: departure from, 152–53, 156; in homesteading narratives, 24–30, 180–81; of liberal religions and homesteading, 105, 270n3; of light and dark, 150; for nature, 4–6, 9, 30–37 (*see also* sacralization of nature); on sin against nature, 219,

305n28; in social crises discourse, 285n27; for visit to Forest Farm, xvi–xvii; for walking, 114–16. *See also* conversion; pilgrims and pilgrimages; Social Gospel movement

Renehan, Edward, Jr.: on Burroughs, 114, 121, 134, 270–71n1, 271–72n8, 274–75n30, 277n51, 293n29; on Ford, 280n96

Republican Right, 16

Rich, Louise Dickinson, 25

Rifkin, Jeremy, 286n46

ritual: celebration of equinox, 224–27; decline of, 32; language of, 54–55; literature on, 241; relocation of, 35–37; reversal of/of reversal, 256n54; ritualization vs., 68–69; role of, 75, 76, 99; sacrifice of nature as, 72; search for, 33–34; of soil, 86–91; use of term, 67–68, 260n1. *See also* sacralization of nature

ritual action: ambivalences in, 201–3; attention to form in, 263n32; eating as, 30, 74–86, 75, 77; farming life as, 30, 35, 65–74; gardening as, 30, 73–74; homesteading as, 64; meaning-making in, 232–33; "playing" at farming as, 65–74, 218; as practice-oriented spirituality, 100–101; role of, 65; sharing food and sauna as, 92–96; utilitarian juxtaposed to, 102–3

ritualization: of daily lived experience, 65, 68–69, 72–73, 100, 135–36; of dissent, 76, 92–93; of domestic practices, 130–31; of farming practices, 67–68, 89–90; of homesteading, 93, 96, 172; meanings of, 66; as response to nature and culture, 83–84

Robinson, Carolyn, 192–93, 204–5

Robinson, Ed, 192–93

romanticism, 21, 230, 233, 282n6

Roof, Wade Clark: on nature and individualism, 97; on religious vs. spiritual (terms), 248–49n13; on sacredness of nature and body, 255n52; on spiritual seekers, 4, 227, 297n60

Roosevelt, Franklin D., 289n75

Roosevelt, Theodore, 78–79, 133, 275–76n35, 280n91

Rose, Vivien, 302n5, 303n14, 304n21

rules: breaking of, 67

rural life: Burroughs on, 110; declining population in, 142, 283n8; Ford on, 134; as promotion from city, 134–35. *See also* city; country

Ruskin, John, 197

Russell, Bertrand, 282n4

Russian Revolution, 159

sacralization of nature: concept of, 30–31; expanded/dissolved self and, 73; homesteading's role in, 50; implications of, 198; meaning-making in, 223–28; process of, 32–37; self-cultivation juxtaposed to, 57–62; as theme, 102–3

sacrament. *See* ritual

sacred: discourse on, 6, 85, 254n49; meanings of, 100, 224–28; sauna tradition as, 95

sacred space: concept of, xviii, 248n11; lived religion approach to, 6–7; nature as, 248n10. *See also* sacralization of nature

Saltmarsh, John: on Arden community, 144–45; on eugenics, 293n29; on *Freeborn*, 290n88; on Scott, 288n61, 290n92, 306n30; on vegetarianism, 86; on woman's sphere, 303n20

salvation: homesteading as mode of, 196; skepticism about, 180–81; in Social Gospel, 147. *See also* redemption

sanctification, 28, 187

sanity, 21, 65

Sauna crowd: ambivalence of, 104; evangelicalism of, 95–96; home-steading's meanings for, 105; limits to, 95; openness and flexibility of, 194; on sacred, 224–27; sense of ritual of, 93; as spiritual seekers, 227–28; as unintentional community, 97–98; use of term, 92; writing of, 299n73

sauna tradition: background of, 76, 92–93, 269n88; as embodied affirmation, 96–97; negotiations of, 95–96; oral history of, 93–94; trust established in, 94–95; unintentional community in, 97–98

Schmitt, Peter, 143, 250n17, 283n10, 293–94n30

School of Living, 182, 185, 186, 194, 251n12, 295n38

schools: alternative vision for, 18–19; overvaluation of, 15–16; reform movements for, 141. *See also* education

Schreiner, Olive, 38

Schumacher, E. F., 186

science: Burroughs's approach to, 112, 124–26, 158, 172, 278n61; ethics linked to, 191; fundamentalist uses of, 306n29; negotiating between religion and, 219–20; Scott's approach to, 159, 172; skepticism about, 180–81

search for meaning: ambivalence about institutional religion in, xx–xxi; choices in approach to, 1–4; cultivation of self in, 55–59; home-steading as lived response to, xvii; in literature, 254n50; sense of place in, 20; social and historical contexts of, 8–9; spiritual practice in, 100–101; transformational experience of nature in, 69–70; ways of working through, 7

seasons: celebration of, 116, 120–22, 224–27, 274n27; eating in time with, 80–81, 185; immortality linked to, 128

secularization theory, 254–55n51

security: search for, 184, 193
seeing vs. being, 57–59
self: blurring distinctions between nature and, 70, 72; body as vessel for, 88; Burroughs on, 114–16; ethical commitments beyond, 232–34; loss/recovery of, 29–30, 32–33, 74, 104–5; mature development of, 251n9; nature as power beyond, 127–28; as part of larger force, 224; possibilities in, 59–62; pursuit of nature and pursuit of, 106–7; as re-born in farming, 89–91; relocations of, 52–54; remaking of, 53–59; social reform vs., 230; transformation of, 32–33, 69–70, 228; understanding of, 198; as vessel for water, 73
self-construction, 71 fig.; commitment to, 230; homesteading as, 54–55; living close to nature and, 8, 104–5, 198; nature juxtaposed to, 55–59, 106–7, 221–23; in religion, 97, 101; as theme, 102–3
self-cultivation ideal and self-culture: as bodily activity, 121; Burroughs's devotion to, 110, 273n11; changes fostered in, 55–59; continuing process of, 202–3; cultural sin vs., 28; differences in, 50; Emerson on, 41, 118–19; farming linked to, 120–22; homesteading loyalties beyond, 198–99; language of, 79; nature's role in, 230; philosophical foundations of, 37, 41–42; sacralization of nature juxtaposed to, 57–62; vegetarianism linked to, 86
self-discipline: aesthetics and ethics of pleasure juxtaposed to, 82–83; ambivalence about, 92, 95–96; dynamics of freedom and, 264–65n51; "least harm to least number" ideal in, 80–81; limits of, 99, 269n103; Scott's, 264–65n51, 265n59. See also asceticism
self-sufficiency: definitions of, 21–22, 53; garden as center of, 42; how-to

booklet on, 192–93; knowledge gained in, 91; land issues and, 175, 292n17; limited commitment to, 136–37; questions about, 245–46n6; of restaurant/homestead, 18–19; Scott's emphasis on, 164; self-fulfillment through, 299–300n80; as spiritual practice, 198; tempered version of, 176–78, 294n30; of Thoreau (or not), 39, 41; as time-consuming, 300n81. See also do-it-yourself pragmatics; food production
separate spheres ideology, 17, 216, 304n25. See also gender roles; domesticity and homemaking; public/private dynamic
Seton, Ernest Thompson, 141, 275–76n35
sexual orientation, 201
Sheffield Farms Company (N.Y.), 26
Sheilaism (concept), 227, 306n36
Sheldon, Charles, 152, 286n43
Shi, David: on back-to-nature movement, 143; on Borsodi, 185, 189, 296n57; on countercultural homesteaders, 296n52; on cultural gestures, 250n17; on Hall, 177; on Scott, 288n61; on simple life, 281n103
Silent Hostess, The, 210–11, 212 fig.
simple living ethic: affirmation of, 2; Berry's choice juxtaposed to, 84–85; Burroughs's emphasis on, 129–32, 289n76; celebration of, 135–36; commodification of, 299–300n80; complexities of, 64–65; compromise in, 54; domestic rituals and, 130–31, 279–80n85; ethic of affluence blended with, 192–93; forms of, 23; as minority ethic, 189–90, 296n57; nature's role in, 30–37; participants in, 305n27; popularity of, 244–45n3; as practice, 190; revived interest in, 141; social good that transcends self in, 232–34

sin: divergence from nature as, 219, 305n28; sense of, 28–30

single-tax movement: communities of, 10, 79, 139–40, 144, 175; Hall's involvement in, 173–75. *See also* George, Henry

Slabsides (Burroughs's cabin): as back-to-nature symbol, 133–38; domestic rituals at, 130–31, 279–80n85; labor in soil at, 131–32; as pilgrimage site, 109, 271n4; retreat to, 129; visitors to, 109, 133–36, 271n4, 280n93

Smith, Jonathan Z., 68, 261n12

Snyder, Gary, 20, 76, 263n33

social change: Borsodi's vision of, 181–88; capitalism and, 146–47; Hall's vision of, 175–78; home as base for, 213; homemaking as model for, 203–4; homesteading as model of, 163–64, 180–81; nature craze as response to, 142; retreat/engagement dynamic and, 198–200; Scott's vision of, 157–58; self vs., 230; stability in, 163. *See also* cultural reform

social Darwinism, 180–81, 293n29

Social Gospel movement: agriculture and, 164; changes in, 159–60; country life movement in context of, 293n24; as form of radicalism, 153–54, 159; participants in, 148, 285nn29–30; salvation concept in, 147; Scott's interest in, 10, 147, 150–53, 172, 244n1; social science as emerging from, 189; use of term, 285nn28,30. *See also* Gospel of Nature

socialism: fears of, 176, 184; George's view of, 174–75, 284n15; limits of, 159; religion replaced by, 156; as religion without God, 287n54; Scott's involvement in, xiii, 1, 140

Socialist Party: candidates of, 157; Scott as member of, 156; Scott's disenchantment with, 287n57; single-tax movement and, 144

social problems: absentee landlords as, 174; language of, 285n27; living close to nature ideal as solution to, 141–44; Social Gospel and, 147–52

Social Religion (Nearing): on afterlife, 157–58; background to, 154; description of, 150–52; themes of, 155

social science: homesteading as experiment in, 161, 170, 182–83, 222; Nearings' understanding of, 188–89; religion based in, 148–49

Social Science Institute, 39, 188–89, 244n2

society and social conventions: concerns of, 24; cultural power of, 107; escape from, juxtaposed with reform of, 129–30, 159; evils of, 163; mature development of, 251n9; optimism about, 149–50; spiritual commitment to, 162–63

Society of Friends (Quakers), 150, 227

soil: hunger for, 120–22, 131–32, 274n27; values based in, 189; walker's relationship with, 116. *See also* Burroughs, John: on soil as food; theologies

specialization: rejection of, 160, 288n65

spirit: nature as incarnation of, 121; nature as symbol of, 119; sauna tradition as habit of, 92

"spiritual": definitions of, 31, 54–55; quest for, 4, 297n60

Spiritualism, xiii, 48, 78, 88, 126, 259n20, 286n46

spirituality: of doing things yourself, 50–54, 100–101; of "dwelling," 232–33; of gardening, 46–47; of getting close to nature, 34–37; in Gospel of Nature, 127–28, 189; institutional claims on, 249n14; maturity linked to, 57; meanings of, 225–26; as multifaceted, 198; religion as distinguished from (or not), 7, 248–49n13; search for, 4, 227–28, 297n60; of seeking, 99–

spirituality (continued)
    100, 233; "shopping" for, 33; of
    walking garden, 46–47. See also na-
    ture religion/spirituality
spiritual materialism, 29–30, 90–91
spiritual narratives: recentering of self
    in, xviii. See also narratives and texts
    of homesteading
spiritual practice: daily life as, 171–73;
    farm-based, 228; homesteading as,
    96–97, 189–90, 199–200, 231,
    235; individualized, 227; nature-
    based, 23; search for, xx; self-
    sufficiency as, 198
spiritual renewal: meaning-making in,
    223–28; nature as place of, 142–
    43, 158–59, 194; return to farm-
    ing linked to, 114–16
Stalin, Joseph, 159
Stewart, Martha, 198, 299–300n80
stonework: at Arden, 139; Burroughs
    on, 130; at Forest Farm, xix, 54,
    245–46n6; gender and, 206; slip-
    form method of, xiv, 42–44; as
    spiritual process, 51; symbolism
    of, 49
Stowe, Harriet Beecher, 290n83
structures of feeling (concept), 107
Sunday, Billy, 155
Sussman, Warren, 273–74n15
sustainability: commitment to, 21, 55;
    possibilities for, 231; as theme,
    102–3
Swann, Robert, 186
symbolic: use of term, 259n21. See also
    religious language and concepts;
    ritual action

Tatelbaum, Kal, 208–9
Tatelbaum, Linda: on body and gender,
    208–10; on compromise, 54; daily
    ritual of, 64–65, 67–68, 72–73,
    100; on marriage, 205; self-
    awareness and reflexivity of, 2,
    195–96
taxation. See single-tax movement
Taylor, Charles, 233, 269n94

technology: attitudes toward, 53–54;
    embrace of, 57, 203; gender roles
    and, 301n2; nature as authority
    on, 219; uses of, 222–23. See also
    electricity; tools
Temple College (Philadelphia), 154–55
Tennessee Valley Authority, 289n75
Tetlow, Henry, 295n43
theologies: of the farm, 35; of nature,
    143–44, 164–68; of the soil, 5,
    86–91, 145–46, 167, 203
theory/practice dynamic: at Arden com-
    munity, 145; in education regime,
    160, 288n66; ritualization in, 68–
    69; in social religion, 151–53; ten-
    sions in, 17–18. See also practice
Theosophical Society, xiv, 214, 289n82
Theosophy: as influence, 78, 259n20;
    Nearings' interests in, 88; tenets of,
    xii–xiv
Thomas, John L., 174, 284n15
Thoreau, Henry David: Burroughs com-
    pared with, 131, 272n8; cultivated
    ignorance and, 58, 219; as cultural
    hero, 37; Dillard compared with,
    61, 260n36; on eating in time with
    seasons, 80; as homesteader (or
    not), 39–42, 63–64; as influence,
    xx, 3, 112, 136, 216, 224, 230,
    233, 257n2, 269n101, 274n23;
    narrative of, 24, 27; reflections on,
    237; self-cultivation of, 41–42,
    189; walking of, 115; woodchuck
    encounter of, 60. See also Walden
    (Thoreau)
time: nature as authority on, 219
Time magazine, 255n51
time spirit (concept), 122–23
tobacco farming, 195, 266n65
Tolstoy, Leo, 15, 194
tools: Borsodi on, 182–83, 185, 196,
    211, 213–14, 295n46; Burroughs
    on, 135, 280–81n100; embrace of,
    57; gender roles and, 301n2; hand
    vs. power, 53–54, 198, 267n66;
    loom and sewing machine as, 183;
    spirituality of, 100. See also electricity

Total Loss Farm (Vt.): eating and food at, 75–76, 264n49; examples of rituals at, 262–63n31; farmers as chosen people at, 90–91; farming practice of, 65–66, 99; gardening at, 73–74; as home, 256n57; maple sugaring at, 66–67; name of, 74; quest for "truly material" at, 29–30; spiritual practice at, 36, 228; success of, 34

traditions: as biophysical and cultural, 233; commitments to, 232–34; of division of labor, 205–8; in family values, 204–5; narrative unity in, 233; progressive ideals blended with, 16–17; Thoreau and Nearings in, 98. See also religion and religious traditions; sauna tradition

Transcendentalism: as affirmation, 40; attitude toward nature in, 282n6; Burroughs on, 112, 128; as influence, 175; lived expression of, 3; selective aspects of, 39; self-cultivation ideal in, 41–42, 80

Trapp, Maria von, 78

Triangle Shirtwaist Factory fire, 284n21

Trust for Public Land, 245n5

truth, 47–48, 220

Turner, Victor, 249n15

Uncle Tom's Cabin (Stowe), 290n83

Unitarianism, 41–42

University of Melbourne (Fla.), 186

University of Pennsylvania, 157

University of Toledo, 157, 287n56

urban areas. See city

U.S. Treasury Department, 108–9, 271n6, 271–72n8

use-economy (concept), 161, 162–63, 176

utilitarianism vs. environmentalism, 221

Vacant Lot associations, 176–78, 292n17

vegan diet, 79

vegetarianism: Borsodi on, 185; commitment to, 86; nature as authority on, 219; Nearings on, 78, 88, 263nn39,41; principles of, 80–81, 83; rationale for, 88; as ritualization of ethics, 78; Sal on, 83; self and other orientations in, 267n71; as symbolic commentary, 28

Veysey, Laurence, 296n52

Vietnam War, 51

vocation: avocation linked to, 160; farming life as, 110–13, 116, 136; as teacher, preacher and scientist, 145, 147, 170, 188

voluntary simplicity movement, 23, 199, 218

Walden (Thoreau): as philosophical foundation, 40–42; as sacred and ideal text, 3, 38–40, 191, 257n1; writing of, 24

walking: as daily devotion, 172; exhilarations of, 114–16; place for, 117–18

walking garden (concept), 45–47. See also no-till gardening

Waterman, Guy, 70–72, 258–59n19

Waterman, Laura, 70–72, 258–59n19

Watson, Frank, 147 fig.

Weber, Max, 7, 221, 249n15

Wharton, James, 85, 86, 267n71

Wharton School, 146, 154, 282n4

White, Richard, 306n33

Whitman, Walt: Burroughs's relationship with, 108, 109, 121–22; death of, 121, 277n51; as influence, 112, 131, 171

wholeness (concept), 79, 82

wild and wilderness: advocates of, 22, 222, 306n33; as desirable/dangerous, 60–61; how-to books on, 191, 298n65; Sundays in, 234–35

wildlife biology discipline, 48

wild nature: use of term, 234

Williams, Raymond, 59, 106, 107

Winter Sunshine (Burroughs): description of, 114–16; Thoreau's influence on, 274n23; writing of, 109, 113

Wizansky, Richard, 34–35, 99

Wollstonecraft, Mary, 213
women: consciousness-raising of, 205; as consumers vs. producers, 213; emancipation of, 214; Helen as mentor to, 215; identity negotiations of, 216; on marriage/partnership, 204–5; motherhood role of, 207, 208–10, 214; Nellie Seeds on, 214–15; in new religious movements, 302n5; *Women and Social Progress*, 214. *See also* domesticity and homemaking; gender roles; separate spheres ideology
Wood, Lyman, 192–93, 298n68, 298–99n69
"Woodcraft Indian" boys, 141
woodcutting: ritualization of, 69–70
work: culture as stage for, 103–4; as currency of homesteading, 52; in daily life, 39; as drudgery, 173; homesteading as dissent from, 137–38; leisure balanced with, 67, 136–37, 281n104; nature as authority on, 219; off homestead, 206, 207, 210; philosophical talk vs., 50–51; playful rejoinder to, 67; "playing at," 65–74, 218; as resistant to culture and culturally determined, 105–7; self-determination in, 129; separate spheres in, 17, 216, 304n25; as symbolic commentary, 28
Works Progress Administration, 214

world-construction and -maintenance (concept), 59
worldliness: critique of, 37
World War I: opposition to, 156–57, 282n4
World War II: homesteading as response to, 191–93
writing: conversion narratives and, 24–27; economics of, 25, 220; farming balanced with, 110, 116; of history, 229; homesteading combined with, 191, 298n65; motives in, 24–25; pleasure of, 265n59; practice vs., 194–95; religious terminology in, 26–27; self-awareness and reflexivity in, 195. *See also* conversion; narratives and texts of homesteading
Wuthnow, Robert: on discipline, 100, 269–70n103; as influence, 249n15; on nature and individualism, 97; on religion, 233; on sacred, 254n49; on search for meaning, 100–101; on spiritual seekers, 4, 227

yeoman farmer myth, 190, 296–97n58. *See also* Jefferson, Thomas
Yurt Foundation, 15
yurts: Coperthwaite's, 13–15, 195; Forest Farm, xix; Sal's, 45–47

Zen practices, 46

Text:	10/13 Joanna
Display:	Syntax
Compositor:	Binghamton Valley Composition, LLC
Printer and binder:	Thomson-Shore, Inc.
Index:	Margie Towery